ON OPIUM

Also by CARLYN ZWARENSTEIN

Opium Eater: The New Confessions

Carlyn Zwarenstein

on
OPIUM

Pain, Pleasure, and Other Matters of Substance

Edited by Linda Pruessen.
"Not Waving But Drowning" (four-line excerpt)
by Stevie Smith, from *Collected Poems of Stevie Smith*,
copyright © 1957 by Stevie Smith. Reprinted by
permission of New Directions Publishing Corp.
Cover, page design, and graphic elements by
Julie Scriver.
Cover image: *Electro Parade from Montreal,
August 2017* by Camille Couvez, unsplash.com
Printed in Canada by Marquis.
10 9 8 7 6 5 4 3 2 1

Goose Lane Editions acknowledges the generous
support of the Government of Canada, the Canada
Council for the Arts, and the Government of
New Brunswick.

Goose Lane Editions
500 Beaverbrook Court, Suite 330
Fredericton, New Brunswick
CANADA E3B 5X4
gooselane.com

Library and Archives Canada Cataloguing
in Publication

Title: On opium : pain, pleasure, and other matters
of substance / Carlyn Zwarenstein.

Names: Zwarenstein, Carlyn, author.
Description: Includes bibliographical references.
Identifiers: Canadiana (print) 20210178817 |
Canadiana (ebook) 20210178841 | ISBN 9781773101811
(softcover) | ISBN 9781773101828 (EPUB)

Subjects: LCSH: Opioids. | LCSH: Opioid abuse. |
LCSH: Substance abuse. | LCSH: Pain—Treatment.

Classification: LCC RC568.O45 Z93 2021 | DDC
362.29/3—dc23

To the family I depend upon, and who can depend on me—Zwarenstein, Levin, Kitai-Rosenthal, Olmos Hernández, and friends who are family. With endless love.

In memory of my grandparents,
Jack & Esther Levin and Sam & Esther Zwarenstein.

Contents

Prologue

Fall 2020

I first learned of the existence of Michael Eschbach, a fifty-nine-year-old man who has become one of my online friends—an internet ghost, he calls himself—from posts he made on Twitter in the spring of 2020. I was working on this book at the time, about opioids and what people need that opioids can provide. It was also when SARS-CoV-2 really hit Toronto, when schools shut and we all went into a semi-lockdown as COVID-19 cases rose and rose, with opioid overdose deaths surging soon after as drug supplies were interrupted, social services shut down, and isolation exacerbated.

At the time, Michael was living at St. Simon's, a men's-only homeless shelter about five kilometres from my apartment. With increasing desperation, he wrote to whoever would listen that infection was inevitable in the shelter due to crowding and the failure of staff to enforce physical distancing. Never mind that COVID-19 was initially spread by those with the means to travel: the pandemic quickly found its way into the endothelia of the working class, the poor, and the most deeply marginalized. In vain, Michael begged the city to move older men like him out and into permanent housing. Eventually he posted a clandestinely filmed video of the closely spaced cots. A couple of weeks later, the city did move him—not into housing, but into a hotel for men who tested positive at the shelter.

Now, after spending two lonely weeks at the quarantine hotel, Michael has been moved again. The City of Toronto has relocated him to another hotel, this one near Toronto's international airport. Here he lives a surreal existence as he deals with persistent post-viral symptoms that arose after he was released from quarantine.

Michael uses a cane due to a bad knee and degenerative disk disease. He is prescribed morphine as well as pregabalin to cover the pain, which otherwise keeps him up at night and renders him suicidal. When he was moved from the quarantine hotel to the shelter hotel, no one bothered to fax his prescription. So he hobbled in pain the one kilometre to the pharmacy in an attempt to sort it out. "It's horrible. You question the point of existence," he wrote me about the agony he experienced while still waiting for the doctor and pharmacy to communicate, all attempts halted over the weekend.

I send him a copy of my first book, a slim meditation about pain, and while he waits for it — the postal service having slowed to nearly a halt during COVID, even though his hotel must be less than twenty-five kilometres from my apartment — he puts on his mask and goes down to the lobby every day to check the mail. "Just like in those old black-and-white movies where the hero or heroine checks with the hotel clerk for secret messages," he says.

Even if you're not living what Michael calls an "ethereal existence" in a hotel in the middle of nowhere, near nothing but the airport — which promises an escape you can't take anyway — it is the strangest summer in living memory, this COVID summer of 2020. Like most of the world, really, I too am trapped.

There are many ways to be trapped: by poverty, by responsibility, by delusions, by racism, by depression, by loneliness, by pride. I have felt trapped since my body began to turn against me many years ago, when I first started to suffer the intense joint stiffness and accompanying pain that would turn out to be a degenerative spine disease, with symptoms that are temporarily relieved by exercise and which worsen with rest. My joints are joints the way a prison is a "joint." They force me to dramatize my lifelong love of travel by being unable to stop moving, no matter how weary I get. And yet travel itself—hours in a car, in a plane, standing in line—is almost impossible like this. For years now I have thought obsessively about freedom of movement, about psychological escape.

Since childhood, books have opened their departure terminals to other realities for me. For those who are trapped or lonely, there's no better escape, if you can concentrate on it. It's no wonder that, as Michael tells me when he says it's okay for me to share his words and his story here, "One thing I learned while I am homeless is this: no matter our condition, be it mental illness, or marital issues, or diagnosed ailments, or undiagnosed, or we simply fell through all the cracks, all of us read voraciously."

Drugs also offer that immersion. I didn't set out to be a psychonaut, those substance-driven explorers of the inner continents. But I did set out to be a writer, which comes to somewhat the same thing. And, for nearly ten years, I have taken an opioid. Like Michael, I do so legally and at a prescribed dose. But in many ways our experience is also not as different as you might think from that of other opioid users at his shelter hotel, the so-called junkies who use illicit fentanyl or heroin, illegal drugs but painkillers just the same. Under the influence of my own painkilling drug, I have found ways to return to the world, to travel again, and to write.

Pain, an MRI tells me, has worn its white-matter grooves into my brain. Likewise, and despite the intense stigma that clings to drugs derived from or inspired by the opium poppy, opioids have opened new paths; introduced me to new people like my hotel-dwelling friend; and changed the way I think about pleasure, pain, dependence, and what we need, all of us humans, to be well in our lives.

I can't book a ticket out of this apartment where I've spent the past six months, twenty-four hours a day, seven days a week trying to write articles and a book, to parent and instruct, to keep my kids emotionally afloat, trying in vain to keep my spine from ossifying due to lack of exercise and, minute by long minute, to get through the way that feels. But I can write, I can read, I can remember, and, if you like, I can take you with me. Let's call it a trip.

PART I

OPIUM EATER
The New Confessions

If the entire materia medica at our disposal were limited to the choice and use of only one drug, I am sure that a great many, if not the majority, of us would choose opium; and I am convinced that if we were to select, say half a dozen of the most important drugs in the Pharmacopeia, we should all place opium in the first rank.

— Pharmacologist David I. Macht, writing in the
Journal of the American Medical Association, 1915[1]

Wynken, Blynken, and Nod one night
Sailed off in a wooden shoe —
Sailed on a river of crystal light
Into a sea of dew.
"Where are you going, and what do you wish?"
The old moon asked the three.

From *Winken, Blynken, and Nod,* by Eugene Field

It might have started when I first noticed myself lurching stiffly as I walked, in the sleepless weeks after my first child was born. Or earlier, when back pain plagued me at my desk job. Or maybe the story only really begins when I was first diagnosed, years after that. But I'd rather start this story a little later, when after some years of being clawed constantly by stiffness and pain, I began trying to claw back the life pain took from me. It's my story, so I get to choose. We'll start there, in 2015.[*]

Today I am flying from Toronto to New York City. Travel — formerly my great delight — has lately become something of an ordeal. My neck cranes forward, pushed by stiff, hunching shoulders. The muscles at the front of my neck are as short and tight as steel cables; a dull burn at the back of my neck radiates down to my tailbone. My lower back feels unstable, an oddly unbearable sensation, as if my spinal column were inadequate to support the rest of me.

I have a spine disease called ankylosing spondylitis (AS). One of the particular torments of this condition is an inability to find comfort either sitting down or standing up. Seated in the departure lounge, I shift and wriggle in my seat.

I take a little pill bottle from the pocket of my coat and hold it in my hand.

---

[*] This section was previously published in a slightly different form as *Opium Eater: The New Confessions* by Nonvella in 2016.

Through the window, the water in the harbour is slate blue, the financial district buildings beside it grey and blue as well, reflecting dull sky and dull water. It's like being in a black-and-white movie — or a cyanotype, rather, blue scale. What a November day. But I am going on holiday. I've left my loved ones at home for the weekend, and now, for the next six hours, I'm about to leave pain behind as well — along with its accompanying stress, sorrow, and existential angst.

I chase the pale yellow pill, an opioid called tramadol, with a bitter sip of coffee.

The radar weather on the TV screen above me shows a shifting, restless display of green-on-green clouds. It's a good metaphor for the feeling I have during the hour or so after the pill: all the weather in me churning and gathering up and clearing itself out. I'm calm but alert. Anticipating. I still feel the pain that dogs me, but already its force is provisional, its minutes numbered. It no longer depresses me as it so easily can do.

At last, with an unforced sigh as I'm released from pain, I finally lean back in my seat. The airport chatter is muted now. There is a faraway clattering of glasses, and the cackle of friends laughing off to my right is now more distant. A man in a blue surgical mask cleans white cups off a table. As I take in the details, I begin to notice my breath going in and out — my stomach slowly rising and falling, air sweeping through my nostrils, down the back of my throat, filling up my lungs. A seagull floats unsteadily on the rough breezes outside.

By the time my flight is called I'm able to stand up briskly, limber and quick. I walk carefully to my gate, smile serenely at the attendant as my passport and boarding pass are checked, and glide into the airplane. The sky has brightened, the cloud cover lifted. As I settle into my seat, successive waves of good feeling wash over me like the surf. My holiday has begun.

In her book *A Field Guide to Getting Lost*, Rebecca Solnit writes of opiates and their effect of turning her "into something almost reptilian." "Opiates," she writes, turn you "into a cool spectator of your own sensations and desires and of passing time, as languorous as all those images of divans and draperies and long pipes had promised."[2]

Yes. For the relief of severe pain, I take painkillers derived from and inspired by opium. I have taken morphine, extracted from the sap or resin of the opium poppy (and so "opiate," a subset of the larger category, opioids); hydromorphone, a strong, semi-synthetic opioid made from morphine; and tramadol, a relatively weak synthetic opioid with a structure similar to codeine and morphine. All three of these drugs temporarily mask symptoms of my condition, against which even unhealthy amounts of Tylenol don't stand a chance. They do so without the major side effects I've experienced with other medicines. Of the three, I like tramadol the best. It works on the brain both as an opioid and also somewhat like an Effexor-like antidepressant. Tramadol relieves pain incredibly well, helps me sleep through physical discomfort, and perks my mood enough to manage the demands of the day.

Ankylosing spondylitis is a degenerative autoimmune disease. A form of inflammatory arthritis, it typically strikes young people in their prime—in my case, at twenty-eight, shortly after the first of my two sons was born. AS is roughly analogous to having rheumatoid arthritis in the spine. My immune system attacks my body, causing chronic inflammation that began in the sacroiliac joints at the base of the spine and for the past ten years has been gradually moving upward.

In his 2001 novel *Austerlitz*, the writer W.G. Sebald describes an ankylosing spondylitis patient:

> Lying down was perhaps even more painful for him than walking, so that as a rule, despite his exhausted state after his constant perambulations, it was a long time before he could get to sleep. Then, through the grille of a ventilation shaft [. . .] he could be heard calling on numerous different saints for hours on end, in particular, if I remember correctly, Saints Catherine and Elizabeth, who suffered the most cruel

of martyrdoms, begging them to intercede for him in the contingency, as he put it, of his imminent appearance before the judgment seat of his Heavenly Lord.[3]

It came out of the blue. The disease and resulting pain have devastated my life. I'm still trying to find my way now, a decade after the first symptoms that foreshadowed it. In severe AS, inflammation causes the vertebrae to fuse together by a process of erosion and remodelling of the bone. If I'm unlucky, bone will form between my vertebrae and I will be left with a completely immobile, terribly fragile spinal column, or "bamboo spine." Two gut-shredding years of anti-inflammatory medicines left me with an ulcer, debilitating heartburn, and various food intolerances, as well as constant fear of potential side effects — like sudden and occasionally fatal gastrointestinal bleeding and heart attacks.

"I will never take those again," I told the rheumatologist, standing uncomfortably rather than sitting in the chair I'd been offered. The doctor wrote me a prescription and handed it over across his desk. It was only after googling "tramadol" that I learned I'd been prescribed my first opioid. At first I thought that meant I was going to die.

The opium poppy has been cultivated for over three thousand years. The Sumerians called it *hul gil*, the joy plant. The nineteenth century — the Romantic and early- to mid-Victorian period — was the great age of opium, with derivative medicines used by patients of all ages for all manner of ailments. Addiction at that time was viewed for the most part as a weakness rather than either a criminal act or a medical condition, and the opium trade itself was a cornerstone of British imperial policy.

Morphine — named for the god of sleep, dreams, and transformation — was first isolated from the sap of the poppy (that is, opium) in 1805 by a German pharmacist's apprentice. Friedrich Sertürner was also an opium addict, and later, not surprisingly, a morphine addict. Morphine is the most important active constituent of opium, and its isolation — along with the development of the hypodermic needle mid-century — allowed for more straightforward and effective pain management. In all cases, an injection makes the drug dramatically stronger and faster-acting, and more dangerous.

Morphine remains the gold standard drug against which all other opioids, including the synthetic ones, are compared; the dosing of all of them is calculated in terms of equivalencies of morphine.[4] Morphine and its derivatives are the most effective and powerful painkillers around today. While legal and prescribed for medical reasons, these substances are related to currently illegal drugs such as heroin—itself synthesized by an English chemist and once sold freely as a cough suppressant (it works).

While heroin was made illegal in the United States in 1925, in the late forties and fifties you could still pick up your prescription for heroin pills at the Boots pharmacy in Piccadilly Circus in London—in fact, under its medical name diamorphine, it is still used in the UK as a strong painkiller and as an effective treatment for heroin use disorder.[5]

As a girl, I loved the Sherlock Holmes stories, and read and reread Arthur Conan Doyle's erotically measured lines about the famous seven percent solution of cocaine:

> Sherlock Holmes took his bottle from the corner of the mantelpiece and his hypodermic syringe from its neat morocco case. With his long, white, nervous fingers he adjusted the delicate needle, and rolled back his left shirt-cuff. For some little time his eyes rested thoughtfully upon the sinewy forearm and wrist all dotted and scarred with innumerable puncture-marks. Finally he thrust the sharp point home, pressed down the tiny piston, and sank back into the velvet-lined arm-chair with a long sigh of satisfaction.[6]

Like him, I enjoy the waiting. Once I have decided that today is going to be a tramadol day, and I've given myself a deadline before which I absolutely will not cave in and take it, my experience of pain is transformed.

Rather than grinding and hopeless, it feels charged, electric. The difficulty I have standing up (or sitting down) begins to feel noble. The constant, miserable, and exhausting stretching I do to relieve pain and stiffness in my joints acquires a warm-up quality.

I am already removed one degree from my own experience and it is a little more observable, a little more interesting. I know that in a little while, after some sore but delicious anticipation, it will melt away in an exquisitely gradual, perceptible way. And then I will feel expansive and happy. The hours ahead are no longer to be endured but rather to be savoured, and this knowledge invigorates me, refocusing my day.

Then there is the actual taking of the drug. If you don't get a high from whatever medicine *you* take, I suppose it is just a medicine. Nobody craves Tylenol or ibuprofen or Lipitor. If, however, the drug you are taking is really, in your own mind, a drug, all the preparation involved is part of a lovely ritual of anticipation. It has a sort of pleasant glow of association. Do this, feel that. A lifelong non-smoker, a cautious adolescent, and the most sober adult at any party, I have nevertheless been fascinated by intoxication, addiction, and altered mental states for as long as I can remember.

I don't think that anyone I know has known that about me.

The flame that licks the spoon. The tightening of the rubber strap and the clinical flicking of a tube with the nails of index finger and thumb. The way you hold the cigarette, even, stretching out your fingers, touching your lips as you inhale. It's all a very private romance.

Unfortunately for my sense of occasion and aesthetics, all *I* do is swallow a medium-sized yellowish pill, chasing it with some water or — more sensibly, given the drowsiness it induces — coffee.

The most notorious drug addict in English letters was a man named Thomas De Quincey. He was born in 1785 and died in 1859. De Quincey was perhaps the best essayist in English in an age when creative non-fiction, as it's called today, was having its moment. He chronicled his vivid memories of the pain and pleasures of medicinal opium in his memoir, *Confessions of an English Opium-Eater*:

> Opium! dread agent of unimaginable pleasure and pain!
> I had heard of it as I had of manna or of ambrosia, but
> no further: how unmeaning a sound was it at that time! what
> solemn chords does it now strike upon my heart! what heart-
> quaking vibrations of sad and happy remembrances! Reverting
> for a moment to these, I feel a mystic importance attached to
> the minutest circumstances connected with the place and the
> time and the man (if man he was) that first laid open to me
> the Paradise of Opium-eaters.[7]

By *man-if-man-he-was* he means the pharmacist. (The humble apoth-
ecary is also described as the "beatific vision of an immortal druggist, sent
down to earth on a special mission to myself.") In his *Confessions*, as he
wrote in a revised edition late in life, De Quincey hoped to "emblazon the
power of opium—not over bodily disease and pain, but over the grander
and more shadowy world of dreams."[8] Blurring the line between addiction
and pleasure, recreational and medical use, he anticipated Freud in his
exploration of the effect of the subconscious on the psyche.[9]

De Quincey's father was a relatively prosperous merchant who
died when De Quincey was a child. Two of his sisters also died when
he was young. He was especially traumatized by the early death of his
elder sister, Elizabeth, probably of meningitis, and haunted by imagined
visions—which returned during the nightmares of opium withdrawal in
later life—of her skull, which he saw (or believed he'd seen) when it was
opened for an autopsy.

As a teenager, De Quincey ran away from his much-hated Manchester
boarding school and decamped to Wales and then London. He nearly
starved to death in the big city before embarking on a career as an
essayist and hack writer, churning out hundreds of essays for the leading
publications of the day. A charming, eccentric, and sometimes pitiful man
as an adult, De Quincey was ambitious, versatile, eloquent, and (as the
number of exclamation points in the above excerpt suggest) often over-the-
top as a writer. And, of course, a nearly lifelong drug addict.

During his life, De Quincey was known for many works, but *Confessions* remains his most enduring. With its focus on subjective experience and individualism, its obsession with dreams and archetypes, and its oscillation between emotional extremes, it's a narrative that sits confidently beside the works of other English-language authors of the Romantic movement, such as Mary Shelley, Emily Brontë, and Walter Scott—as well as those by fellow opium users John Keats and Samuel Taylor Coleridge. (De Quincey was an acolyte of glorious poet and miserable addict Coleridge, who tried to warn him away from the clutches of the joy plant.)

Confessions came out some years after De Quincey moved from being a long-term recreational user of opium to a confirmed addict. The book—which, among other things, ponders withdrawal and addiction, and opium's effect on memory and imagination—was translated into French and adapted by Baudelaire, making it a literary inspiration for the francophone Romantic world as well. *Confessions* and his other works have influenced generations of writers. An essay demonstrating De Quincey's style of black humour, "On Murder Considered as One of the Fine Arts," inspired Edgar Allan Poe as he essentially invented the detective novel. (Poe's work in turn inspired Sir Arthur Conan Doyle's creation of Sherlock Holmes, bringing us full circle.) Jorge Luis Borges considered De Quincey an influence, and Hector Berlioz's *Symphonie fantastique* was based on *Confessions*.

De Quincey first took opium for relief from a blindingly painful toothache—or possibly trigeminal neuralgia, a monstrously painful condition affecting the facial nerves—on the advice of a college acquaintance. It was a wet Sunday in London, and he had been in agony for nearly three weeks. On Oxford Street he saw the shop of a druggist—that "unconscious minister of celestial pleasures"[10]—and went in to purchase his first, fateful dose. He returned to his lodgings and downed it:

> That my pains had vanished was now a trifle in my eyes—
> this negative effect was swallowed up in the immensity of
> those positive effects which had opened before me—in the
> abyss of divine enjoyment thus suddenly revealed. Here was
> a panacea, a *pharmakon nêpenthes* for all human woes: here

was the secret of happiness, about which philosophers had
disputed for so many ages, at once discovered: happiness
might now be bought for a penny, and carried in the waistcoat
pocket: portable ecstasies might be had corked up in a pint
bottle, and peace of mind could be sent down in gallons by
the mailcoach.[11]

This was the beginning of a love affair that lasted half a century. From
his very first experience until his death nearly sixty years later, the Opium
Eater drank his opium, as laudanum: a tincture of opium in alcohol
commonly sold as an over-the-counter medicine. Although he made his
name through publication of the scandalous *Confessions*, De Quincey was
not doing anything even remotely scandalous when he first tried the stuff.
Opiate medication was widely available — then, as now, at the drugstore,
among other places[12] — and it was relatively cheap. This made pain relief,
measured in mere grains of opium or drops of opium in tincture, accessible
to the working poor who could not afford wine or spirits, as De Quincey
noted of a trip he took back to Manchester:

I was informed by several cotton manufacturers, that their
work-people were rapidly getting into the practice of opium-
eating; so much so, that on a Saturday afternoon the counters
of the druggists were strewed with pills of one, two, or three
grains, in preparation for the known demand of the evening.[13]

I too remember when I started taking opioids. As I write this, it's been
over four years. I expect I felt more self-conscious getting my first dose
than De Quincey did, since tramadol requires not only a non-renewable
prescription but the display of valid photo ID to the pharmacist.

If you have ever had a toothache like De Quincey, or dental surgery,
you understand how quickly one can become desperate for relief. Having
some sort of time limit on suffering makes it endurable. It's the same

way that running a marathon is tolerable because you know that it will eventually end. Every step gets you closer to relief. I don't think I'm a lightweight. I like to believe that I'm an expert on pain, thanks to hours devoted to close study of it during the births of my two children — one at home, one in hospital, neither with painkillers. Those experiences taught me that the most intense pain imaginable can be tolerated for a time, and that the way we experience that pain — empowering, terrifying, humbling — can vary dramatically.

And so even childbirth, the most painful thing commonly experienced, doesn't work as an objective measure. There are other sorts of pain, harder to describe. Chronic or recurring pains are insidious. They eat away at energy, optimism, endurance, sense of self. More relevant than a measurement or even a description of pain, then, is the completely subjective impact it has on one's thoughts, behaviour, and physical health. Pain above a "level 5" — moderate pain that dominates your thoughts and to which you cannot adapt, according to one scale designed to measure it — frequently results in temporary personality disorders.[14] At higher levels that continue without relief, personality or other psychological disorders are almost ubiquitous, and suicide is common.

It is pain that now regularly pushes me back to depression — a long-time acquaintance I was happy to forget when pregnancy and breastfeeding turned out to be miracle cures for my apparently hormonal woes. It is as bad as I'd remembered it. If pain were a substance it would be a dangerous, mind-altering one indeed.

But a quest for pain relief that settles on opioids can bring an escape that is more than just physical, as Thomas De Quincey (and I) discovered. As the first person to write publicly and in detail in English about the inner experience of taking opium, De Quincey was to become the archetypal drug-dependent, tormented-but-inspired artist, and the progenitor of a whole new genre of literature — the addiction confessional — later taken up by literary junkies like William Burroughs, Irvine Welsh, Jim Carroll, and many others. And yet, his description is precise and unique-sounding rather than stereotypic. It's also utterly resonant with my experience of tramadol:

> The town of L—— represented the earth, with its sorrows and its graves left behind, yet not out of sight, nor wholly forgotten. The ocean, in everlasting but gentle agitation, and brooded over by a dove-like calm, might not unfitly typify the mind and the mood which then swayed it. For it seemed to me as if then first I stood at a distance, and aloof from the uproar of life; as if the tumult, the fever, and the strife, were suspended; a respite granted from the secret burthens of the heart; a sabbath of repose; a resting from human labours. Here were the hopes which blossom in the paths of life, reconciled with the peace which is in the grave; motions of the intellect as unwearied as the heavens, yet for all anxieties a halcyon calm: a tranquility that seemed no product of inertia, but as if resulting from mighty and equal antagonisms; infinite activities, infinite repose.[15]

Please compare that with the following description of tramadol given by drug user "J.C." on an online forum:

> It's as if the most comfortable, softest, pink blanket is being wrapped around me in both a physical and emotional way. It is like laying back and talking with my best friend. It's like walking outside on the first day of summer and smelling the fresh cut grass. My problems have not disappeared, I have not escaped them, but the little annoyances of life have had the volume turned down a notch. Tramadol has often given me the opportunity to reflect and feel optimistic about the future. [...] The great thing about tramadol, however, is that it does not inhibit my activities at all. It doesn't make me want

to just lie on the couch like marijuana, or immediately run around the world like amphetamines. It just feels natural to continue to do, whatever it is that I do. Doing work is fine, conversations are great, sports are fun, there are hardly any activities that I can think of that tramadol detracts from.[16]

At twenty, Thomas De Quincey left his desultory studies at Oxford every three weeks or so to travel to London, where he would indulge in laudanum, theatre, opera, and long, rambling walks through the ancient city streets. The opiate was an essential enhancer, instilling a peaceful curiosity amid the urban tumult.

As it happens, I was also in London at about the same time in my life. Just before my twentieth birthday, I worked for six weeks in an infectious disease laboratory at St. Mary's Hospital. (Also, coincidentally, this is where heroin was first synthesized, back in 1874.) Like De Quincey, but more sober and more cautious, I wandered through the city. I was in the first throes of what was eventually diagnosed as major depression. I was treated with antidepressants the following year. And yet my state of mind at that point was probably like that of young Thomas: open to everything, romantic, melodramatic, unstable, desperate to take it all in. I like to imagine how it was for him then. The dark buildings and gilding late-afternoon light, the vast and noisy variety of people of all appearances and conditions, the cobbled streets that wind like hilly labyrinths up and down and around. The grandeur of intricate stonework everywhere. You mostly have to imagine much of it, today. Rotting timbers, memories of plague.

Just my height — a bit *under* five feet — and slight, De Quincey was sensitive and precocious, with a blazing talent for languages. He was often torn, like me, between a desire to please and conform and an equally strong attraction to rebellion and iconoclasm. "I used often," he writes, "on Saturday nights, after I had taken opium, to wander forth, without much regarding the direction or the distance, to all the markets, and other parts of London, whither the poor resort on a Saturday night, for laying out their wages."[17]

On these "long, rambling nights amongst London's working class, De Quincey enjoyed the drugged bliss of both sympathy and separation," writes Robert Morrison, one of his recent major biographers.[18] "In knitting together drugs, intellectualism, unconventionality, and the city, he maps in the countercultural figure of the bohemian. Decades before Edgar Allan Poe and Charles Baudelaire, he emerges as the first *flâneur*, high and anonymous, graceful and detached, strolling through crowded urban sprawls trying to decipher the spectacles, faces, and memories that reside there."[19]

De Quincey describes two types of laudanum high. Immersion in an interesting crowd, or attendance at the opera, for example, are made just that much more exquisite under the influence of laudanum. But there is a second level of high where, he says, it is good to be alone in order to fully luxuriate in the sensation. Although the Opium Eater seems to have been the first person to write about deliberately selecting experiences that will be enhanced by opiates, or that will themselves enhance the opiate high, or that somehow together will create an aesthetic and emotional synergy, he's certainly not been the last. And by this I don't just mean avant-garde literati. On online forums, drug users — including prescription users who are genuinely suffering from pain and taking opioids at normal, prescribed doses — repeatedly describe particular music or social settings that seem to enhance the overall experience. I have now mixed morphine and live theatre, morphine with intellectual café chats, morphine with art; hydromorphone with intense one-on-one friend conversation and (on a different occasion) with salsa dancing; and tramadol with an El Greco exhibit, a ballet about Vaslav Nijinsky's descent into madness, and watching Brazil beat Panama at soccer. It has also made rolling out coils of clay in a ceramics class particularly hypnotic.

Dorothy was lulled to sleep in her field of poppies in Oz and lucky to wake up. The brilliant red of the opium poppy, *Papaver somniferum*, has long been linked to death-like sleep or sleep-like death. Fields of poppies covering hundreds of thousands of acres supply the raw material for millions of opioid prescriptions and provide that ambiguous, tenuous exit from the struggles of life. Usually it's a temporary reprieve. Too often it's permanent.

Celebrities die of illegal opioids in droves. The less well-known may also die with needles in their arms, or with bottles of prescribed liquid morphine in their medicine cabinets. Barbara Hodgson's book *In the Arms of Morpheus* looked at the early history of morphine and opium use in medical preparations in Europe and North America. "Fortunately today, since other, non-addictive drugs are available, morphine is limited to short-term use and to palliative care, and dependence on it through medical application is rare," she wrote.[20] That book was published in 2001, but the statement was not entirely true then, and it's certainly not true as I write this a decade and a half later.

Since the early 1990s, pharmaceutical companies have engaged in heavy marketing of opioid painkillers, developing and promoting dozens of new varieties.[21] As a result, prescriptions for them have surged. Drugs once restricted to mostly in-hospital, intravenous, short-term, and palliative or post-operative use are now prescribed in lower (but often escalating) doses over the very long term to patients living with enduring pain. Unsurprisingly, unintentional deaths due to prescription opioid overdoses have also quadrupled in the US over this period.[22] The development has been gradual but accelerating and, as I write this in 2015, has flown largely under the popular radar for around twenty-five years. It's a situation that in some ways mirrors the widespread and haphazard use of opiate-based medicine in the nineteenth century.

Study after study carried out over the past few years points to galloping use of opioids—particularly in North America and Australia—to treat a wide range of afflictions. This surge is often reported in the news inaccurately, incompletely, and with breathless alarm. It's "a problem." It's "a rash." It's "a flood." It's "an epidemic." The "painkillers are killing us." But the headlines are hyperbole mixed with truth. What is true is that more people are now becoming addicted to prescribed opioids, whether their own or, often, someone else's; more people are seeking treatment for physical dependency (different from addiction) as well as actual addiction; and more people are dying of overdoses of prescription opioids.

Some fifteen million people worldwide were dependent on opiates in 2014.[23] An increasing number of these used prescription opioids. (Not all opioids are included in the published data. Tramadol, for example, is not among the six major prescription opioids whose use is tracked by the International Narcotics Control Board—so actual numbers are considerably higher.) The World Health Organization estimated in 2016 that around 69,000 people were dying of opioid overdoses each year.[24]

The estimate includes illegal drugs like heroin as well as accidental overdoses of prescribed drugs—and accidental overdoses of drugs that are legally prescribed to *some*one, but taken by someone else. It is also made blurry by including drugs like fentanyl that are legally prescribed but are also illicitly produced and sold for recreational use, and may be used unwittingly by someone who thinks they're taking illegal cocaine, while drugs like oxycodone are legally prescribed but often procured for illicit use.

It's hard to keep track because the ultimate cause of death is not always obvious, either. But given the numbers of users and widespread availability of opioids, the grim global overdose statistics are not surprising. In North America alone it is estimated that between around 2012 and 2016, roughly 2.1 million Americans[25]—and, according to one researcher, some 200,000 Canadians[26]—were addicted to legal opioid painkillers—these two countries being far and away their greatest consumers.

I have been on tramadol for nearly five months. I was working for four hours a day, I am now doing 10–12 hour days, I concentrate all day long and work performance is effective. My identity has been unchained from desperation and loss of soul. I can once again feel deep emotions, happiness, contentment, enjoyment from achieving good result with my work—on tramadol, it is not the sick kind of happiness as on amphetamines. It is natural—I also get down when there is a reason. Most of the days, although, I feel extreme happiness for having come through. [...] I am in balance, I am free, I am positive and most of all, I am myself—a whole identity.[27]

—a post by a drug use forum member

In New York I make the shift to taking tramadol twice a day, every day. In the process, I have the striking insight that it is better to feel good than to feel bad. I wander with my friend Sonia—she high only on life—around Manhattan galleries and streets, discover magical cafés, have long conversations about art and life. We are nearly forty. But we once did the same thing as privileged young wanderers fresh from our first year of university, when we backpacked in Paris together partway through my London laboratory contract. Then, red wine acted as a more conventional colourant to our bohemian experience. I remember one long nighttime walk to our hostel home. We rambled on enthusiastically about life, about art, about art and life, and life as art. About commitment to social justice causes. About living with intensity. All as one does when one is nineteen and lucky and backpacking in Paris. Of course, we had experienced nothing. Nothing!

Now, wandering aimlessly in the West Village after the bruising experiences of adulthood, we end up after midnight on a quiet street. We notice a restaurant that looks as if it's closing. It turns out that it is open, dusky, impossibly romantic. There are just a couple of patrons finishing their dinners in the back. There is a grand piano, old portraits. The building is a carriage house built in 1767, some years before Thomas De Quincey was born across the sea. As we sit at the bar, the upswell of good feeling becomes almost overwhelming.

"Right now," I say, straining to put this into words, "I feel like there is just as much possibility and adventure in life as I felt all those years ago in Paris."

As De Quincey established, there is nothing better than wandering anonymously through a great and diverse city. The drug is not necessary. But it certainly is complementary. Getting lost, you find yourself.

De Quincey came to prominence during the height of the English Romantic era, which stretched roughly from the late 1700s to around 1850. Robert Morrison writes that "The Opium Eater is bookish, dreamy, and aloof, yet urban, street-smart, and with a keen interest in the macabre."[28]

This sketch of De Quincey could apply to every Romantic. You can spot them by their interest in emotional extremes, in the morbid or melodramatic, and in the action of dreams and fantasies. Romanticism is marked by individualist subjectivity as well as its flip side — fascination with the exotic or Other.

The Romantic craze started, believed Scottish surgeon Thomas Trotter, with dependence on stimulants like coffee and tea — gateway substances along the slippery cobblestone path to the opium den. The new generation of "Romantics," he wrote, were afflicted by "the nervous disposition formerly the privilege of poets, artists, and aristocrats."[29] How much worse, then, the tumultuous, sensation-seeking temperament of the *actual* Romantic-era poet or artist!

While biographers may argue about whether Keats's "Ode on Indolence" —

> Ripe was the drowsy hour;
> The blissful cloud of summer-indolence
> Benumb'd my eyes; my pulse grew less and less;
> Pain had no sting, and pleasure's wreath no flower[30]

— arose from direct experience or not, there is no doubt that English literature in the nineteenth century was absolutely drenched in laudanum. The list of historical users includes a Who's Who of Romantic authors: Lord Byron, Percy Bysshe Shelley, Bram Stoker, Elizabeth Barrett Browning, Charlotte Brontë. It also includes later and perhaps less-expected figures like *Little Women* author Louisa May Alcott, a morphine addict, and Florence Nightingale — that icon of devoted self-sacrifice — who regularly injected herself with morphine during the Crimean War. "I could not get through the day without this wonderful little pick-me-up," she once wrote.[31]

Opium was just one factor at play. Tuberculosis was another. Like ankylosing spondylitis, infection with *Mycobacterium tuberculosis* — the classic microbe of the Romantics — often struck young people in their prime. A second-century description of pulmonary tuberculosis gives the image:

> The youth with the croaking voice [...] the extreme wasting, the nails crooked and brittle, the eyes deeply sunk in their hollows but brilliant and glittering [...] the lassitude coupled with foolish gaiety [...] the shoulder blades like the wings of the birds.[32]

Bright eyes, dreamy indolence alternating with animated conversation, and bodies bespeaking indifference to food — these also characterize what the French refer to as the *opiomane*. By the nineteenth century, prevalent tuberculosis and prevalent use of opium together provided the basis of the archetypal Romantic. Opium, morphine, and heroin eased the tuberculotic sufferings and the passing of Frédéric Chopin, Aubrey Beardsley, Franz Kafka, Katherine Mansfield, George Orwell, and D.H. Lawrence.[33]

John Keats was less fortunate.[34] The great poet, whose work De Quincey later championed as a critic, died of tuberculosis like his brother and mother before him. In his last days, an unusually moralistic friend hid from him the laudanum that could have eased his bloody cough and pain. He died in agony, just twenty-five.

Of course, of course, yes of course: drugs are more likely to be detrimental than improving to literature or art. And yet, some undeniably beautiful and passionate work arose from that drowsy hour — and its release from pain.

Well before pain became an issue for me—always, in fact—I have dealt with setbacks by trying, not always successfully, to follow the writer Neil Gaiman's advice: "Husband runs off with a politician? Make good art. Leg crushed and then eaten by mutated boa constrictor? Make good art. IRS on your trail? Make good art. Cat exploded? Make good art."[35] The breakup, the breakdown, the lousy boss, the crummy landlord, the diagnosis. They're all experiences that I can one day turn into writing. That desire to produce something, anything, that feels meaningful becomes more urgent as the setbacks increase.

So much literature has speculated about the uncertain relationship between opioid drugs and art. Art certainly acts, like drugs, as a form of short-term relief, and helps me put routine pain into perspective. Even better, it's comforting to find that my experience makes me (or lets me fancy myself) part of the long lineage of speculation on the relationship between art and drugs. Still, my own experiences have left me confused about whether opioid-based pain relief—or the other, infamous effects of opium-related drugs—actually improves my creative processes. And about whether pain itself makes me a better writer or a worse one. All I know is that both opioids and writing seem to have become vital to my existence.

Sometimes I imagine my ambitions as circus lions circumscribed by rings of fire. The fire is pain. Pain causes physical limitations; eats at my fragile sense of optimism; confuses my thoughts and imperils my livelihood; deadens the association-making ability from which creative work emerges. Pain makes me strained and cranky as I try to play with my two young children, who can absorb depression just as they thirstily absorb every other influence.

Endurance is possible, but endurance on its own does not equal a full, contributing life. Our purpose in life is not, cannot be, simply to suffer.

I have several times made conscious decisions about mind-altering drugs. The film *Trainspotting* came out in 1996, when I was nineteen. By the time I saw it, I was just learning that depression was an issue for me. The movie was my first introduction to heroin and I immediately understood that it was dangerous for me precisely because it seemed so attractive, attractive as other drugs I'd heard of—cannabis, cocaine, LSD, alcohol—had never been.

So—not that they were handing out syringes on the way out of the movie theatre, but just in case—I resolved at that moment never to try it, or anything like it. Fifteen years later, my inadvertent and unsought experience of drugs has confirmed my instinct that opioids are "my" drug. I echo De Quincey's vehemence in distinguishing between the calm glow of opium and true intoxication:

> First, then, it is not so much affirmed as taken for granted,
> by all who ever mention opium, formally or incidentally,
> that it does or can produce intoxication. Now, reader, assure
> yourself, *meo periculo*, that no quantity of opium ever did,
> or could intoxicate. As to the tincture of opium (commonly
> called laudanum), *that* might certainly intoxicate if a man
> could bear to take enough if it; but why? because it contains
> so much proof spirit, and not because it contains so much
> opium.[36]

Certainly, opioids, unless you take enough to make you drowsy, do not distort thinking. They relieve pain and elevate your mood. This is equally true of Tylenol 3 with codeine, of fentanyl, and of heroin. Though they may be sedative—and numerous users, including me, also note paradoxical stimulant effects—they are not depressants like alcohol. No slurry words or fumbled movements. No coke-like jerkiness.

Patients taking accustomed doses prescribed for chronic pain would be perfectly composed and lucid, entirely normal. A little sleepy, maybe, or conversely, a little animated. The late, great Oliver Sacks describes in *Hallucinations* his experience — as a thirty-second birthday gift to himself — of injecting a significant quantity of morphine pilfered from his physician parents' medical supplies:

> Within a minute or so, my attention was drawn to a sort
> of commotion on the sleeve of my dressing gown, which
> hung on the door. I gazed intently at this, and as I did so, it
> resolved itself into a miniature but microscopically detailed
> battle scene. I could see silken tents of different colors, the
> largest of which was flying a royal pennant. [...] I lost all
> sense of this being a spot on the sleeve of my dressing gown,
> of the fact that I was lying in bed, that I was in London,
> that it was 1964.
>
> Before shooting up the morphine, I had been reading
> Froissart's *Chronicles* and *Henry V*, and now these became
> conflated in my hallucination. I realized that what I was
> gazing at from my aerial viewpoint was Agincourt, late
> in 1415, that I was looking down on the serried armies of
> England and France drawn up to do battle. And in the great
> pennanted tent, I knew, was Henry V himself. [...] I glanced
> at my watch. I had injected the morphine at nine-thirty, and
> now it was ten. But I had a sense of something odd — it had
> been dusk when I took the morphine; it should be darker
> still. But it was not. It was getting lighter, not darker, outside.
> It *was* ten o'clock, I realized, but ten in the morning. I had
> been gazing, motionless, at my Agincourt for more than
> twelve hours.[37]

While it was a magical experience, Sacks resolved not to repeat it. One could easily dream one's life away. The few times I have tried my own modest, oral dose of morphine have not gone very well. At a very low dose, it does nothing. At double that dose, still low, it relieves pain; instills a heaviness that feels almost muscular, and paradoxically painful, even; induces great lassitude; makes time pass mysteriously. I'm drowsy, but when I try to rest my sleep is fragmented and haunted by distressing scraps of dreams. I think Sacks is right: morphine, though helpful for dying, does not seem conducive to actually living—for me at any rate.

My friend Emily and I lie in the grass in the park on a chilly, sunny fall day. I pick at bits of grass as I try to explain my frustration at endless pain, at the limits it puts on my capacities, on the scope of my life.

"When the alarm goes off in the morning," I tell her, "my first feeling is of dread. I'm thinking about the amount of work I'm going to put into just sitting up. You'd rather not wake up."

Em suggests antidepressants, not for the first time. I explain that tramadol feels very antidepressant when I take it. (In fact, it has been investigated for use as a "legitimate" antidepressant.) Yes, I am depressed, but for the first time—notwithstanding many years, now long behind me, of not-very-effective medications—I can decide when to make that leaden hopelessness go away. Extracts of opium, and its synthesized imitations, bind to our *mu*-opioid receptors—proteins present in the brain, spinal cord, intestinal tract, and elsewhere in the body. It took until 1974 for scientists to discover that we produce our very own opioids, called endorphins. The word was a neologism, a short form of "endogenous morphine," because we knew about morphine before we knew that we—clever creatures that we are—produce these magical molecules ourselves, in the brain and pituitary gland. Indeed, the receptors for opioids and endorphins have been part of our genetic makeup since our ancestors first developed backbones 450 million years ago.[38]

So exercise is a natural form of pain relief and mild euphoria. A half an hour of running is, for me, as for many others, a reliable way to emerge from the enervating fog of depression. I'm lucky in the nature of my spine disease, at least in that regard: one of AS's diagnostic features is that stiffness and pain worsen with rest and improve with exercise. Stretching, strengthening, and cardiovascular exercise are fundamental to treatment and improved outcomes.

While I can't stand for more than five minutes or sit for more than ten without pain and obvious discomfort, I can run for quite a long time on a soft, indoor track. Psychologically speaking, this is life-saving. (On real morphine I'm far too lazy for exercise — but I have learned that tramadol mixed with endogenous morphine from a long run is a glorious combination.) I'd heard of people becoming addicted to exercise and had understood it as a mild mania for being fit. In fact, there is a recognized disorder called "exercise addiction" and at least some evidence suggests that the pain relief and euphoria produced by exertion can create a pleasure-seeking feedback loop.[39] In some people this is associated with body dysmorphia, eating disorders, and control issues, but in most this is a mild and beneficial dependency — rather than the sort of thing that leads to robbing sneaker stores at gunpoint.

Will Self, the tall and cadaverous British novelist and essayist, is a former heroin addict. He was once hired by the UK's *Observer* newspaper on the strength of his reputation as an exceedingly literate junkie (and later fired after he quietly snorted heroin in the bathroom of Prime Minister John Major's campaign jet). Self is also a walker, covering heroic distances measured in the tens of kilometres at a time. He wrote this passage many years after leaving off the smack:

> The surrealist poet Louis Aragon wrote a famous book called *Le Paysan de Paris*; in it he describes how at unexpected moments during such a promenade, the walker, if sufficiently alive to the nuances of place and atmosphere, can experience the "moment." What exactly this "moment" is can seem a little obscure, but in essence it's the ambulatory equivalent of the sort of insights the surrealists believed they received from dreams, séances, automatic writing and other methods they used to short-circuit the deadening influence of rationality.[40]

Self doesn't allude here to the resonance with the mental state of the opiated *flâneur*. But it is there. Walk long enough and natural opioids mingle with a pleasant sense of being lost — an ideally receptive, relaxed, and dynamic creative state. The writer Malcolm Cowley was once asked in a *Paris Review* interview if he had any tricks to get him going on his day's writing. He replied: "A lot of people use walking. I wonder if the decline of walking will lead to a decline of the creative process."[41] But walking isn't always an option, nor is it an option for every creative person. There must be other ways to be a *flâneur*.

In the evening, my children are asleep and the house is hushed, save for the wonder of their little bellows-like breathing that fills our apartment. I stand by the fridge and pour myself a mug of milk. Earlier in the day, anticipating this moment, I tried to focus on the exact nature and quality of the pain I experience—wanting to go beyond aversion, to get something out of the experience, knowing that I have the power to banish it later on, when I am ready. That moment is finally here. I swallow a tramadol pill and a few pieces of dark, bitter chocolate to keep me awake for the most magical part of my day. As the pain melts away after an hour, I settle in at my desk.

Alethea Hayter, a British academic, tried to methodically tease apart the creativity innate in an artist and the creativity induced by their use of opiates. When Hayter published *Opium and the Romantic Imagination* in 1968, you could still get a prescription for heroin in the UK—but the dangers of heroin (long prohibited in the United States) and morphine addiction were becoming increasingly clear. She was curious about opioids' reputation for causing waking dreams, reveries, and vivid fantasies, and her book is a thorough analysis of the works of literary users of opium.

In reviewing the work of De Quincey, Keats, Poe, Collins, Coleridge, and others, Hayter concluded that opioids loosen the restrictions on creative thinking—and seem to enhance one's ability to find patterns. My own experience bears this out. Opioids seem to make it easier to derive symbols and metaphors from one's imaginings or from the raw material presented by reality. On tramadol, I range freely in my thoughts. I can draw analogies, coming up with unexpected parallels between disparate things or ideas. This effect on analogical thinking is mentioned over and over in the literature on opium.

But the precise nature of what opiates contribute to the creative process slips hazily through Hayter's fingers, beyond the conclusion that they stimulate metaphorical thinking, providing writers both with dream imagery and the means to creatively interpret it. More important, to my mind, is the calm, playful focus I can achieve with tramadol. It's a state conducive to the odd combination of discipline and freedom that any art-making requires. That dispassionate absorption, more than the discrete thinking patterns that Alethea Hayter tried to tease out of her reading, seems to me to be the key to opioids' influence on creativity.

Of course, De Quincey himself made an important cautionary point about turning to substances for creativity. "If a man 'whose talk is of oxen' should become an Opium-eater," he wrote, "the probability is that (if he is not too dull to dream at all) — he will dream about oxen."[42]

Another white night — no sleep, no oxen — followed by fitful rest. Once the confusion of the morning passes, my dominant feeling is that of dread. I spend twenty minutes (the time I usually stretch while still lying down, reminding arthritic joints how to move) simply willing myself to face the day. Through the day I have the distinct sense of my face as an unsmiling mask, and I feel, both physically and metaphorically, that my skin is too thin.

In the afternoon I give in and take tramadol. After an hour that blessed warm feeling melts the stiffness, dissolving pain along with my black mood. I pick up my children from school and am able to play with them like a good mother. After reading them bedtime stories and kissing them goodnight, I lie down on the floor in the living room to meditate for ten timed minutes.

My mind quickly drifts. Visual imagery assembles itself before me. In precise detail against the clear and familiar background of my living room ceiling I can see the body of some creature, curled up and opened as for a dissection, the viscera in muted, contrasting colours. I then imagine — I am awake, not dreaming, in a sort of waking dream — another creature, smaller, crawling inside the body cavity of the first creature, curling up around the stomach or beside the liver, tucking itself in for comfort and for warmth.

I abort the meditation session before the ten-minute timer rings. This is my first taste of the notoriously dark opioid-induced reverie.

Thomas De Quincey's reveries — something between dreams and hallucinations — were the result of withdrawal at times, and, at others, of using laudanum. They were fearsome, but De Quincey's imaginative power is remarkable. In his dreams, he writes in the *Confessions*,

> I was buried for a thousand years, in stone coffins, with
> mummies and sphynxes, in narrow chambers at the heart
> of eternal pyramids. I was kissed, with cancerous kisses,
> by crocodiles; and laid, confounded with all unutterable
> slimy things, amongst reeds and Nilotic mud.[43]

A frightened obsession with crocodiles — representing perhaps a xenophobic Orientalism, or contrasted with the loving innocence of children, or simply a representation of all that is horror — became a recurring theme in his reveries, in his withdrawal nightmares, and in his writing:

> The cursed crocodile became to me the object of more
> horror than almost all the rest. [. . .] All the feet of the tables,
> sofas, &c. soon became instinct with life: the abominable
> head of the crocodile, and his leering eyes, looked out at me,
> multiplied into a thousand repetitions: and I stood loathing
> and fascinated.[44]

The terrifying image of a coach driver transformed in his imagination into such a beast — a venerable croc, in a livery of scarlet and gold — haunts De Quincey's other great work, *The English Mail-Coach*.

As for me, I have occasionally experienced other waking dreams. Once during a yoga class I imagined riding a flying carpet. The Persian rug pattern, the way it billowed toward me from the air below, a cool feeling from the wind, and most of all, a frightened exhilaration: it was far more real and surprising than an imagined scene, but more within my conscious control than a dream. That one was a gift.

Over the past eight years I have regularly been asked to rate various aspects of my pain — along with fatigue and resulting psychological distress — according to those one-to-ten scales I mentioned. (On one such scale — there are many — ten represents unbearable, unimaginable suffering, the sort that would quickly cause one to black out; one represents no pain: "feeling perfectly normal."[45]) It's a frustrating exercise. Both mental and physical pain are difficult to quantify.

They are best expressed in metaphors: the dark hole, the cliff, the vise, the hot poker, the black dogs. Or in ambiguous phrases evoking the senses: heavy, fine and needle-like, wide or very bright. Loud and metallic. Electric. Soft and creeping. Or more like concrete, like lead, like spiders.

Pain studies could be like wine connoisseurship: "It started with a bouquet of creeping unease, then a full, bloody, vigorous sensation followed by a lingering ache."

So I write this, again, under the influence.

It's a release that I've earned through the sheer effort of waiting for it all day. At last I take the pill, and I begin to focus intently on the pain in my neck and down my back — waiting for the magic moment when it begins to melt away. I watch, feel, and wait. Minutes pass. Is it gone? I think I feel it leave. But no. The pain is still there.

Then, as it always does, at almost exactly the one-hour mark, something shifts. The ropey muscles of the neck that pull my head forward, the tight muscles around my hips, mid-back, and sacroiliac joints (in an X-ray you can see the erosion) — they all seem to loosen at last. I sigh audibly, letting my shoulders fall. I stand up straighter. Gravity stops pounding me into submission. All at once, I seem able to inhale more oxygen than usual. That breath is rich and deep. I'm also breathing more slowly than usual.

I close my eyes almost unconsciously. When I let them close, just for a moment, there's a pleasant weight on my eyelids, as if I were falling into a dreamless, restorative sleep. At the same time I seem to float, perhaps on a pool raft drifting on saltwater waves, with a sort of inner buoyancy. It is wonderful.

I could stay in it forever, like those Victorian gentlemen found after days by worried families — prostrate upon a back-alley opium den couch, obscured in a cloud of stale smoke.

But I open my eyes after a moment because in the infinite peace and wisdom now upon me — right now — I also see my goal: to write, to create, clearly and without stress.

First physical pain recedes, and then emotional pain. I was depressed, and now I am not.

Nothing is hazy or distorted or vague. There is no drunkenness, no lack of balance or blurring. I can once again see all the little worries and big angsts in my life from a bearable distance. And now, taken a little out of myself, I can also see and feel compassion for other people's struggles, am interested once again in their stories. For these few hours I have regained the essential human characteristic of someone who is well and flourishing: a healthy curiosity about everything that is not me.

Not least, the thread of thought I want to track down and record in writing plays out smoothly and I can follow it. Peaceful, concentrated work is the best opioid side effect of all.

I close my eyes again. There are endless variations in the texture of good feelings that keep me here, happily working at my desk. Every time I close my eyes — every time I inhale, deeply, then exhale — these feelings are intensified. This eye-closing, this looking within: it's a subtle action which, over a group dinner or in a café, I've sometimes caught friends catching, to my shame.

But then, why should I feel ashamed?

It's a little glimpse of what is called (as I've since learned, on online forums where drug users and abusers share their experiences) "nodding" or "nodding out," drifting out of consciousness on opioids. The term is also used simply to describe sleeping or the sleepiness associated with the drug — and more generally "being on the nod" is long-used slang for a calm and dreamy opioid high. "Nod" is the Hebrew root of the word for "to wander." The term may refer to the involuntary dropping of the chin into a literal nod, but it carries, too, associations with the Biblical land of Nod and all manner of remixed cultural notions: wandering, desires, creativity, sleep, dreams.

Sunny morning, busy street in Toronto's Little Italy. Alam, the server at the Il Gatto Nero restaurant, nods hello and brings me my coffee, black. Notebook open on the glass-topped, black cat–inscribed table, I sit cross-legged and shift position every few seconds. Rattle, rattle in my backpack: a pen and that little bottle of pills. In my jacket pocket I sometimes feel for its slim plastic cylinder and child-proof top as if I were Gollum fingering for my precious. I order a croissant and begin to work — the expectation of pain relief enough to get me happily through the next hour. In the same vein, the always-ailing Marcel Proust began his day with coffee (a legal stimulant), a croissant, and some opium.[46]

Opium. *Plus ça change, plus c'est la même chose*...only the statistics are more impressive than in Proust's time. The estimated amount of opiate raw materials needed for *legal* (that is, medical) purposes around the world for 2015 was equivalent to some 620 tonnes of morphine. Globally, including non-legal uses (diversion), we collectively consumed 6.27 milligrams of morphine per person in 2013, or over 42,000 tonnes.[47]

That's the weight of 250 houses, 350 blue whales — or a quadrillion and a half poppy seeds.

Once you leave aside (deep breath please): the social costs of addiction; the risk of fatal overdose when drugs are taken in unsafe settings, unsafe amounts, unsafe combinations, or unsafe ways; the horrifying violence that has accompanied a profitable trade in illegal drugs; and the danger of diseases transmitted by sharing needles...set aside all that and the long-term health risks of opioids are actually slight compared to many, or even most, other medicines.

The social context of prohibition makes drugs like heroin incredibly dangerous. But it's true: at low doses, *relatively* few other long-term effects have been shown, particularly for opioids taken by mouth, even though opium has been used medicinally for thousands of years, morphine for hundreds, and even a synthetic drug like tramadol for over forty years now:

> Legal drugs like tobacco and alcohol are directly associated
> with a variety of serious physical health issues, while
> opioids — including heroin — are not in and of themselves
> harmful to the body (unless too high a dose is taken).[48]

Ah, the dose. There's the rub. The Swiss-German physician-alchemist Paracelsus — who incidentally first created tincture of opium and came up with the name *laudanum*, meaning "praiseworthy" — said it first and said it best: *dosis facit venenum*. "The dose makes the poison." For opioids, a "high" dose is too high if it exceeds the opioid tolerance of the person using it. It's a shifting, individual standard.

The problem with prescription opioids can be seen as a problem of dose, in that the initial therapeutic dose rarely remains therapeutic in the long term.

Knowing this — and enjoying the mental effects while depending on the pain-relieving ones — I try, as I've said, to take tramadol sparingly. But effective pain relief requires actually using it. And so I am, like De Quincey, like Coleridge, like so many others before me, falling into the same trap of raising the effective dose.

And now I find that when I'm not feeling very, very good, I'm feeling very, very horrid.

On several occasions I have looked up the number for a local distress hotline. I dial. I hang up. Nothing to say. I'm so locked up in misery I can barely talk.

Feeling that it is somehow dangerous not to stay in touch with people on the other side of the crazy line, I text jokes to my friends. The sillier and more pointless, the better. Sometimes the absurdity actually makes me laugh. I distract myself for hours looking up jokes on the internet.

> Hello, welcome to the Psychiatric Hotline.
> If you are obsessive-compulsive, please press 1 repeatedly.
> If you are co-dependent, please ask someone to press 2.
> If you have multiple personalities, please press 3, 4, 5, and 6.
> If you are paranoid-delusional, we know who you are and
>   what you want.
> If you are schizophrenic, listen carefully and a little voice will
>   tell you which number to press.
> If you are depressed, it doesn't matter which number you
>   press. No one will answer.

But you can't live on silly internet joke forums all the time. So I take tramadol more frequently, without the drug-free days that I had previously carefully interspersed between my hours of relief.

After a few weeks or a month at a particular regular daily dosing of tramadol, the euphoria I've mentioned takes longer to set in and then becomes barely noticeable—more wishful thinking than actual relief. In fact, after someone notes that I seem to be in pain, I note that why yes, so I am. Not only is the opioid no longer doing what it's *not* supposed to do, it's also not even offering the intermittent pain relief for which it was prescribed. I feel miserable and very bleak and I realize that I have reached a fork in the road. In order to get the effects—both pain relief and high—I need to either take less tramadol, or take more.

It took Thomas De Quincey eight years to reach the same fork. Of
that time, he wrote:

> True it is, that for nearly ten years I did occasionally take
> opium for the sake of the exquisite pleasure it gave me:
> but so long as I took it with this view, I was effectually
> protected from all material bad consequences by the necessity
> of interposing long intervals between the several acts of
> indulgence, in order to renew the pleasurable sensations.[49]

Exquisite pleasure aside, too much pain endangers my ability to properly stretch and mobilize each precious joint. It makes it harder to exercise,
harder to get out of bed and face the day. As we've come to understand
that maintaining mobility and circulation are crucially important in many
ailments, pain management has become key to better medical outcomes.
Today, poorly controlled pain is generally considered poor medicine — as
well as a failure of compassion. The latter is a fairly modern concern,
quality of life not having been a major goal of medicine in ages past. Dr.
Thomas Dormandy, a pathologist and the author of *Opium: Reality's Dark
Dream*, writes that "quality of life was an invention of the Romantic Age
propped up by opium."[50]

I don't tell my family doctor that my painkillers make me high — or
alter my experience of reality — and he has never asked. In an enlightened
age of medical cannabis, it wouldn't really be an appropriate question.
Besides, most people taking opioids as prescribed to relieve constant pain
would quickly develop tolerance and lose any euphoric sensations, making
them only early, emergent properties — and as beside the point as the
spontaneous orgasms one patient experienced on Parkinson's meds.[51]

And my doctor is no fool. He prescribes small doses, limited quantities,
and no automatic repeats on any prescription. I ask how to prevent developing tolerance, and he reminds me that it is better to treat pain before
it gets out of control. If, or when, I become tolerant, he can rotate me to
another opioid.[52]

He suggests two trial options, and I choose hydromorphone, a strong opioid marketed as Dilaudid. He writes me a prescription for just ten half-doses. People react quite differently to different opioids: one may produce nausea, another constipation, another itching. It's therefore sensible to let a patient try more than one in a controlled way. I actually just want to know that tramadol will go back to feeling the way it felt before, but I can't figure out how to discreetly ask the question.

Dilaudid is seven-and-a-half times stronger, milligram for milligram, than morphine. It has been implicated in many overdose deaths. I start on a minuscule dose. Typically (or ideally) a doctor will begin a patient on the minimum dose of an opioid and gradually increase it until it brings adequate pain relief. Hydromorphone is considered extremely addictive, and the opioid that (according to those in a position to know[53]) can closely if imperfectly approximate the experience of heroin. The intense good feelings it's giving me this very moment as I write this back that up. I began to feel shivers of pleasurable sensation after about forty minutes.

But, like morphine (and unlike tramadol), it is poorly absorbed through the gastrointestinal tract, which limits the intensity. Just as other patients using it for pain report in online forums, it doesn't seem to me to cause mental cloudiness.[54] Neither, though, do I feel the opening of possibilities that I get with tramadol. Its pain-relieving effect is also very short-lived. On another occasion, Dilaudid seems to do little for the pain, and I increase the dose as my doctor had advised. I feel the soreness dissipate a little and a small burst of positive energy pushes me out of the house. I make it on time to meet friends at the Jean-Michel Basquiat exhibit at the art gallery—yes, the Basquiat who died in 1988 at twenty-seven, in New York, of a heroin overdose. But despite a slight dreaminess and some relief in my spine, I soon find it too painful to stand. While my friends view the paintings, I'm reduced to crouching in a corner.

Every two years or so, we visit my in-laws and large extended family in Mexico City. I usually make a pilgrimage to the sun-lit, fantastically coloured Casa Azul, the former home of Mexican painter Frida Kahlo and now a museum dedicated to her art and life. I've been fascinated by

Kahlo's life story since my first trip there, to meet my then-boyfriend's family, in 2002.

Through her life, Kahlo, who died in 1954, had numerous operations on a spine and pelvis forever damaged by a horrific trolley accident. Her life was filled with hour upon hour of excruciating, demoralizing pain. Through her treatments, she became dependent upon painkillers (morphine and meperidine, an opioid marketed as Demerol) as well as alcohol, which she also used for pain relief. "I tried to drown my sorrows," she wrote, "but the damned things learned to swim."[55]   .

So far as I know, Kahlo never heard of De Quincey, but her life reads as one great Romantic oscilloscope graph: soaring highs and subterranean lows. She might be considered the patron saint of artsy-people-who-suffer-back-pain-and-depression-relieved-only-by-reliance-on-drugs.

"I never lost my spirit," she wrote of a period spent in the hospital near the end of her life, her beloved husband Diego Rivera ensconced for a time in a hospital room beside hers. "I always spent my time painting because they kept me going with Demerol, and this animated me and it made me feel happy."[56] This period — enlivened by the rare presence of unreliable Rivera, and by prescription drugs — was one of many fleeting moments that Kahlo snatched from a life otherwise dominated by physical and mental suffering. Seeing a painting in a gallery, or in the artist's own home or studio, is quite different from looking at it in a book or on a screen. You realize that an actual person — imagining, dreaming, suffering, working — held the brush, made each stroke, set down her brush in weary despair, looked out the window at the sculpture garden, back inside at the anatomy textbooks, the ceramic tiles, the bottle of tequila, or the hypodermic needle. In her diaries, you can see how Kahlo endlessly tried to reason with herself, to find hope when feeling low. She lived large when her health permitted it, collecting illustrious friends and lovers. She also collected votive paintings: folk paintings on tin in which people depict their real incidents of suffering. In detailed images and captions, they thank the Virgin of Guadalupe for intervening — for letting them recover after they were struck by lightning, incapacitated by polio, robbed and assaulted, or hit by a runaway horse. Or, in Kahlo's case, survived a broken spinal column, collarbone, pelvis, and foot—and had an iron handrail ram through her vagina, abdomen, and uterus.

Upon developing my own spine condition, I graduated from interest to identification with Kahlo. Like me, she took pre-med courses with the goal of becoming a doctor, but ended up (as all doctors will, sooner or later) a patient instead. She remained passionately interested in medicine, its tools, and its subject, the struggling human body, and portrayed these in gruesome detail in her paintings. She found solace and meaning in art, while being constantly frustrated by the limits imposed on her by physical and mental suffering.

In periods of great illness and pain, Kahlo dressed with extravagant care, layering on jewellery to distract herself and those around her. When feeling particularly demoralized, I copy her, wearing multiple bright necklaces. One of her paintings is a self-portrait with the spine represented as a broken column, resembling something from an ancient Greek temple. For years, I misinterpreted it for some reason to be the long barrel of a gun running up her body instead of a spine. Either way, it is a searing representation of what it feels like to have a crumbling, grumbling vertical axis where a healthy backbone ought to be.

Like De Quincey, Frida Kahlo exploited her suffering for its inherently dramatic possibilities in art. I recognize in De Quincey's lush descriptions of the pains and the pleasures of laudanum the impulse I see in myself to romanticize my experiences. In Kahlo, I recognize the desperate nature of that impulse.

Some commentators have described Kahlo's ongoing search for medical treatment that might bring physical relief as pathological, attributing her physical symptoms to a misplaced search for love through medical intervention. This is a strain of the frequently unjustified, skeptical response that healthcare providers give to many pain sufferers, particularly women—especially women from racialized groups, or who live in poverty, or who have multiple health issues. They may be dismissed as drug-seekers, disturbed souls, or hysterical. And their pain is vastly under-treated or mismanaged, resulting in further desperation and apparently odd behaviour.[57]

Some doctors speak of pain sufferers principally as "difficult patients" who need to be redirected, spoken firmly to, or appeased. Others talk about the "pain lobby"—a vague reference to overbearing drug marketers in cahoots with lily-livered legislators and pushover docs, along with strident or manipulated patient advocacy groups. I find such voices dismissive, blindingly privileged, loose or selective with evidence, and patronizing, even as they raise valid questions about these drugs and how they are used.

For those few writers who have questioned the authenticity of Kahlo's symptoms and ongoing suffering, I can only prescribe a handrail through the vagina, if any of them have one, in hopes of provoking a more compassionate—and ultimately more clinically effective—response.

Moved by greater compassion and greater insight, Fernando Antelo, a physician, wrote:

> Frida Kahlo's life and artwork can serve as a resource for physicians who want to better comprehend the experience and dehumanizing consequences of pain. Her paintings are a medium to visualize pain and the effect of pain on the human condition. We witness the suffering, grief, and doubt in Kahlo's paintings; through them, we can contemplate the experience of pain from the perspective of the patient. Patients living with pain are acutely aware of their bodies in ways that healthy people may not be. Pain can be discernible and persistent as well as dynamic and indefinable.
>
> Pain, moreover, can bring about a transformation in a person that manifests both physically and mentally. Living with pain can have a paralytic effect on a person's goals and dreams, in addition to family, marriage and career.
>
> Though the practice of medicine often focuses on diagnosis, treatment and education, the role of the physician demands much more. By understanding pain as a complex

phenomenon that affects many aspects of life, we as
physicians can fulfill our role to comfort and heal.[58]

Lately, when I've briefly stopped taking tramadol, I've found that I may
have some physical dependence on it. After a days-long stretch without
it, I experience what could be withdrawal symptoms: abrupt and intense
depression, restless sleep, and stomach upset. I don't crave it, though,
unless I am in severe pain, so I think what I'm craving is the pain relief
rather than the opioid itself. In fact, it becomes a little contest with myself
to see how long I can go without. Upon giving in and taking the drug,
though, it is like coming back to myself.

As addicts say, in the end I am taking the drug not for a high, but just
to feel normal. Or De Quincey: "Since leaving off opium, I take a great
deal too much of it for my health."[59]

I started out taking a pill for severe cramps. That turned
into taking 10–20 mgs on the weekends. That turned into
taking 45–60 mgs every day for the past 7 months. I am a
functional addict; I work full time and have a very successful
Etsy business on the side which I put hours into as a second
full time job. I thought I would never be a daily user but here
I am. It makes me able to work harder, and that extra money
earned goes to pills. I wish I could only use on the weekends,
but now there's always an excuse to use more, to be creative,
to be in a good mood for my bf's birthday coming up, to go
to the gym.

— Another drug use forum post[60]

I write to Wayne Skinner, co-author of a book called *Substance Abuse in
Canada*. He's a social worker specializing in addiction at the Centre for
Addiction and Mental Health in Toronto. The book reflects what is called
a biopsychosocial approach to addiction. In other approaches, addiction

may be viewed as a brain disease, or as a moral failing, or as a "disease" of choice, or as a life sentence meted out in one's genes. I disclose in my email that although I don't currently meet any of the definitions of addiction I'd read in his book, I do regularly take prescription opioid medication.

He replies with grave kindness, and on a cold day in January I walk the ten minutes from my house to his office in the former Provincial Lunatic Asylum. I'm quite nervous but the avuncular Skinner sets me at ease, asking about my kids and telling me about his granddaughter. We proceed to talk for two meandering, challenging hours. I explain that I am conflicted about my use of opioid medications. I also tell him that they have been a revelation in that they give me control over depression. I confide—bashfully—that while I am taking them as prescribed and in modest doses for pain, I do choose *when* to take them more on the basis of enjoyment, especially on quiet evenings to write.

In a way it seems that I'm insistently trying to establish myself as being "on the edge" of being an addict; gently, he pushes back, defining me with equal insistence as a person doing the best she can. According to the biopsychosocial approach to addiction, just because something is highly pleasurable, illegal, or dangerous doesn't mean anyone who uses it will fall prey to addiction (statistics for just about any potentially addictive substance you can think of bear this out). Addiction is far more complex, and results from an individual combination of an experience feeling immediately rewarding, of biological predisposition, of availability of the pleasurable substance, of our relationships with other people, and of physical or emotional suffering that may be relieved by the behaviour or substance. Skinner speaks generally about addiction, which includes behaviours like compulsive gambling or porn addiction. But there *are* substances—like opioids—that seem to invite dependency.

"Addictive substances are appetitive and reinforcing," Skinner says. *Appetitive*, a lovely word, in that such substances satisfy deep appetites for pleasure. And *reinforcing*, because such pleasure carves strong, memorable grooves into the psyche, particularly in people who for some reason feel they need it. "People who are opioid-dependent have higher rates of depression than in the general population. Addiction problems tend to be accompanied by mental health issues," he tells me. It's not that easy to tease out the direction of causality, but there is reason to believe that people seek out the drugs that help them feel okay. "For example, people with anxiety may find relief in drinking alcohol or smoking pot, while those suffering with attention deficit disorders may turn to stimulants, including cocaine, to self-medicate their symptoms." He also mentions that conflict avoidance is an issue for many opioid users. I file that one away to worry about later.

What Skinner is saying relates to effects I observe in myself, and to what I've read about others' experiences with opioids. In my case, tramadol is appealing partly because it somehow firms up the shaky boundaries of my personality. My ego becomes vague and crushable when I'm depressed. But with tramadol it is robust, an adequate container: the expansive inner feeling it generates is soft but resilient, a protective bubble.

I think I now better understand things I've heard about serious opiate addicts — especially heroin users, who, according to the stereotype, may lose interest altogether in making meaningful connections with other people. "Sometimes ah think that people become junkies just because they subconsciously crave a wee bit ay silence," wrote Irvine Welsh of heroin addicts in *Trainspotting*.[61] Indeed, wrapped in the gauzy cocoon of peaceful concentration that accompanies the far less intense hit of a legal, low-dose narcotic, it's not difficult to shrug off the slings and arrows of difficult people and demanding relationships — or the lack thereof.

De Quincey himself attributed his attachment to opium to childhood trauma, and spoke of it as satisfying a genuine need: "I trace the origin of my confirmed opium-eating to a necessity growing out of my early sufferings in the streets of London," he wrote.[62]

The broader world — the one outside my head — confirms this attraction. Despite scarce published data on rates of opioid use among First Nations, Inuit, and Métis communities in Canada at the time I write this (though that will change), a number of First Nations communities have declared community emergencies due to the prevalence of prescription drug misuse and related harms like accidental overdose and suicide,[63] with Canada's Auditor General expressing similar concerns.[64] Many of these communities are already suffering from relatively poor health, just one result of multigenerational trauma resulting from residential schools and a long and ongoing legacy of racism, violence, and culturally genocidal policies.

Tramadol, regarded in 2015 North America as barely even an opioid (that will change too), has become an incredibly popular street drug in occupied Palestine, as well as in other places in the Middle East. In Egypt it has surpassed cannabis and heroin as the most popular recreational drug.[65] In Gaza, under an endless occupation where there is little or no opportunity for advancement or escape and where things lurch from crisis to crisis, people live in a constant state of tension and confinement, leavened by unique incidents of horror. No wonder that a drug that offers a deep sense of peace and elevation is appealing. In 2010, international newspapers reported that Hamas officials burned some two million of the painkiller pills in an attempt to combat rampant addiction—and, perhaps, to prevent chemically induced tolerance of the intolerable. Similarly, in the 1970s the Black Panthers saw heroin as a tool of white supremacist oppression. The title of New York Black Panther Michael "Cetewayo" Tabor's 1970 pamphlet "CAPITALISM PLUS DOPE EQUALS GENOCIDE"[66] is a succinct expression of the Black Panther belief that heroin (dope) acted as, well, the opiate of his people, supporting oppression and ultimately death in Black American communities.

But people seek out painkillers because they are in pain. The Romantics had tuberculosis and rheumatic fever. Today, arthritis pain is one of the principal ailments driving people to use opioids. An aging population subject to osteoarthritis—as well as higher rates of chronic inflammatory diseases like rheumatoid arthritis or AS—is going to be a population with ever-higher rates of daily, maddening joint pain. That's without even considering the impact of a trend toward precarious, literally back-breaking work and unaffordable preventative healthcare upon the prevalence of back pain and other pain conditions. According to the National Institute on Drug Abuse, "the bulk of American patients who need relief from persistent, moderate-to-severe non-cancer pain have back pain conditions (approximately 38 million) or osteoarthritis (approximately 17 million)."[67]

But do we really *need* relief?

Pain does not have to be depressing. There are ways to distance oneself from it. The most helpful I've found is the sort of mindfulness meditation where you actually try to observe pain quite intently, noticing exactly, with curiosity, and without judgment, just what it is like. Over time, you find ways to go beyond just "I hate it, I want it to stop" — that is, to overcome aversion and attraction.

I learned this formally through a structured set of mindfulness-based stress reduction (MBSR) workshops developed by Jon Kabat-Zinn, a professor of medicine and founder of the Stress Reduction Clinic and the Center for Mindfulness in Medicine, Health Care, and Society at the University of Massachusetts Medical School. The approach is based on Buddhist principles, with the mysticism stripped out. MBSR training, sometimes combined with cognitive-behavioural psychotherapy, is now widely offered across North America for the treatment of chronic pain, anxiety, depression, and a host of other conditions. Despite practising mindfulness, however, I find that it remains extremely hard to prevent ongoing pain from veering quickly into complete despair.

My New York insight is that it's better to feel good than to feel bad: I can't tell now whether this represents a passionate rebuttal to the quiet martyrdom of everyday suffering or a sign of weakness, of surrender to the most primitive drives that classify all things according to good/bad, aversion/attraction.

Opioids replace the non-judgment of mindfulness with a powerful attraction to what feels good. Despite the sinful connotations of pleasure-seeking, that attractive sensation of calm observation — Rebecca Solnit's reptilian feeling — is the same empty, comfortable detachment that the experienced meditator may occasionally feel. It's equally analogous to the notion of "flow" as described by psychologist Mihály Csíkszentmihályi: the time-suspending feeling that comes from total absorption in an activity. Flow has, like mindfulness, been popularized to death in a million positive psychology self-help books, none of which mention that opioids can get you there faster—and despite distracting obstacles like worry, sadness, or pain.

The Holy Grail for researchers and pharmaceutical companies: a non-addictive, non-dangerous opioid. They've certainly tried. The really hard part is selecting for analgesic effects while avoiding the deliciously reinforcing reward pathway. Over the decades and centuries, creators and purveyors of pharmaceuticals have enthusiastically marketed such alternatives as:

> morphine (non-addictive alternative to opium);
> long-acting oxycodone (non-addictive alternative to
>   morphine);
> tramadol (non-addictive alternative to oxycodone);
> methadone (non-addictive alternative to heroin); and
> heroin (non-addictive alternative to morphine), among others.

More recently, rising fears about overdose and addiction rates are making former pariah drugs like cannabis seem an innocuous (and profitable) alternative. Indeed cannabis is a very promising alternative or adjunct to lower doses of opioids or other drugs—but its long-term effects are largely unknown, and its effect on cognition and motor skills means that it is definitely not a good option for all pain patients, even when it does work to reduce the perception of pain. Other possibilities gaining increasing attention, investor interest, and a speedy rehabilitation in the popular imagination, even as opioids are increasingly equated with poison, include low doses of LSD, infusions of ketamine, and other non-opioid psychoactives. More interested in profit than committed to a particular substance, some Big Opioid executives have quickly moved on to Big Cannabis, while others have instead contributed to anti-legalization campaigns. Then there is the Butrans transdermal, an opioid patch that is, in the traditionally flippant way, proposed by researchers and marketers alike as a less-easily abused alternative to the strong, long-acting fentanyl pain patch.

In practically every case, the marketing pressures and inducements placed on doctors and government regulators by pharmaceutical companies have been relentless and, often, shameless.

Various research teams are hard at work producing new, powerful opiate analgesics that do not cause physical dependence or reinforcing behaviour (or a number of other common opiate side effects like respiratory depression and constipation).[68] The science behind it is interesting and based on an evolution in our understanding of the diversity of opioid receptors—but maybe only time will tell if these, or other newly developed opium-inspired painkillers, are the long-sought non-addictive opioids.

I wonder if I'm in some new spot on the continuum of addiction severity: the pre-addiction obsessive fascination stage. I think about my opium-eating and what it all means—a lot. There is a phrase I came across when I started googling "opiate experiences" and similar terms. The phrase is "opiate naive." It means someone who is new to using opiates (recreationally or otherwise) and has not developed any level of tolerance to the drugs. It's also a good term for my feeling upon discovering an online world of people with relatively normal lives and surprising drug habits:

> yeah there's no way to tell how often you can use without
> becoming an addict. When I broke my arm I was only taking
> a half to maybe two percs at a time but before i knew it i was
> taking 20 at a time which led to shooting heroin so yeah...
> doesn't matter how you start out because more than likely
> it'll end up being an addiction. Not something you can play
> around with.[69]

As soon as *Confessions of an English Opium-Eater* was published, critics immediately voiced fears that it would inspire others to become recreational opium users and addicts. In one Sherlock Holmes story, "The Man with the Twisted Lip," Dr. Watson describes an old friend who had done just that:

> The habit grew upon him, as I understand, from some foolish
> freak when he was at college; for having read De Quincey's
> description of his dreams and sensations, he had drenched
> his tobacco with laudanum in an attempt to produce the
> same effects. He found, as so many more have done, that the
> practice is easier to attain than to get rid of, and for many
> years he continued to be a slave to the drug, an object of
> mingled horror and pity to his friends and relatives.[70]

Much of what is written about opioids, including rather a lot of the medical literature, conflates the distinct terms "dependency" and "addiction."[71]

Physical dependence, where your body comes to depend upon the opioids and reduces its own production of endorphins, may arise more quickly than tolerance (where over time many, although not all users, find that they need to increase the dose to get the same effect) and is a separate phenomenon — although they often occur at the same time. If you stop taking the drug abruptly once you have become physically dependent on it, you then experience unpleasant withdrawal symptoms.

It's not clear what proportion of the people usually described as "addicted" — in apocalyptic-sounding news reports about the "opioid crisis" — are actually physically dependent (due to the drugs being used for treatment of long-term severe pain) without exhibiting the behavioural issues that define psychological addiction.

Still, the doctor-sanctioned escalation of doses that often occurs as patients become tolerant to their original dose can represent a failure of opioids as a pain relief option if patients are left worse off. Patients could end up chronically taking dangerous doses, trapped by the pains of withdrawal from exploring other options. (And opioids can occasionally, especially at high doses, actually *cause* new pain, although it's not really clear how often that occurs in practice.) Prescribing opioids responsibly requires a very careful hand.

Regardless of how you define it, after a spate of poor health and depression incited him to start taking laudanum daily, De Quincey fell into some version of dependence, and for the rest of his life laudanum was as vital to him as food and water. He chronicled much of this less-transcendent aspect of the drug in a section of his *Confessions* entitled "The Pains of Opium."

Over and over he tried to reduce or stop completely his intake of laudanum, each time bringing on, within a few days, an atrocious list of emotional and physical withdrawal symptoms. ("Cold turkey" refers to the gooseflesh from chills that are one common symptom of opiate withdrawal;[72] "kicking the habit" refers to restless legs, another withdrawal symptom.[73]) Though he happily exploited his laudanum experience in his published writing, De Quincey's suffering with such symptoms of withdrawal and others — violent depression, gastrointestinal upset, terrible nightmares, insomnia, trouble concentrating, and voracious craving for the drug — was genuine and chronicled with much greater desperation in his private letters to friends.

During six months of despair induced by reduced dosages, he wrote in his private journal: "Horrible! that a man's own chamber — the place of his refuge and retreat — should betray him! . . . Not fear or terror, but inexpressible misery, is the last portion of the opium-eater."[74]

Sometimes, with me as with De Quincey, it is hard to tell whether the painkiller is causing or alleviating mental distress, or whether it's not related at all. De Quincey wrote in one letter that:

Whatever I may have been writing is suddenly wrapt, as
it were, in one sheet of consuming fire — the very paper is
poisoned to my eyes. I cannot endure to look at it, and I
sweep it away into vast piles of unfinished letters, or inchoate
essays.[75]

De Quincey's wife, Margaret, and his children would sit with him as he
suffered sleepless nights with the agonies of withdrawal. Robert Morrison
writes,

Margaret attended him through these dreadful sieges of
physical and spiritual despair. His sufferings frightened her,
and when she witnessed the horror of his attempts to reduce
his opium dosages, she was the "first to beg me to desist."
At length De Quincey "grew afraid to sleep." One solution
was simply to stay up the whole night and the following day.
Another was to ask Margaret and the children "to sit around
me and to talk: hoping thus to derive an influence from what
affected me externally into my internal world of shadows."[76]

This stratagem did not work, and he battled with himself, taking
increasingly high, even astonishing doses before making further agonizing
but successful attempts to lower the dose — for a time. His family
remained devoted, and though hectic, his family life was harmonious.
(A serious and long-term addict at a time when the average man lived
less than half a century, Thomas De Quincey died at the very respectable
age of seventy-four, having far outlived his long-suffering wife. He took
laudanum virtually until his death.) A close reading of De Quincey's life
suggests that if he hadn't been continually on the verge of financial ruin
due mostly to addictive *behaviours* rather than substances, his life might
have been a far easier one, notwithstanding the decades-long addiction to
opium.

Book buying, in fact, was the most compulsive of De Quincey's various
addictive behaviours. He would spend money he couldn't afford on books,

let his rooms pile up with papers, and then, overwhelmed at the task of cleaning them out, actually move out and rent new lodgings that sparked more joy. Sometimes for himself and his family, sometimes just for him to quietly live and work.

The result was that despite professional success and a steady output of published writing, he was constantly in debt, to the point that he was hounded by solicitors, legal officers, and dozens of creditors from across England and Scotland (where he lived for years). He was occasionally homeless, often in hiding, and more than once sought sanctuary for himself and his family within the six- or seven-mile circumference of Edinburgh's Holyrood sanctuary to avoid being taken into debtor's prison. Several times he was "put to the horn," in which messengers-at-arms blew three blasts on a horn in the marketplace and then denounced him by name for his debts.

Drawing on De Quincey family papers, Robert Morrison writes that De Quincey, a genuine eccentric,

> often "set something on fire, the commonest incident being for someone to look up from work or book to say casually, 'Papa, your hair is on fire,' of which a calm, 'Is it, my love?' and a hand rubbing out the blaze was all the notice taken." One night a maid reported with alarm that De Quincey's study was on fire. His daughters rushed downstairs, but were told by their father that they could not use water to combat the blaze, "as it would have ruined the beloved papers." Instead, De Quincey entered the room, locked the door behind him, and put the flames out with a heavy rug. "He was not a reassuring man for nervous people to live with," Florence [the middle of the three De Quincey girls] remarked mildly. Margaret [De Quincey's eldest daughter] was more to the point: "for Papa, we are at a constant war with him."[77]

When the pain is too grinding, I sometimes find that if I can go deeply enough into depressive words and music, no longer trying to be upbeat, I at least feel in sync. I listen to Nirvana, the Rolling Stones' "Paint it Black," "Toccata and Fugue in D minor."[78]

The Romantics did not notice their suffering from a distance. They sought it out. They wallowed in it, in its texture and temperature and hue. Could it be a literary form of cutting, in which people may self-injure for the emotional relief it provides, for the self-made opioids[79] the brain releases in response to injury?

If I go into it deep enough, maybe I can make myself *like* the pain.

Well, here it is.

Something has seized the back of my neck and the trapezius muscles down the sides in an impossibly tight grip. It's as if someone were standing behind me, forcing me to bend. It is unbearable. I don't know what my next step will be if I stop getting regular hours of relief with tramadol. Indeed, this is becoming a demonstration not of the slippery slope or downward spiral into addiction but of the impact of ongoing severe pain on mental health, on sanity, even.

Throwing oneself into the aesthetic feeling of misery takes a dangerous level of commitment to experience. Joel Faflak, another De Quincey biographer, writes that aesthetes like Charles Baudelaire "read De Quincey's addiction as part of the exquisite beauty of a life lived too exquisitely, a dangerous literary existence suffused with 'an incurable melancholy.'"[80] I'm all for *saudade*, but this is all starting to feel a little too too-exquisite to me.

I ask my rheumatologist to refer me to the Centre for Addiction and Mental Health — not for addiction treatment but because I'm feeling desperate from pain and, notably, from my despair at the limitations it puts on my activities and aspirations.

I am not managing.

With excessive pain as my underlying spine disease remains untreated, tramadol has become a less reliable, complete escape from both emotional and physical angst. I return to my range of other mental tricks. They are all mindfulness or flow strategies. I've rediscovered piano practice: despite the difficulty of sitting up straight, I welcome the focused distraction as my fingers move through the scales and melodies I used to know. I draw — not to produce anything, but patiently, carefully sketching in every detail of a scene, knowing that the longer I spend on each part of the whole, the more I will be absorbed by the work and temporarily freed of awareness of pain. I exercise, forcing myself through a half an hour of unpleasant warming up of joints before a warm springiness begins to loosen up the tight and painful joints and muscles — and a mental elation (endogenous morphine!) unclouds my brain.

No matter how bad I feel, I take more and more comfort and uncomplicated joy from playing with my children — while simultaneously working hard to focus moment to moment and hide from them my tension and misery. When these strategies work, they get me through another ten minutes, another hour, another day.

Nothing so magical, so *easy*, as the opioids.

I'm on a six-hour hike partway up a volcano, and I'm parched under the blistering sun. I'm in my early twenties, on a biology field course to Ometepe, an island in the centre of Lake Nicaragua. I forgot to bring my water bottle, have no hat, did not apply enough sunscreen and am not keeping up well with the group. But I get there, one step at a time.

What sticks in my memory, looking back, is the moment when we reached our goal, a waterfall halfway up, and our guide took oranges out of his pack and shared out the juicy segments. That simple snack tasted better than the best meal of my life. It tasted like relief, it tasted like life. I think that in the popular image of the prescription drug user, the drugs become a numbing substitute for life, but that is the opposite of my experience.

I don't know how I would manage the unrelenting, ever-surprising trek of a rich, busy family life without the sweet relief of painkillers. Sometimes I feel desperately grateful.

I call in prescription refills regularly. The pharmacist—my unconscious minister of celestial pleasures—is used to my frequent visits. When the doctor once fails to renew a prescription before the long weekend, she re-sends the request, looking at my face and writing URGENT on the fax.

By overlapping doses, I finally—at the very end of the day—feel the weight of my head lift from my shoulders and the burn in my lower back ease. It is wonderful to be able to turn my head without pain or unbearable stiffness for the first time today, but I have to work to keep the clear and focused dreaminess I have been claiming to feel when on tramadol. And—testing, testing—I still feel a painful resistance if I try to lift my head back to look up in a normal way. The stiffness caused by acute inflammation in my spine is simply too much to mask anymore (or at this dose). Though I know that if I hadn't been taking tramadol I would not have been sitting down as I wrote this. Because I simply wouldn't have been able to sit down. Or, for that matter, to make dinner for my family, wash dishes, sweep crumbs off the table, or help my son floss his teeth.

In a revision to the *Confessions*—thirty years after its first publi-cation—De Quincey sums up the ups and downs associated with both physical and psychological need for the drug, and the desire to be free of both opium and pain, as consisting of:

> Manoeuvres the most intricate, dances the most elaborate,
> receding or approaching, round my great central sun of
> opium. Sometimes I ran perilously close into my perihelion:
> sometimes I became frightened, and wheeled off into a vast
> cometary aphelion, where for six months "opium" was a word
> unknown. How nature stood all these see-sawings is quite a
> mystery to me: I must have led her a sad life in those days.[81]

As well as being a fundamental technique for coping with pain — and depression, its mental cognate — mindfulness is one of the newer and most promising strategies for dealing with addiction and its siblings (for example, obsessive-compulsive disorder, anxiety, or eating disorders). In all cases, the issue is one of unbearable sensation.

The unending stress of the Gaza occupation: sensation that comes from the external world. Childhood sexual abuse, whose trauma continues into adulthood, perhaps represents an unbearable internal sensation, and is a common element in the life histories of many serious, hard-to-treat opioid addicts. The remedy for sensations of awfulness that the human psyche — no matter how Romantic — is not well equipped to handle is detached, curious, calm, and focused observation. It's an attitude easily reached while under the influence of opioids, but one that takes hard daily practice — hourly or constant practice, even — without chemical help.

I have briefly known this feeling when writing is going really well and I lose my sense of self in the best possible way, writing down ideas that I know are sure and right, images that feel inspired, as easily as if I were merely transcribing. Not just mental stresses, but physical pain, even, become unimportant in those moments of flow, the effortlessness that comes when completely focused on creation. When I come out of this trance, two hours may have passed in what feels like seconds. Something new has been brought into the world. And I have not noticed that I was in pain.

The actor Alan Arkin writes of the craft of acting, which he describes as his addiction:

> For those few minutes I was living in a state of grace.
> It was a place where nothing could go wrong. [...] I now
> lived not just for acting, for being in front of an audience,
> but for the possibility of that exalted experience returning.
> I lived for those moments when the part played me and I
> was completely out of the way.[82]

As Arkin goes on to say, those moments can occur in acting, arts, sports, or other fields and must be earned by hard and persistent work — but their arrival cannot be predicted or guaranteed. Each of the artists and writers name-checked in this essay has felt it. A slang term for smoking opioids or other drugs, and the pursuit of the fleeting opioid high, is "chasing the dragon" — an evocative phrase that seems better suited to the work of art. A dragon truly worth chasing. I would do almost anything for that feeling.

I meet my friend Derek for lunch. I take tramadol, and it is only partway through the meal that I feel some relief from pain and can finally sit down to eat. Derek practices Shambhala Buddhism, and so it is to him that I come with the question of why my work at mindfulness isn't enough. "I spend all my energy watching my pain without judging it, and so I'm depressed that that's all I'm doing with my life," I complain, tears welling. "And then I have to watch my depression without judging *that*!"

He doesn't tell me to meditate harder. He doesn't ask me what I'm doing wrong. He gives me a careful hug. Derek is the best of Buddhists, the best of friends. "I think you need hope," he says.

Until I can prevent pain from pushing me into hopelessness, it looks like I will be relying on opioid drugs to provide daily hours of relief. At the same time, my six months on daily opioids have only helped me to prove for myself what is already known: there are no quick fixes, no matter how desperately I — or any other pain patient — may need them. A drug that works best when I take it least often is not going to be a great solution to lifelong pain, unless I can find a way to just rely on occasional doses for relief — and for that wonderful, cool transcendence.

I go through many nights with no painkillers, often waking from pain, turning over and over through the long hours in search of a comfortable position. When I wake up to the morning alarm it's with the distinct feeling that I've been hit by a truck. I'll lie in bed for a while as I contemplate turning over — then, still in bed, spend fifteen minutes stretching very, very slowly, with long pauses in between movements as I prepare myself for the next painful stretch.

I don't tell my former interview subject, Wayne Skinner, that I've booked myself in at his workplace, the Centre for Addiction and Mental Health. At my intake appointment, the psychiatrist and I both gloss over the opioid question (low doses, obvious pain). I fill out yet another set of rate-your-misery questions. Hesitate over one.

"Have you ever made a plan?"

At first I don't even understand the question.

Then I get it.

No, no. No! Never. Of course not.

I think about it often, but that's not a plan. I have children I love. I have many dear friends, I have family who care. I am so lucky. I have things I want to do. Far too much to live for. I keep telling myself these things. I know I want to live. I want a life. The intake psychiatrist turns back to his screen and types, "She endorses passive suicidal thoughts." And, "She is capable of caring for herself and is not at imminent risk of serious self-harm."

He sends me out with a list of mindfulness meditation programs to contact, recommendations that I look into mood stabilizers and antidepressants, a referral for magnetic deep brain stimulation. I wonder what I was hoping for.

I trudge homeward through Little Italy and pick up my kids.

There's old Thomas De Quincey, back in nineteenth-century London with his rooms of books and papers, his decanter of laudanum, his watchful daughters, and his hair occasionally on fire. And here, travelling across the ocean and through the years, is Mexico City. It was there, sitting in the

Franciscan church in the elegant central Mexico City neighbourhood of Coyoacán, more than a decade ago, that I really fell in love with the man who would become the father of our two boys. Every old house and taco stand and cobblestone is still luminous to me with that memory. It is with that tender feeling that I return now to the Casa Azul.

Frida's house — the Blue House — is bright, highly designed, and arranged, personal. A collection of pre-Hispanic sculptures sits in the courtyard garden. Cats weave in and out. The museum is full of her paintings. As a visitor years after her death, I can hold in my mind both the pain and the magic of this art that is the pure expression of joy, often, and more often of suffering: *"Mi pintura lleva con ella el mensaje del dolor,"* she said — "my painting carries with it the message of pain."[83]

Looking at a reproduction of her illustrated diary, you can see that near the end of her life her handwriting became lighter and looser. Her painting as well.

"The drugs she was taking," writes biographer Christina Burrus, "in particular the Demerol, caused her to swing between euphoria and despair, also affecting the steadiness of her hand and consequently the precision of her brushstrokes. Her style, which had been a meticulous as a miniaturist's, became more relaxed as a result."[84]

Her body, under the elaborate traditional Tehuana dresses she wore, was covered with injection scabs.[85]

The last image in Kahlo's diary is rather like Vincent van Gogh's final painting of crows under a menacing sky: pulsing with foreboding, devoid of hope. In her sketch, a galloping horse casts a dark shadow under a pitilessly bright day. She writes ambiguously, upon going into the hospital, "I hope the leaving will be joyful, and I hope never to return."[86] Frida Kahlo died of a pulmonary embolism — or, possibly, an overdose, possibly an intentional one. Indeed, pain without end — and here the distinction between physical and mental pain becomes impossible to make — may be too much to endure, even for people used to suffering. Even used to laughing at it, or with it. With the help of her dangerous and appetitive medicines, Kahlo managed to ease her pain just enough to periodically and strongly embrace life. Shortly before she died, she painted her famous, joyous still life of watermelons.[87]

Brilliant colours, with a hand-written message:

Viva la Vida!

To life!

PART II

SATURN DEVOURING
HIS CHILDREN
A Tale of Instability in Seven Parts

Death

Oaxaca City, Mexico. We're sampling spicy, salty grasshoppers and mealworms from a vendor in a quiet cobblestoned street when we hear the deep oom pah pah of a Día de Muertos parade. My family and I have been wandering in and out of raucous, exhilarating Day of the Dead street parties here for the past two days. It's 2015.

Those parades pull in everyone on the street to dance with their stilt walkers and giant, articulated skeleton puppets and costumed revellers. On the sidelines, kids enact murder scenes, the small body of one lying eerily still amid the street chaos, collecting tourists, until its accomplice child appears, plastic knife in hand and werewolf mask on face, to request their loose change. Vendors sell balloons and roasted corn on the cob smothered in mayonnaise and chile. Dancers of all ages wear traditional Tehuana dresses or are got up as elegant ladies and gentlemen, but all have their faces painted white, decorated with stylized skulls and flowers.

As this latest parade comes into view, though, the difference is like the drop in temperature when a shadow drifts across the sun. This one is quiet and gloomy. It is, clearly, not the kind of celebration you are invited to join—nor does it feel like a celebration. A convoy of cars and pickup trucks rolling at the speed of the people walking alongside, it moves slowly, reminiscent of nothing more than a funeral procession. In fact, few of the paraders are in costume, though most are heavily tattooed. Machine guns are part of the display. The music is, indeed, distinctly funereal. Even the skulls are more grim, more realistically *dead*, than anything else we've seen in this joyfully death-mad city. Marchers carry plaster figurines of what looks like the Virgin of Guadalupe, Mexico's beloved version of the Virgin Mary. But her neck is bones. She carries a scythe.

These, it dawns on us at last, are followers of la Santa Muerte, Our Lady of Holy Death.

Santa Muerte is a folk saint who has become increasingly popular in tandem with an explosion of violence associated with an overt "war" on drug cartels across Mexico. Oaxaca isn't especially under the thumb of cartels—the fashion for la Santa Muerte has drifted down from the north. She does appear in the robes of the Virgin of Guadalupe, but instead of the angelic, brown-skinned face of Mexico's most popular holy image, la Santa Muerte's face is a livid skull. She is condemned as a death cult by the Catholic Church (despite its own fondness for graphic crucifixion scenes and penchant for snacking on the body and blood of Christ). In the nearby cathedral, a nun tells us as much, as do posters at the entrance of the church, while a young worker at the San Pablo Cultural Centre, a repurposed seventeenth-century convent, tells me it's just a fad, *un modismo*, and strange rather than fear-inspiring.

Santa Muerte is popular among the disillusioned, perpetually screwed working class, and is associated with the outcast and marginalized, from queer Mexicans and sex workers to both foot soldiers and top dogs in the illicit drug trade. When her votive candles and vestments are amber or yellow, Santa Muerte represents health, and this version may be seen in rehab centres for drug and alcohol addiction. She offers healing and protection against violent death, assault, witchcraft, and gun violence. By March of 2020, cards with her grim image will be in circulation around Mexico. They will read, *Today Santa Muerte assures you: The corona virus will not touch your house or your family, they are covered with the precious blood of christ have faith and don't doubt. Santa Muerte I have faith in you.*[1] This crisis will shake up the drug trade in many ways, but the injustices and dynamics that will play out then are well established now, five years before.

The war on drugs, fuelled by demand for drugs from the United States and powered by guns smuggled in from the US—and kept alive by global prohibition of drugs like heroin, cocaine, and marijuana—has devastated Mexico. The government estimates that 61,637 people have been forcibly "disappeared" in the battle against drug cartels since 1964.[2] Most of this has occurred since 2006, when then-president Felipe Calderón initiated an ill-conceived war on the cartels, one that has been plagued with corruption, deadly errors, and human rights abuses (security forces are thought to be responsible for most of the disappearances[3]). The country is littered with mass graves. Soldiers who once devoted their time to slashing and burning opium poppy fields—a drug war strategy long encouraged by the United States—have now moved to fighting cartel operatives in bloody street battles.[4] With such levels of violence from all sides, it's no wonder people crave la Santa Muerte's tough-minded protection.

She may be frightening and fatalistic, but we could use a Santa Muerte up here in Canada and the US, if only for clarity about what is going on (she is, in fact, popular within and even beyond the Latino community in American cities like New York, Chicago, Los Angeles, and New Orleans). The number of corpses associated with overdose across North America is mind-boggling. North Americans overdose on heroin from Mexico and Afghanistan and, increasingly, on synthetic opioids that are smuggled from China or Mexico or, even, easily produced in a clandestine lab in the United States. There were a gobsmacking 70,237 drug overdose deaths in the United States in 2017[5] (the number in 2018 dipped slightly lower), of which 67.8 percent involved opioids, whether licit or illegal or both. That's twice as many fatalities as from motor vehicle accidents,[6] and represents some two hundred Americans dying of drug overdose every day. It's a similar situation in Canada, where, in 2018, a Canadian died of opioid-involved overdose every two hours.[7]

It was in November of 1987 that Meg, at three years old, found her mom nearly dead on the kitchen floor, an attempted suicide. And it is on another Day of the Dead, in 2019, that she visits her mother's grave here in Toronto. She brings an offering of cigarettes and whisky to this final resting place, her first visit since her mother's actual death more than a decade later. Meg soaks the smokes in lighter fluid and sets them ablaze: a votive candle in memory of the beloved dead.

Since her teens, Meg has been haunted by the idea of her mother's alcoholic ghost battling delirium tremens in the afterlife. Homeless or insecurely housed and addicted to drugs for fully half her life, it has taken Meg all these years to gain enough stability to imagine seeking out the grave. Now, she figures, she owes her mom the booze and smokes so long denied.

Meg is dependent on fentanyl. She cooks up and injects the very strong, illicit opioid every few hours during the day, every couple of hours in the evening. It helps her get to sleep during the long, insomniac night. She does this, now, in the privacy of her own home.

Before that, Meg lived on the street on and off—in a temporary tent city, under a bridge—and in insecure and dangerous temporary housing. Up until a couple of months ago, she paid for her drugs and other needs by car panning—panhandling to drivers at stop lights—for sixteen hour days. Meg also supported herself over the years by busking and regular panhandling, as well as through hard labour in a Christmas tree lot. The weather in Toronto ranges from nearly forty degrees Celsius in summer to nearly forty below in winter.

Although with her long orange hair in a braid, and her eyes framed with chunky glasses, Meg looks young for thirty-five, one can also see the impact of a decade and a half on the street. Her arms are scabbed and bruised from injections. She walks with something like a swagger, equal parts defensive and confident, although her gait might just be an effect of her own chronic pain, from past injuries poorly treated. Despite our dramatically different lives, we live in the same city, know the same landmarks and cultural references. Meg lived, on and off for two years, in the park outside the art gallery where I take my kids; I published somewhat abstract articles on homelessness here in Toronto while she was actually living it.

The drug that Meg takes is the one that regularly sends police officers to hospital with panic attacks. They don't know they are panic attacks; the cops believe they might have overdosed by breathing or touching the illegal drug during an arrest. They are wrong; this is impossible and has never happened, but local newspapers dutifully report "a suspected overdose," and politicians promise to ban legally prescribed fentanyl painkillers to prevent future incidents just the same.

Fentanyl is a well-understood, effective, and safe painkiller for surgery, for toddlers even, or in patch form for pain patients with stomach issues that make oral opioids intolerable. But the chemically identical, illicit version that Meg uses has been implicated in tens of thousands of actual deaths — not due to touching or inhaling it, but to injecting or snorting an unknown quantity. Because users don't know what they're getting, or because they've mixed it with alcohol or another drug that exacerbates its effects, it's easy to accidentally exceed their existing opioid tolerance, overdose, and die.

In 2016, fentanyl or similar synthetic opioids were involved in the deaths of twenty thousand Americans.[8] Illicit fentanyl began to contaminate and then replace heroin in the illicit market in a number of North American cities starting almost precisely after OxyContin, an opioid painkiller, was reformulated to make it hard to "abuse." At the same time, a heavy-handed and poorly thought-out crackdown on opioid prescribing in the United States and Canada made it hard to access far safer prescription painkillers like the drug I still take to cover up the pain in my spine. Many, many people who had used others' prescriptions to get high were forced into withdrawal. They moved en masse to heroin and, inevitably, illicit fentanyl.

Easy to produce anywhere, compact and potent, illicitly produced fentanyl and even stronger versions of it, such as the big-game tranquilizer carfentanil or isotonitazene, one of an infinite series of so-called designer drugs, are the logical next steps in the time-honoured drug policy game of whack-a-mole. In this deadly game, which has occurred since substances were first banned, prohibition of one substance incentivizes the move to a stronger, cheaper, more powerful alternative, along with more chaotic patterns of use. Over time, people who use street opioids have gone from unintentionally overdosing due to unsuspected presence of fentanyl to simply accepting the greater risk, to being dependent on illicit fentanyl and actively seeking it rather than heroin.[9] Meanwhile, death after death after death after death.

This forced shift from a less potent to a more potent substance occurred during alcohol prohibition in the twenties, when low-proof alcohol consumed in homes, restaurants, and bars was replaced by bathtub gin and hard liquor consumed in speakeasies. It occurred with opium prohibition from around 1910, when opium smoking using finely wrought implements in well-appointed opium houses became injected morphine and then heroin in back alleys. With the banning of coca, a mild stimulant, in 1961, coca and products containing it gave way to cocaine and then crack cocaine. Ephedra (an amphetamine-like substance) was banned in 2003, but methamphetamines like crystal meth have since grown in popularity while decreased access to diverted prescription amphetamines like Adderall or Dexedrine may also be fuelling illicit methamphetamine use. In each case, one among many unfortunate outcomes of prohibition has been unnecessary, accidental deaths from a previously *less* risky substance.

This tendency for restricted access to one appetitive substance to result in a move to harder drugs, taken more dangerously, is what's known as the Iron Law of Prohibition. The Iron Law— "the harder the enforcement, the harder the drugs"[10] — has been a consistent feature of the US-led global war on drugs from its earliest days. Prohibition forces dependent drug users to play a form of Russian roulette, where you just don't know which dose will be your last.

Meg in fact prefers fentanyl to heroin, and has no desire to replace it in the five shots she does each day. She uses drugs—especially opioids—to deliberately ward off trauma, including but by no means limited to that post-suicide-attempt scene on the kitchen floor, and her mother's subsequent disappearance into a hospital psychiatric ward. Meg thought her mom was actually dead—she was only three, after all—and believed this for years no matter what she was told.

Later, Meg would pray to God to allow her to die in exchange for letting her mother be happy. A psychiatrist once told her, when she was a teenager, that "inside you there's a little girl who has never stopped screaming." And no wonder.

When Meg was a child, other habits helped her cope. Surreptitiously, the little girl chewed the inside of her cheeks and lips until she severed a nerve. She has been diagnosed, at different times and by different people, with "polyaddictive tendencies," cocaine use disorder, opioid use disorder (the medical term for an opioid addiction), and substance use disorder. But she believes that her first addiction was to the printed word:

> I'd press my feet against the door to keep them out of view
> and sit on the can with my pants up and read. It was so
> peaceful. What the reading DID was give me a measure of
> control. I could not, could not, control what others did to
> me. [...] But suddenly I could control SOMETHING. [...]
> It was... unreal. Unbelievable. I could MAKE IT STOP
> HURTING for the first time since I could remember. Ever.
> And THAT is what I think I got physically addicted to.
> The absence of pain.

Meg's exasperated teachers once advised her parents — her father and stepmother — to confiscate the books in which she was constantly immersed. Her reaction to this attack, she tells me, was physical, similar in its sense of total agony and desolation to her later experiences of opioid withdrawal, body pain included. I can imagine Thomas De Quincey having an identical response to someone taking his books (he and Meg both escaped their dearly loved but disturbed middle-class families and took to the street as teenagers).

As with Michael Eschbach, my friend in the shelter hotel, I first connected with this former street kid after following her writing online for a while (I later learned that while I was scoping her out, she was doing the same to me). Meg attracted my attention due to her heart and obvious writing talent — she may be the first person I have met who seems to share my life-or-death feelings about language and writing and reading—and the fact that she is as addicted to opioids as anyone could possibly be.

Except that the more I learn about *that*, the more unsure I am about what it really means.

Like all writers, surely, I want to spin the straw of life—its beauty, its mystery, its pain—into gold. So long as my prescribed drugs make the impossible possible. My generous, fractured family seems to accept my still-shaky argument, almost totally unsupported by income, that observing and absorbing and writing about life is my job. Haltingly, I'm trying to feel out what a writing life could be, this side of pain, children, loss of both love and money, and the other jarring losses and subtle gains that illness has brought.

I used to support my attempts at fiction and poetry, minimally but adequately, by working as a freelance journalist. I wrote mostly about issues of poverty and injustice, although I studied biology and wanted somehow to write about everything, which isn't a typical newspaper beat. Somehow, I only very rarely touched on addiction or substance use. I followed interests, but I didn't really have a plan. I was young; I didn't think in terms of a body of work. Until my body became my work. As writing became more difficult, I realized I need to get serious. Now, with better pain control than I've had in years, I imagine writing for real again, starting where I am.

I worried so much about becoming dependent on painkillers—and now I am.

It wouldn't be so bad, really. It's just that every time opioids let me expand the scope of my life, I push myself a little too hard and then slam smack into the brick wall of pain which, after all, is only eased for fifteen hours out of every twenty-four.

I have never stopped trying to get out of my own head, out of the brain, where pain is understood. Watching my pain-related thoughts and feelings like clouds passing in the sky, as recommended by mindfulness practitioners, helps me endure when it's really bad, but since mindfulness involves being okay where you are, I get nowhere. I don't want to go nowhere; I want to go somewhere, to be more than my mere existence. Surely the desire for some sort of progress is a basic human feeling? A poem I once loved enough that I know it partly by heart, Mary Oliver's "Wild Geese," comes bitterly to mind during the regular flares in my spine disease, when my immune system attacks me with a vengeance and life again diminishes to mindful observation, counting of breaths, soft ticking of the clock:

> You do not have to be good.
> [...]
> You only have to let the soft animal of your body
> love what it loves.

Right now, I don't want to be placated, to be told that all I have to do is exist, that a stoically enduring potato or a goose has as much value as a philosopher. I don't want to be told that I only need to let this soft animal do what it wants. I want my body to be my instrument. I am too young and have done too little to be content, now, to merely exist. And also I am no longer so young, and I'm scared that time is running out. And then, I need an income again, though after a decade of living well below the poverty line, it turns out that freelance journalism, never a path to riches, is no longer a viable way to rise above it.

Writing about drugs and pain, my current specialties, is also hardly a way to make a living, but I am torn: I want to earn my keep; I want my twenty years of sporadic journalism to form themselves somehow into a career. But I hate much of what passes for journalism these days, and I'm also not sure I'm good enough at it, suspect I'm ill-equipped to compete with my peers for scarce dollars and column inches. I feel like I have too little energy to waste time on things I don't find really meaningful, although being game for any assignment is a sine qua non if you want to get work. One lesson of trying to survive pain has been that meaning is everything. It's a piece of driftwood you cling to, hoping to make a raft.

Still, I know how to do the writing part, at least. When you write newspaper articles, as I've done since I was a teenager in the 1990s, there is an objective tone you strike. This reassuring tone largely derives from the language you choose and how you put the words together, with how you marshal your facts. Not what you say, but how you say it. I strike this tone now. After writing my first book, a memoir about my subjective experience of pain, it feels bracing to write again now in this neutral, authoritative way. At last, it's not my story. No more attempts to wring a narrative from stasis, drama from misery, meaning from a fundamentally meaningless experience. In fact, I try to pull myself right out of my pain-fogged, stressed-out head with these tough, smooth journalist words.

Having asked Meg if I might quote something she wrote about drug prohibition, and then having asked if I could go so far as to use her story in my book about opioids, I now arrange an interview. I pay for lunch; I am gracious and professional. Adequate pain treatment has given me this.

Meg, a writer and opioid addict, and Carlyn, herself a pain patient on opioids and also a journalist, met one day in a little crêpe café on Bloor Street.

I try to describe myself fairly here, neither too harshly nor flatteringly. Ankylosing spondylitis continues to progress in its gradual reshaping of my back, but I hold myself as straight as I can, so what people see is mostly just tension, a pale and taut little person held up by ropy neck muscles and willpower.

I sit down opposite Meg, shifting at first a little and then, as the tramadol wears off, a lot, twisting surreptitiously one way and then the other. Meg is telling me about her first suicide attempt, which involved a broken heart and a bottle of Tylenol with codeine, and which introduced her to the opioid high at age sixteen. I'm concentrating with increasing difficulty as the dual effort of sitting still and paying attention becomes too much to manage.

I hate this. It's not working; I can't get out of myself. Pain takes up too much space.

At last I ask Meg if we can stop for a second. I try to put it in words that will be neither too much nor too little. Indeed, it feels as if Goldilocks's story—getting the porridge just right or nothing works—is the story of my life. Too much exercise and I'm exhausted, too little and I lose range of movement. Too much sitting and I need to stand, too much standing and I need to sit. Too much work and I fall apart, unable to handle multiple responsibilities with minimal capacity. Too little and I sink into depression. Too much caring about others and I'm stretched until I snap, too little and, well, what am I even for?

Meg's fairy tale, meanwhile, is more like that of the child left to wander in the darkest, most wolf-infested of woods. At this moment, she is telling me a story of such emotional pain that nothing in my life is analogous to it, and it deserves my full attention.

"I'm just going to get another coffee," I cut in awkwardly. Then (why?) I confide what I usually try to hide: "I have trouble concentrating after a while."

My notebook sits in my backpack this first time Meg and I meet in real life. I ask a few questions, but mostly I'm just listening, partly because my hands cramp as I take notes. The words I quoted above are Meg's own written account.

The café doesn't have a bathroom so I nip out to use the one in the Jewish community centre next door. I leave my wallet, phone, tablet, and my coat with painkillers in the pocket. When I get back Meg is having a smoke outside. I don't need to check to know that everything is still where I left it. Trust is the first thing my friends ask me about as I get to know people who use illicit drugs, particularly injection users (it's far rarer that anyone challenges me, asking why *they* should trust *me*). None of them has ever met a fentanyl addict. Meg would be like some exotic species if she weren't so obviously not an "addict" but a person (who plays guitar, writes poetry, and uses drugs). We go back in together.

Meg wants to talk. I don't need to say much at all, which is convenient, given how hard I'm having to concentrate just to sit normally. She speaks thoughtfully, with intense pauses as she tries to express a complicated idea, such as the one about the way reading let her blot out everything else. We have a moment of shared recognition, and I tell her I think that's why I can't bear to listen to podcasts or watch videos. With text I get to control the pace of information coming at me, and I love that sense of control. It's a sort of zoning out by zoning in. It strikes me how pathological this all makes reading sound, and how familiar and pleasurable it is to me as well.

Meg's life has been a procession of traumas. But recently, and even as homelessness in Toronto has been growing out of control and contributing to increased drug-related deaths, she has hit the jackpot: a rent-geared-to-income apartment in municipal community housing where she should be able to stay for the rest of her life. On that little raft of security, and the steady if contaminated source of fentanyl she has secured, she is now trying to paddle her way to safety. Getting off opioids isn't part of the plan. Fentanyl, like reading long ago, gives her mental control over the ghosts that haunt her.

And there are so many. Meg has experienced it all: she has been raped, fended off attempted gang rape with a serrated kitchen knife, lived through bedbugs four times, drained her own abscesses, waited patiently for her dealer while sick from withdrawal, sold drugs herself, been arrested, been persistently sexually harassed while begging for change. Two years ago, Meg's lover, J., overdosed on fentanyl. Meg woke up next to her soulmate's naked corpse. If she lived in the United States, she might have been jailed for homicide, as she paid for the drugs for them both. As it is, Meg lives with that loss every day of her life.

Almost all of the people Meg has called friends over the years are now dead. She mentions one who died just last year, crushed in an outdoor clothing donation bin on a bitter winter night.

This one I know. I mean, I remember this case, was shaken by news reports on this particular homeless death, because the victim lived so close to my downtown Toronto apartment. Turns out, Meg met Crystal Papineau when they were both teenagers. Homeless people die on Toronto streets every year, and their deaths pass unnoticed by all but their loved ones and advocates who have held a monthly memorial for two decades, the death toll growing year by year. But everyone who heard about this death remembers it, because the night Crystal died was so extremely cold and because her death was accidental and gruesome.

Meg has recently started seeing a therapist, the same psychologist her parents sent her to once upon a time, when she was an overweight, socially awkward, closeted, bullied teen. Her stepmom, who doesn't even live in the country, has stepped in to pay the therapy bills. With this and her secure housing—and her fentanyl dealer—Meg hopes to build herself a new and better life. *Write your autobiography*, the therapist suggests now: an obvious form of therapy for someone so dependent on words. But the instability and trauma and death are a swirling vortex of pain. Working through it is a slow process.

Jeffrey Turnbull, an Ottawa physician who treats chronically homeless people with opioid addiction, described the unravelling of their compounded, interlocking traumas to me as a process of gradually peeling back the layers of an onion. Whether or not they bring on tears, each causes great pain. It's not something that happens just like that.

Despite my lack of diagnosable opioid use disorder or of this kind of trauma, so much of what Meg tells me about her relationship with fentanyl is familiar to me from the rhythms of pain and relief I experience several times a day. Right now Meg is taking just enough of the drug to ward off both withdrawal and intense post-traumatic symptoms, to be able to function the way I can clearly see her functioning now. Whatever it means to be high, nothing in her behaviour signals it.

I've been wondering about this, actually, as I learn about substance use while using substances. There are other similarities between me and Meg. She uses her illicit painkiller to muffle back pain as well as the symptoms of chronic post-traumatic stress disorder. Meg's had her chronic pain since childhood, but it's been exacerbated over the years by her work hauling Christmas trees, her nights sleeping outside on concrete, and from car panning on her feet despite, at various times, a broken tailbone and foot. Like Meg, I take enough of my prescribed medication to cover up physical pain, to be able to function, but not so much as to be on the nod or seriously risk a seizure (a potential side effect particular to my atypical opioid). And I benefit from the emotional uplift and energy boost tramadol provides, as she does with the drug she injects. Her drug typically lasts her around five hours; so does mine.

When I speak to people living or working on the street in cities across North America, they tell me that something is different now. I write this in late 2019: here at the end of the second decade of the millennium, there's more violence, drug use is more chaotic, people are more desperate than in previous decades. People who have used heroin with relative stability for ten, twenty, even thirty years are now dying of overdose.[11] But the sight of open drug use, homelessness that in cities from Philadelphia to San Francisco to New York to Vancouver to Toronto to Los Angeles seems to be reaching a crisis point, heavy and chaotic polysubstance use, and overdose death after death after death after death are not disasters that have emerged out of nowhere to plague the world's large cities and isolated suburbs and stagnating rural communities. In fact, it's been a slow burn that has suddenly burst into flames.

And not for the first time. Julian Buchanan is a British social worker, now retired and living in New Zealand. Buchanan worked north of Liverpool as a young probation officer in the early eighties. Up to that time, there hadn't been much of a heroin problem in the UK. Hippies and middle-class students sometimes used drugs for mind-expanding experiments. But the working class had no connection to psychedelic drugs or opioids.

Then Prime Minister Margaret Thatcher began closing down the coal mines. Until 1980, villages essentially built around the mines had experienced only very low rates of unemployment. These were folks who worked hard and lived modestly. In a series of policy measures that are now familiar around the world and known collectively as "austerity," Thatcher imposed deep cuts to social programs and public services, which had a devastating impact on the now out-of-work working class.

Suddenly, Buchanan tells me, areas of high deprivation and new unemployment were overrun with teenagers and young adults "off their heads with heroin."

"The young people I was working with struggled in school, couldn't get qualifications. Life was brutal for them and being made more brutal."

They turned, he says, to obliterating their lives. It's important to understand — especially today, when we hear a lot about "deaths of despair" — that these hopeless young people didn't simply set themselves on fire or slit their wrists. Instead, they made choices that may be seen from the outside as despairing or giving up on life, but which made sense in many ways, given the options available to them.

Heroin, and the lifestyle it demands, provided essential things that had otherwise disappeared for young people who had expected to follow a path to employment underground as their fathers and grandfathers before them would have done. Instead, a different form of "underground" offered them "employment" — a seven-days-a-week, fifty-two-weeks-a-year job getting and using heroin. Acquiring drugs and paraphernalia to use them involves basic skills like bartering; shoplifting for money to buy drugs involves cunning, clarity, and dexterity. After the day's genuinely hard work to acquire drugs, they were able to enjoy unwinding with some dope (heroin) — just as their parents would have done with a few beers after work.

"It gave them an identity. It gave them a purpose. It gave them a reward," Buchanan recalls. These are all things that people need. In a sense, heroin didn't just ease pain: it met the set of needs that keep us all emotionally afloat.

Thinking back, Buchanan is convinced he did the wrong thing in advocating abstinence to his heroin-using clients, who often lied to him about their drug use as a result. "I ended up damaging people's lives because they would say [to me] what they're expected to say. I blame me, because I cornered them and set them up to fail by not listening to them."

What Buchanan thinks was missing from his analysis was a real understanding that for his clients, heroin was not the problem: "Heroin is the solution."

"Deaths of despair" is an evocative catch-all phrase for deaths relating to suicide, drug overdose, and alcoholism that have been rising steadily since around the time I entered adolescence — shielded by my whiteness and my middle-class background—in the 1990s. The concept or term was popularized by an economist couple, Anne Case and Angus Deaton. It now garnishes every newspaper article or research paper that observes the persistent associations between lack of economic opportunity or outright misery; depression and other mood disorders; and both poor health and death, whether violent and sudden, or slow and predictable.

Case and Deaton's work is more useful for what it observes than for their tame prescriptions, which focus on "downstream" things like improving college graduation rates rather than on the ultimate causes of misery: the larger structural forces that invisibly shape our lives and opportunities as rigidly as the Fates (Clotho who spins the thread of human fate, Lachesis who dispenses it, Atropos who cuts the thread). Our destinies today are determined by Fates known as Capitalism, Prohibition, Colonialism, White Supremacy, and Patriarchy. By ignoring these, those of us born on the right side of the tracks continue to believe with religious or superstitious fervour in meritocracy, happy endings invented by Disney, justice, positive thinking that veers toward magical thinking, Thoughts and Prayers.

Not everyone is comfortable naming today's powerful, interconnected Fates. Even as he notes that Europeans benefit from a generous, progressive taxation–funded social safety net (including universal healthcare) that protects them from the deaths of despair he observes among Americans, Deaton nevertheless takes pains to emphasize to a *Washington Post* interviewer that "I'm not a left-wing nut pushing for single-payer! It's not because I like socialized medicine. It's just because I think [evidence of despair such as opioid addiction or suicide] is eating capitalism alive, and if we want a healthy capitalist society in America, we've got to get rid of this monster."[12] These researchers have also been criticized for their focus on rising deaths of despair among the white working class, a focus that contributed to the opioid crisis being characterized in the media as a purely white, working-class issue, and to a poorly contextualized narrative about that same population that helped bring Donald Trump to the US presidency in 2016.[13]

The pattern they observe of economic dislocation and ravaged social structures resulting in increased deaths from a range of causes, notably including opioid-involved overdose, holds true across communities, although it can be mitigated by various factors, from a strong social safety net to close intergenerational ties. Like many others who analyze poverty, inequality, racism, stigma associated with substance use and addiction, or other ills inextricable from capitalism, colonialism, and prohibition, these economists' tunnel vision prevents them from seeing continuity between the happy capitalist society they imagine and the monster they describe today (more recently they at last make the link, with a 2020 book straightforwardly called *Deaths of Despair and the Future of Capitalism* in which they finally identify capitalism itself as causing deaths of despair rather than the evidence of despair afflicting capitalism — but they nevertheless again seek to distinguish themselves from what they call the "radical left," instead vaguely proposing, as journalist Zachary Siegel puts it, "tweaking capitalism to be more fair"[14] in ineffectual ways [your billions and trillions are safe from taxes, for example].)

Anyway, "deaths of despair" as a concept risks us missing the great efforts people make to seek fulfillment and well-being and survival for themselves and others, despite the many ways the deck is stacked against them. Far from being passive, poor people and people who use drugs actively struggle to improve their lives. We just often misinterpret what we see. Nevertheless, there is despair, plenty of it. And, yes, there are deaths.

A swirly downward vector like a flushing toilet, "the spiral" tells us that the story of taking drugs goes only one way, that it's unstoppable, that it ends in the sewer or worse, that (contrary to what Oscar Wilde saw from the gutter) the only stars you might see from that vantage point are the cartoon kind that swirl around someone who's just been beaten up and left for dead. The "downward spiral" is such a familiar phrase, it drips so easily off the tongue, that people may use it as shorthand to describe a sense, in their own life, of things going unstoppably wrong.

"My life went spiralling out of control and I lost myself," said Snickerz, a bright, engaging thirty-three-year old woman, when I interviewed her as we sat at a picnic bench a few metres away from the tent where she lived with her partner on the grounds of a Toronto charity.

Or it may be how one describes one's difficult loved one, no longer welcome in the home.

It starts with OxyContin or Vicodin or codeine prescribed for some trifling pain and ends, in the traditional retelling, on the street, in divorce, in separation from one's children, in rags, in an alley, in death. In a death of despair.

Newspaper articles and talk shows could be religious rituals, the descending spiral their sacred symbol. For one thing, drug users who live on or near the street may see it that way themselves. They may see it this way even though the causal relationship between drug use and outcomes like homelessness is not a simple matter of drug use causing homelessness. In fact, most evidence suggests that drug use and housing precarity often share similar causal factors, such as poverty or, more specifically, low wages or income and high costs. As Charles Dickens put it in *David Copperfield*,

> Annual income twenty pounds, annual expenditure nineteen
> and six, result happiness. Annual income twenty pounds,
> annual expenditure twenty pounds ought and six, result misery.

Such a large part of the American population is in this misery situation, in deep debt, one paycheque away from serious housing precarity, it's almost surprising that drug use and overdose rates are not higher than they are. But in fact, many, many Americans live at this level of precarity—with rates rising, as Case and Deaton and many others have chronicled, since the early nineties. Many also use addictive or euphoric or appetitive substances, from prescription opioids and benzodiazepines, to cannabis, to alcohol, to amphetamines. But only a very small proportion become homeless as an apparent result of drug use, and in fact available research shows a relationship between homelessness and substance use that is neither one-way nor direct. Although Snickerz first attributed her eight-year stretch of homelessness to her use of fentanyl, crack cocaine, crystal meth, and alcohol, she later confided that she'd started using drugs to control the emotional pain of abuse she experienced from childhood—abuse that led her to leave her home in Regina, Saskatchewan, and move to Toronto, and the streets.

Decades of research going back to the 1930s likewise show a complicated relationship in which drug use sometimes causes homelessness, through non-payment of rent, for example. Michael Eschbach became homeless, he tells me, after falling into arrears on rent while trying to drink himself to death after divorce, family loss, and other traumas left him deeply depressed. But housing precarity and poverty and drug use can all feed each other. If you are wealthy enough, there is no reason your drug or alcohol use needs to result in losing your home, and the dramatic shift from housing as a right to housing as an investment that has occurred over the past thirty years (what I see both as I travel and in my own neighbour-hood) has pushed far more people into situations in which it doesn't take much to slip over into homelessness. Drug use may actually start for the first time or intensify following loss of housing for unrelated reasons. And drugs may be tools used to, for example, provide a feeling of warmth and comfort when sleeping rough.[15]

The association between opioid prescribing and addiction or adverse outcomes is also not the one-way, reliable link these "downward spiral" stories suggest. True, almost 80 percent of heroin users reported using prescription opioids first (according to US government statistics).[16] And yet, in 75 percent of cases, those heroin users who did begin with prescription opioids (as well as, typically, other substances like cigarettes, alcohol, and marijuana) weren't actually prescribed the drugs themselves.[17] It is extremely rare that a pain patient *without* pre-existing risk factors for addiction or past use of other illicit or habit-forming drugs develops an opioid use disorder, leading them to problematic use of their own prescription or to shift to the illicit opioid market. In the small minority who do have those factors (of the already small minority of long-term pain patients like me unable to tolerate other treatments or for whom non-opioid treatments prove inadequate), the risk of problematic use is a modifiable risk, manageable by education and good communication between doctor and patient. Even where such problematic use develops, it is by no means inevitable or permanent.

When bored and alienated teenagers begin using prescription opioids they find in their grandmothers' medicine cabinet or that they purchase online, get from a friend, or buy from a dealer, this is a solution, for better or for worse, to their boredom and alienation. Other situations similarly replicate the dynamic Julian Buchanan observed with his heroin-using clients back in 1980s Liverpool. When workers at oil refineries separated for months from their families in "man camps," or workers in precarious, tough jobs in construction (with little stability or support in the event of an injury) are prescribed a short-term opioid and find that it helps them manage pre-existing chronic pain or deal efficiently with chronic depression, this, too, is a solution.

When teenagers arrive in the city of Thunder Bay, in northern Ontario, from their small, remote, tightly-knit First Nations communities even farther north to attend school, they are often lonely, alienated, and at loose ends. Mae Katt, a member of Temagami First Nation and a nurse practitioner who runs an opioid addiction treatment program in a high school in Thunder Bay, tells me, "They're just not that street wise...They're coming to an urban environment with well-documented racism [against First Nations people] and deaths and higher rates of overdose... the lay of the land for young people coming into Thunder Bay is dangerous."

Like all young people, these kids need fun activities that keep them busy and promote a feeling of belonging.[18] Family poverty, transportation challenges, and the endemic racism they all too often experience—imagine trying to join a hockey team with no money, no car, and constant unkind and blatantly racist jabs from fellow teens and their parents—make belonging difficult. This makes it far easier for drugs, alcohol, and gangs to step in.

The downward spiral isn't a downward spiral; it's more like a rough road filled with speed bumps, and then creative solutions that flatten out the bumps, sometimes digging a hole in the process. You bump up and down, trying to survive, protectively and even proactively looking for ways to meet your basic, extremely human needs. Harm reduction philosophy seeks to find ways to improve the safety of these improvised responses.

Late in 2020 when I was in near lockdown with my kids but many others were homeless in my city, I "met"[19] (virtually) S., a member of Attawapiskat First Nation, a small community that has endured decades of resource extraction, residential schools, inadequate infrastructure, and a not-unrelated epidemic of suicides among young people. S. is an expressive writer who told me details of her incredibly challenging life in a calm, factual tone that suggests the judicial assistant she was before a traumatic brain injury and related PTSD slowed her down at work, until she was forced into medical retirement. S. was removed from her family and community by the age of four, then separated from her sister by the foster care system a few years later. She was abandoned at sixteen by Children's Aid, which had placed her in a group home, and was homeless while completing high school. S. writes of crack cocaine, which she tried following a date rape that triggered memories of previous severe physical, mental, and sexual abuse she had both witnessed and endured:

> It helped me to feel complete numbness and stopped
> my mind from racing and having constant negative, even
> suicidal thoughts. I gave up custody of my daughter and
> this devastated me, further traumatized me. So it took about
> two years for me to quit, and another year to get her back.

Later, further trauma and her mother's death were the trigger for her first use of intravenous opioids. "These are not excuses, but just events that happened the first time I used these drugs," she explains. S. is currently dependent on illicit fentanyl and would like to get off the drug, if she could find the right support or a safe supply program using fentanyl so she would not be forced back to the street before stabilizing her health.

Despite the intense challenges, including the homelessness and unsafe, unpleasant shelters, hotel shelters, and transitional housing that were the reason I first connected with her, S. is very aware of the context in which her choices to use drugs sit. She tells me, for example,

> I told CRA [the Canada Revenue Agency] I wouldn't file a
> tax return until there is drinking water and adequate access
> to medical and educational services and no more suicides
> in Attawapiskat and was told to just do my paperwork.
> [...] I'm not willingly paying them to commit genocide
> and steal resources.

It can be hard to draw out the very concrete ways in which these things S. names relate to both persistent drug use and harms that aren't .intrinsically associated with the drug itself. But they do relate. For this reason, Indigenous harm reduction looks at the question of how humans respond creatively to trauma from a wider and deeper, culturally specific standpoint that recognizes that problematic drug use is simply one manifestation of responses to centuries of oppression, intergenerational trauma, and both individual and systemic racism and violence against Indigenous peoples.

To only look at the drug use is so reductive as to be self-defeating.

We focus so much on despair that we don't give drug users — like S., like Meg, like others you will meet — enough credit for their ingenuity and survival skills. For better or for worse, opioids and other mind- and mood-altering substances can be expressions of both ingenuity and persistence. They can be a practical response to fragmented lives, impossible communication, and chronic lack of support. Not despair, not lack of self-respect, but the desire to feel better, to transcend pain.

When I chose, twice, to give birth without pain relief, tucked among good reasons for my choices was a kind of macho belief in my own stoicism, my own strength, and a desire to prove it. I don't regret those labours and births. But the subsequent years of chronic pain — miserable, smallifying, meaningless — have taught me to appreciate the life-affirming nature of the desire to feel good. They've also taught me that excessive self-control and self-denial are just as pathological — for an individual person, and for a culture — as excessive consumption and indulgence. Feast and famine: two sides of the same cultural coin.

Meg, like S., is one of several people who use illicit drugs with whom I've begun to blur the lines between journalism source and friend. This is perfectly common within the higher echelons of society where cultural or business or media elite interview each other, hobnob at the same parties, accept each other's philanthropy and awards, and send their kids to the same schools — but maybe less so when your source is a former street kid on drugs. Perhaps this delicate near-friendship would not have happened if we didn't each feel so lacking in the social department. For Meg, that's because her friends are dead, and because, anyway, life on the street can be so transactional that she feels she is learning from scratch how to be a friend. She's pretty good at it.

It's different for me. In an experience sadly common to people with chronic illness or pain, I have lost treasured friendships in distressing ways. In one Spanish study, 22.2 percent of surveyed adults with chronic pain reported that their friendships had been affected by pain. Among those who left regular employment as a result of pain, 44.4 percent reported deterioration in their friendships. Since I have mostly always worked on my own, and since my marriage also did not survive these years, days can now go by for me with extraordinarily little communication with friends or colleagues or even other adults at all. Although I can walk or run and in fact am driven by pain, as well as by having children, to keep going out and to keep moving, in other respects I am isolated, shut in, and limited in my social interactions and mobility. It's like a sort of progressive quarantine, where I am let out under the strict conditions imposed by my local authorities: Exhaustion, Stiffness, and Pain.

We learn to adapt. Gradually, I have begun to establish friendships with people I interact with on social media, that much-maligned cesspool of shallow quips and fake news. When an old friend says, offhand, that they need to get off superficial, delusional Twitter and back to the *real world*, I feel personally attacked. I think of who I speak with daily or nearly every day. Of where I can finally indulge the intellectual, literary conversation I've craved for years. Of which of my friends regularly send me a gentle *how are you* if I've been silent for a few days. With a few beloved exceptions, it is these disembodied friends of the internet ether, this fragile new network of mine.

Meg, who I also met via Twitter, is perfectly able to tell her story herself, and does so there. She recently published her first article in a major Toronto daily newspaper. She is smart and sensitive.

She is also constantly risking death. Whether illicit "down" (a slang term for opioids, which could be heroin, or illicit fentanyl, or most likely some unholy combination) is a solution or a problem or both, the risk of death it represents right now is inescapable. Another thing my old friends ask me when I tell them about my new, delicate friendships with people who use drugs is why, if I'm feeling so lonely, I'd choose to make friends with people who live unstable lives, people who are likely to suddenly up and die on me.

Indeed, if you yourself are part of the community of poor and housing-insecure drug users, you *are* watching your friends die around you. It is eerily similar to the situation for gay men during the early eighties, when entire social networks were ravaged by AIDS-related deaths that the rest of society ignored. People who use drugs, aware that no one will save them if they don't do it themselves, are increasingly organizing, trying to take lessons from what worked during that plague.

In the 1980s and into the nineties, sex came to have the connotation of death. Now, it is drugs: like sex, they chemically induce good and interesting feelings. Just about anything that can be good can, under certain circumstances, instead come to embody risk, contagion, and death. Like sex in that age of unmanaged AIDS and entrenched homophobia, opioids have become agents of death, and using them seems to require a recklessness, a defiance, or a serious need. And the more dangerous they become, the more it seems like the people who persistently use them, for many reasons all related to their painkilling qualities, must be suicidal, or criminal, or deviant, or immature. Untrustworthy, liable to sow chaos. Fundamentally flawed.

To me, that sounds a little like the way you might describe a sick or struggling friend right before you decide that her persistent suffering is inimical to your own relentless pursuit of happiness: *she's negative, she's toxic, I don't have time for this.* Have I been described in this way? I don't know.

Why would I choose friends who are liable to up and die? Well, because I don't choose them from a drop-down menu of fancy options; rather, we find each other. Because friends are not a product or an accessory. Because I am learning to place more and more value on friendships that are intentional priorities, with people who know about loyalty because they know about betrayal, who know about steadfastness because they know about transience, who know about kindness because they know about abandonment. Because I could up and die first, who knows?

While the prohibition of drugs has spawned an increasingly dangerous illicit market, policy measures relating to drug use typically serve to make it even more dangerous: because the sight of many poor people (some of whom use drugs) congregated together is threatening, people with no homes are pushed out of tent cities that make homelessness safer and marginally more comfortable; bathrooms where users seek the privacy needed to inject with care are made less safe by the installation of blue lights that obscure the vein; and substance after substance is banned, leading almost always to more dangerous alternatives. Enforcement of prohibition follows the same systemic and individual racism as other aspects of the criminal justice system, creating still graver dangers for people of colour and Indigenous people who use drugs.

Throughout much of the United States, it's illegal to give someone a sterile syringe to prevent the spread of HIV or viral hepatitis; where syringe exchanges are allowed, it's a strict one-for-one swap that sharply limits the disease-preventing value of clean needles, even though needle and syringe programs have been found not to increase drug use among participants, have been shown to promote lower-risk injection behaviours and, along with other harm reduction measures, may reduce overall prevalence of injection drug use.[20]

Buprenorphine, a generally non-euphoric opioid medication that prevents overdose and effectively treats the symptoms of opioid addiction, is treated under US law as a dangerous substance. Not only do regulations in most parts of the country make it onerous for doctors to qualify to prescribe it, but it's also a crime to divert this life-saving drug to people who want to avoid resorting to illicit fentanyl. In Providence, Rhode Island, for example, an undercover detective faked opioid withdrawal symptoms. In apparently desperate straits, he asked a man in treatment for opioid addiction if he had any Suboxone, an addiction medication that contains buprenorphine—and then arrested the man after he was sold a single film of the drug, a five-dollar crime[21] whose only effect would have been to prevent overdose death. A total of twenty-three people were ultimately entrapped by this cop and charged with narcotics trafficking for doing exactly the same, for the same piddling amounts. Buprenorphine is a legal and effective addiction treatment, and yet people have to sell it on the black market—not so users can get high but simply to prevent overdose death. There are so many stories like this.

Among the medications that have been shown to be highly effective in both treating opioid use disorder and preventing death, there is only one that tends to be popular with authorities—in the correctional system, for example. That's naltrexone (sold under the brand name Vivitrol). It's hard to see it as coincidental that naltrexone has a distinctly punitive effect. To start it safely, you must first "detox"—that is, undergo painful, unpleasant withdrawal for up to ten days—and then only start naltrexone when you no longer have opioids in your system. And then when you are using it, it blocks the effect of opioids like heroin. If, frustrated at not being able to get high or unable to cope without whatever opioids did for you, you stop taking naltrexone, you are then at far higher risk of overdose, and of fatal overdose, than before you detoxed. This is because while you had no opioids in your system, your opioid tolerance naturally dropped. And in fact, naltrexone has, for these reasons, been found to be ineffective at preventing overdose death.[22]

Meanwhile, non-medication-based treatments typically focus on getting people off drugs as quickly and thoroughly as possible, even if this is the fastest way to render them physically and emotionally miserable—and, all too often, dead.

Looking for someone or something to hold accountable for their loved one's death, bereaved and angry family members often seize upon the obvious culprit: the drug itself, which slowed the pulse, dimmed the spirit, rendered the breath more and more shallow until it stopped, greyed the skin or turned it blueish-purple, provoked the death rattle. It's natural to want to overpower the seductively pleasurable substance, to render it unpleasant or dull. But you're attacking an inanimate object—no, not even an object: a mere substance, a collection of molecules.

An opioid has no morality, is neither good nor bad, cannot make amends, does not care, wishes no one harm. It's not the substance itself that craves euphoria, obliteration of consciousness, relief from pain, a little rest, or a good time. A little more rationally, bereaved family members are also angry at the physicians who may have prescribed a drug they see as the start of addiction; the drug companies and marketing executives that maximized profits while minimizing public understanding of how opioids work and coaxing doctors to prescribe them; at the friends who may have bought or shared drugs or enabled their loved one's drug use.

But other grieving parents feel equally betrayed by the language of tough love, by the advice to avoid "enabling" and let one's loved one reach a completely mythical "rock bottom." I call Petra Schultz, a founder of Moms Stop the Harm (MSTH), a Canadian organization of bereaved parents that provides peer support while also advocating for drug policy that would prevent other families from losing their children to preventable overdose (Families for Sensible Drug Policy is a similar organization in the United States). It has been six years since Schultz's son Danny died of an opioid overdose.

"We found a phone number in Danny's bathroom. He died right there where he injected," she tells me. A police officer held the bit of paper with the number. They both knew it must have been Danny's dealer, and that it contained the possibility of legal action against them. The officer wisely told her, "It won't bring Danny back." She declined to take the little note.

In her grief, Schultz was often pointed to self-help literature, which simply added to her sorrow as she read other stories of loss. Instead, she began to research the grief particular to losing a child to suicide or substance use. It turns out that this often provokes what's called complex grief, a form of trauma.

"Even in my grief process, academic literature helped me more than the self-help books," she tells me. Schultz began reading about overdose and substance use. From Johann Hari's history of the war on drugs in his 2015 book *Chasing the Scream*, she learned that there has always been a tight connection between race relations and drug war policies, that human rights of drug users are routinely violated, that it's not just that people who use drugs are burdened with dependence on a dangerous substance, but that the substance is dangerous in large part because of criminalization of users, because their autonomy is so often denied, because they are alienated from families and communities by criminalization or terrible treatment regimens or poverty or shame.

Rather than joining drug warriors like many other bereaved parents, Schultz and her fellow MSTH founders instead decided to work in solidarity with drug user unions and harm reduction advocates, a far better evidenced way to ensure other young people don't die preventable deaths like their children did. I've come to admire the delicate balancing act they must perform as they try not to speak over the voices of people who use drugs themselves, as organizations of bereaved family members often do, even though tortured or abusive family relationships can sometimes be at the heart of compulsive drug use. These mothers also carry out a quieter but fundamental task, which is to support other bereaved and struggling parents. In 2019, for example, they held a photo shoot in Kelowna, British Columbia, for which MSTH members held white crosses in a striking image intended to move others to acknowledge their deceased children as people with valuable lives—and to push for decriminalization as well as harm reduction initiatives including safe supply.

Safe supply and other initiatives that make opioid use less dangerous intervene to prevent the fatal moment when the breath slows to nothing. These, and not the dreadful advice worried parents often receive to push their drug-using children out of the house, to cut off relationships, to stage humiliating and manipulative "interventions," to discourage use of life-saving addiction medications, are what would have kept their deceased loved ones alive.

Sometime after Schultz started educating herself on the war on drugs and its relationship to addiction and overdose, Garth Mullins was just starting up a podcast in which drug users tell the story of the war on drugs, the gimmick being that they are war correspondents. *CRACKDOWN* is a powerful program — with an editorial board of drug users and an advisory board of scientists — that has gone on to win multiple radio awards.[23] One day, Mullins described on Twitter how it felt when he wanted to use heroin. Petra Schultz saw his comment and, in that public forum, began asking him questions about what that was like.

"I wish I could have asked Danny these questions," she tells me now. "I wish Danny could have said, 'Look guys, I relapsed.' I wish we could have said" — and over the phone I hear her voice collapse — "'It's okay, sweetie.'"

She apologizes for breaking down a little, rallies, and continues through tears.

"If we can't do it for our kids, we can do it for others. When you come from a place of love, you don't stigmatize."

So-called tough love, Schultz says, alienates people who use drugs without either dealing with the reasons they use, or providing help with the withdrawal and cravings that so frequently lead people pushed into abstinence back to the drugs, and to fatal relapse, with no further chances.

Schultz saw that Danny's experience was being re-enacted over and over again with different young people as Canada's overdose crisis continued to worsen.

"Stigma and shaming was making things worse," Schultz says. "It drives them to use and die alone."

That Moms Stop the Harm photo shoot struck me because it's both staged and vividly poignant, the sort of cinematic detail I look for when I write. The event was so successful that it has been repeated in beautiful and significant locations across Canada. In the same way, these mothers repeatedly recount the story of their children's lives and deaths in hopes it might stop the onslaught of death and save someone else's child. The second time they staged a shoot, more than fifty grieving mothers posed for photos. Some of these women are PhDs and lawyers, deeply knowledgeable about drug policy and treatment evidence, skillful advocates who hold their own position on the issue but who have learned to work in tandem with drug users themselves, their children's peers. They know that their symbolic weight as "everyday, average moms" allows their beloved children a chance at being seen as human — valuable every second of their lives, including when they use drugs — rather than written off in death as they too often were in life.

The bereaved mothers of MSTH, and their counterparts in the United States, occupy a lonely position in a way. Not fully part of the harm reduction community headed by drug users and frontline workers, they may feel judged by their peers, former friends, and neighbours. Much like the mothers who organize to seek justice and their disappeared children in Argentina, Mexico, or Canada, it is largely the mothers, rather than fathers, who have organized to confront this catastrophe and, always, it is mothers who are judged and found wanting. From my perspective as a parent constantly just hanging in there, I easily imagine that every moment of the constantly fraught act of parenting, every choice they ever made, must be scrutinized for details that might (falsely) reassure another worried mother that *her* child will not suffer overdose, that somehow *they* are different. Were they bad moms? Did they work too much? Earn too little? Stay when they should have left? Leave when they should have stayed? Did they enable drug use by not shutting the door for good?

But these women are practical and focused. By allying with drug user movements, MSTH has been able to support their shared goal of dismantling the system of prohibition that, they have come to believe, criminalized their children, making drug use dangerous and secretive, unnecessarily isolating, and ultimately deadly. And, by allying with these movements, rather than with the anti-drug coalitions or people in recovery who now advocate abstinence as the only option for drug users other than death, they are taking sides in a way that their friends and family may find hard to understand or accept. But there is a comradeship I see between some of the mothers and drug user advocates for harm reduction — between Garth Mullins and Petra Schultz, for example — new solidarity between people with similar goals of advancing human rights and protecting precious lives. A new, delicately built community of allies against the war on drugs is taking shape.

When everything seemed to be falling apart for me, I would leave my own bed and creep in to lie beside my sleeping toddlers and listen to their breathing. Gradually, I would pattern my inhalations and exhalations on theirs and, reassured, would feel the awfulness of everything retreat a little. I also remember when they were just born. I would bend over my tiny swaddled child in the darkness and wait anxiously until I knew that the nightmare had not happened; the air continued to go reliably in and out, it was only in my exhausted dreams that it had stopped, everything was all right. Every mother must remember doing this.

My kids are young adolescents now. I can't bear to imagine losing them. There are no words to even articulate the pain associated with a word like "junkie" in this context. My mind reels and turns away. The brave women of Moms Stop the Harm can't do that. So they stand there, elegant and austere, dressed in black, some holding photos of their babies who barely made it to adulthood or other symbols of their grief. Others stand beside big white crosses, holding them up lightly, or being held up gently by them. Over and over.

The alarm rips me from a disturbing dream, just a set of tangled emotions — I had something, I lost it. When my first child was born I had many dreams like this, hypnagogic hallucinations in which I tried to keep things alive: strange alien creatures, tiny fetal kittens, eggs. The fear of this tiny precious life slipping through my fingers extended from the few, short moments of sleep I was allowed on a two-hour feeding schedule into waking life, which was intense and kind of golden with sleep-deprived, oxytocin-softened love. From those first moments my baby's (and then my second baby's) breath became my metronome.

Petra Schultz and others have adopted harm reduction because of abundant evidence that it prevents death, that it keeps that metronome clicking. And it does so while promoting a caring and respectful attitude toward people too often treated as human garbage. Crucially, it's the approach drug user organizers themselves call for. An example of harm reduction that is well-accepted by most people would be the laws we have requiring seat belts in cars. These are harm reduction because they allow us to continue the intrinsically dangerous activity of driving by significantly reducing the harms that may result from a crash.

When applied to drug use, harm reduction means trying to reduce the avoidable harms associated with using drugs. For example, in pubs and bars, users can imbibe their addictive, poisonous drug of choice in a pleasant, relaxed environment that provides at least some social cues toward moderation, with help at hand in case of excess. Opium dens once served the same purpose, their rich, decadent atmosphere, much like the classic warm interior of a British pub, designed to set you at ease.

Regulations that ensure alcohol is both legalized and quality controlled ensure that what you drink in that pub will not kill you (at least, not quickly). Prescription opioids are likewise legalized and controlled for purity, quality, and dose, which is why they have high street value. "Junkies" are thought to be reckless, impulsive, self-destructive, even chronically suicidal—but the market says otherwise. Prices in the illicit market go up and down depending on a range of factors, but in general a single prescription opioid pill may cost the same on the street as a bag of heroin, or more. The Drug Enforcement Administration (DEA), for example, reported the prescription opioid Opana (extended-release oxymorphone) selling for USD $10 to $80 per pill, and Percocet selling for $7 to $10 per tab, at a time when heroin could be had for $5 to $10 a bag.[24] That's not because prescription opioids give a stronger or better high but because they are safer, thanks to that extremely desirable quality control.

Given that the harms to health, relationships, work, and well-being commonly associated with drug use are far greater than the actual harms intrinsic to a given substance, harm reduction makes intuitive sense. Many people who work one-on-one with clients who struggle with addiction or with poverty and homelessness come to see harm reduction as the most effective and also the most ethical approach to substance use—and the evidence bears this out on multiple measures of well-being. Drug user unions, in which people using drugs organize to advocate for their human and civil rights and for policies that will improve their lives, identify harm reduction practices that can help keep people alive and well even as they may continue to use their drug of choice. These are the organizations that MSTH have come to view as allies.

And yet, such practices are often very controversial. Partly because of the way they are written about in mainstream media, they are associated in many people's minds with a dubious, left-wing political program that seeks to turn attention away from individual responsibility or morality and toward social, political, and economic factors. These factors—the unmentionable Fates we touched on before—are things like race, class, gender, or disability, which assign some people greater power in society than others, dramatically determining health outcomes as well as how drug laws are created in the first place, and then how they are selectively enforced to preserve an inequitable status quo. And although the choice not to use drugs at all *is* on any menu of harm reduction options, a commitment to letting people be the authors of their own lives means that pushing them to achieve abstinence from opioids, other illicit drugs, or drugs in general, at all costs and without actually knowing that is the best thing for a given person, is not one of the goals of this philosophy.

A commitment to a science-informed, evidence-based approach to knowledge is another basic tenet of harm reduction. The body of evidence we have now about people who use opioids or most other common illicit drugs simply doesn't support the assumption that abstinence is either necessary or even—and this is a particularly hard pill to swallow, so to speak, for those committed to abstinence—the best choice for all people who use drugs. But that sounds a lot like advocating that we should all use drugs, and—although the vast, vast majority of adult humans regularly use one or more psychoactive substance of one kind or another—*that* sounds like hippies, commies, and freaks. Or, as Deaton put it, like being "a left-wing nut."

The incredibly high overdose death rate in the US has spurred calls for significant harm reduction initiatives, such as free and over-the-counter access to naloxone, a magical drug if there ever was one, which reverses overdoses of any opioid,[25] or safe[26] consumption sites in cities like Philly and New York—sanitized versions of the pub or opium den, fulfilling the same quality control and death prevention functions. Canada's existing sites have, in this context, become objects of prurient media interest for Americans. It is really hard for many people in the country that invented the war on drugs to wrap their heads around the idea that it could be good for both individual and public health for drug users to have a safe place to use them (and, going further, that a taxpayer-funded healthcare system might pay for and provide safe, legally regulated drugs like heroin? The mind simply boggles, like the inaccurate but memorable scrambled brain on drugs from Nancy Reagan's Just Say No ads in the 1980s). And yet, as I write this, the state of Oregon has decriminalized all drugs, with the city of Vancouver likely following behind. Anything is possible.

In times of loss, my babies' steady breathing kept me calm. One day, perhaps, they may steady my breathing in turn. Although it is unlikely to be needed, I have explained to my children how to squirt naloxone up my nose in the event that I happen to stop breathing and turn blue. This knowledge may also help them save a friend or a stranger's life one day.

It could be one of our neighbours. Just within the first two minutes out the door of my downtown apartment, I pass numerous homeless people panhandling for change, killing time, or sleeping in sometimes ingenious structures set up in doorways or on the sidewalk. Most of them are familiar figures: I know them and they know me.

I've never encountered anyone either injecting drugs or overdosing, and I have no idea who uses and who does not (the US Substance Abuse and Mental Health Services Administration's survey of adults in shelters estimates that around a third have chronic substance use issues, although it's not clear how well that gets at the real number, since not all homeless people use shelters). My naloxone is, for now, mostly a prop, and I'm mostly a tourist, and deaths are, so far, just a rumour for me.

One lovely May day in 2018, I visit a new overdose prevention site (OPS), a supervised drug consumption site with temporary government approval set up in the basement of a community centre in Kensington Market, a gentrifying but beloved neighbourhood near where I live in Toronto. The Market abuts Toronto's Chinatown, was originally a Jewish market, and has hosted successive waves of immigration; the clientele of both the community centre and the OPS thus represent dozens of languages and countries of origin, as well as a significant First Nations population.

I'm writing an article about harm reduction in the city for a small local magazine.

The day before I visit the site at St. Stephen's Community House, a bevy of reporters and photographers have swanned through from the *New York Times*. Later I find the hand-wringing feature they write, asking whether New York is ready for scenes like Toronto's (there are no scenes here in Kensington that I can see). In prurient detail, they describe a user shooting up (St. Stephen's tells me they have not allowed any journalists to watch someone in these private moments).

Tyler Watts, coordinator of the OPS, takes me down to the community centre's basement. The new site has been squeezed in beside the facility's kitchen, which hosts community lunches every weekday. On my first visit, I'm permitted a look at the consumption room. This is a little windowless room outfitted with two steel shelves, each with a chair and a mirror, and just outside that, a cupboard neatly stocked with different gauges of needle, alcohol wipes, rubber ties, and other safer injection necessities; an antechamber contains a few armchairs where users can relax after doing their shot and before returning to the larger room outside, where they mix freely with local senior citizens and young moms.

Watts introduces me to Angela Kokinos, a strikingly vibrant, friendly peer worker at the site. Initially I don't know how to recognize a drug user. It's human nature to fall back on stereotypes to try to categorize people, so I take the more ragged-looking people I see to be probable "junkies." If you are articulate, well-dressed, or healthy-looking, I assume, you must be a staff person, not a junkie. And so, being a newbie drugs writer, it is both surprising and exciting to me when I realize that Kokinos is, herself, a drug user.

My junkie radar seems to have been malfunctioning.

I scribble some notes as she tells me how she recently quit opioids cold turkey. Angela explains that she decided to quit after having accidentally overdosed due to illicit fentanyl in her "down." She is scared of dying. "I didn't want to play Russian roulette," she tells me.

Gradually it dawns on me that many or most peer workers at these sites are present, past, or occasional users of illicit drugs. But here (because, as I will realize later, my understanding of the harms and effects of substance use is actually very poor), I am just very pleased to meet a real-life person who injects hard drugs. Colour! My little plastic bottle of opioids is a warm secret in my pocket. It stays there because it's not exactly the correct time for the exact prescribed dose, despite the stiffness and pain already clawing at my spine. I get that there are similarities between us. But my needs are, you know, different.

Weeks later, I assign myself another reporting field trip, this time to attend a demonstration outside the provincial legislature in support of declaring opioid overdoses an emergency in Ontario. I stand uncomfortably through the land acknowledgement that has become routine here in Canada, an act that has quickly lost its political heat as land remains contested and treaty rights denied. This one is not a reflexive nod to a fake reconciliation, though. Two Cree men, brothers Les Harper and Clay Shirt, each take the mic. In their speeches they say in different ways that their people are now dying of overdose, that the overdose crisis is one more step in a continuing process of institutional neglect, continued human rights and treaty violations, structural factors that set people up to struggle, and governmental indifference that give the lie to pronouncements about "reconciliation" after centuries of colonialism that is still ongoing. Among the many terrible histories that have set the stage for the current opioid overdose crisis, four centuries of rights violations, genocide, and entrenchment of inequitable economic relations for Indigenous people across North America stand out.

Indeed, the Canadian government continues to refuse to mount a serious public health response to opioid overdose even as they promote a narrative in which old wounds are uncovered and healed, leading to a just relationship between Indigenous people and settlers to Canada. Far from it: the Canadian federal government has continued fighting numerous court injunctions requiring them to do their duty toward Indigenous children; similarly, they have touted reconciliation while repeatedly contravening legal requirements to consult before allowing for resource extraction on Indigenous land, including land that has never been ceded. This sounds like a side issue, but in fact historical injustices and atrocities perpetrated against a number of large groups of people — from Black Canadians and Americans to Central American refugees to Indigenous peoples across the Americas — fundamentally shape both the US-led, international war on drugs, and the vulnerability of these different communities to addiction or overdose from prescription or illicit opioids, as well as a huge range of other health-related problems including pain. This is not the past: it occurs through continued oppression, discrimination, and active perpetration of injustice today.

Such historical and ongoing harm is a huge cause of vulnerability to pain as well as withholding of effective pain treatment including opioids where they are indicated; problematic opioid (and other substance) use; difficulty moving out of addiction; greater risk of homelessness and fewer supports to prevent it; greater negative consequences of drug use; dramatically poorer access to decent, kind, and unprejudiced healthcare that can reduce negative outcomes and greater risk of traumatic and harmful healthcare experiences; greater risk of overdose and greater health vulnerabilities that make even surviving an overdose less likely. The list of harms that result directly from injustice could go on forever. *These* are the deaths of despair: but the notion that people are expiring quietly because they can't be bothered to live is both vile and false.

Many people with chronic and acute illness, most notably Susan Sontag but also many others, have critiqued the terminology of the fighting patient: by declaring a "war on cancer," for example, we imply that dying of the disease represents a lack of willpower and fighting spirit, and we downplay the role of both chance and structural factors like inequities that stack the decks against some people every step of the way, from likelihood of contracting the disease to speed of diagnosis to quality of treatment. It is, however, right to acknowledge that those structural factors can represent an undeclared war on patients, including people who use drugs.

As soon as the land acknowledgement is over I go back to surreptitiously stretching, holding myself up with a hand at the base of my spine as people offer further passionate speeches. As we form a circle outside the provincial legislature, I rise to tip-toes, stretching my constantly tight hamstrings. It is a relief when we start marching, taking over a main avenue.

We make our way to the office of Ontario's Chief Medical Officer of Health, the official charged with mounting public health responses to things like epidemics or similar health issues. On arrival, my fellow protestors stage a die-in. The CMOH, David Williams, has seemed oblivious to and uninterested in the overdose crisis, consistently and flippantly refusing calls for a public health emergency to be declared and commensurate resources devoted to preventing opioid-involved overdose. Is it because those dying of overdose are largely poor and racialized people who simply aren't part of this man's frame of reference? As the other marchers fall to the ground, I think that most likely Dr. Williams isn't even in his office. A different physician-leader, Dr. Mark Tyndall, who was director of the BC Centre for Disease Control, told me in an interview about his far more impressive contribution on the overdose crisis in British Columbia that as a young physician working on HIV response in Kenya, he learned essential epidemiological skills that apply equally to responding effectively to a toxic drug supply. You need a swift, coordinated, and thorough public health response, just as you'd treat an infectious disease.

Dr. Tyndall has gone on to become one of the world's best advocates for safe opioid supply, doggedly promoting a biometrically controlled vending machine that distributes stigma-free drugs to people who need them, and arguing for an understanding of the overdose crisis that privileges the experience of those most affected by it. Dr. Williams will become, fatally, the health leader in charge of Ontario's response to COVID-19. We'll check in on him in a few years.

I stand apart, a journalist snapping photos with my phone, not a participant rehearsing death. Indeed, I'm thinking about how to look like a journalist rather than a woman who can't stay still, as the loved ones and allies of drug users who have died of overdose lie on the road.

Death is a constant. Frontline workers, who, like Angela Kokinos, are often people with their own past or current experience of chaotic or dependent drug use, are facing intensely traumatic experiences daily as they intervene with oxygen or naloxone to bring people back from overdose, sometimes to a full recovery and other times to brain damage from prolonged lack of oxygen. Many frontline workers at supervised consumption sites and in outreach to people who use drugs are volunteers or very poorly paid and precariously employed, with no support except each other as they save lives or mourn deaths.

If you are not actually immersed in it, it's hard to convey the extent of what has been going on for years now. On social media, at conferences, and in op-eds, these frontline workers have been trying to persuade the rest of the world of the cascading, rippling harms of overdose deaths, but nothing appears able to nudge governments to take more powerful actions to prevent them. This, even though overdose is not like a mysterious virus with no cure: rather, it is highly preventable with the right interventions, both in the moment and further ahead of time, what they call "upstream." What makes it most surreal is the way no one not directly affected appears to care that several people are dying of overdose every day, that people are being brought back from death on a constant basis, and that there is a baseline level of tremendous trauma and loss across North America that seems like it should cast a pall on life for everyone, all the time. Yet it doesn't seem to even register.

Immediately after saving a life, workers have very little to offer to the homeless or insecurely housed users who really don't have a good alternative. It often makes more sense to continue to use than to subject oneself to a traumatic withdrawal and "treatment" far more often based in moralism than in evidence and best practice healthcare. Long-time users have been through it all already and are perfectly aware that the detox treatment typically on offer ultimately offers no hope of a better life unless their material circumstances were to magically change—and that detox and abstinence actually put them at far greater risk of death in the event of a relapse that, statistically, is highly likely to occur.

"People think in harm reduction that we don't encourage people to seek out rehab or counselling but it doesn't exist, and not in the way people want it to," says Zoë Dodd, a prominent harm reduction advocate in Toronto who founded an illegal OPS in a park before it was accepted and ultimately funded by the government. She explains that all options, including detox leading to abstinence, fall under the umbrella of harm reduction, but the system we've set up in North America to address problematic drug use is adapted from the early peer-based models like Alcoholics Anonymous, which are outside the healthcare system, unresponsive to evidence, and focused on shame-inducing interventions that don't work, or that don't work well enough for enough people.

Although popular culture and talk shows and references to addiction in movies or songs all treat rehab as the correct path for someone who uses alcohol or drugs in a problematic way, the data on get-off-drugs programs is not reassuring, particularly in the context of an opioid overdose crisis frequently resulting in death. We know, for example, that rehab and detox and twelve-step programs like Narcotics Anonymous are *not* effective at preventing death. The most recent good research on this comes from a 2019 study by Sarah Wakeman, an addiction medicine physician and researcher. Wakeman and her team studied a staggering 40,885 adults with opioid use disorder, comparing effectiveness of six different forms of treatment, and found that the *only* treatments associated with a lowered risk of overdose were the opioids buprenorphine or methadone. Not with counselling, but simply on their own. Even though it makes sense that good counselling—particularly the sort of long-term individual talk therapy that no one funds but that is most likely to make a difference for people with complex, long-term trauma—might be helpful, the fact is that if your goal is to prevent death in someone at risk of opioid overdose death, you need to prescribe them opioid substitution medication. Intensive or less intensive behavioural health treatment, inpatient detox, or the abstinence-forcing medication naltrexone (Vivitrol)—these popular, prevalent "treatments" are not treatment at all: they simply do not prevent overdose or death. In the case of naltrexone, you'll recall, it may in fact hasten it.

Evidence doesn't seem to matter, though. The moralistic way of thinking prevalent across North America, and in particular throughout the addiction treatment industry, holds that despite the evidence, the most important thing is to get drug users to stop using drugs—even those drugs that treat addiction, prevent death, and improve multiple health outcomes. Ultimately, policy decisions are being made not on the basis of evidence but on the basis of values, and the values that prevail in North America at the moment are killing people who use drugs. Some see this as an unfortunate but unavoidable outcome of drug use. For others, it's "another junkie off the streets." Either way, we seem to be imagining people drained of life, zombie-like, at death's door, barely human, fundamentally doomed. But studies like Dr. Wakeman's show that existing policy—not inherent properties of the people or the drugs, but bad policies, including promotion of ineffective addiction "treatment"—actively kills these people who do not need to die, who were capable of leading thriving, immensely positive lives.

I am alone in the book-strewn office-bedroom where I spend most of my time, googling around to see if I can find any credible descriptions of people injecting in a Canadian supervised consumption site when, I'm not sure how, I come across an obituary. Angela Kokinos—born a couple of months before me—died in September. It is January. The last name Kokinos rings a bell. But the "Ang" I met this past spring seemed a lot younger than me, vibrant. I scroll down.

I will never forget her smile and how she made me laugh, wrote one of many friends commenting on her online guestbook. *Even in the darkest of times she had the ability to turn tears of pain into tears of laughter.*

All my childhood memories include my sister. Angela was there for me for my darkest days.

She was such a great friend and I feel like part of [my] heart is torn.

She had a large impact on the person I am today. I was so lucky to have a friend like her. [. . .] I am not sure where to start I am truly heartbroken about this.

Angela was our second of four children. Angela cared about everyone else more than herself. Angela helped a lot of people in need. Angela saved lives at work. Angela was always laughing and making people happy.

And some that used the nickname "Ang."

I remember scribbling that name, along with a few quotes, in a notebook that is now somewhere in my closet. I have multiple black notebooks and the odd coloured one. It takes me a while—bending hurts, and moving things off from on top of other things is a ridiculously difficult task that I often give up before I've found what I'm looking for—but at last I find it. A red one.

"I think people are scared," are among her words that I wrote down in May. She was scared. Ang, who I now know was Angela Kokinos.

My source—though I hadn't quoted her in my article in the end—died and I didn't even know. I've already missed her funeral. My provincial government is in the process of pulling funding from overdose prevention sites like the one Ang worked at, instead of expanding them so that there might have been one near her apartment, when she needed it. Tentatively, I use the facts I already know to write an article about the closures of overdose prevention sites, and an awkward tribute to Angela. I know that Ang's co-workers have enough to deal with already, just trying to keep serving clients. So you could say it's considerate of me not to bug them for an interview. But I know that I am embarrassed and craven. I wrote about a beloved member of a loving community moving heaven and Earth to save each other's lives, but I wasn't part of that community. I wandered in to write about the overdose prevention site, then wandered out again. I wasn't engaged day to day, was not connected in a real way. Had no vested interest, no personal reason to care. There was no reason anyone should have thought to tell me that she'd died, and no reason I would have known. Their lives stopped with the shock of it even though the work went on, but I just carried blithely along, oblivious until now. This is a thought about journalism and what I am writing for, about what kind of writer I want to be. Am I in, or am I out?

Months after her death, I finally get the story from Barb Panter and Tyler Watts, Angela's colleagues and higher-ups at work. Kokinos had, unsurprisingly, not stuck with abstinence; she had returned to cautiously using opioids. As with trying to quit cigarettes, it is absolutely normal to require multiple attempts, but the systems that treat addiction tend to stress the importance of staying off drugs rather than making it as safe as possible to keep trying. Imagine that you could die if you removed your nicotine patch or spat out your Nicorette gum and had a cigarette. That's what this is like.

She overdosed in a moment of stress, using alone in her apartment. If she had waited and used at the supervised drug consumption site where she worked, she would not have died. That's pretty much a certainty. Although tens of thousands of injections have taken place at the over one hundred sanctioned supervised drug consumption sites around the world, so far no one has died of overdose[27] in one — not one person, even though the population that typically use them have generally poor health status and so would be vulnerable to things going wrong.

"When Ang died," Tyler Watts tells me, "I wasn't sure we could withstand any more." At the time, the provincial government had pulled funding from that site and others, and St. Stephen's was relying on donations from the community and on temporary funding from the federal government to stay afloat.

"It's frustrating that we have to fight to keep a life-saving service. When our clients pass away and I want to scream and fucking punch things," he says, "I can't let her death be in vain. [. . .] Ang was a tragedy that will break my heart to the day I die but she's also a motivator to the optimism I feel. She believed we could make change so I'm not going to let her down. That grief really binds people. You go through trauma together and those are the only people that get it, that you know you can rely on and trust."

I see my new friends, like Meg, or Joe, who you'll meet later, only occasionally in the flesh. Given the physical limitations that have put such strain on my "real life" friendships, I am grateful to be able to keep in touch with them mostly via regular messages. In some cases, they are friends who I *only* know virtually, like Michael. Still, I speak with them regularly, almost daily in some cases.

All of these friendships — which go beyond the short-term, one-way connection of journalist and subject — come about, in a gradual and natural way, after Angela Kokinos's death. First they are friendly acquaintanceships, then interviews, and then tentative friendships. For each of these new friends of mine, drug policy, substance use, inequities, and the gap between what people need to flourish in their lives and what so many have is not just another social justice topic. It is, rather, the very substance of their lives, the air they breathe, and a daily apocalypse they cannot escape.

In the summer of 2020, a year after Angela died, I will "lose" another source within days of our long, intense phone interview. Mary Duffy, a trained cook in Texas, became homeless after her husband left (taking the house) following years of cancer treatments that left her bankrupt. Duffy describes to me her odyssey through an American dystopia of homelessness and punitive shelters, such as Haven for Hope, a partly open-air "transformational campus" founded by an entrepreneur in private prisons who saw potential in the abstinence-only homeless shelter market. At Haven for Hope, access to a roof over your sleeping mat crowded by hundreds of others on a concrete floor is a privilege, which must be earned. You do that via participation in substance use counselling and drug testing, attendance at religious education classes, and work programs.

Breaking curfew or failing a drug test can put you back in the concrete courtyard. At the time we spoke, Duffy feared she'd soon have no option but to return to Haven for Hope, where she'd previously spent just a couple of sleepless, terrified nights in the open, listening to gunshots in the dark. But, as I will learn shortly after I file my article draft, her luck briefly turned, and she succeeded in renting an apartment. Her sister co-signed the one-year lease.

Maybe three weeks after my article is published, I receive a direct message from a stranger. "Hi Carlyn," he writes. "I am Mary Duffy's neighbor and I have some very sad news. I found her deceased yesterday, face down on her couch."

Duffy, I will learn, had shared the article I wrote with her new neighbour, pointing out the passages where she appeared. Although she did not use recreational drugs and had spoken disparagingly about drug users at the shelters she'd stayed in, he tells me he believes she actually died of a drug overdose, probably of prescribed medications, as the floor of her new apartment was strewn with pills and pill bottles (ultimately "heart attack" was listed as the cause of death).

But here, now, in the fall of 2019, I'm still returning over and over in my mind to Angela's death, while at the same time getting to know Meg. In some ways, she is an intellectual kindred spirit. She's as weirdly interested as I am in parsing out my — and her — different feelings and motivations. Her facility with literary references challenges my own. She asks how I am and I am touched to see that she is interested and responsive to the details of my rarely sunny answer. She is not afraid of pain.

But still, even if I knew her better, I would have no claim on her well-being. As December approaches I am becoming increasingly anxious about her Christmas holiday plans: she will travel to Connecticut to stay for five days with her father and stepmother. This will require crossing the US border while addicted to illicit fentanyl. I can't imagine how she will manage this. She has done it before, wedging the drug in her vagina behind a tampon. The risk involved nearly takes my breath away.

When she gets back from Connecticut, Meg says, she will get a kitten. I just got one — a painkiller coup for me, a previously unimaginable commitment to bending and caring for yet another love — and yet her ambition seems dubious to me. I'm full of vague worries that have practical answers, things like how she will keep the drugs away from a cat (A: in a drawer).

She's had cats in the past. And, in fact, many people who are actually living on the streets find solace and companionship, and sometimes protection, in pets (they may also avoid shelters, which do not usually admit animals[28]). Caring for an animal is an act of responsibility and love that satisfies something many of us, people with pain, badly need. Meg is off the street, but dying of loneliness. Like me, when she loves she loves hard and stubbornly. Her last relationship, which was abusive nearly from the start, nevertheless lasted fourteen years.

I'm antsy. I realize that if Meg can't handle the dramatic cut in opioid dose while she is away and resorts to heroin or fentanyl she finds, somehow, on the street, if she overdoses — or does so on her return, tolerance now dangerously low — I don't only lose a source, around whom I've decided, with permission, to structure part of my book. Far more seriously, I would lose the delicate beginning of a friendship.

I feel intimation of loss with the same crawling dread a dependent opioid user feels as withdrawal looms. And...this is awful...it's...well, because I see how neatly an overdose would work, structurally, for my story here, I worry that I am somehow going to worry a tragedy into being. Every article on substance use begins with a scene of someone injecting, and it ends with either redemption and abstinence, or death. Abstinence is neither likely nor, I think, entirely desirable in Meg's case. Certainly not any time soon. It seems to me far more likely that her extended-release morphine will be inadequate and that over five days in Connecticut she will become physically sick enough to seek out whatever source of "heroin" she can find.

So does that leave death? Is death (or redemption) the only structure a book about substance use can follow?

I tell myself that this here is what pain psychologists call "catastrophizing." Just because she *could* die, just because others in her situation are dying every day, doesn't mean she will. But then, pain psychologists sometimes have trouble recognizing catastrophe when it falls on their clients like a giant anvil.

At the same time, I think that a person who chose to leave her family and live on the street, a person who has taken a baseball bat to bed with her for safety, a person who eventually cut things off completely with her ex-girlfriend, leaving without a trace, is a person who does not want a nagging, anxious, neurotic, lonely writer—a writer-mom, no less—stalking her with my silly, maternalistic fears.

But I could end this book, so neatly, with a funeral. The minute I think the words, I hate my dark, opportunistic imagination. I know I don't have the power to cause harm with my thoughts—but tell that to my thoughts. And then, although Meg is usually very active on Twitter, she goes quiet.

I check the social media platform every few minutes for evidence she is alive.

Finally I can't stand it anymore. If she overdoses, how long will it be before someone finds her? My lurid imagination will not stop. It is indecent. It's intrusive. It respects no boundaries. I can't stop it.

I don't want to write about her death. I want her to survive.

Limits

Balzac drank coffee till it killed him. Elizabeth Bishop used cortisone for asthma and also for writing.[1] Isak Dinesen, like Oliver Sacks, used amphetamines.[2] Susan Sontag, too, used speed, in the form of Dexamyl, a combo amphetamine-barbiturate antidepressant that gave her stamina and concentration.[3] Of laudanum, which she took daily from the age of fifteen, the poet Elizabeth Barrett Browning wrote, "that life is necessary to writing, & that I should not be alive except by help of my morphine."[4]

Even just a few decades ago, then, it was not so unusual for writers to use chemistry to push their limits. Sometimes, hunched over the keyboard, I feel that I am donating my body to literature (or, less optimistically, exchanging it for a bunch of lousy words). Without tramadol to cover the pain in my spine, I don't think it would be possible to write in a consistent way, or to write about anything other than pain, except maybe death.

As it turned out, excessive pain, not excessive opioids, was the cause of the depressive breakdown that sent me to the Centre for Addiction and Mental Health in a futile search for support, or maybe comfort, or hope. With my underlying disease under somewhat better control (thanks to not one but two new immune suppressants), and with tramadol covering the persistent, intense stiffness and pain that are otherwise eased only with constant, exhausting motion, I am no longer depressed, and am now inching closer to a normal life.

So now that I've stretched my own limits, optimized myself with opioids, maybe it's time to consider what the heck I'm doing. How far can I go with this new beat of writing about drugs, of writing about pain?

While the medium has morphed over time — with graphic novels, podcasts, essays, and oil paintings all ways to tell true stories — the exploitation of trauma and conflict, of drama, is a constant in the narrative arts. Describing Théodore Géricault's painting of an 1816 shipwreck based on the account of two survivors, the writer Julian Barnes discusses the process of turning catastrophe to art:

> Nowadays the process is automatic. A nuclear plant
> explodes? We'll have a play on the London stage within
> a year. A president is assassinated? You can have a book or
> the film or the filmed book or the booked film. War? Send
> in the novelists. A series of gruesome murders? Listen for
> the tramp of the poets. We have to understand it, of course,
> this catastrophe; to understand it, we have to imagine it, so
> we need the imaginative arts. But we also need to justify it
> and forgive it, this catastrophe, however minimally. Why
> did it happen, this mad act of Nature, this crazed human
> moment? Well, at least it produced art. Perhaps, in the end,
> that's what catastrophe is for.[5]

I have been willing to exploit myself for the sake of what I hope will be art for as long as I can remember. I would literally draw up ink from my veins if I had to. But writing about this great catastrophe of overdose and misery taking place across North America (and, to a lesser extent, around the world) is different. Journalism relating to substance use purports to be objective. In fact, it is laden with unquestioned biases and assumptions about substance use, addiction, and health, as well as race and class, both of which are inseparable from how drug policy is created and how it plays out in the world. Most journalism reflects societal biases, of course. But when it comes to substances, unstated and misleading assumptions are the norm, and they influence policy in ways that result in avoidable death.

With or without their informed consent, we harvest people's stories, take what we need to shore up the narrative about drugs that's already in our heads, and turn our subjects into one-liners, homilies, or cautionary tales.

It's easy to hide in the writing, though. At first scan, an article that speaks with authority reads as neutral, as smooth as a painting that hides its brushstrokes. Indeed, the objective tone conceals the inflections or descriptors that would tell us who this author is and how their prejudices, experiences, assumptions, and privilege (or, more bluntly, their gender, race, sexuality, immigration status, and class, among other factors) in fact shape the way they use these stories. Let alone the editorial slant of the publication itself, a result of the biases of its owners and investors — and yet that slant can be fundamental. People who use drugs are often quoted misleadingly, described pejoratively, and used as narrative devices in ways that don't reflect their actual experience or what they meant to say. As a result, they can become unwilling to share their stories, as they may be asked to do over and over again — by people like me.

As I've started freelancing again, the power dynamics between who typically tells the stories and who actually experiences them are increasingly jarring. It gets hard to see the difference between seeking out sources to provide a quote and some local colour, and the sort of prurient, profoundly ugly "slum tourism" that brings sightseers and poverty researchers alike to Downtown Eastside Vancouver, just as it has brought similar gawkers to observe human misery in Mumbai, Soweto, Harlem, post-Katrina New Orleans, and other locations where poverty or drug use are visible on the streets.[6] Philadelphia's own Kensington neighbourhood, notorious for open drug use and sales and visible poverty, has been slum-toured by everyone from police cadets to Dr. Oz.[7] Journalists descend on these places, take photographs of people as they live out their worst moments, suck the stories out of them, and then move on to the next hot topic. Is that what catastrophe is for?

It occurs to me that if I want to write about drugs now, I had better be equipped with something more than a pen. I should be, maybe, prepared to *do* something. I'm more of a writer than a doer, but still. So I stop at the pharmacy where, every month, I engage in a delicate two-step of trying to get my prescription renewed on time without seeming too interested in what that prescription is for.

In Canada, the opioid overdose reversal drug naloxone[8] — often difficult to access in the United States — is available for free to anyone who asks for it, including, obviously, people who keep prescribed opioids in their homes. Nevertheless, I'm embarrassed. I tell the pharmacist that I'm a drug policy journalist. So they won't think I'm an addict. I emphasize the word "policy" because it sounds successful, somehow. Old bigotry dies hard. Only after I've made it clear that I'm not *one of them* do I request my naloxone kit and the five-minute explanation of how to use it.

As I start trying to sort through the different things I read about addiction, I am drawn to the work of a few journalists in particular. Mostly Americans, they are each open about their personal histories of addiction, and their understanding of the issue from both inside and outside comes through clearly in their writing.[9] I feel intimidated, as I often do by my peers, as I never am by the great dead writers who I want to see as my literary ancestors.

The work these journalists do on substance use and the opioid overdose crisis is different from most mainstream reporting on drugs, which is typically done by reporters who do not specialize in substance use or have a deep understanding of the power dynamics and history at play. For one thing, these writers I like see the war on drugs and the criminalization of drugs (which is, in fact, a criminalization of people) as a major cause of overdose and drug-related harms, rather than a response to them. And because they see it that way, perhaps, they write about people who use drugs and people who are homeless or down-and-out as people, not aliens. They share both an interest in evidence-based responses to substance use and addiction, and an obvious compassion for people who have been through the same struggles with dope sickness (opioid withdrawal) or cravings or rehab as they have. Philadelphia reporter Christopher Moraff, who kindly answered some very naive questions I had about details of the drug trade, said the following in an interview with another journalist, Mike Riggs:

Most people want to tell you their story, but you can't just go clumsily. You need to spend time around these people, and — this is a problem for some journalists — you've gotta be willing to carry a carton of Newports and hand out a few packs of cigarettes now and then.[10]

When I interview someone on the phone for the first time in years, I hunch over my desk, scribbling notes with quickly cramping fingers. I often have to end the conversation abruptly, as I realize I can't concentrate anymore due to pain or exhaustion. And yet, at the end of even a quick interview call I am electrified with energy, a buzz that doesn't leave me for hours, that opens my mind with that familiar uplifted feeling. Journalism gives me a high that makes me forget pain, makes me nearly forget to take painkillers.

For a long time, I thought that any writing life I could salvage must be a retiring one, focused on books and literature and stories I could invent from my head and write from my room. I always thought I would write poetry — the ecstatic art — and novels, which I still see as the highest form of writing, like directing a film or conducting a symphony: so many parts, such mastery to make them all sing. But poetry abandoned me just as love found me, and novels...well, I'm still working on that. I didn't expect to find such joy in journalism, but it's real and urgent and fills me with life.

Meanwhile, an industry trend toward self-revelation and mining one's personal traumas happens to be well-timed. Given that I'm going to live with this tortured spine until I die, I could just keep panning in that river, turning up little nuggets of pain around which to structure an article I can sell for two hundred bucks. I am the resource I can extract. But the adrenaline surge of connecting to the real world makes me crave more of that, even as I'm also getting a little sick of talking about myself. The rush of a deadline likewise tempts me back toward a profession I no longer have the physical strength or stamina to do well in, and at which only the very few and very productive are able to make anything like a living.

Pain is riveting and, even now, seems impossible to transcend in any sustained way — but I know that my life is relatively easy as lives go.

Looking outward, I see that economic and political changes over the past thirty-odd years have in fact pushed many, many people into lives of extraordinary difficulty. I would like to write about this, but to write about it without repeating tired narratives that—recklessly, it seems to me—refuse to really name the problems I can see in the world. Journalism seems to be a game I don't want to play, where I would need far more success before I'd be allowed the freedom and stability—that contradictory combination of needs that returns, over and over—to cover issues of substance use, addiction, pain, and what people need in the way I would like to cover it. It's a Catch-22 that can only be overcome through great fortune or great energy, and I have neither.

Over roughly the past thirty years, there has been a dramatic, unannounced shift in the distribution of wealth and opportunity—the result of multilateral agreements on investment, the commodification of housing, increasingly mobile capital, and skyrocketing earnings for bosses relative to workers. Economies have been transformed, with full-time and often unionized jobs replaced by part-time and precarious work.

As I begin my tentative return to my abandoned profession, I see that the issues I wrote about as a young freelance journalist near the turn of the millennium—wealth and poverty; racism; mental health; the deep injustices built into criminal justice systems; the social and economic influences that persistently affect health outcomes; global solidarity, environment and migration, even—all are distilled to their most intense, painful, inescapable form when you look at drug policy and its effect on the lives of people who face the greatest intersecting barriers to living a bearable life.

As I barrel ahead in trying to re-establish something that resembles, if not a career, then a vocation, I feel an irritation, like a grain of sand worrying an oyster, reminding me to take care. All too often journalists who aren't part of the communities they write about fail to accurately portray the experiences of people who use substances or to even portray them as real people, instead condemning them or condescending to them, in either case using the drama and tension of the lives of marginalized people as the scaffolding of a writer's own career. I'd like to see more writing by people who, in fact, are actually actively using drugs, rather than only either complete outsiders or writers in recovery from addiction. They are out there, though, and over time, I start to find them: talented writers who also use illicit drugs, who are dependent on them.

And where do I fit in, if at all? Is it possible to write well about illicit drugs without having taken them? I don't have that experience. But I *am* using an opioid, now infusing my *mu*-opioid receptors three times a day with its dreamy, clarifying, painkilling magic.

Actually, it seems to me that pain of many kinds—and its daring opposite, pleasure—are important, neglected aspects of the illicit drug story. I've noticed, for example, that not just some but virtually all of the illicit opioid users I've spoken with—like Meg, for example—also suffer from chronic pain. Experiencing pain never scared me. But I *am* scared that by writing about it, by making it my subject, like Frida Kahlo did, I might be stuck there, allowed only to tell my own miserable story, which means nothing and has no moral, over and over and over. At the same time, I'm scared of having nothing to offer that is uniquely mine. Except, of course, the limits pain causes in my life and the way I transcend them.

Each time my dose is raised enough to cover more hours in the day, my energy, my mood, and then my income nudge up a little. In fact, the story of opioids for pain is, these days, a story of limits, the dangers of exceeding them, the dangers of arbitrarily creating them.

While until recently in North America, opioids were prescribed loosely and often where other treatments were more appropriate, elsewhere the problem has been not of a glut but of a lack of opioids, and a lack of access to them. This global imbalance is exacerbated—caused, in fact—by the US-led war on drugs, which puts pressure on countries to permit less opioid importation than they in fact need to supply legal painkillers to their citizens. But, just as my first book, on pain and painkillers, was published in 2016, so too were new US guidelines for opioid prescribing for chronic pain, by the Centers for Disease Control (CDC) in 2016. These, and similar CDC-inspired guidelines in Canada, have spurred a rapid, dramatic, and poorly-thought-out crackdown on opioid prescribing that has left individual patients in these countries in preventable pain as well.

Pain, like addiction and other health-related conditions, affects people like me who are not from impoverished backgrounds, as well as people from the upper echelons of society. But it is the working class and poor who suffer first and most from the many factors that lead to a higher prevalence of pain. It was many of these people who first experienced enforced tapers or cold turkey discontinuation of their painkiller prescriptions.

The CDC's guidelines were intended to reduce inappropriate prescribing (that is, use of opioids when an alternative would do, or when the harms to an individual patient outweigh the observable benefits). But across the United States, they have been re-interpreted by local health organizations, other quality and standards bodies, government departments, and insurance providers as a warning that opioids are not indicated for chronic pain at all.

In Oregon, restrictive prescribing—for the poor, anyway—reached a point where opioids were to be banned for all chronic pain patients on Medicaid, with no new starts on the medicine and with even existing, stable patients tapered to zero (the vote on this was postponed due to a conflict of interest of one of the advisors on the proposed plan). The DEA has raided numerous doctors' offices, sometimes entrapping physicians by faking a medical condition. And not just the small number who really have something shady going on, but respected physicians who treat patients no one else will take—patients who, after finally finding stability through a steady healthcare relationship and an effective, tolerable dose of opioids, lose access to both physician and drug, plunging every aspect of their lives into chaos. Even in those cases, certainly real, where doctors are dispensing pills with no intention of actually treating pain, or who are prescribing in dangerous amounts or ways, prosecutions have left hundreds, sometimes thousands of patients without a physician. Apparently, no one has stopped to consider or care what happens to the real pain patients in these situations.

Doctors, in turn, abandon high-needs pain patients because of the risk of prosecution, increasingly onerous paperwork and reporting requirements, and disciplinary action if they are thought to be prescribing too many opioids. Prescription monitoring databases, again intended to prevent double-doctoring or prescription diversion to the illicit market—and, more importantly, to help pharmacists work with doctors to alert patients to possible dangerous combinations—are instead being used punitively, with information shared with law enforcement and the DEA, and patients unnecessarily humiliated with urine tests and pill counts. The State of Pennsylvania has set up an online form for anonymous reports of prescription drug abuse. Patients across the United States have been forced to consent to invasive, poorly-evidenced procedures and treatments like spinal epidurals, high doses of steroids, ketamine infusions, or new (and just as dangerous) drug regimens as an alternative or requirement to be allowed to take opioids that they already know work for them.

At first, no attempts were made to find out what happened to American pain patients who were forced to reduce and then stop taking painkillers. Their plaintive, poorly written pleas for attention took the form of sad stories recounted in the comments under articles about lawsuits against Purdue Pharma and other pharmaceutical companies. They seemed largely incoherent, doomed to be ignored, plaintive, angry, impotent. But these people are real, and really suffering.

Pain patients on opioids is a category that has never before represented an organized group of people. They were derided as the drug-dependent puppets of pharmaceutical companies, the patient representative groups they established unable to fund any of their work except through donations from those same companies. One such group collapsed as a result, with no medical or social justice organizations stepping in to fill the gap. Then a few pain patients—unused to advocacy; afraid that advocacy in favour of access to this particular medication was seen by journalists and the public as fatally un-objective; homebound or deeply limited in daily activities by their pain-causing conditions—began keeping an informal list of people who had killed themselves following removal of their opioid painkillers. They documented as many details as they could. I learned of the existence of these lists from Lelena Peacock,[11] one of my new virtual friends and the first who is a pain patient rather than an illicit drug user.

Lelena is a former photographer in North Carolina who suffers from arachnoiditis and Ehlers-Danlos syndrome, the latter only diagnosed recently after decades of life-diminishing pain she was regularly told was "just a little fibro." These days, she is an informal, unpaid therapist, reaching out and coaxing pain patients on the verge of suicide to try to hang on a little longer. She has reached out to me when I've been in despair. One day, I will do the same for her.

Lele, as her online friends call her, is also caregiver to her mother, who suffers from chronic pain as well as dementia. In one discussion group I sat in on, she described her mother, forced to taper off the painkillers she has been taking for years. As Lele typed, she could hear her mother pacing back and forth upstairs, unable to sit still due to the pain, and unable to understand why she was being made to suffer like this.

"She would pace if she could, other times she would wring her hands and weep. It was nightmarish," Lelena writes to me when I tell her how this image has stuck with me. Since pacing in pain is something I'm very familiar with, the image of this old woman, Carol Johnson, haunts me again now.

An informal, pain patient–generated list of suicides holds little weight in a world in which formal credentials are conflated with expertise, and expertise is conflated with evidence. Good scientists, though, understand that an academic title isn't evidence. Neither, they know, is a flawed-but-sciency-sounding study, like some that have been used to push people off opioid prescriptions even where they are the best option for a given patient. But a real catalogue of the deaths of real people? That might well be.

Stefan Kertesz is a Harvard-trained addiction physician who works mostly with homeless veterans in Birmingham, Alabama, and has a long-standing academic interest in evidence in medicine. He's also a humanist, the quietly devout son of a Holocaust survivor and an admirer of the Christian humanitarian doctor Albert Schweitzer. "I clearly resonate with the idea that suffering is unfairly distributed," he tells me.

For him, evidence isn't just throwing controlled studies around (*X percent of people who take prescription opioids ultimately develop an opioid use disorder; more people who take the equivalent of 90 mg of morphine daily run into problems than those who take less*) to prove a point (*taking prescription opioids for pain leads to addiction; daily doses of 90 mg or higher are a bad idea for any patient*). All the relevant evidence must be considered to grasp what's going on, and numbers must be put in context (*X percent of any group of people will go on to develop a substance use disorder; similar factors predispose people to addiction and to pain; over time, the effective dose of an opioid is expected to rise; for a small group of pain patients, opioids represent the best possible balance of benefits and harms*).

Dr. Kertesz saw that as his colleagues congratulated themselves on having lowered the number of milligrams of opioids prescribed, important evidence about the harm patients were experiencing was simply being ignored, or never gathered. Along with a couple of his colleagues, and working with pain patients, Dr. Kertesz began keeping his own list of suicides. He became increasingly distressed at the cavalier way the possibility of negative outcomes—what are inevitably, if charitably, described as "unintended" consequences—of forcing pain patients off pain medications (or reducing doses until they were no longer effective for patients with high opioid tolerance) were dismissed by everyone with influence on the question of the opioid guidelines or how they are applied. Honestly, no one seemed to care.

All along, Dr. Kertesz has been keenly aware of the need for hard evidence. At last, he, along with other colleagues, published an observational study[12] in the *BMJ* that looked at 1,394,102 veterans who had been tapered or cut off their prescribed opioid painkillers between October 2012 and September 2014. Over that time period, there were 2,887 deaths due to either overdose or suicide. Stopping opioid treatment was thus associated with a significant increased risk of death from overdose or suicide. Before assuming that the issue was an overly fast taper, or that suicidality is an independent indicator of opioid addiction or dependence, or that opioid treatment might have caused depression, recall that chronic pain, untreated, is itself very strongly associated with suicide (as well as other negative outcomes like loss of function, family breakdown, depression, chronic pain in children, substance use disorders, unemployment, dementia, and cardiovascular disease among a very long list).

In this case, the longer the patient had been treated with opioid painkillers before being cut off, the greater the risk of them dying by their own hand. That's a strong association with death upon opioid taper (usually either strongly urged or actually forced) among over a million veterans with chronic pain who were previously stable. But the actual number of people who have been forced off prescriptions that they believe have been working for them (frequently without any evidence that they are wrong, and frequently after "failing" other treatments) is far higher, and there are not yet studies that capture that harm in numbers. Instead, we look for the same cries of anguish and calls for help that prompted Dr. Kertesz and others to start keeping track.

Kertesz says, "What concerns me even more [than the numbers of deaths] is how little we understand, or even *seek to understand*, about why they happen." Not until we were four years into the unintended consequences of the 2016 guidelines did the CDC produce a docket on pain and opioids that finally included mention of publicly reported deaths due to suicide. Dr. Kertesz wrote detailed funding proposal after proposal, unable to garner interest in monitoring patients for unintended side effects of such a major change in both pain treatment and the physician-patient relationship, even though you'd think that misery, loss of function, and death would be notable unintended effects. Like patient groups that have attempted to advocate against legislated dose limits and patient abandonment, Kertesz has been accused of being a shill for pharmaceutical companies (he has no relationship, financial or otherwise, with any such companies). The doctor's work continues.

Thousands of private practices, hospitals, insurance providers, and clinics continue to cite the CDC as the reason they are cutting off their patients, lowering effective doses, subjecting their patients to drug testing and pain contracts, even abandoning patients, leaving hundreds or thousands of sick, vulnerable, and disabled people without any healthcare at all.

Racialized and poor patients in wealthy countries, often assumed to be "drug seeking" (a term that should be eliminated from the medical lexicon), have long experienced, on an individual level, the global shortage of prescription opioids, having been denied opioids even where they'd have been appropriate treatment, through most of the mid-to-late twentieth century. Then, following predictable results of loose prescribing without patient education or support, those who did get appropriate opioid pain treatment were first to be quickly and brutally cut off the drugs regardless of whether they were improving function or quality of life or not. In general, wealthier patients have been the last to feel the effects of this crackdown. Of over-prescribing or "pill mill" doctors who have been de-licensed or jailed, many seem to have practised in poorer areas and in largely Black communities, leaving predominantly Black pain patients without medical treatment, and facing far less likelihood of finding another doctor to restore their prescription. A 2019 study in the US found that being female or being Black,[13] or having a higher starting dosage (which might indicate several things, including simply a sicker patient), were all factors significantly associated with tapering, and a high school education alone was, compared to higher education levels, associated with faster tapering.[14]

In British Columbia, where stringent new guidelines on opioid prescribing for chronic pain were accompanied by a surge in illicit opioid overdose deaths, the provincial college of physicians and surgeons was forced to walk back part of them, amending guidelines to prohibit physicians from refusing to see patients for things like requesting an opioid or already being on long-term opioid treatment when seeking a new physician. They also now prohibit doctors from putting hard dose limits on opioid treatment for chronic pain patients, instead requiring greater caution at higher doses and prescription of lowest effective dose if long-term opioid treatment is indicated. Still, there and elsewhere, including where I live, pain patients who continue to receive long-term opioid prescriptions do so in fear and under an increasing burden of stigma. They have the sense—in some cases for the first time; in others a sense reinforced at every medical appointment since they can remember—that they are not trusted by their own doctors, pharmacists, or nurses, or by specialists and emergency room doctors when they seek care for pain, or even for unrelated concerns.

In the spring of 2019, with my own physical limits dramatically extended, I take a short trip, on my own, to Portugal, to attend an international conference about drugs and reducing the harms of drug use, and to learn about Portugal's policy of decriminalization of all substances (a topic I'll tell you more about a little later). While there, I file a minor but cool story for a major Canadian newspaper, announcing release of the first official data on overdoses reversed during five years of a safe consumption site running clandestinely in an unnamed American city. I write up my story in the journalists' private sanctum, the press room at the conference centre, my first time in such a place. I reply to the editor's questions on my phone over a solo steak and frites dinner on a chic downtown street, wander a bit among the crowds, collapse fully dressed into bed at two a.m. Drink coffee, take painkillers, do it again the next day, riding on adrenaline. It is all very exciting, like I am a foreign correspondent. And yet, this is really just a few days of artificially exceeding my limits.

In real life, pain makes everything take longer; stiffness means I need to devote huge amounts of time to exercise; inflammation means everything I do leaves me exhausted. I have to stand and stretch at the back of every conference session. Every interaction, every interview is both invigorating and a painful, tiring effort. As with every other short trip I have taken since I started doing this, I will pay for this one with months of flaring pain, progression in the deformation of my spine, exhaustion, depression. Any deviation from the strict discipline with which I run my life is punished. Stay up late for writing time and I'm in greater pain the next day. Skip exercise to see a friend and I have more trouble moving later on. Stand on a street corner to chat a few minutes with an acquaintance and I can feel the price I will pay for acting normal rather than insisting we sit down on the curb. Everything seems to have a cost. The tiny, endless decisions often paralyze me. The big ones, like travel, are clearly worth the cost, but that doesn't make it any less high.

When the disease flares or I am lazy or opt for spontaneity over routine or try to meet the social demands of daily life, the drug simply isn't enough and those limits come crashing down on me. These five days of ardent work, of no domestic tasks, of masking pain: they are a fantasy. I know it. I love every minute.

On the way home, on the plane, I watch a documentary about Marie Colvin, the fearless American war correspondent who worked for the British *Sunday Times*, a reckless and determined journalist and a striking figure with her glamorous looks and black eye patch, until she was assassinated while on assignment in Syria in 2012. Is that the sort of life (or death) I might have had if I had gone from freelancing to a real job in journalism and not broken things off to support a family and raise children? Would that existence have somehow prevented whatever triggered my mostly genetic disease? Was there any way that my life might have ended up differently than it has? What has pain taken from my talents and potential? What has family life cost me, or choosing to be an independent writer rather than a salaried one? Who do I blame for the fact that I'm not living a more glamorous or significant life? What do I really want, anyway?

I'm not really ready or able to be a Marie Colvin, not physically or in terms of my commitments. It's not just the overwhelming logistics involved, it's also a sense of guilt and a sense of fear. And a sense that if I just try a little harder to meet everyone's needs, eventually there will be room for me to live exactly as I want, and also exactly as I need, to accommodate the implacable demands of my vicious immune system. I am becoming increasingly aware that I may never get that chance though, and the example of other women tells me that if I don't act with determined, ruthless focus on what I require in order to feel free and to write, no one is going to give it to me.

I am stretched as thin as a membrane by my commitments. I can't hear myself think. My energy waxes and wanes according to where I am in the cycle of pain relief, and the lovely rush of ease and optimism rarely coincides with writing. Too often I use that burst of energy to wash the dishes. I hate myself for prioritizing this domestic task over whatever potential I have as a writer. What would I tell six-year-old me? But if I don't do the dishes today, they will be there tomorrow, reproducing and taunting me.

This is what Yeats called the choice between "perfection of the life, or of the work." But women—especially women whose health doesn't hold up the basic functions of the body—have no choice but to choose the life. Alexandra Johnson, who wrote a wonderful account of the diaries of six women writers and their relationship to the eventual production of public writing, described Anaïs Nin, "unsolicited, giving Henry Miller her only typewriter when his broke."[15] Katherine Anne Porter, she writes, said that "I have no patience with this dreadful idea that whatever you have in you has to come out, that you can't suppress true talent."

That "dreadful idea" is actually the quintessential Romantic ideal: the heroically talented individual free of their context. But as Porter knew well, life can crush both talent and its expression in a final product, and it is those who are more enthusiastically suppressed by life whose talent is most likely to be stunted, leached, or hidden as a result. And Johnson demonstrates the way women writers often make it as far as a diary but no further: because they're snuffed out by infectious disease in a concentration camp like Anne Frank (or the modern-day version, perhaps: a refugee with blazing writing talent who dies of COVID-19 in an American detention facility[16]), or because they're torn into pieces by competing priorities, or because their confidence is eroded before it has a chance to grow.

Neither a woman, nor a person facing obstacles of gender, class, race, or other "isms," nor a person with a disability, including pain or dependence on an opioid, can ever be free of their context. It shapes us; it also sometimes destroys us.

The Katherine Anne Porter quote continues, "People can be destroyed; they can be bent, distorted and, all the philosophy to the contrary, we don't really direct our lives unaided or unobstructed."

Not that we always realize it. As prescribing practices are deeply tightened, new patients like me may now believe themselves to be more disabled and more limited than, with proper medication, they might in fact be. They may never know what degree of function would in fact have been within their grasp. I didn't know, for so long. I used to dream about running with my body upright, my head neatly over my shoulders rather than thrust forward and down, running lightly without gravity pressing me down as if I, alone among people here on Earth, endured Jupiter's gravity.

For those patients who never find out, or those who have it taken away from them, it's like denying a wheelchair, crutches, or a walker to someone and telling them that mobility is an impossible goal. They remain under Jupiter's gravity, as I did for so long, when there is a treatment — like other serious medications, a treatment that can be fatal if taken incorrectly, a treatment that can, in various ways, do harm — that can restore them to a more reasonable terrestrial 9.807 m/s^2.

Late afternoon here in Toronto is when the British pain insomniacs come out. The Australians are on Twitter by my lunchtime, tired of tossing and turning, looking for company in the desolate hours.

Adam Maier-Clayton was a Canadian pain insomniac whose Twitter handle I recognized, who I often noticed online late at night. When you spend a fair amount of time interacting with others who share your interests in this online world, you get to notice the people who frequent the same virtual hangouts as you. Maier-Clayton, who suffered from depression and obsessive thoughts as a child, also (as an adult) experienced burning, acid-like pain from what was diagnosed to be the result of Somatic Symptom Disorder, a psychiatric condition. He received endless hours of psychotherapy, and antidepressants. Maier-Clayton became a right-to-die activist who advocated for the expansion of eligibility for newly legal doctor-assisted suicide. He wanted the option to apply to people who felt they no longer wanted to live due to depression or other mental illness, or due to intractable pain.

"Every Canadian deserves this right, the right to have the ability to terminate pain that is chronic, incurable," he told Canadian Press in 2016.[17]

In Canada, there is huge popular support for new legislation that allows people with terminal disease or incurable suffering to seek medical assistance in dying. I have supported it, a close family friend benefited from it, and I know of many others who have been empowered by being able to choose when and how they will die. That's all I knew or thought about it. Later I came to understand that for people who are poor, mentally ill, or physically disabled, the concept can be terrifying, because choice is really relative. There is a very real risk of their lives being considered "not worth living," and of disabled people thus being nudged toward their own deaths, or of poor and disabled or mentally ill people being denied the supports—anything from adequate income to morphine to accessible housing—they need to achieve an adequate quality of life, and instead resorting to this form of euthanasia for lack of other options.

It has taken nearly a decade for me to realize that I am disabled, in that the limitations I experience are only partly caused by ankylosing spondylitis and the resulting stiffness, gradual deformity, and pain. The other part is a society that is unwilling to accommodate difference or weakness. I am physically fit and strong but the very specific limits that pain places on me are insurmountable without friends, family, and a community willing to accommodate my unusual needs and incorporate my remaining strengths. This is an experience very familiar to people with disabilities, both visible ones, for which accommodations can include more familiar things like ramps, wheelchairs, and accessible transportation, and hidden disabilities, which often involve some form of physical weakness, exhaustion, or pain, and which really need a willingness of other people to adapt to your rhythm, to welcome the pacing that allows you to get things done despite it.

Opioids give me the dignified ability to limit the intensity of my suffering without resorting to suicide, an overly long-term solution. Other adaptations to my specific, personal limitations include a very flexible work schedule; friends who stay in daily contact despite me rarely visiting in person; an ergonomic keyboard; yoga adapted for an AS spine; jar openers; people who are happy to sit down or walk with me while chatting rather than standing still; delivery services; courses offered over the internet.

The short, solo escapes I have taken have allowed me to see that it is possible for me to live a comfortable life, but only with the right supports, the right flexibility, the right rhythm and pacing, the right trade-off between energy and pain. And so, since society does not make these things easy, and because the consequences of not knowing that life can be more tolerable, more joyful, even, are so dire, I have begun inching toward seeing my nearly invisible spine disease and the pain it causes as a disability. With the right supports, and the ability to individualize the way I live — what in disability rights discourse are called accommodations — pain needn't be as limiting as, in the *real world*, it is.

The night or a couple of nights before he killed himself, Adam Maier-Clayton sent up little pain flares in the dark. He wrote tweets that no one responded to (I didn't know him, and so said nothing). He wrote on Twitter, as if scrawling on a virtual wall or standing on Speaker's Corner, that he had tried and failed to find a physician who would prescribe him a low dose of the opioid hydromorphone (Dilaudid). For some reason he was specific about this drug and the dose he wanted. Presumably he'd been prescribed it before. Presumably it worked? He wrote of his desperation. He wrote that the pain he felt was intolerable. He'd reached his limit. And he wrote that, because of that pain, he wanted to die.

And so he did, killing himself in a motel at the age of twenty-seven. None of the news reports or obituaries I saw, all of which discussed his right-to-die activism, his suffering, and his "intractable" pain, mentioned that final, lonely, almost unnoticed quest for opioids.

Now, when someone sends out a little cry of hopelessness online, I always respond, whether I know them or not. One day Lelena Peacock writes on Twitter that she is thinking about buying a plane ticket. She would, she writes, like to simply walk into the Jukai forest in Japan. Jukai is sometimes called the Suicide Forest, due to hosting Japan's highest number of suicides, often by hanging or drug overdose.

Lelena has been through a lot. Now she is in despair at ever getting her effective pain prescription restored. A few months earlier, she was summarily dropped as a patient by her long-time physician following a drug screen — a condition for receiving treatment for her health conditions — that tested positive for heroin, which she says she has never, ever used. The test was later conclusively proven through a hair strand test to be a false positive relating to her prescribed medication, but it was too late. Her healthcare and her trust in the medical system were lost. This time it is my turn to reach out with a careful private message, and to try to offer a sense of hope to someone too smart — and too experienced in offering encouragement to others — to be easily appeased.

As part of its war on drugs, the DEA limits the supply of opioids that can be imported into the US. Tighter restrictions mean fewer drugs available to treat addiction and chronic pain, but also fewer for patients on ventilators, for patients in or after surgery, for women in labour, for cancer patients, for those on their way out.

The dramatic shift in thinking about opioids has resulted in pet owners being denied painkillers for their cats because it might just be a ruse to get drugs, and in cancer patients being under-medicated and dying in preventable agony. Or, cursed with permanent pain following life-saving treatment, they discover to their dismay that, once their pain is called chronic rather than cancer pain, they are no longer considered candidates for analgesia to improve the quality of the life that's been saved. Children with serious diseases are pushed to learn coping skills rather than provided medication that would make the issue irrelevant so they could get on with their lives, learning those life skills in time. Old people spend their last years struggling against limitations that could be covered up with restrained but effective doses of painkillers. Short surgeries for teenagers or young adults become major episodes in their lives due to use of less effective alternatives and lack of responsiveness to their expressions of agony — or outright skepticism, accusations of lying, and scorn.

I told you that when I first realized I'd been prescribed an opioid I thought I must be dying. It's as though the very fact that someone thought my pain merited an opioid was scary. Having now experienced pain without treatment, with inadequate treatment, and with essentially palliative treatment, I am no longer afraid to be palliated. It is by far the best-case situation.

Now that I'm on something a little closer to a palliative approach, where the goal really is to use as much medication as needed to enable living and to do the things most important to me, I can't see why we typically reserve this practical mercy for the very end of life, when one's function and time are so limited. To spend years half living when a drug can let you live seems intolerably cruel. Not just cruel. Wasteful. Mary Oliver, who in her poem *Wild Geese* first placated and later infuriated me with the assertion that just being alive is enough, asked in another famous poem, "The Summer Day,"

> Tell me, what is it you plan to do
> with your one wild and precious life?[18]

One of many popular sayings of Día de Muertos is *"Todos hombres mueren. No todos viven."* All men die, not all live. I have not been living.

On another Día de Muertos long ago, I travelled with my then-boyfriend to the island of Janitzio in Michoacán, Mexico. The lake was filled with floating candles. The celebration of Day of the Dead is a sombrely or raucously joyful one, with stylized imagery of dancing skeletons, and intimate gatherings of families around the graves of their dearly departed, sharing a bottle of tequila or, on the family altar, placing food they would have enjoyed in life: *pozole* or *pollo mole*, sugar-dusted bread, flower-strewn sugar skulls. Everywhere, armfuls of long-stemmed marigolds, bitter and pungent. Death in Mexico is personified as a woman and given tender nicknames, comfortable terms of endearment. There are more than a hundred of them. Death is *La Patrona* (The Boss). *La Democrática* (The Democratic One). *La Liberadora* (The Liberator). *La Pelona* (The Bald Lady). *La Llorona* (The Weeping Woman).

I thought I had two essays here, one about death and one about limits. About how other people die, and about how I crash into my physical and emotional limits, how I try to transcend them or how I might make them irrelevant. But try as I might, this question of limits inexorably turns back into the question of what makes life worth living. Death insinuates herself back in at every turn. Opioids can cause death: no doubt about it. But for some of us, their role is irreplaceable: striking that delicate balance—not just a life, but a life worth living, one that makes us choose to stay alive.

Vertigo

6 6 Is anyone else feeling our desperate sense of urgency?" asks Garth Mullins in the first episode of *CRACKDOWN*. This, you'll recall, is the multiple-award-winning podcast that attracted the attention of Petra Schultz in the aftermath of her son's death — the one in which drug users report on the war on the drugs the way war correspondents like Marie Colvin report from battle. Mullins was an injection heroin user in Vancouver during an earlier overdose crisis, in the 1990s, and has now been stable for many years on methadone.

Before 2020, when much of the world found ourselves either trapped in quarantine or forced out to work in a world of constant risk, loss, and horror, speaking with drug users and the people who work with and love them brought home to me that a dystopian reality has long existed parallel to the ordinary world of people whose day-to-day concerns are not about life and death. For those on the frontlines of the overdose crisis, daily life involves attending funeral after funeral, memorial service after memorial service. Frontline harm reduction workers at supervised injection sites or community health centres spend all day helping people whose lives are a constant calamity, bring people literally back from death, restarting their stalled metronomes, and still find the strength and composure to be emotionally present for the many moments of touching intimacy, of connection between two humans, that are the true work of harm reduction. Zoë Dodd, the Toronto harm reduction advocate I mentioned earlier, tells me in 2020, "I can't believe how long I've been working in this hellscape." It's a hellscape few outsiders recognize as such. As I speak on the phone with Dodd, a fire engine siren goes off in the background. When I tried to speak with her the night before, she was on her way to a funeral. The morning we finally connect, she has just learned of the overdose death of another colleague.

In an illuminating interview, Mullins tells writer Dawn Paley that, as he began hearing the sirens of ambulances rushing to respond to overdose calls in Vancouver in 2014, "I felt like I was standing on the edge of a cliff and having vertigo: like I was about to fall into something else."[1]

One morning in the winter of 2017, I wake up in pre-dawn darkness. Something is wrong. The air, the quality of darkness, is off. It's something to do with the depth of the small bedroom around me, where I now sleep in a single bed, though often with a small person creeping in to join me in an early morning cuddle as I begin the slow stretching that gets me out of bed each day.

As I walk stiffly to the bathroom, the world shifts. I can't tell what is up and what is down. I clutch at the bathroom floor so that I don't fall off. My stomach churns. I retch but everything becomes worse as I try to bend my head over the toilet. I am cold, sweating and shaking. After some confusing interval of time I lurch back to my bed, where I struggle to understand what is happening, as I hear my kids begin to stir.

I try to get up again and am thrown back against the bed as if by force. I regret my rule against keeping my phone in the bedroom. It has felt, since I became a single parent (and even more since I became trapped by my own body), like my only link to the outside world. But this is different. I call wretchedly for my twelve-year-old to pass me the phone so I can call his father. Just typing out my SOS brings me close to vomiting again. The risk of throwing up my painkiller adds urgency to keeping the inside inside.

I am completely helpless. I've been pushing toward independence, self-direction, reclaiming my life. In fact, in just six weeks I am due to travel, on my own, to Venice. But what control I thought I'd gained over my body and my life shows itself to be nothing now that I am waxy-white as a candle and shaking and unable to move. After one false diagnosis and a couple of harrowing trips to the doctor I learn that I have a relatively common condition linked neither to my spine disease nor (an obvious first question) to the opioids I use to manage pain. In the kind of vertigo I have — benign positional paroxysmal vertigo, or BPPV — little crystals of calcium get loose from the gel in which they're supposed to be embedded and wander around in your ear drum. It is amazing to realize that such a tiny thing can throw off your intuitive grasp of the law of gravity.

I have them in the right inner ear, in the posterior canal, causing me to spin when I lean too far to the left.

The treatment for this condition is entirely mechanical: I need to have my head turned in such a way as to dislodge the bits of mineral from their disorienting position. But the treatment brings on the vertigo, and when the doctor tries the most basic manoeuvre, the spinning that is supposed to stop within a minute or so doesn't stop. Two hours later the clinic is about to close and I still can't walk in a straight line across the doctor's office, so I'm mailed across the street to urgent care, from where I sign myself out against medical advice. I hold onto the walls all the way to a taxi, which deposits me at home, where my kids require even a nauseous, drunkenly lurching version of me. Vertigo is probably the worst physical thing I have experienced. In the six weeks that it lasts, I cannot walk in a straight line, I feel constantly nauseous, and I sleep sitting up every night, an excruciating and permanently damaging experience for my spine.

I suspect that Venice is not a good place in which to have vertigo. I worry about the bed I'm to be provided with — can I get extra pillows to ensure I lie upright, as I have been sleeping for one week, three weeks, four… is this ever going to get better? Somewhere on my bookshelf, which I must scan carefully in order not to bring on more queasiness, is W.G. Sebald's first novel, *Vertigo*. I add it to my tiny carry-on suitcase. His narrator arrives in Venice on October 31, and on the Day of the Dead he wanders around, thinking about Casanova, who was in Venice at the same time of year. By contrast, I am going in spring, and I hope this all signals that I am leaving the limitations of daily life, and the extra hardships of both vertigo and winter, in favour of art, and beauty, and freedom.

Though the bed still rolls as I lie in it, still at sea; although I still have flashbacks when I'm walking on the sidewalk and the ground will shudder for a moment before going still again — I am ready to go, armed with opioid and passport: the two possessions I must not lose, no matter what.

Magic, I want magic. I want to experience it, I want to make it happen. Reckless, irresponsible, passionate magic. For years, despite the joys of seeing life through the eyes of two children, despite my attempts to see myself as a Romantic, for the most part every day has been a long and painful grind. So I'm casting for ways to experience it now. I'm sure everyone's idea of a fantasy life is unique to them. For me, it's largely about travel, immersion in a different world, and about beauty. And it's very much about literature or art or imagination of various kinds and a sense of commitment to it, the commitment that made me throw myself heart-first into a love affair, and then into being a mother, committing with every atom of my being. But now it's my lonely, unsettled self, just me, in need of direction, in search of new, enchanted ground.

In an early attempt to find a new direction for my deracinated life, I went to art school, dropping out after two crushingly painful years. But somewhere during the nervous breakdown that resulted, I learned that although I am poorly suited to a craft that requires both spinal flexion and physical stamina, I love intaglio printmaking. So, having been bewitched by a fairy tale version of Venice I read about in Jeanette Winterson's novel *The Passion*, I wrote to Lorenzo de Castro, the head of a printmaking school in Venice, to enquire if a writer who is only an amateur printmaker might nevertheless come on a short, self-funded "artist residency." I plan to work on the novel that has been mouldering in my hard drive for years. To make an imaginary world that feels real.

Lorenzo said yes, and I negotiated a week, including travel time, away from my regular life — leaving five days to make progress on the novel, five days to absorb a thousand years or so of beauty. I transferred money intended for retirement savings. I booked a flight to Venice. And now, still barely recovered from the six brutal weeks of vertigo, I am here.

There is something marvellous about the way ordinary medieval walls rise up directly from the green-blue, glassy ocean water of the lagoon. I walk around, stopping at each canal bridge, amazed that it all looks like in the pictures, only more so. Now that I am seeing Venice in real life it is like some new part of my imagination has been opened forever, so that I can see it in my mind in a way that, for example, I can't see Kyoto because I've never been there. Books and other forms of art are such a brilliant substitute for first-hand experience, allowing you to feel like you are somewhere you've never been — another planet or universe, somewhere you simply cannot be, even — and yet there is something profoundly different about actually experiencing a place, and I am so grateful to be able to do this again.

At every canal crossing I walk over, there's a boat of tourists holding selfie sticks a few feet from their faces. Increasingly, Venetians can't afford to live in the city where they were born, and must commute from the nearby Veneto region. Although there is still a real life of real Venetians here, it has become almost hidden beneath the tourist version of itself. It's easy to forget that the city has its own genuine culture and subtle atmosphere.

And despite the tourist dollars, the city itself is gradually sinking into its lagoon, at a rate that is getting less gradual all the time. I get to see Lorenzo Quinn's massive sculpture of hands reaching up to support the Ca' Sagredo hotel — a statement about the climate change and consequent rising sea levels that put the long-term survival of Venice in doubt. The white plaster hands — giant, and sculpted with the same creases and lines I can see on my own — rise lovingly and urgently from the waters of the Grand Canal to hold up the building.

In a restored, old Venetian house turned into a temporary exhibit space called the Pavilion of Humanity, a series of installations by artists Michal Cole and Ekin Onat suggest that "home" is not the politically neutral space we often assume. In the small, homely kitchen designed by Cole, I look into a saucepan on the hob. A woman's mouth, mysteriously projected inside the pot, opens and screams silently. Same thing in the teapot on the elegantly set table for two. I feel it. During these six days I have only myself to feed, no school lunches to make or breakfasts to prepare even if I stay up, as I do—jet-lagged and desperate to make some kind of creative progress after an evening spent wandering the magical city—until two in the morning to write at my narrow desk. It makes me scream internally at the thought of the petty things that sap the energy I could be putting toward making art of some kind. My children aren't a burden—never and never and not at all; I feel like I need to keep saying it, swearing this—but the domestic details that come with them, even when I often enjoy them, take up time and stamina I can't afford.

My host, Lorenzo de Castro, is the printmaking school's director of international programs. In his spare time he's part of a group of Venetians trying to push back against the incursion of giant cruise ships into this delicate ecosystem of culture, nature, and ravenous tourists like me. All these things you can understand from a few days of watching and walking and talking with the people who live here. A real understanding of what it is like to be a resident of Venice, though, is not something you can simply absorb through a few days' osmosis. I'm just skimming the surface, dancing on the meniscus of people's lives. It is such a short trip; already I start dreaming of returning, in January or February or March one year, when there are fewer tourists, when the city belongs to the people who live here.

In a shop I buy a plague doctor mask that now sits on the shelf above my desk as I write this, beside an articulated papier mâché skeleton from Oaxaca.

On my last day I finally find my way to the Piazza San Marco and visit the Doge's Palace. Below the building are the dungeons, and it's interesting and sad to see these unpleasant little cubicles that smell like the word "dank." There are very many of them.

I have always enjoyed historical displays, easily imagining myself experiencing what I see, moved by the knowledge that they are evidence of something that really took place. I wander round and round, letting myself into the misery of the lives of the individual people who languished here, most of them never emerging from history with a name or a personality for me to remember, for me to say out loud to make them live again. Then, as a tourist does, I will let myself out of their lives again and let them slip back into the darkness of history.

It was busy elsewhere in the palace, as it is always in Venice, especially right now, as I've accidentally arrived in the middle of the Venice Biennale. The bloody tourists with their bloody selfie sticks have been pervasive as barnacles. But there are fewer of them down here right now, and as I wander on, I am actually alone for once, so it's easier to imagine. I'm in the "vivid and continuous dream" that novelist John Gardner thought a novel ought to be.

Casanova, the great lover, was one prisoner of the Doge's Palace who somehow escaped the suffering of being here and lived on beyond it through his words. This is the immortality you hope for when you write. I can't remember how I know that; if there was a placard or display indicating his tenancy here I haven't found it yet.

Eventually, I realize that I am going in circles, passing what seem to be the same cells over and over no matter which way I go. The pleasant wandering feeling stops abruptly. I have left my painkillers in my backpack, and my backpack in my room. Amid the endless list of things — my kids' and mine — not to forget to do or take when I leave the house, I try to keep one priority ahead of all the other priorities: *do not forget the tramadol.*

I have forgotten the tramadol.

The experience of running abruptly out of oomph is a common one for me. It happens when I've stopped to pick up groceries and realize I'm carrying too much and am too sore and tired to get home. Or when I'm with others and become anxious because I need something — to stop — and yet can't figure out what I need and insist on pushing on. I've begun to train myself: don't panic, stop, get something to eat and some coffee, painkillers, rest. I tell the kids: *I'm not angry; I just need to get home. And I can't talk. And I can't listen. I need to stop. It's not your fault. Please stop talking. Hurry up.* Sometimes I don't even need the drugs; I just need the break. Again and again I overextend myself — often because I'm trying to save energy by doing an extra task now rather than later—and become trapped in a situation I don't know how to escape, utterly overwhelmed.

This is the only time I've had this experience in a dungeon though.

I don't have the energy to go on, but if I don't go on I will be stuck in this place—alone, in a top tourist attraction, during the Venice fucking Biennale—forever. This is ridiculous. *Obviously*, I am not going to languish here until my twisted bones are found decades from now. And yet, I cannot find the way out. As I round what I am now sure is the same cell for the tenth or twelfth time, panic wells up. I am so tired and sore I just want to lie down or even just crouch down, but fear of the other people I wish were here seeing me is inhibiting and I just keep stumbling along.

I finally bump into one other museum visitor, who ushers me confidently in a direction that again sends me in pointless circles. I feel like I'm stuck in some sort of Kafka novel. I am no longer holding myself up properly. Normally I fight to maintain a straight posture, but who cares now? I stumble forward at a forty-five-degree angle to the ground.

I wander for the better part of an hour before, for some reason, the passageway releases its exit. I have no idea why I couldn't find it before. Maybe—as I sometimes find in my writing or in the various life tasks I struggle to complete in a constantly sleep-deprived and uncomfortable state—I simply repeatedly followed the same train of thought, leading me to retrace one path multiple times while thinking I was wandering more freely. Sometimes I fear I've accidentally erased a bit of writing but then find that the version I've recreated is almost a word-for-word match to what I thought I'd lost. I often worry that I've lost my keys and then find them in exactly the place I always put them for fear of losing them. Despite wandering often through my big city and despite not working in an office, I actually keep to the same basic grid of streets, my routine circumscribed by daycare drop offs and pickups, grocery stops, exhaustion, and a rigid exercise routine. I think I am free but I am not free.

I sit in the museum cafeteria and drink an espresso before I feel able to walk home. At last I make it there and, after one heart-stopping moment when I reach into my backpack and don't feel the bottle, I do find the tramadol exactly where I left it. I take the pill and wait. How wonderful it would be if I could just inject this stuff so that it would work right away. At least now I know relief is coming—in about as long as I spent wandering in the dungeon of the Doge's Palace. As the burning in the base of my spine begins to ease at last, I finally begin to appreciate the humour of the situation.

I lie on the bottom bunk of the monastic little bed I've been given in my monastic little cell—uncomfortable for sleeping but so perfect for writing that I stay in it when given the option to move to a grand, airy room overlooking the piazza. I flip through *Vertigo* to find its short section on Venice, and I learn that Franz Kafka actually drew on his own experience visiting the dungeons of the Doge's Palace—and Casanova's account of his imprisonment there—to write his later accounts of frightening and faceless punishment by uncaring bureaucrats and Byzantine systems of arbitrary rules. It must have been in a previous reading of this book that I learned about Casanova, yet another thing I have read and forgotten but that sits somewhere in the mysterious structures of my brain, waiting to be activated.

When I later begin to move beyond just my own futile experience of seeking help for pain and for the depression it caused and start learning about other people's Kafkaesque journeys in search of real support—not just for the misery of physical pain but also addiction—it strikes me just how similar the stories are, with their details of bruised and battered people stuck in an apparently uncaring, needlessly convoluted system. And it seems to me that for people dealing with addiction and dependence on illicit drugs, Kafka's dungeons and corridors become less metaphor and more literal description.

"Let's say you wanted to come up with the worst possible system for people who use drugs and are traumatized, you'd put them in jail. We've created a system where recovery is almost impossible," Mark Tyndall told me when I spoke with him about the opioid crisis in 2018. "I think the most glaring thing was this major disconnect between what the community is asking for and what policy-makers are saying. Ninety per-cent of the problems people have with drugs are obtaining [them] illegally. On their own they're not terrible but we've made them terrible."

In the systems we've created — systems for criminal justice and law enforcement, social services, and healthcare — we make the most vulnerable and least supported people in society run through a ridiculous maze of practical obstacles and moral injunctions that make life more stressful and more dangerous. The situation people face really is often Kafkaesque, often absurd. Where they desperately need a break from stress, pain, and fresh trauma, instead we pile these on at every juncture.

During the two and a half years that follow my own Kafkaesque experience in Venice, I begin to regain capacity. Flashbacks to vertigo, though persistent, gradually diminish in frequency and are easier to dismiss. With pain under better control thanks to my wise family doctor and specialists, who helped me sort calmly through my options and settle on a more effective, slightly higher dose of tramadol, these are relatively good years. I begin to do things that were too difficult or exhausting with unmanaged pain, and that were impossible during those weeks when the world turned upside down and spun around. The Venice trip is the start of many short but glamorous travels: I go to Buenos Aires, to Paris, to Reykjavik, to Mexico City, and, as I've mentioned, to Portugal, where in the city of Porto I played for a few days at being a foreign correspondent or an intrepid travelling freelancer. I take the family to visit my aunt and uncle in the Netherlands and to see other family in the UK. I tell the kids that after we get back from London, we will get the cat I have told them I wasn't well enough to handle. I really wasn't. I thought I'd never be. And now, I think, I am.

And then it happens again. Thirty-one months after that first episode, I fall over attempting triangle pose as I try to stretch my spine after returning, the day before, from a truly triumphant trip to London. The world lurches, the plague mask I bought in Venice rolls past my gaze, and then I'm looking down instead of up, clutching the floor so I won't fall off. It's baaaaack.

It is as though the world is moving, while I am still. Once I am trapped on a street corner, holding onto a wall so that it doesn't slide away from me. I lurch from construction hoarding to a bench to a tree planter. Anything I can hold on to. My world, which pain made small and painkillers enlarged, closes in, again. I must sleep sitting up so as not to trigger the spinning. I walk my son to school, struggling to concentrate on our conversation about superheroes while battling nausea, trying to extend my spine, which has been hunched as I sit up all night, and wondering whether I will make it to school before the walls and ground start to run away from me, a non-positional vertigo apparently induced by weeks of brain-scrambling positional vertigo. All the freedom I have gained over the past couple of years of better pain control is lost. Again I am trapped in my own body, a prisoner of the unhappy and unstable connection between my brain, my eyes, and my inner ears. Every attempt to push my way through it results in greater dizziness later on, just as pushing through pain eventually has a rebound effect. Day after day, my conversations with adults are limited to the shortest and most basic of interactions.

Desperately lonely, I resort to posting a call for help on Facebook. In Stevie Smith's 1957 poem, she writes:

Nobody heard him, the dead man,
But still he lay moaning:
I was much further out than you thought
And not waving but drowning.

I post that poem. Within a few minutes my post has garnered eleven cheery thumbs-ups.

I scheme, fantasizing, for another short escape I might take from single parenting. Sometime between January and March Break of the coming winter, if the vertigo ends, I might be able to get away. I'll still be lonely, but at least I'll be surrounded by beauty. If vertigo has come back to me, I will go back to Venice. Winter 2020 it is. The plague doctor mask still sitting on the shelf above my desk, I start writing to the printmaking school. Will they take me back?

I have always been interested in infectious disease. I studied it briefly in a lab, wrote about plague literature, illustrated the process of a white blood cell dismembering a tuberculosis bacterium for *Nature Reports*. So I pay slight early attention to a flu-like disease that has appeared in China. But mostly I'm thinking about Italy. Perhaps I can take the kids over the summer as part of my continued plan to spend every penny I earn or have saved in order to see beauty now, while I just barely can. It's important, I feel, not to waste time.

Quake

We are in a corner store looking at plastic masked wrestlers when they begin to fall off the shelves. Then everything else falls off the shelves. Then the shelves fall.

It feels like this has already happened, like some secret memory always contained a great fear like this one that makes me try to pull my baby out of his stroller even though the other shoppers are all telling me to leave him in it, it's safer, because I feel like this is it, it's happened before and here it is again and I must hold him tight and close to me because I don't know what else to do. But it is only an earthquake, in the end, in Oaxaca, Mexico, a part of the world where they are common. This is years ago. No pandemic in sight, nor much foreshadowing of the losses of the decade leading up to it. I'm married to the love of my life, and my children are small.

There are many things I don't understand. *Why* have I always been so susceptible to what the writer Norman Rush calls, in his 2003 novel *Mortals*, "the opening up of the mouth of hell right in front of you, without warning, through no fault of your own"? This is what he calls "hell-mouth": In medieval mystery plays the entrance to hell is portrayed as a gape-jawed monster. It was a little booth from which actors would pop in devil costume, and smoke or fireworks would emerge. From inside the hell's mouth you may hear the wails of the damned. The idea, I think, is that hell always exists, but it takes some destabilizing event for most of us to become aware of it, for its great maw to truly gape before us. The Four Horsemen of the Apocalypse were Pestilence, War, Famine, and Death. Those and other challenges to our most fundamental sense of stability, of normalcy, are the substance of hell-mouth. Some of us are very attuned to its existence, and all signs are warnings.

It is my natural sense of hell-mouth, I think, that gives me a glimpse of what some of the people I interview have gone through. It's an instinct that many would call anxious or pessimistic, and I would call realistic. If you are uneasy with pain, with darkness, with bad news, you may have trouble being sufficiently realistic. You may turn away from suffering because it troubles you, or avoid dealing with a looming issue in the hope that positive thinking will make it go away. Although I don't really know why I am the way I am, I understand in my bones that just because you don't like a worst-case scenario doesn't make it any less likely. Could it be from inheriting the anxious genes of my Jewish forebears who were alarmist or far-sighted enough to leave Eastern Europe for an unknown continent decades before the Holocaust? Or a post-traumatic effect of my grandparents' generation learning from afar of the massacre of any family who stayed behind? Who knows. Earthquakes are new to me, though.

This quake, which measures just 6.3 on the Richter scale, stops eventually. I am shaken enough that I don't sleep at all that night in Puerto Escondido. The next day, at the unbelievably beautiful beach, I can't relax. I watch the ocean anxiously for signs of recession. If it suddenly seems to be sucked away, that's a sign of an oncoming tsunami. I calculate the time it would take to stumble up the cliff that makes this beach so stunning, pulling a four-year-old and a one-year-old along with us. I am scared and sleep badly, ever alert, until our plane takes off from Mexico City and we head back to solid Toronto ground. And that's all, for a while.

By the end of that year I'm an unwilling single mother.

In the months after I became the single, sick parent of two young children in a home plagued by the sort of endless problems that plague low-rent housing in a hot rental market, I began to experience a strange set of symptoms. I would be lying in my double bed, in which I reluctantly learned to unspoon and spread out like a starfish, trying to take up space I never wanted, that I couldn't yet imagine learning to want. Unexpectedly, the Earth would shift, my vision would jerk, I'd feel like I was falling. I would think we were in another earthquake. I would see the little plastic wrestlers tumbling over each other, falling off the shelves, the shelves falling.

Then, just as panic seized me, the surface of the bed would right itself again. Everything would be still. No earthquake, no world-lurch. This shuddering happened over and over, the little wrestling figures tumbling from their shelf again and again as, I suppose, I relived the losses of the past months and years: my love, my family, my body, my work, my income, my freedom—treasured friendships, even. In *The Ground Beneath Her Feet*, Salman Rushdie wrote a tremendous scene of an earthquake in Mexico where he captured so perfectly how this feels:

> Caught also in the grip of the fear of the unforeseeable
> and the anguish of loss, in the clutches of this hated
> metamorphosis, the appalling silence of a way of life at the
> moment of its annihilation, its transformation into a golden
> past that could never wholly be rebuilt because once you have
> been in an earthquake you know, even if you survive without
> a scratch, that like a stroke in the heart, it remains in the
> earth's breast, horribly potential, always promising to return,
> to hit you again, with an even more devastating force.[1]

The persistence of events that exacerbate the losses—the difficulty earning an adequate income, in particular, has all sorts of destabilizing effects—makes it impossible to find my footing, the ground beneath my feet.

Watching a two-year-old trying to reach the stuffed animals gazing mutely back from inside the plastic bags in which they are quarantined for months to keep out bedbugs, for example, is an experience I wish on no parent. During the ten years in which we lived in our affordable, spacious apartment before being evicted,[2] we endured six rounds of these vile pests that are attracted to your every exhale, that caused massive welts on my midriff, and that locked us in the most secret isolation; and, finally, we were stricken by a plague of mice that the landlord allowed to reach Biblical proportions, babies running squeaking along the countertops.

I would wake up and think the bed was moving. I would walk down the street and the Earth would seem to shudder. I would flinch at the sound of shouting, sirens, running, bumps. Eventually I realized I was experiencing some sort of post-traumatic symptoms. I still find it embarrassing that they're so bluntly metaphorical.

No single, terrible trauma; but cumulative smaller losses, destabilizing events that pile one upon the other, can, it turns out, result in similar symptoms to PTSD. We know from many studies that adverse childhood experiences increase one's likelihood of substance use problems, with everything from injection drug use and prescription opioid misuse to nicotine and alcohol dependence appearing to increase with the number of traumatic and difficult childhood experiences. This has led some researchers and writers on addiction to come up with a bold, socially conscious counterargument to the brain disease model of addiction that dominates research funding. Gabor Maté's *In the Realm of Hungry Ghosts* posits that the heavily heroin-dependent and addicted patients he cared for as a physician in Vancouver's Downtown Eastside are suffering the effects of childhood trauma, and that drug use is a misplaced coping mechanism. Addiction, writes Maté, who is revered in harm reduction circles, is "a forlorn attempt to solve the problem of human pain." He goes on, "Hence my mantra: 'The question is not why the addiction, but why the pain.'"[3]

It's an appealing argument echoed by journalist Johann Hari and others, and one that rings true to many who work on the frontlines with people who use drugs and suffer from chronic homelessness and poverty. Certainly, early childhood trauma, such as Meg's, can lead people to self-medicate with opioids, covering symptoms like depression, anxiety, insomnia, suicidality, or constant, exhausting alertness.

Maté also believes that trauma and repressed or poorly processed emotions and their behavioural consequences are behind disease and especially chronic pain. In an earlier book, *When the Body Says No*, Maté builds on Hans Selye's important experiments showing the physical effects of stress. In this book, Maté offers profiles of different composite patients. I page through, wondering if by chance there might be one with ankylosing spondylitis. And there he is: a labour organizer whose back is deformed in a physical manifestation of his attempt to carry the weight of the world's problems on his shoulders — a grotesquely simple archetype with the psychology-lite answer to why I happen to have acquired my progressive, largely genetic disease.

Less sophisticated writers than Maté make the imagined, simplistic connection between inferred feelings, beliefs, or experiences and complex physical conditions more explicit. Self-help legend Louise Hay, for example, promotes the science-free idea that the devastating disease amyotrophic lateral sclerosis, or Lou Gehrig's disease, comes from one's denial of success and low self-worth; that babies with asthma suffer from a fear of life; that tuberculosis results from selfishness; that hurt and resentment lead to cancer.[4]

Seen through this lens, drug use is viewed specifically as a "misguided" coping mechanism, regardless of the complex story and choices or lack of good choices available. This assumes, despite evidence to the contrary, that all "hard" drug use is a tragic response to trauma. "Not why the addiction, but why the pain." The question is asked of people who use drugs, whether they want to stop or not. It is not asked of *all* people who use drugs, though, not even of all who use addictive drugs.

Carried too far, this framework patronizes people rather than responding to their attempts to dismantle structural barriers. It replaces the "addict as monster" trope with the addict as patient, or as child. As people infantilized by pain. Less like Godzilla, more like needy little ghosts. It can also, as we'll see later on, contribute to the further marginalization of injection drug users or users of "hard" opioids like heroin or illicit fentanyl that occurs in a strictly medicalized model.

A single, early traumatic event can be the origin of a wound that can only be assuaged by drugs that relieve psychological and physical pain. But while a valuable counter to theories of addiction that focus too much on personal responsibility, Maté's view tends to promote a paternalistic view of people who use drugs that can prevent drug user organizing, diminish interest in policies that respect user autonomy and informed choice, and be reductive, improbably pinning all addictive behaviour on unresolved psychic wounds or, even less credibly, on trauma-induced damage to brain receptors.[5] In some of Maté's other work, he likewise reduces physical suffering to trauma and creative psychological theories that simply lack evidence.

An exclusive focus on early childhood trauma as explaining addiction (or pain) risks overly minimizing the outsized impact of ongoing traumas like poverty, poor-bashing, racism, and homelessness; the impact of prohibition itself, and even the revolving-door, poor-quality, paternalistic addiction treatment system; or the way addiction treatment is rarely based in good evidence and even more rarely based in empowerment and rights for people who have been chronically oppressed (to his credit, Gabor Maté has actually written and spoken very eloquently about all of these and their impact on the health of his patients and the rest of us as a fundamental cause of trauma and pain[6]).

Meg, who knows all about early childhood trauma, nevertheless writes on Twitter: "*Trauma is cumulative.* I feel like I should have a gif that flashes that sentence in neon red; it's that important."[7] Her mother's suicide may have been the fundamental trauma, the origin trauma — but poverty, homelessness, and prohibition have been the causes of years and years of cumulative harm.

Framing drug use as a misguided response to trauma also ignores the inconvenient fact — if you favour a Just Say No approach or are convinced that abstinence is the only worthy goal of treatment for people who use drugs — that the vast majority of those who try opioids, whether medically, recreationally, or for self-medication, never become addicted.

And of course, pain patients, too, are thought to be infantilized by their suffering, unable to accurately understand or express their own needs. We have discussed the way in which the climate around prescription painkillers has changed from overly warm to frosty.

A crackdown in my home province of Ontario on inappropriate opioid prescriptions has yet to affect me. But even here where I live, poorer patients, those with co-existing substance use issues, and those who are for one reason or another assumed to have substance use disorders, have been cut off their long-term pain prescriptions, often for no reason, detonating their often very hard-won stability as if you'd planted a bomb underfoot. I've seen evidence of this personally in distressed emails from pain patients who read my first book and who describe how they are now being denied pain relief that worked for them for years. They don't understand why something that seemed to work is no longer considered effective. They have not found or been guided to an alternate treatment that actually works for them; they are simply left in pain, struggling to cope as I did until painkillers made it all bearable. As Dr. Kertesz and others are increasingly finding, the result is sometimes misery, and sometimes death.

There is almost no one who has not heard that evil pharmaceutical companies and gullible doctors conspired to hook tens of thousands of patients on opioids. Some of the collusion has been proven in court, and certainly the tactics used to promote opioid painkillers were calculating and atrocious. The backlash, though, has been reckless, moralistic, and equally loose with the truth. Increasingly, patients are scared to use the drugs after surgery, fearing that they, too, will become "hooked." And the rhetoric around chronic opioid therapy for intractable pain has moved from "they're dangerous" to "they're instantly addictive" to "they don't work anyway" to "accept your pain."

Headlines about the opioid overdose crisis, as well as the lawsuits themselves, frequently refer to the scandalous profit-seeking of the big pharmaceutical companies. Having spent twenty years criticizing laws and policies that put profit over people's well-being in my non-opioid journalism, I have trouble seeing Purdue or other pharmaceutical companies' profit-seeking as unique. In fact, a corporation is duty-bound to seek profit. Just as corporations may be staffed by people with good hearts and an interest in improving lives with the products they sell, so too it makes sense that they would *also* be staffed by people willing to push the boundaries of what is legal and definitely of what is ethical because of the immense, inherent pressure to squeeze out as much profit for shareholders as humanly possible. I don't see opioid makers as uniquely bad: in fact, they are doing exactly what you would expect a company to do — to promote its products in whatever way is most likely to result in greater profits, and to work to the very limit, and sometimes beyond, of the law. We see this in areas ranging from mining to for-profit nursing homes to transportation, and most definitely with pharmaceutical makers of all kinds, the many, many bad-apple exceptions serving to prove a rule about getting away with what you're allowed to get away with.

I have watched from my relatively comfy position in Canada as pain patients I've met online are forced to taper down from opioids that have kept them going for years. Patients with unpleasant diseases like Lelena's arachnoiditis (where the membranes that surround the spinal cord nerves feel like they're on fire) or interstitial cystitis (which produces a burning in the bladder) who have been able to control unbearable pain are now told that the drugs don't work. They may be told that the pain is mostly the product of sensitization of the central nervous system and that analgesics are not the right solution. Research, which in recent years has accurately exposed an ever-growing set of potential harms associated with opioid use, nevertheless supports far more cautious and limited conclusions than these patients (and medical students) are often led to believe. A systematic review of various studies may demonstrate pretty well that, say, an opioid is not superior to an anti-inflammatory for osteoarthritis of the knee. Or an individual study may find that many chronic pain patients and, to a greater extent, opioid use disorder patients can show signs of oversensitivity to pain as a result of opioids — but only when you poke them with heat or cold, not with electrical stimuli — or in their ability to detect gradually increasing painful stimuli. (I definitely do not like being poked with cold, but the relevance of this to what I feel in my spine is pretty unclear.[8])

While an accumulation of studies like that does suggest greater caution needed in prescribing opioids than was common at the turn of the millennium, far broader and definitive conclusions are delivered with bland confidence, medical jargon, and few specifics. This is *not* to argue for what has been somewhat bizarrely described as the "dark side of postmodern pain medicine,"[9] in which whatever the patient wants to believe about different medicines is true, regardless of the evidence or objective reality, and in which expertise and evidence count for nothing.

But physician and public health official anxiety about the overuse and risks of opioids has resulted in lack of balance and clarity in how evolving evidence is presented to patients, decisions that are not justified by the evidence, and a lack of interest in the facts about what happens following forced or coerced opioid tapers.

I know how the world lurches for them when they are pulled off the treatment that stepped in when their lives were most untenable, and told that they are wrong about their own perception of pain relief. I feel the slight lurch every time I'm due to renew my prescription and the doctor is away, or I wait too long to request a renewal and am left rationing my pills, or when a pharmacy assistant who hasn't seen me before looks extra-carefully at my ID. Could this be leading up to The Talk, in which I'm carefully told that the medicine I count on, that has made my life bearable after years of real and wasted suffering, is in fact not medicine but poison, and that it's time for it to go?

The last bit, about the opioid actually causing new pain, is a reference to a phenomenon called hyperalgesia. We don't know how often it occurs, but it is not common. By increasing the dose of opioid and seeing whether this resolves the pain, a physician and patient can determine whether it is the drug itself, or simply tolerance to a given dose or increased underlying pain, that is actually going on.

Then there is a vague assertion about something called "dependence pain" — not hyperalgesia, and not the underlying pain for which the opioid is prescribed, but pain associated with the fact of being physically dependent. There is little or no evidence that this exists as a separate phenomenon from the three other possibilities (that the original pain for which opioids were prescribed is being inadequately treated at the current dose; hyperalgesia; or withdrawal pain from tolerance and inadequate dose). There's no scientific justification for an extra concept, which mostly serves to further pathologize dependence, a reflection of physician discomfort with their role in creating it, and a potential tool to relieve them of its burden by re-classing it as a sickness in itself rather than a side effect of treatment. But even without this problematic idea, these other three possibilities make it challenging to figure out what is

causing continued pain and whether increasing or reducing dose, adding
a different medication, or tapering off the opioid altogether is going to
be the best approach for the patient. That can only be done by close and
trusting collaboration between the informed physician and the unafraid
patient.

Medical professionals and authorities who have gradually tightened
control over prescribing have appealed to authority, citing evidence. It
does not, however, take much work to see that the evidence used to justify
indiscriminate forced tapers and more generally the demonization of painkillers is shoddy and selective and misleading, and that what patients are
told is rarely an accurate or contextualized story. To actually understand
what evidence supports concerns about the risks of opioids (and there is
indeed a huge amount of good evidence on risks and harms) and what
claims go well beyond available evidence to simply justify a move away
from opioids (and, inevitably, toward other medications, treatments, and
decisions that come with their own sometimes serious risks and harms),
we need to look at it much more thoughtfully.

Historically, in fact, opioids have been used by many people in largely
non-problematic, culturally-relevant ways. A slightly different approach
would give far greater credit to poor people who use drugs for their survival
skills, for balancing the pursuit of security and the pursuit of autonomy
in the most difficult of circumstances. Existing healthcare, addiction
treatment, and social service systems all put up barrier after barrier to
them. These range from smoking bans for people who are now asked
to withdraw from heroin or illicit fentanyl and nicotine simultaneously,
to barring family from rehab or withholding contact for minor rule
infractions. All for no reason except, it seems, to humiliate and remind
people that "once a junkie, always a junkie" — that is, that by being poor
and having used opioids, you have forfeited basic rights such as being
treated with the respect we accord to other human beings.

In the mythology of Mexican masked wrestling there are *técnicos* — the
good guys, who play by the rules — and cartoonish bad guys, or *rudos*,
who don't. In real life, as in the ring, the participants are not equally
matched. Face it: the game is rigged. They say that addiction doesn't

discriminate, that it's a disease that can touch anyone, that anyone from any walk of life can be prescribed an opioid for an ankle sprain and quickly find themselves hooked, transformed into a manipulative, shifty pariah who alienates their family, injecting HIV-laced heroin with dirty needles. In an alley. In the rain.

The valuable notion—accepted by most people who have experienced opioid addiction, whether or not their ultimate solution is abstinence, addiction treatment, trauma therapy, or prescribed painkillers—that pain of one kind or another is at the root of opioid use needs to move to a different level, one that acknowledges the agency of people who use drugs and that honours the wisdom of decision-making under impossible circumstances. Legally or illicitly, as a best-case scenario or recklessly, we use dependence-inducing drugs to treat pain. But what then? What, given that that choice has been made, for better or for worse, do we need now to be well? What is the best way to conquer that sense of the Earth shifting dangerously, of instability, of the ego's perilously thin walls, of shattering despair?

When my children were young, I told them about a famous study by Stanford psychologist Walter Mischel, conducted beginning in the 1960s and continuing through the 1970s. Three- to five-year-old children were given a marshmallow and told that if they could be patient enough to wait ten minutes before eating it, they'd be given a second one. Mischel and his colleagues kept tabs on which kid did what, and followed them on to high school and beyond, with a follow-up conducted in 1990. Kids who were able to resist gobbling up their marshmallow right away were found as adolescents to have greater ability to tolerate stress and frustration, executive functions that were in turn believed to predict success in one's later career and relationships, and to score higher on cognitive and academic performance as measured by standardized tests. The conclusion I shared with my children was the one the researchers posited: they needed to learn to postpone gratification, to show some self-restraint. If they could, they'd be more likely to do well in life. If preschoolers could be taught greater self-control, the researchers argued, they might do better, be more successful in their later life. Conversely, the Ivy League graduates, the successful

doctors, lawyers and executives, the CEOs.. they all must be successful due
to having these skills, skills acquired by as young as three years of age. We
do indeed live in a meritocracy! A marshmallow meritocracy.

But in the past decade, as my children have grown up and as many
classic psychology studies have suffered the indignity of new researchers
failing to replicate their results, some took a stab at the marshmallow
study.

As it turns out, the assumption of a level playing field is based on overly
broad conclusions about human behaviour, potential, and needs that are
spun off limited, highly selective studies that actually show nothing of the
kind. The marshmallow test is one of them.

In 2018, three researchers replicated and extended the 1990 marshmallow study, and upon reading it I had to go to my now thirteen-year old
and ten-year-old and tell them I'd unfairly withheld their marshmallows.
It turns out that when you control better for the environment in which
the kids grew up — in that higher family affluence changes things for children — affluent kids are more likely to be able to wait a few more seconds
for that second marshmallow, and the correlation between that ability and
adolescent achievement is far weaker. It seems that being raised in a more
affluent family results in preschoolers who are less convinced that a marshmallow in the hand is worth two in a social scientist's pocket. Writing in
the *Atlantic*, Jessica McCrory Calarco explains that the later study's find-
ings suggest that "the capacity to hold out for a second marshmallow is
shaped in large part by a child's social and economic background — and,
in turn, that that background, not the ability to delay gratification, is
what's behind kids' long-term success."

Our most prosperous and powerful, whatever their endearing personal
qualities and however smart, ambitious, or hard-working they are, are not
self-denying saints who prospered on their own merits and nothing else.
In a marshmallow-starved childhood, a bright child knows that it's better
to scarf the marshmallow while you can. And a kid who can afford to
let a potential marshmallow just sit there, getting stale, is a child whose
parents are there to pay for private tutors when they fail a course, to ensure
they can concentrate on their studies rather than working to pay for their

university, to introduce them to other powerful people who will grease the wheels all the way to the top, to buy two new marshmallows for every one they let a researcher gobble up in front of them. I have what looks like good self-control, and why not? Nobody's ever stolen my marshmallows. I've never even had to share.

Likewise, we look at poor or working-class people who use drugs and, if we're compassionate, infer emotional pain (by contrast, we don't give any undue attention to the many well-off drug users who rarely suffer any negative health or legal consequences). But along with pain, we infer weakness, poor judgment, impulsivity, laziness, deceit. We don't realize that what we understand to be health and success in any person reflects their relative freedom from a host of factors: structural racism, poverty, trauma, violence, insecure housing, precarious work — or special situations, qualities, or connections that allow them to advance despite them. We are all like those little wrestlers who struggled to find their footing in the quake. Strong, but easy to topple, hard to put back without help.

But we don't see that. And so we think that if we just push them a little more, maybe they'll work harder, do better. Not noticing how firm the ground is beneath our own feet, we give them a little nudge.

Over and over the Earth shakes and they tumble down.

Monsters

With my head forced forward and down, my pelvis forced forward, I suck in my stomach in an attempt to imitate a normal spinal curve and hold myself up. My legs move stiffly. My spine feels unstable. All in all I feel lumbering, ugly, deformed. Monstrous. Every second involves concentration to stay upright. Suffering, what it does to my body, what it does to my mind, and the effort required to transcend it: all of these things make me feel like a monster.

Monsters: they live in books, under beds, and, to my mind, in museums. These days, museums are often bright, slick edutainment machines. It was different when I was a kid in the eighties. Back then, going to the Royal Ontario Museum in downtown Toronto involved a thrillingly dark subway trip that brought us to a romantically dusty collection of mysterious artefacts from both the natural world and human culture.

As an adult I studied biology and got to know the range of hominid skulls very well in a physical anthropology class. In comparative vertebrate anatomy I came to enjoy dissections, where you can actually see and compare the intricate, individual inner workings of the creatures endowed with *mu*-opioid receptors (all the creatures with backbones, as you'll recall). And then I married into a Mexican family and learned to see joy in merry depictions of skeletons and skulls. But as a child then, my fear of monsters, and most especially skulls, was very real. I loved the museum because a museum was basically a romantic, three-dimensional, voluminous book. But I was also afraid.

Creepy feelings rise up in me now, even, as I recall the display where a realistic head of a human ancestor would, when you pushed a button, rotate away, disappearing in darkness, only to reappear de-fleshed, so we could see what the anthropologists found before they created their reconstruction. The anticipation I felt as the skull emerged into the light was unbearable.

A galloping horse skeleton, derived from a scene in a fantasy series I loved, chased me repeatedly in nightmares. The idea that I, like the early hominid, was also full of bones was frightening. Worse was the knowledge that my loved ones also contained skeletons — that we, in fact, were monsters wearing masks of flesh and skin. In fact, most likely it was also to challenge the remaining traces of that fear that I enrolled in the kind of biology courses where you get your latex-gloved hands sticky. And well that I did, because bones have become very significant in my life.

The ankylosaur is a turtle-shaped dinosaur with armoured plates and, in one species, a spikey club for a tail. At some point in my teens, I happened to see a picture of an ankylosing spondylitis patient in a book somewhere. I have a knack for remembering random, useless stuff, especially if it's related to language. And I had seen the ankylosaur at the museum. The dinosaurian name of the disease, the monstrous way the patient was bent over by his condition, back hunched, the bones ankylosed, or fused, just like the dinosaur's. When, after my first child was born, I experienced the very distinctive AS pattern of stiffness and pain relieved by exercise, and when lab results suggested a form of inflammatory arthritis as a likely cause, the twin images of that ankylosed patient, and the ankylosed dinosaur, rose up from my memory vault. By the time I stepped into a rheumatologist's office, I'd lived a summer of secret horror, using the internet to retrieve endless images of patients deformed by the bone disease I already knew I had. That September, I held my breath as the rheumatologist diagnosed me with AS in a matter of seconds, told me irritably when I tried to ask questions that, "Well, it's not going to *kill* you," and walked out of the examination room, leaving me reeling, and with a prescription for anti-inflammatories that ultimately burned a hole in my esophagus.

Over the years, I've adjusted a lot. And now, in the same way I make a pilgrimage to Frida Kahlo's house when in Mexico, I visit the museum here in Toronto — no longer dusty and romantic, but still full of wonders — on a special pilgrimage to see *Zuul crurivastator*, "destroyer of shins," a beautifully preserved skeleton representing a new species of the beast who nearly shares the name of my disease.

Like Zuul, I try to stand up straight but instead curve forward as if my vertebrae were already fused into one bumpy carapace. I try to push my rib cage forward where it belongs but it sinks back, instead bulging into a curve at the back where no curve should be unless your name is Zuul. The gentle C-curve of my neck is flattened out, as an X-ray confirms. Still, the slow deformation of my spine appears to be sparing me the full question mark shape of the untreated AS patient, for whom surgery may be required to allow for a forward rather than downward gaze.

When my doctor wrote a letter to the federal tax agency on my behalf, describing the worsening *deformity* of my back, the word weighed on me for days. I catch my reflection behind the dance instructor as I move stiffly through a Zumba class and see myself as Quasimodo.

When tramadol is not at its peak effect, I project tension, anxiety, or discomfort — and constant frustration — making me quiet, edgy, and drawn. I don't know how to tell people what I need, and my many attempts to do so clearly and gently have rarely improved my relationships, instead leaving me more exhausted and more alienated. Because I'm able to not only walk but run, it is hard to translate the fact that I cannot stand in one spot for more than a few minutes without discomfort curdling to pain into an understanding that I am dealing with a disability. Acknowledging this, as I am gradually beginning to do, means I can start to see that which enables me to do things despite pain as a tool or accessibility aid, and my ability to access it as an element of disability rights. Still, I often feel misunderstood and shut out of regular life because even though I can enter it, I can't do it with the constant smile that lets others feel comfortable.

It occurs to me that in journalism, and in casual speech, we often "monsterize" human beings, conflating the physically non-conforming with perpetrators of morally unspeakable acts, by describing both as

monsters. Zuul, like other artefacts of nature, is a morally neutral monster, but he or she shares the term in popular thinking with serial killers,
animal torturers, child abusers, and people who use drugs.

On Twitter, I have found other monsters: pain patients like me who are
all too often characterized as strident, demanding, grotesque, and difficult,
gross stereotypes of the barely literate, endlessly consuming American.
And then, despite the fact that a psychoactive substance, like a dinosaur,
is morally neutral, when certain people use drugs they get the full monster
treatment, making it impossible to recall that we are describing a human
being, and often one in pain. Drugs journalism, or pulp horror fiction? It
can often be hard to tell. Take this real news article, for example:

> OPIOID HELL: The Zombies of a USA City with a Hopeless
> Addiction That's Set to Come to UK
>   A city ravaged by an opioid epidemic last night gave a
> chilling warning to the UK.[1]

And indeed, you can find these zombies — monsters by definition —
lurching in the street; you can find them skulking in the doorways. You
can find them crowded into shelters or loitering in parks.

The stereotypes we hear about people who use illicit drugs are atrocious. Like all stereotypes, they are malleable, changing through the years.
Rather than the drug being criminalized, it is actually the people who use
it who are maligned, defamed, and criminalized through drug laws.

Unlike Meg, who has faced armed robbery charges that were ultimately dropped, my friend "Joe"[2] is a convicted felon who at nineteen spent
eight months in the clink, followed by house arrest and probation. We
have talked about that, but these days spend more time — through detailed, nearly daily emails, mostly — discussing homelessness, cats, the
way Toronto is changing in tandem with other big North American cities,
and our shared experience of chronic back pain. We first discovered an
affinity on Twitter and begin chatting privately. Joe never asks me direct
personal questions, although he's a good listener who seems to really care
about the answer when he asks how I am. Nor does he ask to meet once

we discover that we both live in Toronto. But he'll check in discreetly, if I disappear for a few days, with a gentle "how's by you?" Nothing more. He answers all of my questions, though.

Joe's life story has been a nightmare, with many terrible details I won't share here, because he has become my friend, not my subject. There is no romantic or sexual subtext here: he is in a very committed relationship which, after a decade when his beloved cat was his only companion, has given meaning and purpose to a life previously shot through with despair.

Over the course of months of sporadic conversation, Joe becomes my most regular correspondent after my mom. We meet in person for the first time, at my suggestion, in a café where I used to hang out during university. I moved into my university residence the year Joe moved into the Don Jail, a now-defunct, notorious Toronto institution that looked, he says, like the set of a horror movie. I remember standing outside it for some article I wrote years ago and he is right, but of course I never saw it from the inside.

Joe knows this café too. He spent time here when he was a teenage drug dealer, selling marijuana and LSD at his high school around the corner. That school happens to be where my son has just started grade nine. We are exact contemporaries born a few months apart, and so we have even more shared cultural touchstones and memories of the city than Meg and I. Joe lives now, with his partner, in Toronto's Gay Village. They live in rent-controlled Depression-era red-brick housing that he describes as a revolving door of "dead-ender" tenants and the odd student from small-town Ontario, stunned to have ended up smack in the midst of urban decay. "We have some wild tenants around here," he writes. "I mean wild as in feral, barely domesticated, probably struggling with housebreaking." His neighbour on one side calls the rooming house on the other side the Murder House. Joe keeps a large combat knife by the door in case someone breaks into their unit.

He recently helped the property manager cart a deceased tenant's possessions to the curb. Joe suspects the tenant died of an overdose. He describes drug deals taking place nightly in the alley behind his house and picks up discarded methamphetamine and fentanyl needles (he can tell the difference) to keep the place clean and safe. They have had bedbugs. The apartment is actually falling apart, and whenever it rains Joe and his partner must run around plugging holes. They've flooded so often they now store their possessions in plastic containers. There's nowhere else to go.

"We're the junkies," he writes to me. "Doesn't that say it all?"

Joe has not, however, ever injected drugs. His partner is a younger trans man who was injecting heroin when they became neighbours, and who transitioned to the addiction medicine buprenorphine after friendship sweetened to love. Having survived abandonment, domestic violence, dislocation, incarceration, and poverty, so far, Joe's main focus now is on keeping his little family—which still includes the great orange cat he rescued from under a truck as a tiny ball of fluff—well and whole.

Joe may have dabbled in drug dealing as a very troubled teenager, but he did not come to opioids until adulthood. Upon leaving prison, the only work he could get was manual labour. This exacerbated back problems and, as was common in the nineties, he was prescribed opioid painkillers. They not only allowed him to continue to work his back-breaking job, but he quickly discovered that, especially when insufflated (snorted) rather than swallowed, they also provided a calm he'd never experienced, a normalcy. With OxyContin, he was at last able to manage his debilitating symptoms of chronic post-traumatic stress syndrome.

After we've been chatting for a while, I notice, because I'm facing the door of the café, that a woman is struggling to push her baby carriage through the heavy double doors and up a single step. It's an awkward entry I remember well from when I tried to do the same with each of my kids, at some resting point during the long walks I took with each of them all over downtown when they were babies. I slide off the uncomfortably high, backless stool I've been sitting on and go to open the door for her. It's difficult to manage because of the orientation of doors and step and stroller, and soon Joe has joined me. The little, underemployed hack with the hunchy back, and the underweight, ponytailed ex-convict together holding a door for a new mom and her baby strikes me as an odd scene. But monsters are surprisingly public-spirited.

Returning to the story, when prescription opioids became impossible to obtain, Joe made a fateful decision to avoid the unpredictable illicit market. By seeking a safe source of (non-euphoric) opioids through the addiction treatment system, he has been made to take on the stereotype of the junkie, the monster in flesh and blood.

"People think of methadone patients," Joe tells me, "as dirty, zombie-like shuffling semi-humans already crawling with disease. They have a poor sense of who actually goes through clinics."

To get the medication that keeps him well, Joe must travel to a distant Toronto suburb, where his methadone clinic is hidden behind an auto body shop. By the time he arrives there in the morning to stand in line or squeeze into the little waiting area, he is in serious withdrawal, sweating and shaking. Every week, he must provide urine samples. Joe sends me photos that he took from inside the bathroom where he must pee in a cup (in the US, this process often involves observed screening). Although at least he is allowed to lock the door, there are four cameras, some fixed at groin level, to ensure he does exactly what he's told.

The writer Elizabeth Brico, in Florida, experiences a similarly dehumanizing process when she undergoes *witnessed* urine drug screening as a requirement for receiving buprenorphine, one of the two most evidence-based treatments for opioid use disorder: "She watched, annoyed, while I pulled up my panties, tugged down my skirt, and sidled past her out the bathroom, empty cup in hand."[3]

Ultimately Brico relapsed with heroin as a result of her inability to pee under scrutiny.

Although some clinicians claim there is a safety value to patients in knowing what's in their urine, the tests are notoriously unreliable and easy to mess with despite the punitive precautions, and there is no evidence that they improve patient care in any way. They allow doctors (even in single-payer-healthcare Canada) and laboratories to bill, often exorbitantly, for provision of the test, and in fact constitute an entire industry devoted to surveillance and reporting of the contents of people's piss and marketing of ever-more-creative ways to monitor human fluids. These include new, privacy-shredding ventures such as apps[4] that allow for observed, recorded alcohol and drug screening.

Philadelphia harm reduction advocate Bill Kinkle, a former nurse who was addicted to heroin, also describes the trauma of this dehumanizing practice, in which he has regularly been forced to relive the helplessness of past sexual trauma and incarceration, including being raped in prison, as part of mandated addiction treatment. Never, he says, has his urine screening been witnessed by an observer of the same sex. He wrote to his case manager under Pennsylvania's nurse monitoring program,

> I want to be as clear as possible here so there is no confusion. What happens every time I am selected for a screen is intense anxiety, cold sweats, an overall psychological heaviness. While I am preparing to go into the restroom I begin to shake and sweat more, most times I joke with the staff to cover the growing impulse to cry and leave the facility, while in the restroom I can smell the jail cell the night I was raped. I can feel the texture of the wool blanket over my face and hear the muffling of sound. My heart races, my voice cracks, and I have to work extraordinarily hard not to spill the specimen as I hand it over because I shake so profusely.[5]

Piss tests are just one, emblematic example of the way vulnerable people are routinely dehumanized and re-traumatized in the name of treatment. As it turns out, whether in treatment or actively using, to most people, you're a junkie for life, or at least for as long as poverty keeps you neatly slotted into their mental category of the worthless, untrustworthy, un-redeemable drug user.

The media-propagated narrative has been that innocent, naive (white) people are prescribed a painkiller and quickly find themselves hooked, ultimately turning to heroin, the true maker of monsters. But people like Joe complicate the reality. So too do statistics on prescription opioids and heroin use. Or the fact that, despite common denial of appropriate opioid pain care to Black patients with serious conditions like sickle cell anemia and other pain conditions, the rates of overdose are now increasing more quickly in the Black community than anywhere else.

It is perhaps natural that pale and privileged people like me would have trouble separating the cause of suffering and its effect. We have a vested interest in not doing it very well. The language of monstrosity that exists so often around drug use reflects the position that certain drug users hold in society and tells us that drug use is deviant, unmanageable, foreign or even alien, and frightening.

The tight connections between white supremacy and the war on drugs run the gamut from the scapegoating of Chinese immigrants in Canada by means of the first opium prohibition laws, to targeting of Indigenous people for enforcement of minor drug crimes today, or the persecution of Black heroin users. The vocally anti-racist jazz singer Billie Holiday, for example, was hounded by Harry Anslinger, the notoriously racist head of the US Federal Bureau of Narcotics in the 1930s and prime mover of the war on drugs[6] that endures today in much the same form he first laid out. More recently, media are quick to report the drug status of Black people killed by police, and police are just as quick to cite drug use or sales or suspicion of either as justification for indefensible and apparently racially-motivated violence. In 2020, for example, we were told that drugs were relevant in the death of forty-six-year-old Minneapolis native George Floyd, who had a non-lethal dose of fentanyl in his system when a police officer knelt on his neck for nearly nine minutes, as he called for his mother and repeated that he could not breathe; or in that of twenty-six-year-old Breonna Taylor, who was shot six times in her own Louisville apartment during a drug investigation.

Over and over since the very start, prohibition or harsh enforcement of it for certain drugs but not others — often even versions of the same drug, as with the chemically identical drugs crack and cocaine — have targeted the racialized minority associated with it, with stereotypes and exaggerations monstrifying different ethnic groups: crack babies, Yellow Peril, drunken Indians — these are all racist constructions that have nothing whatsoever to do with the actual harms of the drug in question.

The racially associated danger of the drug often has to do with either loss of control or insidious control. Where ruthless Colombian and Mexican drug lords mastermind the enslavement of innocent Americans with cocaine, sly Jews control the legal pharmaceutical opioid industry.

In Robert Louis Stevenson's story of Dr. Jekyll and Mr. Hyde, a medical doctor "swallows a potion that transforms him from a rational, intelligent human into an evil monster,"[7] write two veterinarians with PhDs in *American Veterinarian* magazine. The article where this appears is about how to recognize the pet owner who is using their dog or cat to score opioid painkillers — for themselves. "Opioids — the modern equivalent of the doctor's potion — can create dependency, transform people into strangers sometimes given to harmful deeds, and bring on the distinct possibility of death," they continue.

For family members whose loved ones have become "strangers sometimes given to harmful deeds," it can be seductive to describe the drug as such a potion, creating a split personality and turning a beloved child, sibling, or parent into a monstrous creature who exemplifies characteristics like selfishness, manipulation, deceit, and unreliability. "When she's on drugs she's just a monster," says A.Y.,[8] mother of a young woman who uses methamphetamines. An FBI feature film purportedly about drug users' experiences includes a composite user musing on his experience with oxycodone 80s.

> It just turned me into a monster. I never thought any of this would happen to me. I'm a criminal. I'm an addict. [...] the minute that chemical hits your bloodstream, you lose control of what it does in your body. You can't control it. Nobody can control it. And I ask them, of all the drugs they've ever tried, what's the most addictive drug. And without a doubt it's oxycodone.[9]

Others have said the most addictive drug — without a doubt — is heroin; cocaine; crystal meth; or nicotine. *Time* magazine reports on a scary new drug (it's always a scary new drug) based on the opioid codeine. It's called krokodil, or the "zombie drug" (there are many zombie drugs).

It comes from "Siberia and the Russian Far East," and it is the "world's most dangerous drug," causing necrosis of the skin. And, of course, "There are now alarming stories that the monster could be at large in the U.S."[10] Other scary "new" drugs that have each had their turn in the tabloid sun have included flakka, bath salts, monkey dust, jenkem, Tik, and Gray Death. Inevitably, reports like these prove to be nothing but alarming monster tales: moralistic, based on fantasy, intended to scare. When I was a child, we feared that our Halloween candy was laced with LSD (it was not). Now, drug users are apparently giving away cannabis edibles in order to get our children stoned or psychotic (they are not).

With monster language comes suspicion, vigilance, xenophobia, and fear. Monster language serves, repeatedly, as the scaffolding that holds up discrimination and routine rights violations. The moral of the story is that monsters are not to be trusted: they must be quarantined, killed, institutionalized, silenced. Exterminated. Reporter Susan Zielinski quotes Alberta resident Symantha DeSchiffart on a drug user:

> He's walking like he doesn't have any bones. He's right
> messed up. It's scary. He's trying to talk. You don't know
> what they're going to do when they need money. This right
> here is a zombie apocalypse in this area. It's not safe for
> anybody.[11]

The result of commentary like this in this particular community has been closures and defunding of existing supervised consumption sites, moving drug use from a safe, supportive location to alleys, parks, and Burger King bathrooms and resulting in preventable death.

At its worst extreme, framings that effectively reduce people who use drugs to zombies propel regimes like that in the Philippines, where President Rodrigo Duterte openly questions whether drug users are human (his drug war policies and support for extra-judicial killing have resulted in the deaths of tens of thousands of members of the urban poor, with poverty and drug use being repeatedly conflated and subject to similarly hateful and dehumanizing descriptions by the president). Shortly after coming to power in 2016, Duterte told reporters that "Hitler massacred three million Jews. Now, there are 3 million drug addicts. [...] I'd be happy to slaughter them."[12]

Donald Trump, an open admirer of Duterte's approach to drug policy, and his militarism and authoritarianism, likewise advocated capital punishment for drug dealers, while using both "animals" and "drug dealers" to refer to Hispanic migrants and renewing the truly undying global war on drugs. The cost of media recklessness in reporting on drug use without picking apart the racism and poor-bashing inherent in these framings is the cost of human lives.

We — or rather, the wealthy minority who control access to land, resources, services, perspectives — have put together a Frankenstein's monster of a society. In North America, the gap in incomes between rich and poor is worse than in 1913 Europe; globally, the wealthiest have commanded a greater share of incomes, as well as overall wealth, since the 1980s,[13] and market forces play the tune to which we must all frantically dance. According to French economist Thomas Piketty, inequality in the United States is "probably higher than in any other society at any time in the past, anywhere in the world."[14] That's the society we live in, a true monster with every condition necessary for poor mental and physical health, physical pain, addiction, and misery. Like Dorian Gray, whose face remained pristine while his hidden portrait accumulated all the monstrosity of its subject, or like Frankenstein's monster, the creation is thought to have all the bad qualities that are in fact the worst qualities of its maker — in fact, if anyone were to listen, it is more eloquent and humane than its creator. We punish this poor beast of a society for lumbering around, seeking shelter, medicating its pain, worrying its own tail, doing its best to live and find its own meaning and beauty.

Really, who is the monster?

Dross

During the apartheid era in South Africa, my maternal grandfather was a scientist with the country's mining industry research and development organization. A delightful, witty letter writer, he was the family author as well, having produced an elegant history of his employer. He had a great appreciation for words. One that he might never have thought of in metaphorical terms, but which he quite likely used at some point in his work in metallurgy, is *dross*. You can get meaning from context: dross is something like *dregs*—the undesirable, the contaminating. Where dregs form on the bottom of the barrel, dross rises to the top. In this context, dross refers to the undesirable scum that forms on the surface of a molten metal such as gold. It is, as we might guess, the unwanted product of something precious: refuse, garbage, waste.

Dross also happens to be the correct term for the residue left after smoking a pipe of opium. In China, the history of largely moderate, widespread opium use predates the Opium Wars in which the British Empire sought to consolidate its control of the vibrant international opium industry. (Thomas De Quincey's son Horace died of malarial fever while serving in the first of these wars.) Dross was, like cigarette stubs, recycled for use by the poor and used as an extender, the way you might water down a good wine.

Prohibition policies banning opium were enacted unevenly by various governments for hundreds of years before, but they really kicked in in the twentieth century, as an international coalition spanning a range of interests[1] pressured governments to turn away from the incredibly lucrative industry. When prohibition came to China, the lower, dross-dependent classes of drug users were suddenly reclassified as criminals.

This reclassification of social status in China, and wherever opium prohibition came into effect, had direct and dire impacts. People who previously used dross or opium to manage the routine stresses of life, including harsh working conditions (just as De Quincey described workers doing in London and in the countryside during the mid-nineteenth century), were pushed into a more desperate way of life, the way of life we associate with "junkies" today. Meanwhile, wealthy opioid users continued to enjoy the highest-quality opium in use patterns that remained generally moderate and manageable.[2]

Simply reclassifying drug users in this way also had profound, concrete, and lasting effects on their human rights: to liberty and security; to fair trial; to freedom from torture and inhumane or degrading treatment; to freedom of thought, belief, and religion; to freedom from arbitrary detention, forced labour, and slavery, and many more. As criminals, the dross users were considered dross themselves, and not entitled to the same respect, to the same standard of healthcare, to enjoyment of life or autonomy in deciding the direction of their lives.

Occupying an even lower rung on the socioeconomic ladder in North America today, drug users are our society's dross, in the sense that they are not simply seen as bad or unwanted, as monstrous — but that they actually play a lowly but essential role in the social ecosystem. Drug users under capitalist prohibition keep whole industries alive — in their case, these are industries like policing, incarceration, treatment, and surveillance. All this happened historically, and it happens today. The poor, criminalized drug user gives charities miserables to fundraise for, religious groups sinners to save, the state children to apprehend, and politicians scapegoats to blame.

Drugs, or, rather, pharmaceuticals, in fact share an etymological root with the concept of the scapegoat. In his dated but fascinating 1974 book *Ceremonial Chemistry: The Ritual Persecution of Drugs, Addicts, and Pushers*, Thomas Szasz writes of the original scapegoat of Ancient Greece:

an actual goat, or a dog, or a common criminal. The scapegoat was called *pharmakos*, meaning "remedy," on which a community's sins or impurities are cast, or absorbed, as with a sponge, and then purged when the creature is sacrificed, burned, or cast away. In Wikipedia's semi-trustworthy telling, the *pharmakos* is not the scapegoat itself, but the ritual: "A slave, a cripple or a criminal was chosen and expelled from the community at times of disaster (famine, invasion or plague) or at times of calendrical crisis."[3]

The *pharmakos* was also, Szasz says, called the *katharmada*, meaning "that which is wiped off," and it's easy to see how easily this slides into the meaning of "scum" — all that is disposable, impure, and shameful.

It didn't used to be this way. The image of the truly destitute drug user, the stereotype of the down-and-out junkie, was not born until opium, the sap of a plant that grows to this day in gardens across Canada and sometimes in the US,[4] became illegal. Human dross did not exist until we reclassified and penalized the smokers of dross, until we created it.

We think it is the demon drug itself that makes the zombie, the junkie, the crackhead. We are wrong. Each of these words reflects a dehumanizing, stigmatizing, and unrealistic view of drug users. But as well as recognizing that we are wrong to speak of human beings in this way, we need to understand that prohibition policies have actually *created* criminals, *created* people without avenues to meaningful work and a dignified standard of living, *created* behaviours that are then studied, written about, and firmly believed — whether punitively or compassionately — to be fundamental attributes of people who use opioids or other drugs.

The implicit connections between rubbish, human beings, and poverty create a powerful form of bigotry that gives the lie to the idea that addiction affects everyone equally. The image of the poor, homeless, incoherently intoxicated, irrational, untrustworthy, and barely or sub-human junkie is the archetype that emerges when, for example, neighbours are brought together to discuss providing services to people who use drugs.

Inevitably, journalists carefully interview homeowners upset about the possible presence of a halfway house, a drop-in, or a supervised drug consumption site in their community while describing the potential clients of these services as transient interlopers. We forget all too easily that the people who use drugs are also residents, voters, community members, neighbours, and taxpayers, fellow humans with the same human rights as everyone else. We never solicit their opinions on how a supervised injection site may prevent needle waste in alleys or parks, how a drop-in lets homeless neighbours meet and socialize, or how affordable, supportive housing makes it easier for them to work or volunteer in their communities. Instead, we may describe, with disdain, a person injecting heroin in public. Or we creatively describe the lack of dignity, of healthy shame, that we intuit in the eyes or in the clothes of a person we notice on our way to the community meeting we report on, a meeting at which drug users are thought to be better expelled from the community, like the *pharmakos*. Better thrown from a cliff than invited to a community meeting, or to provide an informed opinion.

Like dross (or its synonym, scum), poor drug users are treated — in overt policies and in individual acts of unalloyed hatred — as the unfortunate residue of society. As I have, over the past few years, clawed my way back toward a relatively stable, almost middle-class life with the help of opioids, I have become increasingly aware of how, while I get relief, they get…dross.

Although the "addict" or "junkie" archetype does not reflect reality — and certainly does not reflect the majority of people who use any drug you choose — it is the one that dominates and that haunts conversations about what people need. Metaphors that evoke the image of dross easily strip away any possible empathy, making it easy to forget we are talking about human beings. But analogy is also the way into empathy and recognition of shared humanity.

"It was like a knife cutting into a banana," writer Ivan Turgenev said of an 1883 operation he endured,[5] casting himself as the banana. His friend Alphonse Daudet, who suffered pain due to syphilis, wrote a gorgeous book, *In the Land of Pain*. It is full of fragmentary bits of writing about his life in pain, stories he confided in full colour in writing but which he rarely mentioned to his friends, to avoid hurting them, or being a bore:

"Armour is exactly what it feels like, a hoop of steel cruelly crushing my lower back. Hot coals, stabs of pain as sharp as needles"; "No general theory about pain. Each patient discovers his own, and the nature of pain varies, like a singer's voice, according to the acoustics of the hall"; "A terrible pain in my back and the nape of my neck, as if all the marrow was melting," he writes at different points in what today's relentlessly upbeat culture would call his "health journey."

Similes like these tell us what something is like. But metaphor goes dangerously further, allowing us to believe that a thing *is* what it's compared to. Through metaphor, we can seem to experience someone else's subjective joys or pain or other sensations. Their pain (or joy) is ours. That's what reading does.

Later in the course of *In the Land of Pain* and the cruel progression of his disease, Daudet is more direct, and we feel it: "In my bed my legs are made of stone which feels pain."[6]

As I've been from specialist to specialist, logging endless hours pacing in waiting rooms or lying unbearably still in the sarcophagus of an MRI machine, I all too often feel like an object to be moved and repositioned, poked and prodded, used as a teaching tool for medical students or given words of sympathy that are short and rote. Add that to the self-esteem shredding nature of a disease that makes you feel and move like a ninety-year-old in your thirties, followed by the actual physical changes it wreaks, and it is easy to feel like a most miserable, unwanted, unattractive object indeed. My physical misery feels repellent, even. There is often nothing I want more than to puncture the professionalism of the professionals I depend upon, to hear them share some vulnerability in return for mine, to feel that my pain hurts them too.

When in Venice, an important stop on the old opium trade routes, I forgot about the city's most famous imaginary resident: Shakespeare's Shylock, the moneylender who may have financed some of that trade, as other professions were barred to Jews, who were then scapegoated as financial parasites and grotesquely stereotyped. Shylock asked rhetorically, magnificently,

Hath not a Jew eyes? Hath not a Jew hands, organs,
dimensions, senses, affections, passions? Fed with the
same food, hurt with the same weapons, subject to the
same diseases, healed by the same means, warmed and
cooled by the same winter and summer as a Christian is?
If you prick us, do we not bleed? If you tickle us, do we
not laugh? If you poison us, do we not die?[7]

At the end of a phrase like *do we not bleed* we hear the silent words
"like you": Shakespeare turns *us* into the simile. Sometimes I'd like to do
that to my healthcare providers, so they'd understand, by imagining how
they would handle my life, just how bruised I feel. I'd like them to know
how frightening it is to be so vulnerable, before they poke me or prod me
or pronounce on my not-especially-interesting case. Their case, my life.

My craving to sense empathy from the people on whom I depend to
help me be well leads me to identify not only with my fellow pain patients
but with others who have struggled emotionally (as I have), and with people
who use illicit drugs. The outright contempt certain healthcare providers
frequently express toward these overlapping groups, but most severely toward the latter, is disgusting and damaging for their patients' health.

Of course, a surgeon, say, who empathized so deeply with her patients
that she felt their pain, would be unable to operate. Professional distance
isn't all bad. As a writer I also need the correct amount of empathy, bal-
anced by a bit of distance, an area where I feel like opioids contribute to
my professional development. A little dissociation lets us hold up pain, ours
and others', like a jewel, to examine every facet under a harsh clear light.

And anyway, there are hard limits to empathy, just as there are to the
ability of metaphors to bridge the gap between our subjective experience
and that of another person. I can measure these limits through my sense
of loneliness, my sense that few people understand, or wish to understand,
my experience with pain. But we see these limits, too, in the difficulty
people have in taking drug users and pain patients at their word when
they speak of suffering—or, in some cases, of how opioids relieve that
suffering.

Snow is falling outside as I look through the hospital window to the street. It is 2011, and I'm alone for a moment in a room upstairs from the clinic that treats my degenerative spine disease. I'm here today as a volunteer participant in a study into the effects of long-term pain on certain regions of the brain. During this harsh winter when I become a single parent, reporters also look out their windows and write mocking newspaper headlines about the idea of global warming. In another part of the same hospital, years ago, I waited anxiously while my husband had his appendix removed. Days later I learned that I was pregnant with our first child.

The neuroscientist comes back into the room. He is a little younger than me, good-looking, and kind. I am susceptible. I nearly cry as he gently and deliberately inflicts pain, applying heat and cold until I ask him to stop, then making a note of each time I give in. I imagine him taking an interest in me. After the study he will email me the MRI scans of my brain, unreadable to me (and the research team will miss the seven or eight vascular malformations that are already, secretly, there, that must have been lurking in my head since birth—but more on that later). Still, the image is an accurate if inscrutable picture of the contents of my skull at the time it was taken. The researcher's goal is to determine whether my chronic pain condition, as revealed by brain changes seen on the scan, might make me more susceptible to pain stimuli than others. But I don't believe he can distinguish the effect of his heat and cold or his poking from the pain of rejection and longing that suffuse my every cell.

Without that level of sensitivity, we can't count on others to know what we need. And the differences separating those who set policy on drugs and on pain from those who endure it are significant. A majority of people who die of overdose, who suffer incarceration and family separation due to war on drugs policies, whose pain is inadequately treated, or whose drug use is intertwined with adverse life experiences like domestic violence, housing insecurity, or poverty are non-white. The minority who can afford to attend higher education and amass degrees, and who ultimately occupy leadership roles in organizations that work *with* people who use drugs, are white. What we see as objectivity or professional distance is all too often bias based in class or race, formative experiences of life we don't even recognize as shaping our views.

When I describe a "movement" of people who use drugs, I'm talking about the drug users themselves who actively save each other's lives; speak out at memorials and funerals; organize into unions, demonstrate, and advocate for policy that responds to people's self-expressed needs; spread the word about "bad batches" or reliable dealers—this is the vastly larger group rarely considered a meaningful social movement by those who report on them, and it is predominantly non-white, working class or poor, Black, Indigenous, Hispanic, queer. Many of its true leaders are women.

To most journalists writing about drug policy or substance use, their views are considered niche, special interest, or radical: fatally subjective.

Then again as we have seen, many users of opioids prescribed for pain are increasingly being treated as "drug-seekers" as well, ultimately resulting in a sense among pain patients that they, too, are being viewed as a kind of dross.

As public opinion has turned against the medical use of opioids for long-term pain, a similar if more subdued process has occurred with pain patients as took place when opium was prohibited and all use of opioids (at least among the lower classes) began to be seen as abuse.

To white and middle- or working-class patients who have maintained a certain level of function and quality of life on long-term opioid treatment, the shift in attitude has been jarring. Pain patients who use opioids are considered to be delusional, neurotic, difficult, and prone to lying to themselves. The stereotype of the angry pain patient demanding opioids reflects the fact that anger is typically a response to a perceived violation of one's rights. It's not surprising that people who may not have previously experienced such violations as a routine part of life may not have learned to be strategic in how they respond. Unfortunately, policies such as unnecessary and humiliating urine drug testing, pill counts, and one-sided pain contracts as well as straight-out abandonment of opioid-dependent pain patients by their healthcare providers constitute, over time, an unpleasant education in injustice. Patients learn, through brutal experience, that they will be punished rather than rewarded for being honest and straightforward about side effects, concerns about dose or use, or fluctuating pain levels. They learn, skillfully or not, to be circumspect, or to be manipulative.

Also unfortunately, pain patients frustrated at the change in their status have taken to social media with campaigns like *#patientsnotaddicts*, by which they seek to distinguish themselves from the "addicts."

"We are over being treated like scum," writes one pain patient[8] calling for presidential candidates to defend access to pain medicines.

"Too many people are forced to live in unrelenting chronic pain. They take meds 2 survive not to get high," writes another,[9] drawing a distinction that reflects outrage at the suggestion that pain patients do not in fact take our medications precisely as prescribed, but which also reflects the belief that people who use illicit opioids do so to reach a state of blissful intoxication for recreational, and thus morally indefensible, purposes.

"I don't even drink have i ever yes every once in a blue. I just don't find any point in it. I like to be in control of myself & my surroundings," stresses a pain patient who finds herself bedbound two years after being cut off her oxycodone prescription.[10]

"There were years when I couldn't have been a productive employee/mother/citizen w/o opioids,"[11] writes another patient, whose Twitter bio says she suffers from trigeminal neuralgia, the facial nerve pain that likely afflicted Thomas De Quincey. Where *our* use of opioids is measured, careful, rule-following, and instrumental (enabling a positive life of community involvement, honest work, and traditional domestic activities), she implies, *theirs* is aberrant, out of control, self-indulgent, and inevitably destructive.

We are being treated as junkies, those pain patients say. It's not fair. It's not right. But a better argument would be that *no one* should be treated the way "junkies" are routinely treated.

I do indeed take my pain medication exactly as prescribed. But the distinction many of these patients make between worthy pain patients and unworthy (and worthless) addicts reflects societal misunderstandings of drug use. And it's punching down: attacking a group facing even greater discrimination in hopes of distinguishing ourselves.

Lelena Peacock, my first pain patient friend, grew up in Winston Salem, NC, home of R.J. Reynolds Tobacco Company, makers of Camel cigarettes — a town where through the eighties, she tells me, high school seniors were handed packets of cigarettes; a city, she says, "literally based on two things — faith and addiction." Like so many others, Lele started out as an online pain activist by emphasizing the constantly misunderstood but real distinction between physical dependence on a medication and addiction. But gradually, that changed.

"It dawned on me," Lelena writes, "that Patients Not Addicts was just AWFUL after I realized how loaded it was to say that WE were patients, but folks with addiction weren't."

"I had thought that we were making a distinction about pain patients not suffering with addiction, all the while not even realizing just how stigmatizing and invalidating...and downright hateful Patients Not Addicts was."

My online worlds now blend pain patients, active drug users, and others. Now I notice that Lelena, this pain patient from North Carolina who uses emojis and capital letters to soften her already gentle words, is making the online acquaintance of Meg, my friend who injects fentanyl and has lived under a bridge. They both comment in response to things I've posted online and then begin trading opinions and observations with each other. And why not? They both love cats. They are both determined and caring. They are both, oddly, unfailingly and unfashionably wellspoken and polite. They both know about pain. They both, in their own ways, want to reduce the pain of others, the total measure of pain in the world.

For all the metaphors (or, even worse, supposedly objective 1–10 pain scales) we can use to help us imagine what it's like, to feel like we're actually experiencing what it's like, there is a fundamental difficulty in knowing what pain — or anything else — feels like *for the person experiencing it.* The impossibility of experiencing someone else's experience of a subjective phenomenon (that is, any experience that is not your own) is a philosophical problem of consciousness and of our personal experience of things as diverse as pain, pleasure, the taste of cherries, the colour blue (what philosophers call "qualia"), and it is why there is not and never will be a biomarker, a machine, or a test that will tell us what pain feels like—how bad it is, for example—*for another person,* which is, after all, the aspect that makes pain pain. You've followed me so far, but you can't go all the way. No matter how I flatter myself that I can write a good description, it will never be good enough, never be magic. Like my friends, my family, my doctors, you, my readers, will ultimately never understand what it's like for me—or Lelena, or Meg—to live in pain.

Because of this fundamental limitation, a physician *must* listen, must supply medical information that can be tested against the patient's self-reported experience, must ask, "are you coping?" rather than searching endlessly for the truth, the deceit or delusion, the confession, behind the patient's cry for help. A wonderful thing my family doctor once said to me is "you're coping amazingly well." It's an acknowledgement I treasure, one I'd ached for years to hear from someone, anyone. It made me cry. Then again, the doctor's office is the only place I regularly burst into tears.

And yet, when many patients come bearing their pain and the 86,400 daily seconds they cope with it, day in and day out, before seeking help in the clinic or in the emergency department, all too often the subtext they hear from their doctor or nurse is "are you lying?" It could be simply that pain patients are whiny, paranoid, neurotic, and aggressive and so hear a subtext that doesn't exist. And yet it's not always even subtext. On social media, it is all too easy to find physicians and nurses making cruel fun of patients who rate their pain as 11 out of a 10-point scale, or who claim to have "very high pain tolerance," assumed to be a ruse to acquire drugs. The clever doctors who point out that 11 out of 10 is impossible deliberately miss the point of what these patients are saying. They laugh at the melodramatic words or actions of some of their patients rather than understanding what they are saying, and with good reason: "Pay attention to me. I am suffering. It's really bad."

By genuinely paying attention, by making sure they have not missed any possible sources of the pain that could be treated, by being clear and honest about what they don't know without again accusing patients of lying about what they say they feel—and then by providing as much pain relief as will allow the patient to cope while meeting their realistic life goals and responsibilities, doctors will discover that many patients have no interest in trying opioids at all, and that other treatments may work better and with fewer side effects for a good majority of them. For others, drug seeking is indeed drug seeking, and a serious physician would find out what they need from opioids or other drugs — relief of physical pain, relief of withdrawal, relief of psychological pain — and do their best to meet that need, exploring the options sensitively with the patient, rather than humiliating them for the crime of asking a doctor for medicine.

But then, what doctor wants to believe themselves to be unmoved — disgusted, even — by true suffering? Not a good look: they'd seem to be people in the wrong profession. Best to assume the patient, truly dense, simply doesn't understand that it is impossible to have a pain level of 11 out of 10. Or, assume that they are lying. To get drugs. (No wonder, perhaps, that a common cause of [self-reported] prescription opioid *misuse,* according to both the Substance Abuse and Mental Health Services Administration [SAMHSA] and the CDC,[12] is to treat physical pain, the reason for which the medication is prescribed. A 2015 redefinition of such misuse, in fact, includes use of a prescription pain reliever to relieve pain in the person to whom it is prescribed, rendering the term meaningless[13]).

Once you have decided they are really just a junkie masquerading as a human being, treating the drug-seeker with dignity and kindness is no longer required. They are dross! And so people in pain are humiliated every day in hospital ERs for their withdrawal symptoms, expressions of agony, or attempts to gain relief. The less middle-class they look, the less articulate their English, the less white their skin, the more dehumanizing the treatment.

Is it, perhaps, simply impossible to feel empathy without literally having been in another person's shoes? Because white, middle-class pain patients like me are extended empathy — and trust, and belief in the accuracy of our own account of our own pain — far more readily than those who are poor, who are therefore seen as somehow closer to being the stereotypical and undeserving junkie. Hung out to dry by an inattentive prescriber of his legal morphine pain prescription, Michael Eschbach wrote in despair on social media:

> Why would a whole medical satellite clinic at [I've removed
> the hospital name] ignore my pleas for prescription renewal?
> I know you are just people like me, kids, wives, a life of your
> own, i get it. I had that, in a world far removed from me.
> Why would you let the coverage lapse, to inflict pain?[14]

Simply by virtue of their income — even in Canada, where it's low relative to the private sector, or in one specialty relative to another, and even, in most cases, despite the burden of student loans — physicians' earnings and social status put them on a different planet from so many of their patients in terms of their day-to-day experience. By that measure, it would be best if most doctors (like most policy-makers) were not charged with the well-being of their patients who are poor, or in pain, or dependent on or addicted to opioids. That's because keeping these patients well and, in fact, keeping them alive really requires that physicians understand that the patients' self-identified needs drive health outcomes. Too often, due to their simple inability to predict or understand the material conditions of patients' lives, they effectively, if often unintentionally, treat these patients as outcasts undeserving of either compassion or a deciding role in their own lives.

The discrepancy between official leadership and genuinely represent-ative leaders is true also of chronic pain patients. Low-wage workers with physically arduous jobs make up a substantial proportion of people who have chronic pain, but may not have the childcare, transportation, or leisure time required to take in-person pain education classes or attend support groups or the financial resources to pay for massages, home help, prepared meals, or other things that can make a practical difference to someone living with daily pain, nor to join volunteer boards, act as patient representatives, or otherwise advocate for the interests of the poor majority with pain and for the policies that best serve their interests.

This is all bigger than opioids, though. A minority of people in the world make the decisions and control the resources that determine the lives of the vast majority. Their relentless pursuit of profit has decimated the Earth, unleashed disease and Biblical weather events, ransacked entire peoples and regions for the natural resources that have built and consolidated this minority wealth, and then provided loans to these regions on the condition they butcher social programs and buy the products and services and weapons of these same creditors. Physical pain — from literally back-breaking work at inhuman hours for unlivable pay, from injuries untended and diseases untreated, from histories of discrimination and childhoods of violence and neglect — results from these fundamental drivers of every social condition in our lives. And so does emotional pain. It sounds wild-eyed and radical to blame capitalism, colonialism, and systemic racism or white supremacy for the need for opioids as well as for the raging illicit market and overdose deaths. It *is* radical at least, in the sense that it goes to the real root of the problem.

We need to somehow convince the relatively very small number of largely white, wealthy, abled, solipsistic, and male decision-makers in the world to effortlessly understand and care about the rest of us, to actively want to diminish our pain. Or we need to upend the current structures of power.

Politics have little or nothing to do with the gene variants that made me susceptible to ankylosing spondylitis, or the unnoticed virus that may have triggered the disease, or the migration of immune cells from my gut to my spine, where they have harassed me ever since. But so much of physical and psychological pain, and also our ability to live well despite it and to mitigate its impact on our lives, is a deeply political issue. The interconnected problems of crime, chronic disease connected to poverty, addiction, and mental illness have their roots in the way society has been organized and developed, the way our lives have been shaped by prohibition, capitalism, and colonialism. To prevent and mitigate pain, we need to unmake and remake these structures that shape our destinies, that treat some people, or certain groups of people, as the waste products of society.

By contrast, without changing the relationship of these human beings to power, new pain patients and new drug users will continue to be created.

Rights may one day be given because the powerful suddenly learn to empathize with the oppressed. But then, if my grandmother had wheels she'd be a skateboard. A society in which pain is both rare and more easily managed is one in which workers are paid a living wage; oil is left in the ground so poor and racialized communities won't suffer the ever more dangerous and wide-ranging effects of global climate change; executive salaries are reduced so workers can afford to rest; social welfare programs ensure no family is stretched beyond endurance; and punishment provides no opportunity for profit. Rather than relying on philanthropists and billionaires and the comfortably wealthy to determine how much tax is paid and what it funds, to build affordable housing and fund mental health research, inmates must take charge of the asylum, so to speak. The so-called scum, the dross, the flotsam and jetsam of society—these are the people whose knowledge must drive policy relating to the problems that affect them, with research evidence serving experience rather than presuming to know it.

This is a roundabout way of saying "Nothing About Us Without Us." The phrase, a slogan first used in English[15] by South African disability activists Michael Masutha and William Rowland, has been firmly adopted by drug user movements. Like the disability rights movements with which they overlap, drug user movements are uprisings or organizations of people who are persistently denied the fundamental right to self-determination. They take their bitter experience of being treated as dross—and insist on their rich and precious humanity by whatever means necessary.

Pain, and our experience of pain, must be allowed to guide us in deciding what we need for our own lives. What we need to be well.

Saturnalia

Sick and tired of being sick and tired, eager for glamour, when Sonia and I had the idea to celebrate our twentieth anniversary of friendship with a short trip, I pushed for us to go to the farthest, most outlandishly distant and exciting destination possible. A grudging concession to reality meant giving up on Japan, South Africa, and New Zealand, but I was still keen on Buenos Aires, a thirteen-hour flight.

(My spine used to hurt so much at rest that I dreaded a twenty-minute car ride.)

So we opted for an equally ridiculous plan: six days in Spain, including the overnight flights from Toronto and New York.

(Secretly, I refused to give up on anything. I tucked Buenos Aires away in the mental compartment where I put dreams I intend, although I have no idea how, to will into existence.)

And so, one sombre week after Donald Trump was elected president of the wealthiest and most powerful country in history, I left my family for what was at the time my third and longest solo trip.

(And in fact, things were going a little better. As often happens, time and stability—a break from attacks on my sense of safety in my own body, in my relationships and in my home—healed the open wounds. Efficient, effective reduction of the number of hours spent in serious pain has done much of the rest.)

I fly via Amsterdam to Madrid, where I meet up with Sonia, who has come from New York. The cognitive techniques I have learned, such as distraction and mindfulness, are much more feasible when I don't need to be responsive to young travel companions. I read the news on my phone, I name capital cities starting with each letter of the alphabet, I daydream or I focus tightly on the air going in and out of my lungs. Of course, I also fortify myself for line-ups and the overnight flight with tramadol, Tylenol, and sedating anti-nausea drugs. I could not physically sit still for so long, or stand in one place for so long, without having an adequate dose of the opioid on board. Still, an important analgesic that gets me through the rigours of travel is excitement. With AS under better control, I'm able to get an extra kick of energy out of my sense that I'm realizing a dream that has to do with the kind of person I am. The kind of person who is independent, adventurous, dreamy, and a little glamorous, not to mention privileged with both resources and passport. But really I just want to be reckless. The tingling feeling of being on an adventure hits me the moment I'm in a taxi zooming along the highway to the airport.

Despite the drugs, I pace the aisle and fidget through the night and arrive in Madrid not having slept a wink. This might be the perfect state in which to think from a distance about the coming Trumpian dystopia, to explore the moody, psychologically acute art of Velazquez, El Greco, or Francisco de Goya from the stable vantage point of a bohemian getaway with no responsibilities. Five days of all the intensity of philosophy, politics and art, none of the consequences.

On the plane, I've still got dark thoughts on my mind. If Romantic art and literature capture the highs and lows of pain and pleasure, it is far darker literature — of the twentieth century, for the most part — that better reflects the grinding nature of chronic pain, and the absurd or so-called Kafkaesque experiences of pain patients and people who use illicit drugs. Both, but especially the latter, live in a world governed by capricious rulers and arbitrary laws. The search for relief is inevitably punished, self-determination is impossible, and effects create cause rather than the reverse.

I first saw Eugène Ionesco's *Rhinoceros* as a drama student in high school. It was part of a unit on Theatre of the Absurd, a style of theatre developed in Europe in the 1950s that used ridiculous, repetitive, and absurd situations and characters to explore existential issues and show what happens when there is a breakdown of communication in society, when authority can't be trusted, and when life has no meaning. In Ionesco's play, rhinoceroses represent the infectious nature of mob mentality, in particular the attraction of Nazism in 1930s Romania. The central character becomes paranoically obsessed with rhinoceroses as, one by one, the people around him turn into them.

"An example of collective psychosis, Mr. Dudard," Botard says of rhinoceroses. "Just like religion — the opiate of the people!"

In Nazism, Adolf Hitler likewise created a type of cult or collective psychosis. The comparison with Marx's analogy about opiates stands up, as the Nazis ostensibly sought to replace the moral degeneration of free drug use and loose prescribing of morphine and heroin in the pharmacies with "a transcendental state of being well." In the words of journalist Norman Ohler, who excavated the Nazis' bizarre relationship with drugs in his book *Blitzed*,[1] "They hated drugs because they wanted to be like a drug themselves."[2]

For them, he writes, "there could be only one legitimate form of inebriation: the swastika."[3] And so, when the Nazis came to power in Germany, they initially used racial hygiene laws to carry out a *Rauschgift-bekämpfung*—a war on drugs. Ohler cites reports from staff surgeons to support his assertion that drug users, including long-term pain patients, were sent to concentration camps following a judge-ordered, unspecified-duration confinement of such patients who were found to have unfavourable "hereditary factors" (the others, whose parentage was less suspect or, presumably, more Aryan, were forced through cold turkey withdrawal).[4]

Until this time, German chemical companies had actually been world leaders in the production of morphine, heroin, and cocaine. As in modern-day North America, prescription of psychoactive substances was normalized. Recreational use of drugs, too, characterized the socially progressive Weimar Republic. And in 1925, major companies like Bayer, which marketed heroin, united to form the conglomerate IG Farben—an early, legal example of a drug cartel.

According to the Nazis, the Jewish pharmacist soberly purveyed all this decadence. The focus on evil, conniving personalities is a trope that has powered anti-Semitism since the age when moneylending was one of the few professions open to Jews (like Shylock), and they moved smoothly from being seen as Christ-killers liable to kill Christian children for their blood to being seen as financial parasites, bloodsuckers of a different kind.

And yet, dramatic quantities of alcohol and, later, methamphetamines powered both the euphoric mass gatherings the Nazis liked to hold and the violence in concentration camps, in the streets, and in the battlefield. Ohler demonstrates with glee the way drugs were used by the Führer and the entire apparatus of the Nazi state, from the higher-ups down to soldiers, from concentration camp staff to the prisoners who were experimented upon. Opium may not have been the specific or only opiate of the people, but in practice drugs of many kinds fuelled the Nazis' attempt to "be like a drug."

IG Farben is of course now mostly synonymous not with heroin but with its far more dangerous product, Zyklon B, which was used to gas Jews (including, presumably, the Jewish employees expelled from the company by 1938[5]) and other "degenerates" in Nazi death camps. As part of the IG Farben conglomerate, Bayer officials were responsible for medical experimentation on prisoners at Auschwitz, Dachau, Buchenwald, and other concentration camps.[6]

First among those sent to the Zyklon B showers were mental degenerates, a category that included drug addicts and specifically opioid users, whether prescribed or recreational, and whether or not it was an IG Farben company that hooked them on morphine or heroin in the first place. As Ohler chronicles, in 1935 a Marital Health Law forbade marriage if one partner suffered from "mental disturbance," a category that included narcotics addicts. Another, the Law for the Prevention of Hereditarily Diseased Offspring, explicitly aimed to prevent reproduction by people with addictions. In the first years of the war, unknown numbers of those considered "criminally insane," a category that again included people who used drugs, were euthanized (murdered), sometimes by an overdose of morphine.[7] With similarly absurd irony, the United States, the Department of Justice, and various states have recently considered the use of fentanyl to achieve the same purpose in executions.[8]

Postwar, IG Farben was split up in West Germany. Its successors that have survived to thrive today include, once again, Bayer (they continue to produce analgesics, including Aspirin, Aleve, and the cannabinoid painkiller Sativex), and Sanofi.

Like Hitler, today's admirers of authoritarian leadership — a collection of reckless, bombastic, unpredictable, and irritable men — have a complicated, hypocritical, self-serving relationship to substances, often invoking drug users as bogeymen to support various suspensions of civil rights. In particular, I'm thinking of Rodrigo Duterte, the president of the Philippines. Of Jair Bolsonaro, president of Brazil, and, of course, of Donald Trump, who brought America's excesses, violence, and hypocrisies, long recognized and suffered by the rest of the world, into focus for many Americans for the first time.

I arrive first in Madrid, drinking coffee and chocolate in the airport at what would be my four in the morning. I am wired on exhaustion and excitement and caffeine. When a cab driver says that he can't take me into the city because of something to do with the king, I figure out the metro instead. Riding subways in places that are new to me, figuring it out, feeling competent, noticing the little differences from one city to the next, is one of my favourite things.

It all goes relatively smoothly, although I feel almost dizzy with exhaustion, and I check into our Airbnb. This is my first time using one, and I am confused by the small, chic reception area. Wasn't this supposed to be about staying in a local person's apartment, living like a local, being a virtuous traveller? This, here, is clearly more of a hotel, and it seems I'm never going to meet the person who is officially my "host." Somehow I thought I'd be making adoring Spanish friends. Still, there's a cute antiquated lift and the apartment is stunning.

Later, when we get to Barcelona and come across graffiti that says *Kill the tourists*, I am confused again. I thought I was the good guy! It's not until I get home and notice that Kensington Market, a favourite neighbourhood of mine, is being hollowed out by short-term rentals, leaving working-class residents unable to afford a place to live, steadily increasing the number of people living in the streets, that the penny drops.

The gentrification of neighbourhoods like the ones I stay in in Madrid[9] and Barcelona, or all over Toronto, is related to evictions and homelessness, which is in turn related to an increase in overdose and in the so-called deaths of despair. These trends — worse in North America because of the relatively weak social safety net, among other reasons — have risen in tandem with other trends in capitalism: toward precarious and inadequate work, high rents, low housing security, high academic debt, high medical debt, alcohol use disorder, opioid use disorder, stimulant use disorders, misery, mental illness, and musculoskeletal conditions causing chronic pain. People are being pushed to the edge in multiple ways, making it easy to end up without a place to live, and making drugs sometimes the only peace a person can find. A collusion between real estate industry players and high-level drug trafficking is another aspect common to gentrifying cities, with drug money being laundered in real estate in Vancouver and most likely in Toronto,[10] and vacant flats called *narcopisos* being used in Barcelona[11]:

> Despite recurring calls from the City of Barcelona, many banks and speculative funds engage [*sic*] property mobbing, neglecting apartments that are eventually occupied by drug dealers as a tactic to allowing [*sic*] them invisibly evict tenants and flat owners so that entire buildings can be sold to foreign funds, and rehabbed for wealthy foreigners.[12]

Against this background, we could see opioid use among the poor, as Thomas De Quincey did more than a century ago, as a little wedge of resistance to the ever-more-demanding and ever-more-poorly-compensated demands of work and productive citizenship. Or we can see it as a Band-Aid that covers suffering to allow us to play our assigned role in the labour market. Indeed, opioids are only part of the story. Along with prescription uppers and downers of all kinds, illicit stimulant use is also on the rise. The use of multiple drugs has become common: a way for people to modulate the demands of untenable life circumstances, sleeping despite stress or rising without rest for another day of work at the bottom of the steep socioeconomic pyramid.

We have only this one night in Madrid. I leave my suitcase and a note for Sonia and head out immediately to find *Guernica*, the Pablo Picasso masterpiece that lives in the Reina Sofia museum. I can't go directly to *Guernica* because I have to first get through a multi-room exhibition on the history of art about fascism, of which Guernica is just the most renowned example.

There is a line of thought (and action) about the disposability of different groups of people — with the overlapping categories of drug user, homeless and visibly poor, disabled, and mentally ill being first in line for this ruthless minimalism — that links fascism under Hitler with fascism as it has resurged today.

Authoritarian leaders around the world have, like Hitler, found profit in using the war on drugs to eliminate political opponents and social activists, carry out murders of the most marginalized, and cover up and excuse the excesses of police, military, and paramilitary forces. When Rodrigo Duterte, in the Philippines, talks in one breath of being addicted to fentanyl himself and in the other of murdering drug users, it's hard not to see the scapegoat ritual being literally enacted in this country in which by 2016 some twelve thousand people — including political opponents, poor people, at least fifty children and, presumably, a few drug dealers — had been massacred in extra-judicial killings under the aegis of a war on drugs, the Philippines' jails full to beyond bursting with prisoners. Another prominent politician wrote publicly that year that

> I believe that the Drug Menace is so big it needs a FINAL SOLUTION like the Nazis adopted. That I believe. No rehab.[13]

Shortly after saying this, he was made Philippine ambassador to the United Nations, and then Duterte's secretary of foreign affairs. That particular politician has also paraphrased John Lennon with a call to "Give Fascism a chance." It is, he says, an elegant philosophy.

In Brazil, Jair Bolsonaro likewise admires the fascist, militaristic aesthetic and indulges in a wide range of social bigotries, suggesting that poor people should be sterilized, that drug use causes homosexuality, and that police should happily shoot suspected — never mind proven — drug dealers. In 2019 a member of his military detail en route with him to the G20 meeting in Japan was found with thirty-nine kilograms of cocaine (he was not shot).

For an article I wrote about harm reduction initiatives around the world, I spoke with Leon Garcia, a psychiatrist in São Paulo who worked on a project in which drug users (mostly homeless or barely housed under-thirty-year-olds with serious crack cocaine habits) were asked a rare question: What do you need? Dr. Garcia and the other researchers did not expect the answer they got — "We need homes" — but they set diligently about fulfilling the need, stabilizing their subjects' lives with tiny accommodations in hotel rooms, along with employment. Drug use didn't stop, but it levelled off, and people began to move effectively on with their lives.

Unfortunately, once elected president, Bolsonaro slashed harm reduction programs as he enacted his extreme right-wing political philosophy in which the poor and dependent are not given houses: rather, they may get forced rehab in private, unregulated, and religious "treatment" centres. Dr. Garcia and his colleagues were able to maintain funding for part of their newly housed population. The others, a group that never did well with the chaos of shelters, quickly dropped out of sight.

Beyond the graphic and extreme version of the war on drugs that we see in the Philippines, a similar ritual is carried out in other countries, most notably the United States. Here too, the war on drugs, which has focused on enforcement of low-level drug offences, again targeting the poor and marginalized, has fattened America's prisons to levels of crowding inconsistent with any possible public health goals, causing trauma through families torn apart and children raised without their fathers or mothers. People are held for extended periods without even having been found guilty of a crime, as they cannot post bail; people of colour are dramatically over-represented in prisons; the overdose crisis is fuelled directly as drug users are force-detoxed and then overdose upon getting out. All this sets the stage for further poverty, infection, homelessness, and crime.

According to the Center for American Progress (CAP), one-fifth of American prisoners are serving time on drug charges, and 1.3 million people were arrested for possession in 2015, one every twenty-five seconds,[14] with Black Americans representing only 12.5 percent of substance users but thirty percent of drug-related arrests. Latinos are also dramatically over-represented, and 80 percent of people incarcerated for federal drug offences are either Black or Latino. Canada's drug war may seem a little softer, but our own historical and ongoing oppressions are re-enacted in the enforcement of drug laws. Although we don't keep race-based statistics on arrests, VICE News used Freedom of Information Act requests to discover that while rates of cannabis use are similar among racial groups,

> Indigenous people in Regina were nearly nine times more likely to get arrested for cannabis possession than white people during that time period [2015 to the first half of 2017]. Meanwhile, black people in Halifax were more than five times more likely to get arrested for possessing weed than white people.[15]

All I want, as I race to get through the museum before the tramadol wears off, is *Guernica*. But the range of work is actually compelling, and I slow down to check it out. There is music: the singer and flamenco dancer La Argentinita singing lyrics by Federico García Lorca, who accompanies her on the piano himself. It's an original recording from 1931, five years before the great Spanish poet was, it is believed, shot and killed by Francisco Franco's fascist Nationalist militia. There is a 1938 video of a flamenco dancer, signifying I don't know what, but it sets the pre-war atmosphere.

Further on, a poster shows a hand scratching a red swastika to reveal a green, ghoulish face with blood flowing from its mouth and vacant eye. There's a whole wall of Spanish Communist Party posters illustrated by different artists, each image designed around the hammer and sickle. I feel jittery. Constructivist pamphlets. Surrealist paintings. A delightful Miró. An offset print by Ramón Puyol reads *¡No pasarán! Julio 1936, Julio 1937¡Pasaremos!* (They Will Not Pass! July 1936, July 1937. We Will Pass!) *¡No pasarán!* was the rallying cry of Republican troops defending Madrid against the Fascists, but by July of 1937 García Lorca was dead and Madrid still under siege. And Guernica, a little Basque town, all civilians, had been bombed from the air by the Nationalists and their allies, the Nazis and the Italian Fascists.

At last I make it to the *Guernica* room. The piece is massive. Imagining little Picasso creating this great thing over three intense weeks, you can feel the physicality of it, the immense energy and physical drive to complete the work of simply covering the canvas. But beyond that, what I notice is that there is not a lot of graphic violence in the painting. Rather, there are a few striking scenes that emphasize fear and suffering, focusing on the chaos of war rather than the sadism of it.

The next morning, Sonia and I visit the Prado. Back when I was studying printmaking, I read a book by the marvellous British writer Julia Blackburn, *Old Man Goya*. Between 1820 and 1823, Francisco Goya, the painter and printmaker, created a set of the darkest paintings ever made, painting them in oils directly onto the walls of a house he left soon after.

Some of these works, removed from the walls and given a canvas backing, are here, in a room in the Prado. In *Old Man Goya*, Blackburn, too, visits the Prado:

> Then I was in the rooms that hold the so-called Black
> Paintings lifted from the walls of the House of the Deaf
> Man and fixed on to canvas. I did not yet know that Goya
> was deaf, but I remember it was the sound of the paintings
> that struck me first: a great hollow booming reverberation
> like a mixture of thunder and human voices. And it seemed
> to me then as if it was the paintings themselves that were
> brave; as if they had dared to look into the face of all this
> and had survived.

Finally, we come to the Goya room ourselves. The paintings emerge from a richly hued shadow. They are varied, but all extraordinarily dark, in terms of the palette: all dark golds and yellow ochre, black, grey, and the occasional livid flash of white to highlight staring eyes, or gory red for blood. Unlike Blackburn, for me it is the darkness and the colour emerging from it that strikes me first, before I begin to focus on the figures themselves.

Two men fight to the death, not with swords, but with clubs. They are alone under a bright, cloudy sky in a softly grassy meadow, with the great swing of violence in the full arc of their arms and bodies. A gargoyle-like character yells into the ear of a calmly listening old man leaning on a cane. In *The Dog*, a great area of light goldish tones takes up almost all the space of the painting. The little dog's head almost submerged, near the very bottom, by an expanse of undefined golden brown (quicksand, maybe?) that seems to cover it like a blanket. The creature gazes skyward in a silent, futile plea for rescue.

Despite a mordant sense of humour that can be delightful in his lighter work and that even comes out here, it's natural to see Goya as deeply bitter and a pessimist. He's best understood as a realist, though. He began the Black Paintings, most likely, in 1820, having survived a severe illness of unknown nature in 1819 (his second) thanks to the ministrations of his doctor, a specialist in plagues. Disillusioned with the tumultuous politics of Spain at the time, weary from the traumatic experience of the Napoleonic Wars, and fearful of the return of illness (the first serious sickness left him partly deaf and alienated from the hearing world), Goya retreated to the Quinta del Sordo, a house outside Madrid named not for him but for its previous deaf owner, and began to paint the walls of his dining and living rooms with untitled murals never intended to be displayed or sold.

And here it is, *Saturn Devouring His Children*. The word "Saturnine" means gloomy, melancholic. It's used to refer to a dark expression, like the face of someone who lives with pain, whose internal suffering appears pessimistic and gloomy, a bad attitude that seems both wilful and a deep, inalterable personality trait. The association comes from medieval alchemists who attributed to the planet Saturn a heavy, slow, brooding character that was then said to belong to those born under its astrological sign.

Despite the name, a saturnalia is the opposite of a saturnine state of mind: it's an occasion of wild revelry in which the regular order is subverted: as at the Jewish festival of Purim and similar festivals in other cultures, at the ancient Roman saturnalia rulers were mocked, those without power (children, for Purim; slaves in ancient Rome) were given temporary freedoms and power.[16] Rituals like this are — like the more daily consolations of religion, spectator sports, or entertainment — what Karl Marx called the opium of the people (Marx, of course, was thinking specifically of the palliating but illusory effects of organized religion on the oppressed in his time). Marx's contemporary Sigmund Freud[17] wrote about festivals like saturnalia in his 2013 book, *Totem and Taboo*, noting that they provide a "license for every kind of gratification" within a socially sanctioned framework. It's kind of a case of the exception that proves the rule (of an orderly, hard-working, obedient, and stratified society). Drug users, however, break the contract that lets the poor and powerless enjoy occasional wild celebrations and regular, more sober sublimation in controlled ways. We imagine drug users as saturnaliac. We resent and fear the idea of the high, which can both mask pain and unmask painful truths.

A couple of days later, at an outdoor café table in Plaça del Sol, a tranquil plaza in Barcelona's Gràcia neighbourhood, we talk about Sonia's work in labour organizing and with precarious workers, about the frustrations of my halting writing career. We talk about friendships, and the challenges of long ones. I try to convey to Sonia my feeling of constant struggle and frustration with daily activities, that I am bone tired every single day, that I can't bear the knowledge that I must go home in a few days and start it all over again. That I feel like every bit of joy I have is a guilty, desperate pleasure I have snatched from my life. Sonia asks kind and caring questions and it comes out somehow that I can't actually imagine things becoming easier. That in some way I fear loss as a sort of punishment for ease of the sort drugs provide, or the privileges we're enjoying right now. She suggests, I think, that this vision might be trauma-induced, not real. That even as we oppose injustice, we are still allowed pleasure. I start to cry as I realize I might possibly be wrong that life is about enduring pain. That beauty and pleasure and ease could be rights we're all born with, and not transgressions to be punished by loss.

At night it's easier to accept the vision Sonia and I generate through these long, back-and-forth conversations of a meaningful and joyful life. Easier surrounded by gentle darkness, with the smells of wine and tobacco, fried potatoes and the wet-clay smell of old buildings, and a soft, multilingual murmur of lively, contented conversations in the air, a jingle of dog collars, and clinking of glasses. I write notes to myself: *discuss desire for more pain relief with my doctor; when lonely or sad: read or write; teach the kids to be good travellers; learn about trauma.* We both come home stronger.

Day after day, in the months and years that follow, I remind myself to commit to this vision of creation, of unconflicted joy. And nine months plus one day after that trip, Sonia gives birth to a little girl. The two-part name my friend and her partner give their daughter means "auspicious." And it means peace.

The Saturn of Goya's fearsome portrait is neither saturnine nor saturnaliac. Just as the legend of Saturn, or Cronus, says, he is doing what needs to be done: it having been prophesied that one of his children will overcome him some day (perhaps aghast at his day-to-day cruelty and excess), he takes precautions by mechanically — his face fixed in unresponsive horror even as he does it — swallowing one child after another. His eyes are wide, his hair is wild. He clutches his son tightly by the waist and headless, bloody torso above a cute bum as he stretches his mouth to bite off an arm.

According to text accompanying the painting, "Generally presented as a negative character, here Saturn may personify the markedly human emotion of fear of loss of power."

Saturn Devouring His Children, with this horrifying, mechanical, fearful violence, is a vision of Donald Trump and the concentration camps he set up to counter a bizarre idea of foreign invasion by drug gangs in the form of Central American refugees. But it's equally a vision of Rodrigo Duterte, of Jair Bolsonaro, of the murderous austerity policies that have corroded British life from Margaret Thatcher down.

Or take Grenfell Tower, the substandard social housing complex in a London suburb in which seventy-two people including babies, all what we call "low-income" and almost all people of colour, were burned or suffocated to death in a fire on June 14, 2017. (One survivor was given a suspended sentence after investigators combing through his burnt-out flat found he was producing cannabis oil illegally. Despite the possibility of charges of corporate manslaughter against multiple organizations that failed the tower's residents, at the time of writing no one and no organization has been held accountable; by 2018, journalists were reporting rising rates of alcohol use disorder and exacerbation of existing substance use problems among survivors.)

Adapted to today's world, Goya's Saturn might be a vision of capitalism eating its own, while blaming them for being so tender. It is the cause of the chaos and suffering Picasso portrays in *Guernica*. It is the neighbours hurling insults at people without homes. It is cartels and pharmaceutical companies raking in billions while poor mules spend their lives behind bars, or children being taken from their parents at birth because their mothers use drugs to handle trauma. It is companies that run prisons getting into the homeless shelter business.

It is drug cartels with military budgets and armoured tanks holding shoot-outs with corrupt police while somebody is charged with homicide for sharing drugs or arrested after calling 911 to save a friend's life. It is subsistence crops being sprayed with carcinogenic pesticides in the name of a war on drugs that criminalizes the most vulnerable. It is the least powerful being stripped of every bit of control or pleasure in their lives while the most powerful do what they want to whom they want, even as they lecture the poor on self-control and industry. Here — thoughtless, rapacious, greedy even to the point of consuming its own future — is a system embodied in a person. The stereotype of addiction — in this case, to power and consumption — better embodied than any real human can do.

The one ray of hope lies in Saturn's white staring eyes. Goya's terrifying work is indeed a vision of the fear of losing power, of losing control of the narrative. It's of a horrifying system that knows, deep down, that it is weak.

PART III

THE QUARANTINE OF
THE OPIUM EATER
Notes on Getting Well

This book is dedicated
to everyone who ever
did anything
no matter how sane or crazy
whether it worked or not
to give themselves
a better life.
     —epigraph to Samuel R. Delany's 1979 memoir,
      Heavenly Breakfast: An Essay on the Winter of Love

When Gregor Samsa woke up one morning from unsettling
dreams, he found himself changed in his bed into a monstrous
vermin. He was lying on his back as hard as armor plate,
and when he lifted his head a little, he saw his vaulted brown
belly, sectioned by arch-shaped ribs, to whose dome the cover,
about to slide off completely, could barely cling. His many
legs, pitifully thin compared with the size of the rest of him,
were waving helplessly before his eyes.
    "What's happened to me?" he thought. It was no dream.
    — *The Metamorphosis*, by Franz Kafka[1]

Dependence

I was eleven or fourteen and flying to South Africa. The moving map told us we were off the Cape Verde islands, its little airplane arrow inching toward my grandparents in Johannesburg. I had flown often since infancy, but for the first time I suddenly grasped the situation: there we were in a tiny capsule over the vast Atlantic, with no strings holding us up and no net to catch us. In the same instant that the enormity of it hit me, I realized that it was very, very important to stop this train of thought. If I thought too hard about how vulnerable we were—held up by a few flimsy laws of physics—the fear that would bloom right there would contort my life, which, as adventure and fantasy and even just regular books had told me, was going to be a life of adventure, though I did not yet have a sense of what kind. But I could see the danger of that fear. I felt it, for one trembling second.

I stepped mentally back from the precipice. In the years since, I haven't been able to turn off other fears using sheer willpower any more than I've been able to conquer pain that way. But it worked that one time (plus, of course, I did go on to learn about the mechanics of flight, which is mostly reassuring knowledge).

I am forty years old now, in February of 2018, and life is actually all right. I am on a plane again—on the last leg of a thirteen-hour flight to Argentina. For a week, I will be an artist-in-residence at another print-making studio, this time in Buenos Aires, writing and printing and learning to combine text and image. It's been a couple of years since pain pushed me to nervous breakdown. I still take opioids, and they still work. I close my eyes for a second, to look inward. I seem to feel the tramadol doing its gentle tango on my *mu*-opioid receptors. As a result, I no longer attract attention with my odd behaviour. I sit, imagining myself pacing the aisle the way I would have done a year ago, the exhausted woman who, like Lelena's mother, couldn't stop moving due to pain, like Jacob Marley or the Wandering Jew, cursed to roam without cease, without rest, worn thin as a wraith from endless motion.

Before, I dreaded a half-hour car ride. Opioids have restored my ability to travel, and my ability to rest. The familiar strain tugs at my joints, though. I calculate how many hours have passed and take my morning dose. I'm up to a little white pill and a half at a time now, so I break one in two with my teeth. The bitter flavour thus released has already become a Pavlovian harbinger of relief.

I've always liked bitter, just a little, to bring out the sweet.

The sun has returned and now we are over the Andes. The sky is perfectly clear and we are flying low enough to see the landscape. The view is shockingly dramatic, staggering. And, suddenly, that childhood almost-fear returns and I am convinced we are going to crash and die.

I wish I'd stayed home with my family. No one made me come here; in fact, this trip and similarly glamorous schemes are part of a conscious decision to seize the day—*carpe diem*—prompted by years of limits and fear of the future stoked by the gradual contortion of my spine and by repeated, unwelcome medical news. But maybe I've overstepped. Maybe I'm too greedy. I have trouble not believing I can jinx myself by wanting too much.

I am getting too anxious to concentrate on the book I am reading. There is stupid music on my earphones, not something I want to die to. Ahhh . . . risk is all very well when it's just numbers: you're more likely to die of a heart attack, choking on food, falling down the stairs, or catching a virus than in a plane crash. But I look at those vast, pointy mountains and see there is no possible place to land if something goes wrong.

As anyone would, I now think of Uruguayan Air Force Flight 571, whose survivors in the Argentinian Andes resorted to cannibalism to survive.

These days I do think a lot about risk. I never expected to get an unpronounceable disease. I took anti-inflammatories without questioning the likelihood of side effects that, it turns out, are not all that rare and which badly screwed up my gut and my life. And though I'm a cautious person, I now live with risk by default. If you don't get on a plane, you can't die in a crash (or be forced to eat your cabin-mates). If you don't take an addictive drug you can't become addicted, or overdose.

The supply-side drug policy argument that underpins both the war on drugs and the increasingly restrictive regime for prescription painkillers focuses strongly on theoretical risk, estimated by looking back at a population of people who've used opioids for pain and seeing what percentage are ultimately diagnosed with a use disorder, or what percentage die of an overdose that includes a prescribed or illicit opioid. If you cut off supply, some argue, making sure no one has access to temptation — whether of opioid painkillers or of heroin or illicit fentanyl — potential addicts will instead remain productive and happy workers.

I think of my fractured family, the elements of whom are all home, taking care of each other so that I can go to Argentina. By narrowing my life, pain has forced clarity about my choices. With careful prioritizing; with supportive family; with the various privileges of race and class and citizenship that let me be a traveller for pleasure, not for refuge or exile or work; and with opioids, always opioids, some things have become possible again.

I change the music. Now I'm listening to Jeff Buckley singing Leonard Cohen's "Hallelujah": ethereal voice, soaring chords. I am abruptly distracted from my fear by fascination at the overwhelming grandeur. The sun casts shadows that fall in interesting patterns over the white angles of the mountaintops below us. The mountains are terrifying and magnificent. I feel that swell of well-being I know well. I press my face to the window for the best possible view.

No fear, only wonder.

Hallelujah, sings Jeff Buckley in that transcendent voice of his. Love, Leonard Cohen's lyrics tell us, is cold and broken. And yet despite or even because of all that, it's a joyous paean to God, to life, the hallelujah. Tim Buckley, Jeff's father, died of an overdose of morphine, heroin, and alcohol. Jeff, though, drowned in a perfectly sober accident while on a spontaneous and surely beautiful nighttime swim. You never know. There's risk, and there's failure. And then there's hallelujah.

Cavernous angiomas, or cavernomas, are rare malformations in the brain. I have the hereditary form, both more rare and more dangerous, producing multiple little berries of thin-walled vessels scattered through my brain. It may be that they will never cause problems by bleeding into the fragile architecture of my thoughts and memories, my impulses and desires, my sight and my senses, my pleasure or pain. Or it may be they already have. Cognitive testing shows a dramatic disparity between my results relating to working memory and attention and everything else. Then again, pain can do this too. I think most clearly when tramadol is at its peak; as it wanes, so do my attention and focus. That's my subjective impression, but objective testing shows this as well.

These newly discovered little brain bombs — on my temporal lobe, frontal lobe, occipital lobe, and various other precious parts of my brain — aren't themselves related to ankylosing spondylitis or to opioid painkillers or to depression or to anything else. Yet another one of those things about which you can ask *why me*; or, more reasonably, you can ask *why not?* Why on Earth not me? When struck by the luck of good health or of wealth or of talent, of privilege, being born with the body or race or skin colour or sexual orientation that makes life easier, who asks *why me?* You just take it and run with it.

While these vascular malformations in the brain may grow, their delicate walls slackening, as I age, I must have been born with them: they're a congenital condition. To my list of specialists I can now add an ear, nose, and throat specialist for the (also supposedly unrelated) positional vertigo; a neuropsychiatrist, charged with assessing any damage being done to my treasured circuits; and a neurosurgeon. The last of these doctors is a disconcertingly hearty-looking man who may one day plunge his strong gloved hands into my skull to cauterize or excise a bleeding little brain bomb before it destroys everything in this precious compartment that holds my everything.

Or not. Hopefully not.

I have a panic attack the first day I travel to see him. But nothing happens at that appointment, or subsequent ones. They're just another one of those things, like vertigo, that may leap out and attack me at any time, or that could leave me alone. And for now, I'm very lucky. All that happens, really, is that yet another doctor — at a loss for anything else to say in the face of my anxious wish to know and control my future — tells me to "go and live your life."

Every time I hear that phrase, I go home, eat a big piece of chocolate cake, and then transfer money from retirement savings into my travel fund.

The pain in my spine wakes me in the night. I try every possible position but cannot lie still in any. This distinctly AS sensation feels like having "radioactive badgers and termites chewing on your bones,"[2] an image devised by Dawn Gibson, a patient advocate and writer with ankylosing spondylitis who runs a popular online chat group for people with chronic pain and invisible illness. It is a very good analogy. I can't stay still, I can't stay still. The badgers.

Eventually discomfort outweighs exhaustion.

I clunk out of bed and root around in a coat pocket for my precious plastic bottle. I take my morning dose of the drug just before dawn. I wait.

First I feel an ease creeping into every part of my body. It's as if the very membranes of my cells are slackening, letting down their constant guard. I mean this as an analogy, because this is how it feels as the drug settles in. As it happens, though, the interaction of a drug and the receptor it targets does happen at the level of the cell membrane, as well as within cells, giving rise to research articles and grant applications with marvellously war on drugs titles like "Membrane trafficking of opioid receptors."[3] If they could, I'm sure the DEA would post officers in our very cells to prevent any such thing.

At a slightly less intricate level of analysis, as a result of its embrace of my *mu*-opioid receptors, the opioid inhibits the nerves that produce chemical signals causing my brain to interpret and respond to signals of pain. Smooth muscles throughout my body that would otherwise contract relax,[4] blood pressure drops, respiration slows (not so you'd notice). Because mine is an atypical opioid, norepinephrine and serotonin are also suddenly more available to do their work of transmitting signals along the nervous system, as if I'd taken both morphine *and* one of the class of antidepressants that act on those two brain messengers; Effexor, for example. Then — complete, blissful oblivion as pain retracts its claws and I drift back to sleep. If you haven't spent the better part of more than a decade awake and writhing through the night, its slow seconds stretching out into eternity, you may not appreciate this word: *oblivion*. Even the word itself tastes like honey. The feeling of this nothingness is dark; its sound is sweet.

I wake up with the alarm an hour or so later. There is a feeling of softness, almost a gentle glow in the air. On mornings like these and no others, I get out of bed without my usual grim stretching routine, and breakfast with my family has a light and relaxed feel. The price of this is of course that I run out of tramadol earlier in the day. The bottle says "take three times a day, as needed," but since each dose reduces pain for just five hours, there is still a certain amount of rationing and endurance involved, and endless choices and trade-offs that force me to make constant calculations just to manage daily activities. Still, that tender start seems to make everything run more smoothly. I can depend on it.

The magic pill is how I get to Argentina, and other places before that. Gradually I have extended my answers to the fundamental questions of *how long I can sit?* and *how long I can stand?* After New York City, my first successful "escape" from responsible, normal existence, I start forcing my life into the shape I want, arranging experiences. Until I adapted to pain by using the behavioural technique of pacing myself, effectively restricting my life, I wasn't able to manage it. But with adequate doses of tramadol my reach is far greater before the pain takes over or the energy runs out: work a little more, attend an event, make carefree plans to see a movie, visit a friend rather than relying on people travelling to me for my entire social life. With each new activity, I become more ambitious — and then crash painfully against my physical limitations. A little more opioid provides the surge of energy and ease to again raise the bar. My overall dose remains relatively low and relieves pain for about fifteen hours of every twenty-four, but it's enough to let me spend much less time struggling to get through the hours or to accomplish basic household tasks.

All these years I'd somehow not realized how much function is tied to pain relief. I'd assumed the level of energy and function I had was the limit of what was possible at this stage in my slowly, inconsistently degenerative spine disease. But taking enough tramadol makes all the difference. Now I see that this drug, which doesn't cure, can make the disease less relevant. The secret to greater function lies in taking an adequate dose to cover the pain — not intermittently, not with the ascetic restraint I have practised, but enough that I am rarely aware of pain, don't need to try so hard to rise above it, reframe my thoughts about it, or breathe through it.

I ask the doctor if I can raise the dose in order to meet my goal of working full-time hours at writing again. He knows and I know that while to date I've been able to easily lower or skip my dose without ill effects, suggesting little or no physical dependence, the longer and more regularly I take the drug, the more likely physical dependence — getting "hooked" — becomes.

Doctors and other healthcare professionals as well as patients have been quite rightly appalled by a growing reliance on chemical constraints in psychiatry and in healthcare in general. Often, they serve to replace the chains and manacles of an earlier age in mental healthcare. In fact, since waves of poorly managed de-institutionalization in the late 1970s and '80s, these chemical straitjackets have been employed more and more; in Mike Jay's *This Way Madness Lies: The Asylum and Beyond*, he notes that while de-institutionalization went along with a shift in public attitudes toward what were now seen as horrifying examples of the worst institutional care for mental illness, the closure of public mental health hospitals was in fact "driven by larger and more impersonal forces: economics, and the transfer of healthcare responsibilities from the state to the private sector."[5]

In the place of public asylums, anti-psychotics and sedatives are used excessively on the elderly or children, inconvenient or troublesome populations, and disproportionately deployed against people of colour and Indigenous people. These drugs, along with antidepressants and opioid painkillers, take the place of steady compassion, serious reform, or radical (meaning, you'll recall, "going to the root") responses like giving people housing, fair work, childcare, and other supports that allow them to cope with life and be less likely to be driven off a mental cliff.

There is good reason, moreover, to be appalled at a consumerist society where pharmaceutical and medical-device corporations are able to promote quick-fix solutions to serious social and population health problems, make vast sums of money selling them, downplay risks and play up benefits, and take no accountability for the ways people may be harmed by too much medicine or the wrong medicine. Here, too, psychiatric and other psychoactive medications, including opioids, seductively fill in holes left by trauma or poverty or simply a rotten society, leading to an escalating series of medications, side effects, interventions, and personal and social harms.

Too many medications can interact in unpleasant ways. Too much medication can have unpleasant effects. This is all true. And so we have what's called the "de-prescribing" movement, which suggests that less is more, that we should choose medical interventions with great restraint, that if it ain't broke, don't fix it. I support this informal movement, but it can go too far, expressing a puritanical moralism on the part of the proponent rather than a cautious and wise attitude toward patient well-being. All too often, de-prescribing advocates assume that non-intervention, or non-pharmaceutical intervention, is always a wiser and, significantly, a worthier choice than the disputed intervention. And de-prescribing may invoke highly unscientific magical thinking, where people are asked to leave prescriptions and to deal with the sometimes severe consequences for their well-being by believing they're not really in pain, being told for example to *believe*, and to *keep an open mind*[6] about various forms of brief psychotherapy or mindfulness promoted as evidence-based practices, and so not a matter of faith (and even if their experience after giving it a good try is that, nope, it doesn't work).

Sure, taking a pill to solve a problem is a Band-Aid solution. An easy way out. A quick fix. In my case it is, indeed, a fix.[7]

It's a fix that extends me. The Band-Aid allows me, like nothing else, to cope with the unfair burden of parenting and housework that still falls predominantly to women, providing great fulfillment in many ways but sapping already-limited energy. It's a problem that almost all women writers and other artists with children face even without the exacerbating factors of single parenthood, depression, stiffness, the strange disability of being unable to stand immobile, and pain. The quick fix, several times a day, helps me get a little closer to having it all.

Now that this is my life, I feel affront at caricatures of the 1950s housewives who relied on meprobamate (Miltown) to chill out and sublimate their frustrations. Miltown, the first "minor" tranquilizer, paved the way for other mood-altering drugs, such as Prozac or Valium, that generally preserve alertness and function better than their predecessors. This allowed them to be marketed widely as mild psychiatric medicines, now seen as distinct from (and, despite also causing physical dependence, less morally fraught than) other mood-altering and easily overdosed drugs like opioids and barbiturates.[8] The thing is, short of revolution or cloning myself, I don't have a better solution. And in fact—and this is what we fail to consider when we describe drug use as a misguided coping mechanism, an unsavoury dependence—*there may be no better solution* under the circumstances.

I am not the only person in the world to find better living through chemistry. In a sense, we all do it.

You could picture the human body as a Rube Goldberg machine, with an endless series of cycles and interactions that serve to maintain a dynamic balance, or *homeostasis*. An actual Rube Goldberg machine is a mechanical contraption that does simple things in an absurdly, delightfully complicated way. The absurd complexity is the point and the joy of it. A series of interactions fuel movement through the system, offering suspense and tension, surprise, point and counterpoint, conflict, repetition, variety: all the elements of a great little story. In this story, we're all like little Goldilocks, using the chemicals that make up and fuel our bodies to keep ourselves not too hot but not too cold, not too stimulated but not too sedated, not too wet but not too dry.

Put a marble in the teacup and watch it roll down a hill, landing on a balance that lifts to strike a series of dominoes that fall, sounding out the musical scale, say, and striking a lever that turns on a kettle that boils water for your tea: whatever ridiculous outcome you want. The little steps —one thing does something that triggers another thing that stops another thing that sets off yet another thing—get the job done.

As we've seen, the euphoric effect of opioids result from interactions between our *mu*-opioid receptors and molecules that bind to those receptors—molecules that could be a drug like morphine, or could be the endorphins produced by the body itself in response to pain or stress. This causes neurons to fire in "hedonic hotspots," certain very specific regions of the brain within areas called the nucleus accumbens, the ventral pallidum, and the parabrachial nucleus of the pons, as well as possibly in a couple of other brain regions, reducing the experience of pain and producing that of pleasure.[9] It also continues the domino effect, preventing a neurotransmitter, called GABA, from doing *its* job, which in turn allows for the release of dopamine, a molecule that reinforces the experience of opioids.

Previously, dopamine was thought to be *the* pleasure molecule, until we learned in the 1980s that you can kill an animal's dopamine cells and it will still experience pleasure. If you're a primate like me, for example, you might still enjoy the taste of sugar, like the dark, sweet flavour of the maple syrup I've used to sweeten the coffee I'm drinking as I write this. In fact, dopamine is more of a motivation molecule, encouraging you to keep seeking that good sensation — a learning process that in part explains why addiction has been described as a learning and developmental disorder.[10]

Oddly, there is far more research out there on the neurobiology of addiction, and on the experience of pain, than there is on pleasure, or on the intense feeling of pleasure that we call euphoria. And yet the first definition in English of this word, *euphoria*, has to do with medicine: in a 1706 dictionary, it is defined as "the well bearing of the Operation of a Medicine, i.e., when the patient finds himself eas'd or reliev'd by it."[11] Whether medically induced or not, euphoria is well-being, positive excitement, and happiness. This glorious feeling can be triggered by exercise (not only our endogenous or self-made opioids, but also endogenous cannabinoids and, believe it or not, endogenous amphetamines; each play a role in this); both sexual activity and specifically orgasm; psychoactive drugs both stimulant, like cocaine or crystal meth, and downer, like opioids or alcohol; positive social interactions; romantic love; laughter; making, dancing, or listening to music; mania and hypomania; fasting; and otherwise typically unpleasant medical conditions like migraine, epilepsy, and multiple sclerosis.

Like long-distance running or tasty foods, dancing in a group has been found in experiments to activate endorphins, reducing our experience of pain. The way researchers figured this out is by giving some patients naltrexone, which blocks endorphins. When this drug was administered in one of these studies, not only did the dancers miss out on the reduction in pain that is part of an endorphin high, they actually experienced greater pain.[12]

When you experience trauma or intense stress — or dancing — your body releases endorphins, diminishing your awareness of pain and in particular dampening socially stressful perceptions such as rejection. Those who are chronically stressed — in particular, people who experienced adverse childhood experiences such as maternal separation, displacement, deprivation, abuse, or death of a parent — may show greater sensitivity to rejection of various kinds. In fact, early childhood trauma can result in a tendency to release cortisol, the "stress hormone," in response to situations where others might not feel as stressed. Cortisol, an important player in the constantly dynamic body machine, provokes release of our self-made opioids. Rejection can be intensely painful, and chronic endorphin release can promote a sense of detachment or numbness. In animal models, at least, opioids such as morphine can essentially fill in for the social connection that is vital, biochemically speaking, for development. Likewise, when a human infant is born physically dependent on opioids due to exposure to the drugs in utero, the best treatment for the pain of withdrawal they experience is close contact with mom,[13] sometimes with tiny doses of morphine gradually tapered down until mother love fills the gap. (Horribly, a more common response is for babies with this condition, neonatal abstinence syndrome, to be removed from their mother's arms and custody, often permanently. This sets up a lifetime, and even lifetimes, of trauma for both parents and children that plays out in behaviour and in biochemistry alike.)

People who respond intensely and needily to opioids might not be suffering from too few endogenous opioids but from too much stress (and, of course, those whose lives began in trauma or adversity all too often endure further adverse experiences at every step as they grow into adulthood).

"For me," writes Joe in one of our frequent direct message exchanges,

> sober is a miserable state, anxious, light sensitive, on my
> toes. [...] Part of it is how sharp my vision is. When I'm
> cold sober everything feels like the Sharpness setting is
> too high. Things are soft and a bit fuzzy optimally. [...]
> High is relaxed and calm (sort of, as much as I get). I can

feel a slight swimmy feeling in my head when I'm "right."
I guess I've reached a point where it takes a fair amount of
"high" to get normal again. Now, tell a bunch of sobriety
purists you like your head a little buzzy and watch them go
apeshit about how you're not really living.[14]

Imagine being the only one in pain in a world of people happily dancing. Of course not everyone will find their way to opioids as a solution. But for those who do, homeostasis — balance — feels restored. Here's Joe, again (I added the italics at the end):

I'm definitely high, no denying that. I could go shopping,
do physical labour, or probably even handle a job interview
like this. Few people would know I was high except to see
my pupils, but that wouldn't grab most people immediately.
[...] I'm definitely intoxicated, but after decades of practice
I'm fully functional like this. Sober or not? [...] Thing is
I don't really feel life sober, I have really bad PTSD, I feel
pain and fear, coupled with an exhausting kind of hyper
awareness that takes boatloads of energy to maintain. Is
that normal?[15]

I begin to notice, as I speak with people who use drugs, that many of them — whether current users or former — talk about heroin saving their lives, or keeping them from suicide. The association of heroin with love is not new, the seduction of it, but all we hear about the drug is that it leads to death. So why, I wonder, do so many insist that at an especially low and vulnerable time in their adolescence or early adulthood, heroin stopped them from killing themselves, that it kept them from despair? Turning the question around, I start to ask myself, why don't we simply *believe* people when they say this? Is it possible that what people say about the most important good and bad feelings of their lives is true?

I'm lying flat on my face. If my vertebrae eventually fuse completely, daily prone lying is supposed to ensure they do so in a sort of straight rather than bent-over way. After a while my spine begins to hurt, to feel as if it's being extended backward rather than simply lying flat. But sometimes it does feel like a healthy routine, kind of like a siesta. Upon getting home from my morning of café writing and painstaking exercise, I collapse onto the bed with relief. Today, though, when I try to get up, I find that I can't. I can't figure out how to move.

My body has become heavy and weak, my muscles painful. I feel profoundly bad. Perhaps I have the flu. I have a phone interview, in an hour, with an organization interested in having me as a keynote speaker — to talk about prescription opioid use, and how sparing pain relief has allowed me to ward off dependence, and how despite my worries, my opioid story is working out okay. It really feels like I have the flu. I think I had better cancel the call. But the phone is miles away.

Time passes, horribly. Everything hurts. This is not the usual, specific pain from inflammation in my spine and shoulders, which is accompanied by stiffness. *Everything* hurts. Back hard as armour plate. And at last it dawns on me: I forgot to take tramadol this morning in my usual stiff-jointed rush to get everyone out the door. It has now been nearly eighteen hours since my last dose the night before.

It doesn't *feel* like I can't get up; I try and it turns out that I actually can't, as if there were weights pinning me down on the bed. I'm a turtle on its back, a giant beetle, a ninety-one-pound beached whale, Gregor Samsa.

With painstaking effort, I force myself to turn over. Blindly, I reach beside my single bed — when we left the pest-ridden apartment in which my marriage ended years before, I opted for floor space over mattress space. I feel for the coat I took off just before collapsing here. It takes every bit of willpower I have to complete this small action. My fingers scrabble in my pocket for the little bottle, I swallow the bitter pill and a half without sitting up, I wait. The metamorphosis that occurs as the drug is gradually absorbed through the gut feels slow, but from outside it would seem like an astonishing transformation. I'm glad there's no one here to see it.

Five minutes before the scheduled interview, I feel power returning to my limbs and I haul myself vertical. I'm like a Rose of Jericho, the "resurrection" plant that unfurls from a miserable, desiccated ball when placed in a dish of water. The effect is as magical as my helplessness was pathetic, and frightening. I make it to the phone, which is now less than a metre from my bed. I talk my way competently through the interview.

It seems right that "metamorphosis" and "morphine" should share a root to do with shapes and creation (the name of Morpheus, the god of dreams, means maker of shapes, while metamorphosis refers to changing shape or form). I have changed, been reshaped, into a machine that runs on morphine.[16]

So. So now I run on opioids. Chugga chugga choo chooooo. Okay. A new stage. Something else to adapt to. With a degenerative disease, adaptation's the name of the game. Just when I think I'm on stable ground, there's some new rumble and shift, and here I am, reeling again. But when it comes to opioids, specifically, I'm also easing into a trope. "One morning you wake up sick," writes William Burroughs in his prologue to *Junky*, "and you're an addict."[17] Throw a stone into a pool of newspaper articles about addiction and you'll hit a million headlines that say the same.

American psychiatrist Karl A. Menninger wrote, not about drugs, specifically:

> When a trout rising to a fly gets hooked on one and finds
> himself unable to swim about freely, he begins with a fight
> which results in struggles and splashes and sometime an
> escape. Often, of course, the situation is too tough for
> him. In the same way the human being struggles with his
> environment and with the hooks that catch him. Sometimes
> he masters his difficulties; sometimes, they are too much for
> him. His struggles are all that the world sees and it naturally

misunderstands them. It is hard for a free fish to understand
what is happening to a hooked one.[18]

In general use, we understand the term "hooked" to refer to being
psychologically drawn back to a drug, over and over, despite great harm.
To flailing, a junkie trout caught on a heroin hook. We *also* use it to
describe physical dependence resulting in withdrawal symptoms. To most
people, the distinction doesn't matter: you act like an addict, so you must
be hooked. Or you're hooked, so you must be an addict. In fact you must
act like an addict. However you act. 'Cause you're an addict. 'Cause you're
hooked.

But despite his first-hand experience, Burroughs is — most people
are — wrong. You can wake up sick and not, in fact, "be an addict."
Menninger, though, is right. A person's struggles are all the world sees,
and, as we have seen throughout this book, it misunderstands them, and
journalists reporting on substance use and poverty issues feed public opinion, reinforcing and perpetuating that misunderstanding. And the history
of prohibition and the roles that the disciplines of medicine and criminal
justice have each played in shaping our understanding of the harms, benefits, and effects of substance use have made it impossible to see clearly and
with true balance.

My own experience of using a legal opioid in a non-disordered way,
and then what I have learned about the strikingly similar subjective
experiences of people who use maintenance doses of illicit opioids (and
so are inevitably considered to be addicted to their drug), has made me
increasingly question whether we even know what we mean by addiction,
and whether we're properly understanding the relationship between
opioids and the struggles of people who use them.

I *still* do not have an opioid use disorder, nor do most long-term, daily
prescription opioid users — even though now I, like most of them, have
a level of physical dependency. If we stop using the drug suddenly, we'll
experience withdrawal symptoms, like my sudden "flu" and far worse.

The fact that having such symptoms and trying to regain access to
the drug so closely resembles the symptoms of opioid use disorder can be

interpreted in different ways. Perhaps psychological compulsion to use a drug—even when that has profoundly negative effects on our lives—is really just a social construct, determined by a combination of physical dependence and reduced access. Or, perhaps, a pain patient who loses access to the drug and chooses to replace it in the illicit market or tries desperately to restore access is in fact addicted—was, perhaps, addicted all along.

I try to imagine what would happen if I were no longer allowed to use tramadol. Surely I would just return to the miserable, martyr-like existence I lived before? Think positive, reduce my activities, get into prayer? Or, now that I am learning more about illicit drugs and have started forming friendly relationships with former and even current drug users, would I cross the line? Is that choice what determines whether my physical dependence is an addiction? How, in that case, can we distinguish being "hooked" from the natural, admirable human impulse to improve one's condition?

Since cannabis has become legal for recreational use in Canada, attitudes that used to be deeply hidden can now be paraded on TV shows or podcasts, on social media posts, in the most casual conversation (though freedom to share without repercussions continues to depend on your race and other issues). No longer is it shameful to say, "I'm feeling anxious, so I'll just smoke a little weed to calm down." It's the same with caffeine, where caffeine dependency or coffee addiction jokes are a morning office staple; or alcohol, where "wine o'clock," "mommy juice," and other jokes about alcohol and parenting are ironic but unrepentant declarations of psychological dependence on a habit-forming substance.

Scientists are still teasing out the details of the vastly complicated ways that opioids affect us. It does seem, though, that being physically dependent—"wired" to your drug, is how illicit drug users put it—changes you in some basic ways. Studies in rats, for example, seem to show a difference between rats who have never taken an opioid and those who are dependent, like me, and who are then deprived of the drug until they go into withdrawal. They differ in the way opioids cause the brain to release the chemical messenger dopamine in a specific region.[19]

Physical dependence isn't a great thing—mostly because it makes me dependent on my prescriber and pharmacist, in that sense leaving me less in control of my own life. And if, on the balance, it were making my life worse, it might be worth trying to get off tramadol (which, if done gradually, will not trigger either withdrawal symptoms or cravings). But since I've already tried all other treatments for pain and have gotten back so much function from this drug and nothing else, there's no real reason to do so. It's not a cure, so if I'm not taking it, I lose the pain relief that has allowed me to reclaim so much of my life. The price of that greater control of my life is this need to ensure that, as for someone dependent on heroin — or on any other substance that produces physical dependence, including medications like benzodiazepines, anti-epileptics, and antidepressants in addition to every opioid, from codeine to methadone — my source remains stable. Is it possible that the behavioural aspects that make up a diagnosable substance use disorder are merely predictable artefacts of a situation where dependent people are deprived of the drug they physically require? That people with addiction to opioids like heroin or illicit fentanyl are really just physically dependent but denied a level of access I have to the drug I need?

Is it possible that addiction to a drug like heroin, as the pathology that ties into all the stereotypes we as a society hold about the personalities and motivations of drug users, doesn't really exist? Meg, my interview subject-turned-friend who is dependent on illicit fentanyl, has been wondering exactly this. Our first meetings coincided with us each starting to gain confidence in our instincts on the issue. She says that while she has been truly addicted to cocaine, her need for opioids is a different beast. She distinguishes between self-medication of trauma and pain, and addiction. Increasingly, and although, like her, I'm still trying to put words to the observations and thoughts shaping this distinction, I'm inclined to agree.

Everyone is talking at the same time and their words are rattling around my head, banging inside, shouting back and forth like someone's playing a mad game of squash in my skull. I feel this sense of urgency, of emergency. It's an urgent emergent submergent situation. I'm submerged in it, choking.

Or I'm a stringed instrument but all the strings are fraying. All seventeen of my lovely children are asking me to do things, listen to things, help with things. All of them at once. Someone has me by one ear, someone by the other, and they pull in opposite directions. *Please lower your voice*, I say, trying to hide the tension as I speak, but the voice is like a fork scraping a plate, a full set of nails scraping a blackboard; someone is throwing their entire weight at my ear drum like a horde of taiko drummers. I just want it to stop, I need it to stop. Stop stop stop. I am a wire and I am going. To. Snap.

I hear myself in the sudden silence.

Even the quiet reverberates, every vibration magnified a thousand times.

I'm a monster (late for my dose).

When does a friendly acquaintance become a friendship? Since I met Meg last year, she has come in and out of my life. My close friends Sonia, Sven, and Fred — all in different countries from me — do the same. Not the sort of friends who are there, even if just by text, every day (which is still a thing I don't seem to do well without), but intense and deeply caring and present when they drift back into my orbit. That's one kind of friendship, the travel kind. Always there to be picked up when you are in the same city. Always with a genuinely warm and happy feeling when you connect long-distance from time to time. The difference with Meg, compared to my other friends like this, is that we live in the same city, if in two often different realities. And that if I don't hear from her for a long time, I start to worry that something has gone horribly, fatally wrong.

It's different with Joe, who, although it's almost only and comfortably a virtual relationship, is someone I touch base with very regularly. He's never intrusive, always busy trying to keep the chaos of his own life under control, but around, mild and friendly. Other than us both knowing Meg, having each met her in person at around the same time, we have no friends in common and no stake in each other's lives. I was touched when, during the COVID-19 pandemic, he offered to walk across town to bring me alcohol wipes, which I need for my immune injection and that were on back order everywhere I looked. Maybe he warmed toward me when I first started to use the word *friend*, clarifying: You are not my source, you are not my story. You are my friend and the friendship comes first. We have had some intense, real-time written conversations about our inner lives, about relationships, about failures, about childhood. But most often, I ask about his spoiled, beloved orange cat, and he suggests kitten-wrangling strategies once I get my own. I get his update on the latest outrageous neighbour behaviour; he asks how I'm feeling—"How's by you?" he asks, if we haven't spoken in a while. We talk often about poverty and Toronto's accelerating affordable housing crisis. We talk quite often about drugs. We may, sometimes, move into a longstanding semi-argument where he tells me that if he has opioid use disorder, so must I.

He is wrong; I do not meet the criteria to consider my opioid use pathological, a disorder. But he is also right. Joe is another user who seems to blur the neat boundaries we'd like to draw between recreational and medical use. He was originally prescribed OxyContin for back pain resulting from hard manual labour. A quick study, he figured out right away that the medication worked like nothing else to soften the anxiety and depression and other symptoms of complex PTSD (C-PTSD), a type of post-traumatic stress syndrome that arises from severe or chronic trauma. So for greater effect, he snorted the drug, determining the dose that worked for him and allowed him to manage work far better while high than not, including in finicky, detail-oriented jobs like working for a locksmith.

The only reason he is treated as someone with a drug problem rather than as a pain patient is because he made the sensible decision not to move on to street drugs when his supply of prescription opioids was cut off. Instead, he sought a safer alternative: medication to treat addiction. But choosing to enter the shady, unregulated world of addiction treatment has subjected him to medications that produce side effects no one seems to care about, to humiliating rituals of control and surveillance, to untreated pain, and to dehumanizing treatment in a system where poor people get poor treatment (even here in Canada).

Being high, for Joe, means his medication is having an effect. And the effect means that he is well, not subject to the litany of symptoms brought on by abandonment, poverty, domestic violence, and nightmarish instability from childhood on:

> For me high is medicinal, as is the case for millions if not actually billions of humans. Life is rough for most of the species, a really privileged few "don't need drugs to enjoy life" because they're lucky enough to have "enjoy life" on the fucking menu in the first place. I have no idea what that's like, thinking I could just have it all at my fingertips if I just quit using drugs. I have quit, the list of options never expanded to include Be Infuriating Happy Go Lucky Dickhead With Zero Perspective. If life is so kind to you that you don't have to cushion the blows with a few milligrams of bioactive potential obliviousness then more power to you, and more available dope for me. I don't particularly want to have to stretch the dwindling supply any thinner. Just don't expect the same from all of us, we don't all stumble on the Happy Sobriety that is in far shorter supply than dope.[20]

When I met him, Joe was languishing on his addiction medication, a buprenorphine formulation that had left him badly underweight and sapped of energy. When he switched to methadone, the entire mood lightened. Still, what he feels would really work to let him live well with opioid dependency — a condition he intends to maintain until he dies because he considers it psychologically beneficial — would be an opioid like the ones he started with: oxycodone, or morphine, or hydromorphone. Though he has not had regular access to drugs like these in years, he believes that if he could return to them he would be more functional, more able to participate in society, more able to work. This personal testimony is the sort of thing typically discounted and flattened under the narrative of the pain patient who got hooked (or of the junkie whose explanation for why he uses is always assumed to be a cover for something else).

If he could manage his complex post-traumatic stress disorder and chronic pain, he would like to study to become a veterinary technician. Having spent his post-secondary years incarcerated, and confident in his intelligence, he has no particular interest in getting the high school diploma he didn't collect. But now he imagines supporting himself and his partner, rather than struggling to survive, and doing so by working with animals like his cat, which he rescued from under a truck as a kitten.

Joe would do anything to be able to get back the self he had when he had access to "real" opioids. Anything except risking fentanyl-contaminated street opioids. But to be prescribed real opioids, you need to have a worse case of opioid use disorder than he is considered to have. How would you demonstrate that you are sick enough with addiction to qualify for an opioid substitution program? Well, you'd be someone who persistently uses street opioids.

What Joe thinks he needs doesn't come into it.

No, he mustn't think about it, or indeed about anything,
and especially not about heroin, because heroin was the only
thing that really worked, the only thing that stopped him
scampering around in a hamster's wheel of unanswerable
questions. Heroin was the cavalry. Heroin was the missing
chair leg, made with such precision that it matched every
splinter of the break. Heroin landed purring at the base of his
skull, and wrapped itself darkly around his nervous system,
like a black cat curling up on its favourite cushion. It was as
soft and rich as the throat of a wood pigeon, or the splash of
sealing wax onto a page, or a handful of grass slipping from
palm to palm.

The way other people felt about love, he felt about heroin,
and he felt about love the way other people felt about heroin:
that it was a dangerous and incomprehensible waste of time.[21]

Every opioid user with whom I've shared this excerpt from Edward St. Aubyn's autobiographical series of novels agrees: he has perfectly captured the feeling of heroin. The metaphor of the chair leg, in particular. Heroin (or fentanyl, or morphine, or hydromorphone, or Vicodin, depending on who you talk to) perfectly fills in what is necessary and missing. It lets them stand.

I understand it too. I don't know what is missing for me. I don't think that my pain medications instantly filled in a hole that was always empty in my life. But as someone who often experiences a gaping emotional void, I too enjoy the clear calm, like a still blue sea, that comes from satisfied *mu*-opioid receptors. Endorphins give this feeling; comfortable love gives this feeling; the absorption of writing or walking or art gives that healthy clarity, that *right*ness — and so do opioids.

Without the drug, you are gravely sick: physically sick, emotionally sick, and in a pain that spans the two. Once the opioid molecules bind cozily back to your starving opioid receptors, you are restored to function and health. You rejoin the dance.

No wonder the slang phrase for relieving opioid withdrawal by taking opioids is "to get well." As an outsider to the world of illicit drugs, at first I thought the phrase was ironic. But it is used literally, not for tragicomic effect, and for good reason. Once physically dependent, without the drug you really are sick, and it is impossible to carry on a normal life while seriously ill.

In the early hours, you wake with withdrawal already setting in. Having, if you are lucky, slept away four or six or eight hours on the street, you're now on the clock. You have a dangerous deadline, measured in hours, to acquire the drugs that will keep you well. Much petty crime as well as armed robbery charges relate to this frantic search.

In an unremarkable building in a suburb of Canada's capital city, the patients at the managed opioid program (MOP) run by Ottawa Inner City Health (OICH) are able to sleep in for the first time in years.

The twenty-one clients of the MOP program all have severe, longstanding opioid addictions. Each of them has endured multiple, agonizing, unsuccessful attempts at traditional twelve-step rehab programs, detox, and other addiction treatments such as buprenorphine or methadone. They have also all experienced chronic homelessness. These people, all of whom tested positive for viral hepatitis and many of whom are HIV positive, are at the highest possible risk of overdose death. The illicit drug supply in Ottawa, as elsewhere in Canada and the United States, is dangerously unpredictable and contaminated. Not using opioids is not a realistic option. They have tried, and tried, and tried.

(We say "they failed the treatment," just as, in order to qualify for insurance for my expensive immune suppressant medication, I first had to "fail" two trials of anti-inflammatory medications. My failures involved the drugs making me very sick, with effects that lingered for years. A "failure" of addiction treatment, by contrast, all too often leaves the patient dead. It is high time we put the responsibility where it belongs: the treatment failed the patient.)

Under treatment here at the MOP, the lives of these formerly homeless, deeply drug-dependent people first become stable, and then begin, tentatively, to expand. Hours of the day that were once spent seeking drugs, a task requiring more energy and focus than any CEO's long day in the corner office, now weigh on them. Gradually they begin to fill up the time with activities: volunteer work, playing guitar, learning basic life skills that life never gave them a chance to acquire, reconnecting with family—estranged children, aging parents—and, mercifully, catching up on many years of lost sleep.

But treatment here does *not* mean getting off drugs. On the contrary. These patients are, in fact, provided with high doses of hydromorphone. It is prescribed to them, and they inject it up to seven times a day, in addition to long-acting morphine that they take orally. MOP residents are all on different schedules for their injections, but with nurses available twenty-four hours a day, seven days a week, they can take their dose whenever they need to. Acquiring drugs no longer requires committing a crime, hustling, waiting in agony for a dealer to respond, or taking public transit while in full withdrawal. Instead, MOP clients leave their individual bachelor apartments and pad down to take their shot at their convenience, without ever leaving the safety of their first home in many years.

The MOP is the brainchild of a celebrated Ottawa doctor named Jeffrey Turnbull, who I mentioned earlier with his analogy of addressing traumas gradually, as if you were peeling the layers off an onion. Before he developed this program, Dr. Turnbull co-founded OICH and their equally controversial managed alcohol program (MAP). That program, started officially in 2001 after a few years of preparation, and inspired by a small initiative in a Toronto shelter that in 1995[22] became the world's first MAP, reduces binge drinking and prevents life-threatening alcohol withdrawal by providing small amounts of wine every hour to people with severe alcohol use disorder. The MAP has been incredibly successful in helping people with chronic, very serious dependence on alcohol to gain stability in their lives and make substantial improvements in their overall health. People like the late Inuit artist Normee Ekoomiak, a survivor of Canada's infamous residential schools whose work hangs in both the Canadian Museum of History and OICH's office, and who was Dr. Turnbull's first MAP patient, his artwork a colourful reminder of the value of this slow, multi-faceted approach to addiction that focuses on gradually rebuilding shattered lives, very gently unpeeling that onion of pain — rather than on saying no to drugs. People who previously resorted to drinking mouthwash can turn their attention to other things.

The MOP arose after Dr. Turnbull began to wonder if the initially counterintuitive practice that works so well with MAP — simply giving a substance-seeking, substance-dependent person a quality-controlled version of the very substance they are seeking — could work for opioid-addicted patients as well. Since opioids involve similar issues of both physical and psychological need for the drug on which the person is dependent, it makes sense that it might. The drugs prevent the withdrawal symptoms an opioid-dependent person would otherwise experience when attempting to leave off street opioids like heroin and illicit fentanyl. The additional benefit for opioid users that isn't an issue for the alcohol-dependent is that a prescribed opioid is legal. A prescription for the opioid they can't do without instantly releases them from the need to commit crime, whether in acquiring the drug or in using it. They can begin to disentangle themselves from the criminal justice system and the many ways it can wrap itself around a person's throat—especially a person with few economic or social resources, especially a racialized person—and not let go.

Unlike the addiction treatment medications buprenorphine or methadone, though, hydromorphone doesn't just quell withdrawal. It is a full opioid agonist: it gives users a similar high to heroin.[23] As Stephanie Muron, the nurse coordinator for the program, told me when I interviewed her for an article[24]—initially provoking a real sense of shock I had to hide—"We *want* them to feel some kind of rush."

Regardless of my tender sensibilities, this is essential. The goal is to support patients in abandoning the contaminated, untrustworthy illicit opioid supply, rather than in setting abstinence-based goals that are then routinely broken because the patients are not able or willing to meet them. Methadone or buprenorphine, of course, are effective, life-saving, and well-evidenced treatments for many opioid use disorder patients. But other opioid users in treatment routinely supplement these prescribed medications with street opioids because although methadone and buprenorphine prevent withdrawal, they don't provide the high. If an opioid like hydromorphone, morphine, heroin, or fentanyl is the medicine that "gets you well," these treatments can be a pale substitute for what you really need.

Ideally, in fact, the MOP would actually use prescription heroin (diacetylmorphine or diamorphine); hydromorphone is a substitute that simply has fewer legal barriers to make it accessible (in Canada, as in a number of other countries but in contrast to the United States, there is very limited access to prescription heroin, or diacetylmorphine). Currently just a few programs use it; most notably, the very successful, very hard-to-access Crosstown Clinic in Vancouver. In part, the inexplicable lack of expansion of a highly effective program has to do with red tape, and with stigma. But there is also the fact that in Canada there is no domestic production of opium,[25] whether to ensure a reliable, domestic supply of essential painkillers or to provide this addiction treatment. It must be imported from Switzerland, even though opium poppies are grown illegally by poor farmers in Mexico, and eradicated enthusiastically by Mexican troops, whose war on drugs efforts have been funded, equipped, and trained in large part by the American government.[26]

In the managed opioids program, drug-seekers are supplied with safe access to something very like the drug they are seeking, while simultaneously addressing their other basic human needs: for shelter (residents rent their own apartments in the MOP building), companionship, healthcare, safety, respect, and privacy. It's a bizarrely straightforward solution.

I speak by phone with a couple of people in the program, and they tell me about how their lives are, well, ordinary now. Heartbreakingly so. Ricky Bélanger, who used heroin and morphine for fifteen years and has overdosed numerous times, is now gradually reconnecting with both her children (she's actually a grandmother) and her parents. When I spoke with her, she was babysitting a puppy. She no longer buys opioids on the street at all.

But this is not a story of recovery, at least not in the conventional sense. For Bélanger, a better life also — and, quite frankly, most critically — includes those multiple daily injections of prescribed opioids. These keep her from resorting to a ubiquitously adulterated street supply and from breaking the law constantly in order to meet her brain's persistent need for the drug.

Injecting with nurse-approved technique in a safe place surrounded by caring people and then returning to your stable, affordable apartment — I can't see how that doesn't represent recovery for Bélanger, who lived on the streets through Ottawa's freezing winters and broiling summers. A number of MOP participants ride bikes from their quiet residential neighbourhood back downtown, where they volunteer at the supervised injection site where their less fortunate peers must still inject or snort illicit, unpredictable drugs.

Dependence is in fact the least of Bélanger's problems, and dependence on opioids, far from being an obstacle keeping her from fulfilling her potential, has become one of many supports that together allow her to have an increasingly good life. The obsession with abstinence forces endless, unnecessary struggle and death.

The dichotomy isn't between addiction and abstinence. It's between chaos and stability.

But although this is a very resource-intensive program, since nurses are available to supervise injections twenty-four hours a day, it's not the cost of the program that anyone expects to be controversial. Rather, it is the idea that people who use illicit drugs are allowed to get high.

If it's that hard to accept the abundant hard evidence that medication involving opioids might be the best treatment available for people with a diagnosis of opioid use disorder, imagine how much people struggle with the idea that patients — junkies, addicts, society's dross — might in any way enjoy the experience. While the rates of adherence and improved quality-of-life measures with programs that provide full agonist opioids like hydromorphone or heroin are exceptionally high — seemingly[27] higher than for the less-euphoric opioids methadone and buprenorphine — they are seen as radical and last-resort programs even where they are offered (not in the United States, at all).

At the time I wrote my article about the MOP program, opioids were dispensed, and injections supervised, by a nurse. By the time I followed up with Dr. Turnbull a year later, they'd relaxed the rules somewhat. Dispensing had become more flexible and responsive, with patients able to take their medication with them if they were visiting a friend, for example, or needed to take a dose at work. Increasingly, adult patients are treated like adults. It's not that they have earned some previously unearned right to be trusted or treated with dignity. It's just that the program has matured.

And the drug they are taking retains its function. "Opioids," one patient who asks to just be identified as "R" tells me, "make me not want to kill myself" — yet another of the many people who have told me the same. He explains that they're "not just a drug, they're a tool." R has flourished here, practising guitar and volunteering downtown at a supervised injection site. Although healthcare providers have emphasized to me the importance of abandoning the sometimes-transactional relationships of life on the street in order to recover from opioid addiction, R is clear that he remains friends with the people he was friends with before. But he doesn't have to keep up any less genuine interactions now.

For someone who struggles with himself enough that suicidality is a constant, R took an amazing step by agreeing to our telephone interview: he has become a patient representative, speaking freely about the program to journalists like me, and advancing patients' perspectives with program staff, resulting in changes that allow the program to better meet residents' needs.

Which is what the MOP is all about.

Meg and I meet regularly now, not for me to interview her, but as, yes, friends. If I have planned better than the first (and second) time, I'm able to sit comfortably through the few hours we spend together, and to focus and interact without disappearing into pain and compulsive stretching.

Despite her newfound housing stability, Meg is barred (like me, only far worse) from regular life by the need to get home for a quiet injection of a drug that is barely keeping her going. She is waiting to get onto a program with the potential to change her life in a way that even stable housing could not do.

Sometimes her dope isn't the good stuff. Sometimes she's on a four-hour leash with fentanyl cut with benzodiazepines and caffeine. On these occasions, she is the one who starts showing the subtle signs of back pain before I do. She has learned, just like many pain patients, to hold most of what she is feeling inside, like a cat. But I easily catch the surreptitious stretching, since she looks like I always feel. It is also difficult to hide the slight sheen of sweat as withdrawal symptoms set in.

What do you depend on, I asked.

"I am dependent on my family and it is my favourite dependency as my family deeply supports and cares for me and I love to do the same," wrote Jordan, a young man in his twenties who injects stimulants and opioids, from his family home in Edmonton, Alberta. Jordan was also, he told me, dependent on an indifferent boyfriend, and on the doctors, nurses, and pharmacists who prescribe opioids to him as an addiction treatment, replacing much though not all of his illicit supply and reducing his risk of overdose death.

It was a revelation for Jordan when he first discovered drugs as a teenager. Those early experiences with ecstasy, or MDMA, which, like cannabis, he discovered before moving to so-called hard drugs, came as a sudden relief from a lifetime of emotional struggle. It was, he tells me, "an indescribable and relieving feeling of calmness without the constant thought and brain fog I was used to due to the intense depression and anxiety I experienced daily." Like many people who use drugs, Jordan now uses uppers (like methamphetamines or cocaine) and downers (like opioids) to modulate his mood and activities, the way users of more conventional drugs start the day with coffee and end it with a glass of wine:

> I am dependent, I believe, on the opioids for filling up
> that space for where people were meant to be validating
> of my existence growing up but instead invalidated it
> and traumatized that space, so somehow the opioids fill
> that spot to grow from, a space where I dont need to die
> to escape my life, I can face it and the speed of cocaine
> gives me that energy kick and drive and focus to then do
> what I need to do.

It was when he was able to access Edmonton's iOAT program — injectable opioids that are prescribed as a treatment for addiction — that Jordan became able to live in a less chaotic way, to begin repairing relationships, to abandon risky work environments, and to move on with his life after so many unstable years. Like R, he's returned to old creative loves, rediscovering passions for singing, creating dance music with piano and guitars, and writing poetry. He works out now, has a new and caring partner, and is catching up with friends from whom he used to hide.

"I work on being that way even without the substances and that will happen but for now I chase that as I don't trust reality to be safe enough without it," he writes.

> I always want that backdoor towards safety and trust and
> losing loneliness but I also know I want to put effort towards
> these pieces in my life as the drugs don't just magically solve
> the issues but they help give that bit of trust and self reliance
> to deal with them.

Will Jordan at last leave opioid dependence behind? For many people, this is *the* question. They worry that opioid dependence, even if it stabilizes people's health and reduces their overdose risk, means leaving a person who uses drugs—an addict who either has an opioid use disorder, or who is in denial about having an opioid use disorder—in the same bad place they find them. The idea of replacing a dependency on one drug with a dependency on another is deeply disturbing to them.

People who have themselves left a very bad part of their life behind and whose model of recovery depends on treating the drug as forever forbidden to them may be particularly invested in the importance of getting unhooked, of freedom from what they see as "a crutch."

Needless to say, they see a crutch as a bad thing.

Independence

I used to avoid coffee. I liked it, but I didn't want to find myself depending on that bitter taste and chemical optimism to start my day. If I had a headache, or the deep sciatic ache that has tormented me often since childhood, I preferred to suffer than to take Tylenol. I'm attracted to freethinkers and people who pursue an independent vision, even at personal cost. I don't trust easy success; at university I sought out the subjects I found difficult, not those in which I could easily excel. I dislike team sports; I love the independence of long-distance running, which brings an expansive mental feeling even before endorphins kick in. Independence is wonderful! I'm more comfortable interviewing than being interviewed, offering help than accepting it. This runs deep, and self-mastery is something I have, at times in my life, taken too far.

For my first several years of opioid use, I chose carefully, rationing relief so I would not develop tolerance. But I wasn't just being wise and cautious. There was a moralistic element as well. I took perverse pride in the adherence to suffering that kept my doses low. Abstinence and control were anorectically linked. I say anorectically because, during a few confused years of my adolescence, I would feel a pride that exploded into a kind of euphoria when I denied myself food. I felt sharpened by hunger.

You can be sharpened by pain, too. Into a knife, or a needle, or a tooth.

There's nothing healthy or virtuous or redemptive about it. Pain cuts you off from the outside world and forces you inward where only the most sensitive and loyal of friends dare follow.

Father, give us courage to change what must be altered,
serenity to accept what cannot be helped, and the insight
to know the one from the other.

This is American theologian Reinhold Niebuhr's 1932-33 prayer, which morphed into the better-known Serenity Prayer popularized by Alcoholics Anonymous and Narcotics Anonymous:

God, grant me the serenity to accept the things I cannot change,
courage to change the things I can,
and wisdom to know the difference.

It seems sometimes that we are asked to do everything, anything, but demand change in the world that caused and perpetuated traumas. For this reason I am stuck on which version of this saying I should follow, the one that starts with fighting for change, or the one that starts with serene acceptance of the world as it is. How do you know the difference, and how do you recognize when there is something that must not be accepted serenely, but that must be altered, in oneself or in the world? When what's required isn't serenity and acceptance, but courage?

I first spoke with Jordan, who lives in Edmonton, and who told me that his favourite dependency is his family, in 2019. The following year, the right-wing United Conservative Party government in Alberta shut down the program that had allowed him access to prescribed, injectable opioids. Like other such governments, they seized on visible evidence of poverty and drug use to put in place further and often brutal cutbacks to programs that actually helped and empowered the most vulnerable, that named injustices and sought to redress them. Eleven participants of the program are suing the government. Shuttering the clinics that have allowed them to become independent of the illicit drug supply, they argue, violates their right to life, liberty, and security of the person and the right to not be subject to cruel and unusual treatment (all guaranteed in the Canadian Charter of Rights and Freedoms). They further contend that this constitutes discrimination on the basis of physical and mental disability.

They may well win their case. After all, in 2014, twenty-one graduating participants of Canada's first trial of heroin-assisted treatment in neighbouring British Columbia won their Charter challenge against the Conservative Party of Canada–led government's decision to cancel a legal exemption that would have maintained their access to the substance at the heart of the life-saving program.

Like other right-wing governments, and particularly those that share evangelical Christian and social conservative outlooks, Alberta's United Conservatives hew to a very specific notion of "recovery" from addiction. It's abstinence-based, and in many ways religious, a notion in which the implicit narrative involves renunciation and redemption. By leaving off any veneration of substances in favour of the clean, wholesome intoxication of God, you become a worthy citizen in their eyes. Never mind if the treatment doesn't work. Never mind if recovery in practical terms means a miserable quality of life. Never mind, even, if the sinning junkie ends up dead before they get the chance to surrender, as Narcotics Anonymous advises, to a higher power than evidence-based medicine.

Pain patients are also often seen as in need of a kind of quasi-religious redemption. "Pain acceptance" sounds like what a frontier medic might tell their patient before pouring a slug of whisky down their throat, stuffing a stick between their teeth, and proceeding with the amputation — but it's actually yet another behavioural pain science trend, a response to patients who complain that, despite a heavy diet of mindfulness meditation, gratitude journaling, and cognitive-behavioural therapy (CBT), they are suffering too much, or have lost function, once denied effective analgesia.

Pain acceptance, as a concept, hinges on the assumption that patients who, despite learning the techniques intended to promote a curious, non-judgmental attitude to pain, still see their pain as "suffering," are fighting against the idea that their pain is indeed intractable. Persistently continuing to suffer, they demonstrate a misunderstanding of pain, identifying it unnecessarily with suffering, taking on suffering like martyrs who secretly love it. They fail to grasp that pain itself won't kill them. Fearfully, they avoid exercise and other healthy lifestyle measures, preferring dependence upon palliatives, the easy way out. They fail to accept that their life can be meaningful and joyful despite constant or near-constant pain. That is, they are actually causing themselves suffering that is not intrinsic to the pain itself. Not just loving it, then. Inviting suffering, even. Begging for it. Fail fail fail.

Pain patients, in this understanding—because the doctrine of acceptance seems predicated upon the existence of inadequately accepting patients—insist upon full palliation of our symptoms, on comfort and pleasure, on divans and grapes tipped into our rosy mouths, upon Soma, upon soft bodies and underused muscles, upon not experiencing any hardship, challenge, or twinge. We refuse, stubbornly and angrily, the idea that we might be forced to live with a little bit of pain. We want magic. We are infantile, seeking oral gratification, demanding quick satisfaction of our bodily desires. We stubbornly refuse to accept that opioids, a treatment long known to soften awareness of physical agony, do so at a cost that is not worth paying, as one physician writes scornfully in the journal *Practical Pain Management*:

> The present mentality is one of instant improvement with
> a magic pill. The population is too influenced by television
> where incredible things are resolved within an hour, including
> within the commercials. Reality is quite different.[1]

The magic pill is poisoned, we are told. The magic pill doesn't work anyway, they say. Or, they insist, the magic pill works well for some, but isn't right for you.

To use opium today in the United States requires: independent thinking, relative financial freedom and freedom from surveillance, and a willingness to be alone.

Matthew is a software professional in his forties with a master's degree who lives somewhere on the West Coast (Matthew is his middle name). He writes music in his spare time and has a girlfriend who currently lives in another state. There must be tremendous risks involved in acquiring and smoking opium in the United States in 2019, when we start talking about it, but we both know that those risks are dramatically different for him — white tech guys like Matthew get a pass on eccentric drug habits — than they would be for someone who is Black, for example, or Hispanic, for someone who is poor.

The opium Matthew gets in the mail looks like chunks of dark resin. Other than in photos, the only opioids I've ever seen are my own. Using an encrypted chat service, he sends me photos of opium and of the beautiful opium-smoking paraphernalia he finds on French auction sites or on the Dark Web. Describing anything without simply using the thing as its own definition requires analogy: metaphor or simile. "It's pretty unique," Matthew says of the smell of refined opium.

"The way coffee or wine or other things have a taste that's not duplicated elsewhere," he manages at last. "It's kind of sweet, heavy, ripe, and almost meaty in a way."

As for how it feels to smoke it, here is Matthew's description of how he spent November 3, 2020, the day of very significant US elections:

> I basically did some work yesterday, then before lunchtime, I smoked three pipes. So...the first was a sort of a euphoric rush, where I set down the pipe, and looked at the lamp for a while letting it come over me. Really. Not a single thought about the election or...much of anything, besides how nice it feels, and how nice it is to lay [*sic*] there next to the lamp,

and...not have to bother regarding things like Donald
Trump. After that settled down, it was really relaxing...
take the feeling of having a really nice stretch and amplify
that. A lot.

The pleasures associated in literature with opioids involve a bewitching
mix of the unfamiliar and the warm and cozy; of feelings of peace and
feelings of separation. "The experience [of using opium] has been pretty
positive overall. The downside is really the external factors around it,"
Matthew tells me. "It's not a thing that's easily shared."

And yet, before prohibition, opioid use in China was a social activity,
not something to do on your own. "I missed my real calling running an
opium den for expatriates somewhere along a Golden Triangle border
frontier. (As problematic as that is, I know)," Matthew writes.

He suggests that if I'm interested in opium, I ought to read a historical survey of the substance in China called *Narcotic Cultures*, by Frank
Dikötter, Lars Laamann, and Zhou Xun. A carefully documented, measured history (if controversial because of its conclusions), *Narcotic Cultures*
makes a strongly argued case that opium smoking was a generally positive or neutral, culturally entrenched practice both recreationally and for
medical reasons in China, as elsewhere, well before the Opium Wars to
which Thomas De Quincey's son gave his life and which allowed Britain
to assume control over the lucrative opium trade.

As Dikötter and his co-authors put it, the cure was far worse than
the disease. We've discussed the way criminalizing a previously accepted
practice created a marginal, criminal class of people. Prohibiting opium
smoking didn't just push users to more potent substitutes like morphine
and to injection drug use; it also forced treatment that killed a proportion
of the patients; used torture, forced labour, and physical restraint; and
often involved substances like strychnine, arsenic, and high doses of
caffeine.

The result was the establishment of a thriving illicit drug industry;
dramatically expanded, eerily similar incarceration and treatment industries; increasing disparity between the poor and the wealthy in the negative

impacts of drug use; and ever more potent sedatives like morphine and heroin, as well as the first explosion of legal and illicit stimulant industries that endure today.

As the authors of *Narcotic Cultures* demonstrate with carefully documented primary sources, opium use has a long history in China, as in other countries from Turkey to Japan and beyond. In China, it was used both as the most effective treatment (not cure) for many ailments and for moderate, chronic recreational use in a cultural context that generally defined the limits of consumption.

Opium and then morphine and heroin were also abundantly available in Europe and America. The heroin often came in pill form and at sometimes homeopathically vanishing strength. While the drug caused dependence in some and killed the odd child, the British Empire and American republic barrelled along perfectly well during this entire period when essentially every person would have had significant exposure to opioids in various forms.

When he was a child, Matthew's parents had a book called *Secret Paris of the 30s*, by the photographer Brassaï (Gyula Halász), a Transylvanian immigrant who came to Paris in 1923. *Secret Paris of the 30s* brought the Paris underworld to darkly luminous life (Brassaï was originally a painter, and took inspiration from Henri de Toulouse-Lautrec, who recorded similarly artistically documentary scenes of a similar, earlier Paris).

Brassaï's secret Paris book hits all the Romantic, counter-culture notes that appeal to me for reasons I don't really understand, just as it did for Matthew. I quickly acquire it so I can see the photographer's studies of opium dens, those culturally regulating, supervised consumption sites of the long nineteenth century. The book even features self-portraits of Brassaï lounging in these sites that had become, by the time they arrived in Paris, notoriously louche clubs, although they still served the safer, supervised-consumption function of their earlier Chinese counterparts. I flip through the pages of dark, gleaming nightlife to the very end, looking for photographs taken in the clubs. These must have had an outsized impact on Matthew's childish imagination, because there are disappointingly few of them. In fact, it is in the context of the rest of the photos and the text that I can see their significance. While the opium den Brassaï was able to get into was actually in the home of a wealthy Parisian, the other photos in his book authentically reveal the real demi-monde, that world where several identities — sex worker, opium smoker, immigrant, actor — are thrown into a single pile because of their shared excommunication from the "regular" society of daylight and legal commerce.

It's no different today, when distinct identities such as, for example, sex worker, fentanyl user, Indigenous person, poor person, trans woman, or homeless person each increase the bearer's exposure to systemic injustices. The more they overlap in one person, the more injustices and barriers that person faces as they try to live out their lives, and the more likely they are to be pushed into the demi-monde where solidarity may well exist in the shadows, but where rights are violated in routine and flagrant ways. Audre Lorde, the Black feminist thinker associated with this concept of *intersectionality*, coined by Kimberlé Crenshaw in 1989, expressed it well when she said, "there is no such thing as a single-issue struggle because we do not live single-issue lives."[2]

"I can only hope Carlyn can enjoy what is left of her life…," wrote a well-meaning reader of my first book, *Opium Eater: The New Confessions*, which came out when I was, for crying out loud, only thirty-nine.

Reader, I do.

Not despite pain, though. Nor because of it, but largely during the moments when its relief allows me to live my life more fully.

Of the various mental framing or philosophical therapies out there for enduring pain, I find one called Acceptance and Commitment Therapy (or ACT), the easiest to, well, accept and commit to. Although it *is* often taught as yet another blame-the-victim technique in which patients are told that the reason they are struggling is because they have failed to "accept" their pain, and that any reaction that involves seeking less pain is further evidence of this failure, my reading of it is quite different. ACT starts with an existentialist understanding of the world:

> Bad things happen in life. Plus we continually lose the things we love. Then, we die.

ACT asks each of us to come up with our own response to this unsatisfactory situation using the one thing we can control: acting according to values. Not just anyone's values, but the values that represent, for better or for worse, our own deepest belief about what is important.

I was already practising mindfulness as well as CBT techniques, inadequate but still-valuable basic skills for coping with pain. After reading a book on the subject of ACT and warming to the individual-values aspect that seemed missing from those two techniques, I sought out an ACT therapist. At the time, I was having real trouble coping with pain, uncertainty about my health, loss and limitations, and unbounded loneliness. I'd go to our sessions and would ask what he thought I should do about *this* thing that was tormenting me, or *that* thing that was tormenting me. He would just sit there — for a hundred dollars an hour — until I got fed up and told him what *I* thought was important.

It was very annoying.

But, in fact, using ACT to focus insistently on what is really important to me and to no one else has led me to a few conclusions, to a budding independence of thought about my own life.

Other than family and friends, writing is the most important thing to me. It's more important than any hypothetical romantic relationships, sex, sleep, money, prestige, comfort, or even physical health. I am willing to do almost anything to make it possible, except sacrifice my family or friends. And as it turns out, my ability to write and to manage the other important things — my function, that is — is improved by better pain control.

I didn't actually realize this until my doctor and I agreed to increase my dose of opioids to the extent that I was actually comfortable much of the time, rather than just getting by, because I'd started to notice that I was able to work more when I was in less pain. Pain relief made me not just less despairing but also more productive and active. It really hadn't occurred to me that it might work that way.

And so, after more than a decade of active engagement with suffering, as a result of adherence to a technique taught to help people live with enduring pain, I've actually chosen to pursue a *less* stoic existence. The way to do that is by using these risky chemicals to cover up the pain, releasing me from the need to endure. It's not a choice that is open to everyone with chronic pain, and for so many years, it was not a choice I even realized I had.

And perhaps it won't be a choice for me forever. I worry about that constantly. Does my opioid-given quality of life have a best-before date that comes far before my actual expiry date?

ACT doesn't give me an answer to this. But because I accept this pain as my reality, and because I commit to acting from my own values, for now the answer is *carpe diem*: seize the day.

Canadian literary critic Amanda Leduc writes about disability, and the way the world does not yet accommodate difference or the tools we use to manage it, leaving disabled bodies to be looked on as either, in her words, "an object of pity" or "an object of tender fascination." Or a monster (from her essay called "Monster or Marvel"): "Navigating the world with our guide dogs and scooters and other supports — augmentations that aren't sexy like the claws that come racing out of Wolverine's hands or the arc reactor in Tony Stark's chest or the impossible body that gets to be Steve Rogers's, but are nonetheless tools that we use to make ourselves be more."[3]

A crutch, a wheelchair, an antidepressant, an amphetamine that treats attention deficit disorder, an opioid that fills in where one's own endorphins don't soften and brighten the harsh world enough on their own. We might focus on changing society so that it meets every need — indeed, in a world of such blatant inequality as this one, we must. But in the meantime, so long as pain-causing diseases exist and so long as children are traumatized and so long as so many needs go persistently unmet in adults as well, access to a treatment that effectively eases pain, both physical and emotional, is a disability right. Not because, as pain patients sometimes say, they have the right to pain relief, but because, like everyone else, we have the right to accommodations that afford us the chance to realize our potential.

Matt Johnson, a Toronto harm reduction worker, leads me to a café around the corner from the community health centre where he works. He's previously given me a tour of his centre's supervised injection site. Low showers where homeless clients can wash their feet before they look for a vein. Little stainless steel tables — shelves, really, with chairs. Mirrors so harm reduction workers like him can discreetly check that their clients are still breathing after they legally inject themselves with illegally acquired, illegal drugs like heroin. Or, more likely, an unholy mix of fentanyl, caffeine, and any of a wide range of possible extenders and adulterants marketed as heroin or down. Oxygen and naloxone are at hand.

It's September 2018, and the Canadian government, along with Mexico, has just this very morning re-committed to the American-led war on drugs. This war is widely believed to be a failure in every possible way, so it seems an especially strange thing to sign on to for a country (Canada) that has just legalized recreational cannabis, and another one (Mexico) that has just ejected a president associated with corruption, incompetence, and a renewal of his predecessor's bloody, useless war on drug cartels.

We're just half a block but a world away from the lives of the drug users Johnson works with. He tells me about the negative effect the new statement on international drug policy goals may have on those mostly homeless clients here in Toronto. He strikes me as comfortable, outspoken, and a person who, unlike most of his clients, is in a good place in his life.

While we are talking, I am wondering the thing I wonder every time I interview someone or am interviewed myself. How awkward, how attention-getting, would it be to take the pills that are burning a hole in my coat pocket right now? It was too early to take them before we met. But now it's getting late. The sitting I'm doing so competently is going to turn into squirmy discomfort and irrepressible stretching pretty soon.

If I wait much longer, I'll also start simply fading, my interview questions growing less and less concise and my conversation more flaccid as my focus becomes derailed by pain in my spine and neck. This has caused me to cut interviews abruptly short or to wrap up with vague statements, concentration already lost, as will happen two years later during my early interviews with Meg.

I need tramadol now as definitively as I need lunch. More, in fact. Because my body requires the morphine-like substance released as tramadol is broken down in my liver, missing doses is no longer an option. At least, not unless I'm willing to unleash not only pain but withdrawal symptoms as well.

Johnson is familiar with withdrawal, because for many years he was addicted to heroin, just like his clients. He has, indeed, not always been in the good place in his life in which I find him. As a gay teenager in a homophobic environment, he considered suicide. When he started using drugs, he tells me, he went directly to heroin, convinced he was likely to die either way. Like many other heroin users, he feels that the drug prevented him from killing himself. That doesn't mean he didn't run into problems with it. He was addicted, but ultimately kicked the habit and is no longer dependent on opioids.

And yet, Matt Johnson last injected heroin last week: he is, in fact, an occasional, recreational heroin user.

But he no longer physically requires opioids, as I do. Thanks to therapy and self-examination, he has learned to be careful, these days, not to use opioids as a substitute for healthy relationships and meaningful work. They are, he tells me, more like a holiday, one that takes preparation. Where he carefully injects fentanyl-laced "heroin" about every three weeks, I take my little heroin pills[4] three times a day. Where he takes his for a brief vacation from life, I take mine on schedule no matter what.

What Matt Johnson practises now is a way of using heroin that was popular during the 1950s, called "chipping," where you take great care to avoid acquiring physical dependence by spacing out what De Quincey, who initially practised this a hundred years *avant la lettre*, would have called his "debauches" and what Johnson calls a holiday, recreation like any other form of recreation. With care, a stable lifestyle, a home that offers a calm, well-lit place to inject, and knowledge of how to mitigate the risk of overdose, it is, despite the terribly dangerous, unpredictable illicit market, maybe safer than, say, hang-gliding or mountain climbing. A risk, but a calculated one. If the drugs were tested for purity and composition, this risk could be lowered to something closer to the risks involved in medical use of fentanyl in a hospital setting, which are negligible.

Marcus Aurelius became emperor of Rome in 161 CE. As well as leading a vast empire, he also found time to become a major figure in Stoic philosophy. During those periods when my world contracts to a little pupil of pain, I tend to read a lot of Marcus Aurelius. "If you are distressed by anything external, the pain is not due to the thing itself," he wrote, "but to your estimate of it; and this you have the power to revoke at any moment."[5]

Taking medication of any kind isn't a choice made lightly, but I've experienced permanent harm from years of stoic, miserable non-treatment. Stoicism was the inspiration for the founding of cognitive-behavioural therapy. But stoicism is both more profound and more moderate than that pop psychology technique. Perhaps even the stoic emperor himself would have found something immoderate, something excessive in the strict and punitive self-reliance that led me to avoid a tool — pain medication — that I already knew made it easier for me to exercise, made it possible to work, and allowed me to handle multiple responsibilities without taxing my body beyond what I could cope with without emotional breakdown.

Although he was probably the world's most powerful person, and during a time of relative peace at that, Marcus Aurelius didn't have to invent torments to help him practise his philosophy. He suffered from chronic stomach pains, despite an austere lifestyle that avoided the rich and decadent meals of later emperors. But there is one thing I did not learn until recently. Marcus Aurelius's personal physician, Galen of Pergamon, prescribed him a preparation called theriac, consisting of "viper's flesh, opium, honey, wine, cinnamon, and then more than 70 ingredients."[6] The emperor took this concoction daily, perhaps because he was dependent on the opium (or, who knows, the viper's flesh).

When they teach stoicism to pain patients, they *always* forget to mention the opium.

"I only know one thing, and that is to shout to my children, 'Long live Life!'" writes Alphonse Daudet, the writer who suffered from syphilis.

"But," he adds, "it's so hard to do, while I am ripped apart by pain." And he also writes, as pain reduces his field of vision, his range of movement: "Pain, you must be everything for me. Let me find in you all those foreign lands you will not let me visit. Be my philosophy, be my science."[7]

I have lost years, years when my children were sweet and little, years when my marriage would have benefited from less struggle, years when my income gradually dwindled and I was no longer able to do the hustle a freelance writer's career depends on, years when my world shrank just like Daudet's, years when no one could understand how hard it was to do *any*thing, when I turned to reading Marcus Aurelius, when I tried to detox myself from dependence on normal human needs like feeling okay.

At moments I am riven by anger that nobody *really* told me about opioids. Sure, that they can be addictive and destroy my life, that they can have side effects, that they can kill me or my loved ones, that they don't even work for chronic pain: these messages that are all typed neatly on bright stickers plastered on every prescription I pick up. They are further inserted helpfully in the paper pharmacy bag in leaflet form as well. "Anti-stigma" ads on bus shelters warn that anyone may have their boring, stable lives suddenly run through a blender as a result of their prescription painkiller, that it's a short walk off the plank between the ship of pain relief and the ocean full of pharmaceutical sharks, a short walk from the doctor's office to the darkly lit McDonald's bathroom or alley where, without warning, you may find yourself injecting heroin in your groin.

Somebody should have used their positive thinking skills when writing these leaflets. Because I wish, now, that somebody had instead emphasized how badly pain can fuck up a perfectly good life, regardless of how hard you work to transcend it or accept it or reframe your thoughts about it. If I'd been less afraid and less moralistic about these drugs, I might have spent my thirties living rather than earnestly transcending suffering while trying to hold onto joy and love and life for myself and my loved ones.

All this time, I didn't have to suffer so badly. Marcus Aurelius didn't.

Medicalization of opioids, like medicalization of other aspects of life that have both individual health and social causes and effects, has for over a hundred years been an issue of control, with the medical profession extending its area of practice to encompass many things that were previously considered part of the criminal justice system, or simply part of general culture. Moving addiction and substance use into the realm of medicine and public health is often seen as a way to look at them from a more gentle perspective than the punitive way law enforcement sees it.

And yet control — and patients' resentment of being controlled, and physicians' anxiety about their responsibility to adequately control their patients — looms large for both pain patients and addiction patients. The exertion of control over what substances people use and how they manage physical and emotional pain became a preoccupation of the medical field from the time opioids were first banned except for medical use, so that the nineteenth-century equivalent of convenience stores had to stop selling mild opioid remedies to anyone with good coin. Henceforth, opioids could only be acquired with physician approval, which could always be revoked. They also now required a diagnosis, meaning that their legal use could only indicate a pathology, and could never be a normal, healthy human activity anyone might choose. And, further, opioids were now a form of relief awarded to some patients and denied to others — sometimes for very valid reasons, and sometimes simply as a result of the doctor's prejudices.

The modern dynamic of control and resentment of it starts early, with evidence suggesting even medical trainees find people with chronic pain to be frustrating and "unrewarding" patients. Meanwhile, chronic pain patients consistently report that their physicians or other healthcare providers lack empathy, listen poorly, and are dismissive and disbelieving, often assuming they are "drug-seekers," "malingerers," or emotionally disturbed (for reasons unrelated to distress from poorly treated pain or appalling healthcare interactions).

One study of physician attitudes toward prescribing and tapering or stopping (also called "de-prescribing") of opioids, in which wildly varying attitudes of family physicians on the topic were gathered using structured one-on-one interviews, included the observation that "For some, there was more comfort when prescribing short-acting opioids because physicians perceived a sense of control, or a *'leash'* on patients."[8]

> Others who were more established in their practice (i.e., > 20 years of clinical experience) felt that they could manage opioid prescribing in a way that met the needs of their patients — a confidence that was largely attributed to their clinical experience and strong therapeutic relationships that reduced the perceived potential of adverse consequences. Previous experiences, such as working in the shelter system or an addiction facility, and opioid-specific training also bolstered confidence.[9]

This is a Canadian study. In the United States, it is increasingly difficult for pain patients to find a doctor who will take them on for any sort of care, let alone to continue an opioid prescription, regardless of how well it appeared to work or whether or not there were unacceptable side effects (one quite representative pain patient says she was told, when she was abandoned by her physician, "I'm not going to lose my licence over you"[10]).

It is hard for a free fish to understand what is happening to a hooked one. Things that seem surprising or shocking to those of us who do not have experience with illicit drugs, especially in intersection with poverty and housing insecurity, illustrate why it is ridiculous that people who use drugs are not considered *the* experts on what they need. For example, I learned that drug users and informed allies often call for assisted injection to be allowed at supervised consumption or overdose prevention sites. For people like me who were uneducated about all this, it seems like a step too far. After all, we have already bent our delicate sense of morality to allow for users to have a safe place to use illicit drugs on which they are dependent. Now we are asked to further accept the scandalous, enabling idea of allowing a friend or a nurse or any other person to inject this delicious poison for them! But assisted injection and safe injection education are in fact vital elements of disability rights and women's rights. Women may be held virtually prisoner — speaking of leashes, speaking of hooks — by their need for opioids and dependence on their pimp or partner to do the injection. So may people with physical disabilities and chronic illness, of whom there are very, very many among the street-involved community. Being able to seek assistance for the sometimes extremely difficult task of finding a shy vein, and injecting with proper technique to prevent abscesses and other injection-related harms, frees this person from their dependence on a particular human. And then, being taught how to safely inject on one's own is like the adage about teaching a man to fish rather than simply giving him a fish. These can be first steps to becoming financially and physically free of an abusive and controlling relationship. By working with people who use drugs in their actual (not theoretical) lives, harm reduction workers consider what is going to help them move forward with both autonomy and support in the moment, and what will most effectively reduce the potential harms associated with drug use in that moment. Assistance and education to more safely do what you are going to do anyway no matter what is one important way to do so. If this causes an uncomfortable feeling to rise up like bile, a distaste at the idea of such dependence, this would be a good example to use to explore your feelings about what independence really means.

Over the years, attempts to prevent addiction by developing new, safer opioids or addiction treatments have typically focused on ways to make drug use less pleasurable and, if possible, more painful, while exerting as much control as possible on the person who persistently chooses the short-term pain relief opioid drugs provide. This can involve messing with genes and neurotransmitters to reduce drug users' ability to experience pleasure; a constant search for non-pleasurable opioids; and devices or implants that block any possible good feelings or impose painful or unpleasant feelings when drugs are used. Even evidence-based, life-saving medication-based addiction treatments are made as disruptive and unpleasant as possible for the patient taking them: methadone typically requires daily attendance at a clinic and urine tests under observation, whether by a human or by a camera. Buprenorphine likewise often involves intrusive testing and daily attendance, sometimes allowing users to earn "carries" for good behaviour, rather than simply buying their medicine at the pharmacy and taking it privately and without vigilance like the rest of us. Justifications for this level of scrutiny can include patient safety, risk of diversion, and simple inability to trust "addicts," even those under treatment, but there is no good evidence that patients are better off being treated in this way.

The ever-eloquent Garth Mullins writes:

> "Compliance" [is] the secret ingredient in all these
> medications. A little subversive agent that sneaks into
> your system. Methadone has a scold baked in — maybe
> a school nun. Suboxone has a cop baked in. Sublocade
> seems to have a prison warden baked in.[11]

The popular belief is that if you are not abstinent, even from medications that treat addictive behaviour, you are dependent. And if you are dependent, you are weak of will, sick of body, corrupt of spirit. You are not sober. You are still a junkie. But for a person with physical dependence on an opioid, a reliable source of untainted, known-dose opioids can be not only stability-restoring but a profound tool to enable independence. If Meg were on safe supply, she would become essentially like me: housed, medicated, stable, and not constantly risking sudden death. She would achieve this without needing to detox, to face cravings or a resurgence of disabling post-traumatic symptoms, or to endure endless Narcotics Anonymous meetings. It is important to recall that NA and similar programs that rely on abstinence do not protect you from death in the event of a relapse, a highly probable event. While Meg's back pain could likely be treated by something other than an opioid, fentanyl is of course effective for that as well. By simply moving onto safe supply, she could continue to receive pain treatment without needing to go through another trial of other medications. Life, we both know, is short, and this would let her get on with it.

And so, now that she has a home, Meg begins to look for a doctor who can continue working with her to further stabilize her life. There is a doctor who we both follow on Twitter who is involved in safe supply; we'll call her Dr. X. She talks a lot about anti-oppressive practices in medicine, about decolonizing the profession, about avoiding what she calls "medical violence." Just before heading off on that Christmas holiday trip I was so worried about, Meg writes to her out of the blue and convinces her to take her on. Patient and doctor connect right away thanks to their mutual desire to question power relationships in healthcare (Meg studied nursing for a time—impressively, she's a high school, college, *and* university dropout—and has seen first-hand distressing power dynamics among different healthcare providers, as well as between doctors and patients). The clinic's approach is not lax or reckless. It's practical and focused on practising medicine in a way that is evidence-based, effective, and compassionate. To start, Dr. X's medical team addresses Meg's anxiety about her visit to her family. They propose increasing her dose of long-acting morphine, which she already receives through a city harm reduction program, a safety measure for people otherwise subject to the illicit market. Instead of crossing the border with fentanyl wedged into her like a tampon, she can, with this higher oral morphine dose, travel the way I do: with a labelled, legal prescription bottle in the carry-on that doesn't even raise an eyebrow as it passes through baggage checks. Long-acting morphine does not give her the high she requires to control trauma symptoms and feel okay, but by increasing the dose, she is able to at least get by for those few days without resorting to fentanyl, experiencing only mild withdrawal.

Upon her safe return in the new year, though, Meg must wait to actually get on the safe supply she really needs: prescribed hydromorphone (Dilaudid) in tiny pills that she can crush and inject. In the absence of an expansion of Canada's prescription heroin program, or of anything to provide prescription fentanyl for people dependent on that drug, hydromorphone is, as I write this, the pinnacle of safe supply in this country.[12]

Since I first met Joe and his partner, they have spoken about their dream of getting accepted to a safe supply program. They both know from experience that hydromorphone, when they can get it via a diverted supply (Meg, for example, bought morphine from a cancer patient early in her opioid career), allows them to function a million times better, to feel and act normal, to be themselves (buprenorphine taken long-term caused unpleasant side effects for them both, and the prescribing regime for methadone is both restrictive and infantilizing). Unfortunately, since they are receiving addiction treatment that works well enough to prevent them from constantly overdosing on street drugs, they can't demonstrate that they need hydromorphone badly enough to qualify for it. Although their past experiences with opioids, without opioids, and with buprenorphine and methadone suggest it would work better than the drugs they are taking in restoring both normalcy and health, access even here in Ontario where it does exist is restricted to those likely to die imminently without it.

And even for people like Meg who are perfect candidates under the current rules, there is an extremely long waiting list of drug users who would like to stop depending on the illicit supply and who want to be part of the hydromorphone safe supply program. Weeks of hope stretch into months of anxiety as the clinic Meg has found must contact others higher up on the list to offer them safe supply first. Meg has stopped car panning, effectively removing her last real dependence on the street — other than the dealer she continues to see and trust with her life — but the money will eventually run out. Safe supply is also a financial, and therefore a class, issue. As the months go by and she is buffeted by the vagaries of her illicit supply, I can feel her tension twanging over the invisible lines I imagine connecting us via direct message.

And then at last...she gets the call.

This time, the dramatic structure of Meg's story is more of a tragicomedy than tragedy, or just an anticlimax, a bad one. After weeks of trying to transition on to prescription hydromorphone, after months of waiting for it, after years risking her life on the black market when it wasn't an option ... turns out Meg is allergic to hydromorphone.

At least, as a natural philosopher, Meg seems to get some pleasure from the irony. After finally achieving the Holy Grail of medical treatment for opioid users in Canada — hydromorphone prescribed to ingest as she sees fit — it turns out that it's no use to her. She has finally, finally, reached safe harbour and she can't disembark. The illicit drug supply that she knows may kill her at any time, that shifts and shudders without warning, leaving her in sudden withdrawal from a bad batch, or zonked out from a tainted batch, never able to find her footing, is all there is for her. It is heartbreaking.

And yet there seems to be very ample evidence that people who use drugs respond in a very variable way to the available treatments. The most effective treatment for opioid use disorder is going to be whichever treatment the patient can follow, can stick with, that will keep them alive, and that will improve their quality of life.

Buprenorphine, increasingly promoted as an alternative to other opioids for chronic pain patients because it is thought to have less risk of addiction (because of its lower "likeability"), is a lifesaver for those at high risk of overdose. But for some people, likeability is the essential factor in being able to stick with a treatment, and without a substance with high likeability they are simply unable to function in their lives.

But there are other issues as well. While many people are stable and able to continue with their lives once on buprenorphine, other patients report not feeling well on this medication over the long term. Joe lost weight and energy on bupe, and took it miserably in order to stay off the illicit market, and because his C-PTSD was unmanageable with no opioids at all. He was skinny, ill, and depressed, unable to work, sluggish, and cynical when I met him.

Despite a typically difficult regimen, methadone works very well for many former heroin users. Thousands upon thousands find it effective over years or decades, incidentally providing excellent evidence that opioids can indeed work long-term, including for pain.[13] But others simply don't want to be chained to an unpleasant dispensing system (not, of course, an intrinsic problem with the drug, but a socially constructed feature that could be changed), and still others find its side effects not just unpleasant but intolerable.

It's unlikely, though, that many people who have sought and used heroin illegally would reject its prescription version. And so it seems to me that there are only two reasons for it to remain the rare exception — a highly limited treatment considered radical — rather than the most sensible standard of care for people seriously dependent on it.

One reason is the fear that if prescription heroin were widely available, people would seek it out, even if their addiction were transient and could have been managed in some other way. There is evidence to suggest that this is unlikely. In Portugal by the nineties, practically every family had someone who struggled with heroin addiction. And yet after decriminalization and harm reduction policies were implemented in 2001, most people did not remain entrenched in problematic drug use. Most of them moved on. Likewise, of American soldiers who returned from Vietnam in 1971 with heroin addictions — 43 percent of returnees reported narcotic use while in Vietnam, and half of those reported becoming addicted to them while there — only 2 percent became readdicted back in the United States, despite many reporting that they knew where to access narcotics if they wanted.[14] And for all the concern about them being irresistibly "likeable," most people don't like prescription opioids, either. In trials of opioids for chronic non-cancer pain, a 60 percent drop-out rate over the course of a twelve-week trial is not unusual,[15] because people experience side effects they don't like or can't tolerate, or simply because they don't like the way opioids make them feel.[16] What feels like the missing psychological chair leg for some, or like blessed relief from pain for others, is actually unpleasant to the majority of people who try it (another fine reason to prescribe non-opioid analgesics first when pain relief is needed, and only try out a lowest-effective-dose opioid if they are intolerable or ineffective).

The other reason to ignore the strong evidence in favour of prescription heroin for addiction is that providing the most sought-out, most pleasurable drug to people who are willing to risk their lives to seek it is just not what we as a society are comfortable with. Far better, we think, to punish people who are dependent on heroin but who fear death from overdose by providing dependence medications that are unsatisfactory, unpleasant, and energy-draining. Far better to discourage heroin use by making sure it's as dangerous as possible. And far better to ensure that people who are so starved for the sensation of pleasure that they will play Russian roulette to get it do not have any access to relatively safe sources of pleasure.

I ask Meg about all she has been through to get hydromorphone, and she replies:

> You asked me earlier if I'd really gotten anything out
> of all my effort, if my body won't handle dilaudid [the
> hydromorphone]. I had a bunch of half answers at the
> time, but there was something really obvious I knew I was
> missing. The answer is: Dr X. I don't know what she might
> or might not be able to do. But I do believe she'll try her best,
> & I know she's willing to use her powers of prescription in a
> way no other doc I've met has been. But that's what will make
> this whole thing worthwhile, really. Having her as my doctor.

Just having a trusting relationship with a physician is a big step for any drug user who has been belittled, treated with suspicion, denied proper medical care, and both controlled and abandoned for years or decades. Meg doesn't know what's next, other than remaining dependent on the ever-more-risky, expensive illicit market, but she can now talk to Dr. X about obstacles to living a safer and more comfortable life, and together they can brainstorm options to overcome them.

Other than my prescribed opioids, taken as prescribed, I don't know much, experientially speaking, about recreational drug use—even though mind- and mood-altering substances (alcohol, sedatives, cannabis, and caffeine, for example) are used very widely, almost universally, in modern society. And yet, while I may be more naive about recreational drug use than many, I am not the only one to feel uncomfortable even thinking about the idea of substances that may be disinhibiting, that may let down our guard, that may loosen or soften us, that may change our visible rhythm. I'm too self-conscious to enjoy most drugs. But the joylessness goes deeper than that, and further than just me. Because we live in a society completely shaped by prohibition, because none of us or our parents have lived in a time or a place where prohibition didn't exist, we are very trained to see pleasure through substances as a poisoned chalice. And then, there is simply a lot that we don't know about the joys of drugs.

I mean this not experientially, but factually. We as a society actually know very little about how or why people use drugs for pleasure, even though that—and not trauma, moral weakness, or brain disorder—is the main reason people use them. Here are just a few of the things we don't know:

- We don't know how or why it is that most people who use drugs never run into the problems that have given them a bad name.
- We don't know what factors can allow someone who is vulnerable to addiction to avoid falling into damaging patterns of use, or to quickly get out of them and moderate their use.
- We don't know who benefits most from which currently illegal or scheduled drugs.
- We do know that both the dose we take and the context and frame of mind in which we take it meaningfully change the way we experience psychoactive drugs, but we don't know what settings or doses make them safer, less safe, or more beneficial for a range of potential issues.
- We do know a lot about what combinations of drugs are unsafe, but we know little about how to mitigate dangers. The combinations that may safely enhance pleasure or other effects

users seek are secrets shared on internet forums and whispered from one user to another.

- We do know a lot about the dangers of drug use, but little about its potential to help people manage the effects of trauma or mental illness or even the physically damaging effects of unjust societies.

The reason that we know so little is threefold: one, certain powerful drugs are illegal or are scheduled in ways that make them hard to study; two, inaccurate assumptions about substances are so ingrained that we have trouble neutrally considering both potential risks and potential benefits of all substances; and three, a single organization funds the vast majority of scientific research on psychoactive substances in the entire world.[17]

"Everyone knows that if you write the words 'harm reduction' in a proposal [to them] it will not get funded," says Sheila Vakharia, deputy director of the Department of Research and Academic Engagement at the Drug Policy Alliance. "They're only interested in people who have problems. Abuse is in their name."

Indeed it is. The bias that the American organization that funds 90 percent of research on drugs worldwide[18] brings to its work is right there in the name: the National Institute on Drug Abuse, or NIDA (although it would take more than a name change to change this bias). Abuse, then, is the fundamental issue that guides almost all of the research that is done about psychoactive substances, and the risk of abuse is the guiding framework for most research questions about drugs.

Psychiatrist Nora Volkow, the head of NIDA, has emphasized the brain disorder concept of addiction. In a profile in the *Lancet*,[19] she is quoted as saying, "My mission is scientific, not political."

Volkow, who was born in Mexico City, happens to be the granddaughter of Leon Trotsky, the Russian revolutionary who promoted the idea of permanent revolution by means of mass action by the working class in advanced capitalist countries. Trotsky and his wife took refuge in Mexico from his political opponents, he had an affair with Frida Kahlo while they were there, and he was assassinated with an ice pick in the Mexico City house where Volkow was raised.

Compared to all that, I can see how her work could seem pretty apolitical. Still, her comment is disingenuous. Drugs and addiction have been political ever since the prohibition of opium (and before, actually), and given the influence that the American-led war on drugs has upon numerous aspects of the life and fortunes of people around the world, her role — which determines most of the research done on psychoactive drugs globally — is deeply political.

"Instead of abstinence, we are devising ways of treating addiction in which the individual is trained to think that the environment in which they were consuming their drugs is no longer pleasurable," Volkow tells the *Lancet*. Guided by NIDA's research and communication focus on abuse in pursuit of irresponsible pleasure, we attribute all sorts of harms to drugs that are not in fact inherent in the substances themselves. As a result, drug use in general is conflated with addiction, or disordered use, which in turn is considered to derive from problems in the individual rather than seen as one response of creative humanity to difficult circumstances — circumstances like poverty, colonization, family separation, homelessness, or racism — that result from inherently political policy decisions. And so the response and the entire way of understanding drug use focuses on control, forced change, and ensuring, as we have seen, that the experience of drug use is no longer pleasurable. Or, even, that it is punitive.

Volkov's comment about making drug use environments less pleasurable is a bit of an understatement. Researchers and policy-makers have developed everything from fiendishly ingenious ways of making drugs themselves painful, unpleasant, and more dangerous; to ways to render the consumption environment not only not pleasurable but dangerous, traumatizing, and unnecessarily lethal; to creating so-called treatment systems that consistently punish, humiliate, and oppress people seeking help, and indeed are, yes, dangerous as a result. And then, the brain disorder concept of addiction pushes drug users from a coercive criminal justice system to a coercive and controlling medical system on the very inadequate basis of a few studies of functional MRIs relating addiction to patterns of activity in the brain.

So there is a major lacuna in the research literature, left by a funding body focused on problems, control, and suppression of a basic human response to basic human needs and desires. In response, Dr. Vakharia and her colleague Ingrid Walker began a project to solicit and fund scientific research that would ask the sort of questions NIDA is unlikely to fund. Walker is an associate professor of American Studies at the University of Washington Tacoma, who researches and writes about drugs and ways to conceptualize drug use beyond the familiar ones of criminalization and medicalization.[20]

To start, the pair identified key subjects relating to drugs where research is notably lacking. These include the role of pleasure in drug use; self-moderating drug use; and what a post-prohibition world might look like. Might it involve more pleasure, for more people? Might it involve less pain?

"Right now, people of privilege can experience pleasure [with drugs]," Vakharia notes. As they have always been, the wealthy are allowed to indulge in intoxication, altered mental states, and enhanced moods, whether using legal or illicit drugs, with remarkable indulgence — regardless of the official legal regime. De facto decriminalization and safe supply exist among white and wealthy communities in every country and under every type of regime in which the privileged can buy their way out of consequences for breaking the law. These are, of course, groups that anyway don't suffer from the over-policing that targets the poor, people of colour, Indigenous people, and immigrants for severe and punitive enforcement.

The very word "indulgence," according to teachings of the Catholic Church, refers to a way of reducing the amount of punishment you must endure for your sins by buying your way out of it. When it comes to the sin of altering one's mood or experience of reality using psychoactive substances, only some of us can afford to indulge.

It's still very early days for this project of Vakharia and Walker's. But there is a world of pleasure to discover. Despite more than a hundred years of propaganda that says otherwise, not all of this pleasure must come at a cost. Not all pleasure, even of the truly exquisite kind, must needs be guilty pleasure.

I have come to rely on short escapes, one or two a year. It's been a while, and as usual I make a wish inside my own head and then set about trying to make it come true. I plan to go back to Venice. It's been three years. It's time. I will go in late February or early March, just as winter thaws into spring. I'll see what it all looks like when the tourists are gone, except me. But I delay booking my flights, making arrangements. There has been too much indulgence and I feel like I can't go ahead with it. I need an excuse. I wait. I can't write, I can't think, I am dull and fenced in and the isolation of being at home is so much less rich and free than the wild, proud loneliness I feel when I travel by myself. It's me or them, I think about my family. I need to go. I delay a little longer.

Delay too long and the opportunity slips through your fingers. In this case, though, it's good I did, because I would be in quarantine in Venice as I write this. Instead, I'm in semi-lockdown with my children in Toronto, going into my fourth month of 24/7 single parenting with no relief.

The last interview I do in the real world before the COVID-19 pandemic puts a stop to them is for a short series about homelessness that I've sold to an online magazine. One part looks at the criminalization of poverty, where poor people are blamed and persecuted for being poor, and, in particular, a trend across North America and beyond to the establishment of tent cities, and then to those proto-shantytowns being dismantled by authorities. There is a single tent remaining from one small tent city in downtown Toronto, and it's on the grounds of a homeless-serving organization called Sanctuary.

I have been fretting about this interview, because I'm worried about COVID infection—I take two immune suppressants, remember—and don't want any homeless people I interview to think that I'm refusing to shake their hand because I'm assuming they are dirty or infectious. In fact, the only person who tries to shake my hand is a Sanctuary worker, who I dodge, explaining awkwardly about the immune suppression as the handshake turns into an equally awkward elbow tap. I speak with a young man who lives in a doorway. And then I go out to the back and wait for Snickerz to finish doing her makeup, in her tent which is so sturdy and reinforced with layers that it resembles a nylon igloo. I stand, walk around, try to stretch without looking like I'm stretching, wonder how I can be a journalist like this. As it turns out, this interview is great. Connecting with people is great.

But isolation, distancing, and quarantine will soon be watchwords for all of us, shelters will have multiple outbreaks of COVID, and encampments — groups of tents, which allow people who use drugs to avoid infection from close quarters without leaving the communities and harm reduction services they need — will pop back up everywhere, filling the Sanctuary backlot and every public park, despite the city's attempts to dismantle them.

The last time I visit with Meg before I stop visiting with anyone, our conversation turns to the pain that can occur when family members turn on each other, or when one is cut off for marrying the wrong person, or other infractions. We talk about racism and ostracism, *-isms* that have touched each of our families (my extended, her close family) going back a couple of generations. So not too close to home for me — but abandonment by family was part of the pain Meg's grandmother and then her mother held and that Meg couldn't make go away, no matter how much pain she took upon herself. Why, she asks, in a world with so much pain, would you create more of it? We turn the question around and around. Why do people do that? Why wouldn't you try to ease pain wherever you find it? Why make more pain?

We walk toward the subway together before she heads one way and I head the other. We hesitate on the corner. I make a little choice, and I reach out to offer a hug that she readily returns. I'm not a hugger.

It's the last embrace I can remember giving anyone outside my household before COVID-19 puts a stop to embraces.

Interdependence

Just as old bones and plant matter can be crushed into diamonds under the weight of time, isolation, hardship, and pain all cause a transformation. I enjoy stories in which this process occurs. The genres that do this, fiction or non-fiction, that have always been my favourites include the literature of prisons, plagues, and quarantine, desert islands and shipwreck, hiding, and madness (I'm thinking of the dramatist Antonin Artaud, who was addicted to opiates and who spent much of his life in mental institutions). As I write this, I'm aware, like every person alive, that I'm living through history—though what is remembered by the time you read this depends on many things. Regardless, right here, right now, we are in a story, and the quarantine is one of its guiding, contradictory metaphors.

The prison and the desert island and the quarantine can each represent many things at once. Despite the life-destroying losses of the COVID-19 pandemic, our personal quarantine may be privileged, protective, cozy, and safe. By limiting, it reduces choices, and clarifies, essentializes—much like pain. Though, like pain or addiction, such solitude may be lonely, a vast pit into which we can fall and lose ourselves. COVID-19 has been devastating, death-dealing, soul-destroying for most people on the planet in this little moment of history—but it has also laid bare a lot of truth. About who is essential, and who is treated that way. About who you can count on, and who you cannot. About which structures in society are necessary, and which deserve to burn to the ground. About what should grow in their place.

The resolution of any of these forms of isolation narrative involves the return to society. You wash up on the mainland. You step out of prison. The world is new and different. After so, so long, you hold another human being in your arms.

As I write this, I am in lockdown with my little family. Every day we see or read the news. We learn of new betrayals by corrupt leaders and resource-stealing elites; of acts of solidarity and care by others rehearsing a more co-operative world; we learn of predictable calamities and visions of tenderness. Some of us are shut in by our immune systems, illnesses, depression, or lack of access to medicines; subject to violence, cut off, or in pain. Conversely, others are denied the safety of quarantine, of social benefits, of timely vaccination, condemning us to years or lifetimes of suffering. We all wonder: If and when we get out of here, how will we connect? Will we still know how?

Writing in 1925, Antonin Artaud defended the unrestricted use of opioids for pain of all kinds:

> We know the soul's dosages, its sensibilities, its marrows,
> its thoughts. Leave us in peace. Leave us to our illness, we
> ask nothing else of men. We ask only for a respite from
> suffering. We have evaluated our own lives, we understand
> the restrictions we have placed on ourselves and others, we
> understand the enforced flaccidities of life, the renunciations,
> the paralysis of subtle functions that our disease imposes on
> us daily. We are not quite ready for suicide.
> In the meantime, fuck off.[1]

As that last line suggests, Artaud's vision was explicitly anti-social, and brutally realist. But the quarantine story, like the prison story and the desert island story—and the opioid story—is, in the end, about imagining the world anew. And, as I'm not the first to note, it's about being able to rely on each other again.

And all should cry, Beware! Beware!
His flashing eyes, his floating hair!
Weave a circle round him thrice,
And close your eyes with holy dread,
For he on honey-dew hath fed,
And drunk the milk of Paradise.

The great Romantic poet Samuel Taylor Coleridge wrote "Kubla Khan (or, a Vision in a Dream. A Fragment)," perhaps the most famous opium-inspired poem of all.[2] And yet, he was always ashamed of his drug use and struggled against it for decades. Whereas laudanum doesn't seem to have substantially damaged Thomas De Quincey's literary potential, and it certainly made his name, for the elder poet, opium was a liability even in artistic terms. Largely due to the secrecy he tried to maintain about his habit, Coleridge's behaviour was erratic, and he was driven into unwelcome isolation and deep loneliness. In his private letters, he reveals a pathetic subservience to the drug. And yet, like De Quincey, at other times he fancied himself easily able to master his chemical nemesis. Coleridge once wrote with bravado that he could wean himself off opium within a week, that it would be, a "trivial task." "Is indeed Leviathan so tamed? In that case the quarantine of the opium-eater might be finished within Coleridge's time and with Coleridge's romantic ease,"[3] wrote De Quincey, knowingly, about Coleridge's vain hope of such a quick and easy, permanent detox. De Quincey had been in awe of Coleridge's literary powers since he was a hopeful young acolyte of the poet — but he was far more in awe of opium's dual power to inspire and to oppress its subjects.

"The quarantine of the opium-eater," then, is this loneliness and isolation that the drug, or perhaps just the stigma of opioid use or of addiction, produce. It's also the "halcyon calm" and detachment De Quincey described opium producing in him. Or what "Lena," a drug user commenting on her experience in an online forum,[4] calls a "geometrically precise version of solitude."

Privileged, even coddled by his family so he could write, and gifted at conversation with people of all stations of life, De Quincey nevertheless struggled with contradictory needs common to writers and other artists who require time spent in their own imaginations to get anything done: the need to keep people away, and to hold them close. In a way, the quarantine imposed by laudanum became De Quincey's excuse and the condition for both. As he expressed in his early, mythologizing writing about opium, there is an aspect to this quarantine that is not just tolerable but magical. So many drug users — from De Quincey to the psychonauts on drug forums like Bluelight and Erowid — have described this dual quality of opioids. There is no question that modern-day opium eaters experience the quarantine, for better or for worse, to varying degrees. With his fortuitous phrase, the "quarantine of the opium-eater," my old friend De Quincey hits once again on the perfect expression of the problem.

Frida Kahlo, who spent many, many hours alone due to pain and illness, if not literally quarantined, used to write lying down, and to paint self-portraits using a mirror mounted above her bed. How very lonely she must have been. How lonely she was.

I so often ache for someone close to me to ask, genuinely, how I am. I crumple inside when someone asks me that question in a perfunctory way while informing me with their body language that they would prefer the TL;DR answer, or ideally just good news.

By its very definition, a degenerative disease involves gradual losses. But everyone likes a good triumphing-over-adversity story. Sympathy can curdle into boredom and irritation when the adversity continues to gradually triumph over me instead. Having previously understood friendship as a safe, reciprocal place to share one's joys and mourn one's losses, I've been confused and hurt at some friends' lack of interest in joining me in the latter.

And I want to curl up and hide my wounds when an actual effort at honesty (for, I think, how can we be friends if you don't understand my life?) is rebuffed. And in fact, sometimes when I ill-advisedly try to express the pain this causes—a last-ditch attempt to avoid allowing the gap in understanding to grow until we can't see each other from our respective sides of it—the friends themselves may be hurt or angry, and they may distance themselves. This is a pattern I have found, and it's not at all unique to me: in fact, it is common among people who live with long-term pain. The choice becomes: hide pain, keep friends, feel alone; or share pain, lose friends, be alone. An alternative, which Alphonse Daudet and fellow writer Marcel Proust both settled on, is to hide pain from friends, spare them any sympathetic suffering, or boredom—and save the stories for their readers.

"Be regular and orderly in your life, so that you may be violent and original in your work," said Flaubert. Ha, easy to say when you're the bourgeois-hating but nevertheless bourgeois son of a surgeon, with a non-live-in lover, brothels a-plenty, and a preference for what one Flaubert biographer calls "remote intimacy,"[5] (meaning epistolary, long-distance, mourned, longed-for, or unconsummated relationships), when you live with your mom and don't start work till one p.m.! And yet it's good advice.

As for Kahlo, for Marcel Proust, and for countless other writers and artists confined by their bodies to cork-lined rooms and worlds of the imagination rarely disturbed by visitors, my epistolary friendships have assumed for me the role that work friendships and daily interaction with a romantic partner play in the lives of my busier friends and acquaintances. It's a little like communicating from a desert island by bottled message.

Fortunately, I've always been at my best in writing. It is, in fact, perhaps the perfect setup for a writer and an introvert and a Romantic: solitude broken mostly by written communications with correspondents of my choice, unlimited by geography. It gets me close to Flaubert's writing ideal.

I crave conversation and contact. I crave new and glamorous and intellectually or aesthetically stimulating experiences out in the world. But at the same time, there is so little of me to go around. With so many demands and priorities, I must limit the scope of my life if I really want to write.

For better or for worse, the opium eater's quarantine — both isolation and loneliness, and the boundary-strengthening, solitude-enriching effect of the drug itself — gives me a chance to step away from the conventional, domestic, coupled, and healthy life I once lived.

It took me months to choose a new duvet when my bed became mine and mine alone. I could not remember what I liked. What was my style? What was me? The process felt like an amputation. Among the now-cryptic, years-old notes I scrawled in one of my many notebooks, I find one from 2016 that's easy to parse: *Sleeping w X — womb, cave like a bear, utter peace. vs. the earth quaking when that peace was disturbed.*

But here, years later, I have new walls, a protective bubble, a coldness, an identity that is all mine and from which my unique vision, my individual spirit — the original meaning of the term "genius," something each and every one of us possesses — can emerge. I don't think loss or pain are meaningful or improving in themselves, but without them, I might have woken up at the end of my life and discovered I never found the time, or the necessary cold loneliness, to devote to my art.

Thomas De Quincey wrote:

> At no time of my life have I been a person to hold myself
> polluted by the touch or approach of any creature that wore
> a human shape. I cannot suppose, I will not believe, that any
> creatures wearing the form of man or woman are so absolutely
> rejected and reprobate outcasts, that merely to talk with them
> inflicts pollution [...] for a philosopher should not see with
> the eyes of the poor limitary creature calling himself a man
> of the world, filled with narrow and self-regarding prejudices
> of birth and education, but should look upon himself as a
> catholic creature, and as standing in an equal relation to high
> and low, to educated and uneducated, to the guilty and the
> innocent.[6]

But De Quincey's attitude was not common in his time, and it is not common today. And so those who most need the halcyon calm of opioids are forced by society, rather than their own lack of social skills or interest, into the most brutal of quarantines, making opioids all the more necessary to survive, and, in solitude, all the more dangerous. A quarantine (shut in) and an exile (shut out), in which those doing the exile seem to think the normal laws of civility and decency no longer apply. S., the smart, perceptive, and thoughtful Indigenous woman you met earlier, tells me, for example, that she has twice been asked *if she is a rat* while visibly experiencing symptoms of withdrawal.

A vicious circle, indeed.

Joe spent most of his life profoundly alone. "I generally avoid people in order to avoid being a toxic presence in their lives," he says. "I grew up as the kid nobody wanted and so I've always felt like a walking carcinogen." Joe spent ten years with only his cat for company — an experience that, he feels, taught him how to love. Now, the ways in which he also cares for his beloved (let's call them "Alex") are endless. We talk, as friends do, about frustrations and communications difficulties in our day-to-day relationships too. But Joe's personal experience of trauma has given him an insight, and a loving patience, that I wish I were better at bringing to my own friendships and loves.

With wry humour and hard-earned stoicism, Joe continues to share with me, too, stories of his daily struggle to deal with the atrocious neighbours, the constantly flooding apartment, the pests that come and go. Being poor is an endless series of challenges and indignities. Being poor and disabled and part of the addiction treatment system is almost the bottom of the barrel (so many options: be the dregs on the bottom or the dross on top). Not every relationship can survive far more minor obstacles. But for Joe and his partner, steady, unconditional, reciprocated acts of caring have gradually improved both their lives despite the way everything seems stacked against them.

As they care for each other in quarantine while recovering from probable COVID-19, the couple play video games:

"I'm playing *Uncharted Waters: New Horizons* and sailing around naming everything after my partner. I also named a ship for my cat," Joe writes on Twitter. He lists some of the places he's named:

> Alex Bottom Bay
> Alex Harbour
> Alex's Landing.

If love is, as I believe, an ongoing commitment to action rather than a transient emotion you feel, Joe is the best practitioner I know. On the other hand, the kind of patient, caring support he offers his partner—beginning with quietly cleaning up heroin syringes at a low time in their life—is pretty much the opposite of how families are told to respond to loved ones who use drugs. It's also at odds with the way pain patients are encouraged to focus relentlessly on our individual mindsets and coping skills when we may ache to just be surrounded with love and care—even though our conditions aren't the sort of thing that inspire people to send flowers. Unconditional, loving support is also the opposite of what people who use drugs find when they seek help for addiction, or are forced into the addiction treatment system.

For this reason, harm reduction advocates and people who use drugs use the slogan "support, don't punish." They commonly cite Portugal's drug strategy, in force since the summer of 2001 and notorious for its decriminalization of all substances, including heroin.

The empty windows of this old stone farmhouse outside of Porto, Portugal's second-largest city, frame a piercingly blue afternoon sky. The sun shines hot through the space where its roof used to be. Standing with me in the sunlight, Sérgio Rodrigues, an activist who is a founder of CASO, the Portuguese drug user union, tells me he grew up nearby. He knew the family that lived in this farmhouse, and he played soccer here where grass now grows amid the stones of its ruins and garbage litters the grounds they farmed, and where people who use drugs like heroin and crack cocaine come for privacy.

A few minutes away is an old schoolhouse that, also abandoned in the years after Rodrigues attended high school there, was once popular with drug users as well. It provided a safe, enclosed place to use and to sleep. The structure is under construction now though; it's being turned into a fancy health centre that will cater to a different class of patient.

I am here with a group of journalists on a trip organized by APDES, a Portuguese NGO. Rodrigues, who also works for APDES, takes out his phone to show me a picture of his young son. A few years ago, when his child was in utero, Rodrigues made a cameo in journalist Johann Hari's popular book about addiction, *Chasing the Scream.* Then, he was a methadone user, stabilized on the medication after eleven years of addiction to heroin and crack cocaine. It's been a year or so since he weaned himself off methadone and began carefully experimenting with smoking heroin. Not every day. He doesn't smoke in the presence of the little boy, who is now a gorgeous five-year-old. Nevertheless, he plans to talk to his son openly about drug use when he's older.

"I try to show a beautiful life," he says. "Drugs exist. They bring benefits and harm. [...] Prohibited is more appealing... talk, so [it's] not hidden."

I wish I spoke Portuguese. Even in English, his second or third language, Rodrigues's eloquence comes through, but it's harder for me to get down on paper. With translation help from another APDES worker, I also manage a conversation with someone who uses this unofficial drug consumption site, a woman named Carolina Padua. She holds a crack pipe in her hand — a clean tool supplied by APDES to protect against the spread of infectious disease — and tells me about the Portuguese system, under which she switched from heroin to methadone, dispensed by a bus that makes daily stops in a few locations around the city. Padua is rail-thin, which gives her the figure of a younger woman and the face of someone much older than her forty-nine years. But what we think of as the "look" of the drug user has no relation to the intrinsic properties of a drug, whether heroin, methadone, or crack cocaine, though it may have plenty to do with living rough, or with chronic pain. Rodrigues, for example, doesn't have it, nor, actually, do any of the drug users I have met who've spent little or no time on the street and who have stable, decent housing and income.

I arrived in Porto on Día da Liberdade, the April 25 national holiday commemorating the 1974 Carnation Revolution, a coup and popular uprising that overthrew the authoritarian, right-wing Estado Novo and put an end to its secret police, the isolation of its population within a more liberal Europe, and ultimately to its colonial wars and empire in Africa and Southeast Asia. In a store, I am handed a carnation — citizens who joined the revolutionary soldiers on the streets did so holding red carnations, symbols of socialism and communism — and a small bottle of port, the city's most famous export. At the shop entrance, a man plays Cuban revolutionary songs on a guitar. Wandering down the Rua da Cedofeita, I snap a photo of graffiti that reads "É URGENTE PENSAR NO AMOR" — *it's urgent to think about love*. Red carnations are strewn on the road from a parade earlier in the day.

I am here to attend the biennial conference of Harm Reduction International (HRI). The organization holds their conference in different locations, but it's special that this year they are holding it in Portugal, home of the nearly two-decades-old, daring experiment in the decriminalization of all drugs.

Portugal's drug problem arose from, or following, dictatorship. During the right-wing regime of António de Oliveira Salazar, the country was isolated within Europe. Like South Africa under apartheid, which remained culturally stuck in the 1950s as the rest of the world entered the Swinging Sixties, the authoritarian government in Portugal suppressed cultural change, even as the rest of Europe began to experiment with psychoactive drugs. When the dictatorship fell, heroin use exploded in the country. Injection drug use became widespread and open drug use common. A traumatized population with no experience with recreational drugs and no cultural context for generally moderate use quickly became heavily dependent on the substance, to the point that just about every family, from whatever social class, was affected by heroin addiction. HIV rates climbed until Portugal had the highest rates in Europe relative to its population size.

In the year 2000, a group of eleven experts — drawn from an unusually creative range of disciplines — was given a broad mandate to completely rethink Portugal's approach to substances. As theoretical physicist Alexandre Quintanilha, one of these experts, recalls at the HRI plenary, they held public hearings in cinemas across the country, up to a thousand people in attendance, people sitting on the floor. With so many touched by heroin addiction, the population was eager for a new way to understand the issue, ready to make the shift from seeing people who use drugs as criminals to seeing them as patients, and then simply as human beings.

The policy enacted the following year decriminalized possession of small, personal use amounts of any drug and replaced the criminal justice–based response to drug use with an approach focused on harm reduction and healthcare. Critically, looser drug laws were paired with stepped-up access to addiction treatment (using methadone) and harm reduction for safer use. The results were striking. HIV and viral hepatitis rates plummeted, injection drug use declined rapidly (and those who continued to inject increasingly did so with sterile equipment and safer technique), and drug use rates have remained below European averages for twenty years now. After a low of eleven overdose deaths in 2011, rates have risen more recently. There were thirty such deaths in Portugal in 2016, a year in which 63,632 Americans died of drug overdose (42,249 of those involved an opioid).[7] Since Portugal's experiment, some twenty-five to thirty countries have adopted at least some version of decriminalization, although few have gone as far.

Before I came here, I tried to pitch an in-depth story that would draw on interviews I'd already done with Canadian experts on substance use and addiction, adding what I learn in Portugal, to propose a Canadian adaptation of the Portugal model. I meant it to be a practical, informed response to the federal government's assertion that such a model cannot possibly work here in Canada. The more I learn, the more it seems to me that some model beginning with decriminalization is essential to address the fundamental causes of the current overdose crisis (so long as they are limited in scope, both prescribed safe supply and supervised consumption sites are more like emergency measures to prevent death within a prohibition system).

After trying and failing with every major publication in the country, I booked my flight anyway. While in Portugal, I do manage to file one article for a Canadian newspaper, about an American story: the first official data, announced at the conference, from a clandestine supervised injection site that has been operating somewhere in the US. But mostly I am just absorbing, meeting people, and learning that the way things are in North America (and much of the rest of the world) is not the way things have to be.

When I meet Ricardo Baptista Leite, a physician and centre-right member of Portuguese parliament who heads an international network of parliamentarians working on policies to reduce infectious disease, I have the strange feeling that I've met him before. We chat about Portugal's decriminalization policy and about his party's decision to push for legalization of cannabis (a step beyond decriminalization toward legal regulation of the substance). Portugal is, he tells me, watching closely as legalization plays out in Canada. Our form of legalization is clearly garnering huge profits for a small group of already wealthy investors, but scant attention is being paid to public health or to redressing decades of harms to racialized communities that resulted from criminalization of weed. I'm still trying to figure out why I recognize Baptista Leite as we talk. Bluff, confident, dark good looks . . . ah yes. He looks disturbingly similar to my neurosurgeon, the one who may one day plunge his gloved hands into my memories, my appetites, my thoughts. I try to concentrate on his words.

Portugal's policy of decriminalization is based on clearly articulated values—pragmatism, humanism, evidence, and participation—that are distinctly different from those underlying the American-led prohibition regime. It is also decidedly paternalistic: the state aims to provide firm but loving guidance to people falling into bad patterns in their relationship with substances.

All day I talk with drug users and harm reduction workers, activists, policy-makers. I meet the drugs editor at VICE, and BBC reporters, and a Colombian journalist, and many doctors, won over to harm reduction by the evidence that it prevents infectious disease and other health harms. I have dinner one night with Scott Bernstein, a fellow Canadian and a lawyer who directs policy for the Canadian Drug Policy Coalition, which holds the ambitious goal of moving Canadian drug policy into an entirely new, post-prohibition era of legal regulation of substances. At one plenary, Baptista Leite says words ready-made for a headline. I scribble them down: "Harm reduction and love share a common denominator. For it to truly work, it needs to be unconditional."

I hear similar language from many others — here and among harm reduction workers in Canada. One of my first interviews upon my return to Toronto, for example, is with an overdose prevention site worker, Franky, who tells me: "People who use drugs deserve the best." It's a controversial statement. While in Porto, I buy a T-shirt made by Release, a UK charity focused on drug law and policy. The shirt reads, simply and factually, *Nice People Take Drugs*. Back in Toronto, my nearest and dearest are uneasy with me wearing this tee outside the house. This, despite being informed about harm reduction and in favour of human rights for people who use drugs. It's too much of a pro-drugs statement, they say. Like, say, wearing a hat with the letters MAGA, Make America Great Again.

By no means everyone who uses drugs, but the poor, the Indigenous, the homeless, the sex workers, the disabled, the queer and trans — in short, the most marginalized drug users — are regularly told and shown that they don't deserve "the best." That they deserve neither healthcare nor pleasure. That they don't deserve life itself.

"I've been called names all my life. Sticks and stones may break my bones but names will never hurt me. My mother used to tell me that. It helps a little," S. tells me.

I do feel anxiety, every time I wear that shirt, about having to be ready with my speech about why people who use drugs don't renounce their human rights or membership in the human community. But how can it be more shameful to suggest that people who use drugs are nice people than it is to proclaim one's allegiance to the movement that tore refugee babies from their parents' arms, that sets crosses on fire to chants like "Jews shall not replace us" and "white power"? This is the context that makes Dr. Baptista Leite's statement, and Franky's, radical and important, that makes it so important to think about love.

In Porto, I also get away from the formal plenaries and meet people who use drugs who are setting out their own agendas and figuring out what form their movement will take—not always in a comfortable relationship with the non-governmental, medical, and bureaucratic organizations that have such prominent presences here, or even with former drug users who identify as "in recovery." These participants are more critical of the Portugal model. They tell me and other journalists there that, partly due to its success in reducing injection drug use rates, this model has stigmatized injecting, driving drug users who persist in this practice into the shadows. They tell me that the rights-violating control exerted by law enforcement in other countries is replaced here in part by an overly medical model where substance use is pathologized, where all use is seen as addiction and mental disorder. They tell me that austerity policies enacted during the economic crisis resulted in funding for community-based harm reduction initiatives being drastically reduced, while other aspects of the drug strategy did not suffer similar cutbacks. This one-on-one work, though, in which harm reduction workers meet drug users wherever they are—at an abandoned farmhouse, for example—and form relationships of trust and care by being trustworthy and responding to what users say they need, is really central to harm reduction, and irreplaceable by more formal, clinical interactions, however well-meaning.

Most nights, after the conference wraps up for the evening, I escape from so much social interaction and find a restaurant to eat in on my own. I respond to edits on my piece while I wait for my dinner. I imagine a different life where I'm a foreign correspondent and my plane out from Porto takes me on to Uruguay or Mozambique or to New Zealand. There's a wraparound program—providing everything from shelter to methadone to training in human rights—for women who use drugs, and their children, in the Mombasa region of Kenya that I'd like to check out and write about, and a women-led organization in Barcelona that tries to flexibly respond to the varied needs of women who use drugs and who have experienced violence. There's a whole world of creative responses to explore. And just, a whole world. On the plane, it feels like I could go anywhere.

And then I am home, back with my children, in damaged North America, and I write about Angela Kokinos, who might not have died if she lived in a place with a sensible drug policy like Portugal, despite the ways it's due for an update after twenty years of impressive successes. Unbelievably, in just a year the state of Oregon will decriminalize all substances. Others will follow.

"The opioid piece is probably the least challenging of all of it, to be honest with you," says Dr. Turnbull. It's been a bit more than a year since my article about his managed opioids program was published. I called him back to ask what has happened since he gathered those twenty-one patients at extraordinarily high risk of overdose death.

"No one thought [these patients would] be alive a year later," he says. That's how unwell and at risk they were. That's how they were selected for the program.

And yet they have just held an anniversary party.

The neighbours — who I'd been told last year were having some trouble adjusting to a bunch of sometimes rowdy and definitely not property-value-enhancing people living next door — have "slowly embraced them." One resident of the program facility started up a dog-walking business, offering a service people need and a bridge between the yuppifying neighbourhood and these distinctly lower-socio-economic-bracket residents.

No one here is dying from opioid use anymore, even though the overdose crisis continues to claim increasing numbers of victims in the province and even in this city.

"I can't think of the last time there was an overdose," Dr. Turnbull says.

Residents are engaging in volunteer work, advocacy, or paid work. One young woman has left to live with her mother, while another returns to the MOP now and then between living with her boyfriend. She gets "carries," injectable opioid she can take with her and administer on her own. Some residents have said they wish to continue to inject their drugs, while others have now switched to oral (pills) Dilaudid. Dr. Turnbull doesn't really care: he's more interested in other goals than whether or not his patients are taking opioids or in how they're taking them — goals like connecting with family, a common one among the group. Staff may facilitate family sleepovers, or almost daily family visits with residents.

"It's kind of getting boring here," Dr. Turnbull tells me. Patients have finished their courses of treatment for hepatitis C and their physical health is generally stable. With assistance from program staff, they have gradually sorted out their judicial records, freeing themselves from endless involvement with the judicial system for petty crimes they no longer need to commit. They have learned basic skills they never got a chance to learn: things like laundry or cooking pasta. Things are so stable, the nature of the doctor's work has changed. He's not running an addiction program anymore, not really. While it's boring in the ways that really matter, it's still chaotic in other ways.

As an example, Dr. Turnbull recounts an incident that had occurred that morning. A resident who had been carrying crack cocaine panicked when a police officer paid a visit to tell another resident that there was no outstanding warrant for their arrest: a good-news house call. But, knowing perfectly well from experience that cops equal danger, the panicked resident quickly ducked into a bathroom and hid the baggie of crack in her vagina. And then could not get it out.

"I didn't ever think in my whole career I'd be fishing a bag of cocaine out of someone's vagina," says Dr. Turnbull, who did, after all, train in internal medicine. "My gosh, it's weird."

No longer is he trying a seemingly risky strategy to keep desperately addicted, extremely unwell people alive one more day. The strategy is not risky, and it continues to work. But now he is running a group home for people who have endured profound adverse circumstances throughout their lives. No one escapes unscathed from what these people have been through.

"Not one little bit of this has to do with their opioid dose," says Dr. Turnbull. "[We are] undoing damages done by society over twenty years."

It takes a long time, he explains, for residents to reset their balance, to find enjoyment in other things than drugs. He mentions one resident for whom it took a full year of emotional work before dinner with family became at last an enjoyable experience, rather than an occasion that inspired only dread.

"This isn't a fentanyl crisis or an overdose crisis," "Lauren" tells me. "It's a prohibition crisis."

I am speaking—via Signal, an end-to-end encrypted messaging and call service—with a woman who is a member of a heroin buyers club. In 2019, the British Columbia Centre on Substance Use (BCCSU) released a white paper outlining how a safe, affordable heroin supply could be achieved, at a time when the illicit market is so dangerous, by the establishment of what they call "heroin buyers clubs." The daring idea is to combine the strengths of buyers clubs and compassion clubs. The former were pioneered by AIDS activists to buy expensive HIV medications in bulk, while the latter arose in Canada during cannabis prohibition to supply the drug to patients who used it to control epilepsy or other conditions.

Under her real name, Lauren is an important organizer in the drug user–led movement for overdose prevention and better drug policies in Canada, but she needs to go by a pseudonym if I'm to tell this story. I am terribly worried. Unlike some of the writers whose journalism on substance use and drug policy I admire, I've never done anything like this before, and I distrust my own eagerness for a juicy story. I am trying hard to be worthy of the trust people are placing in me, but what if I'm not? We spend a lot of time talking about the protections she needs in order to be able to answer my question. Her conversation with me is the least of her worries right now though, she says.

Lauren is in the process of talking with drug dealers, trying to find someone who will provide a reliable source of uncontaminated (illicit fentanyl-free) heroin. She thinks she has found a person they can trust. Lives are on the line.

The idea is that her group, which consists of four women and one man somewhere in Canada, will jointly purchase heroin at a group rate—like Groupon for hard drugs. They will test it for purity, using the sophisticated mass spectrometer technology available at a few medical centres in their region. Then the co-op members, who include working mothers, will be able to inject the heroin upon which they are dependent with the same regularity and confidence (and privacy) that I inject my immune suppressant or take my prescribed oral opioid painkiller. As with the patients at Ottawa Inner City Health's managed opioids program, these are largely people who have tried alternatives—including detox, including methadone, including twelve-step programs. All have resulted in a return to fentanyl-laced heroin and a life of constant risk. Unadulterated heroin, for these users, means stability—if only they can reduce that risk, a risk that we associate with heroin but which is not actually intrinsic to the substance. "You have to have the support but you don't need a medical system," Lauren says. "We are there to support each other through . . . anywhere from sourcing drugs to going into detox."

Lauren tells me that this club began with a single acquaintance of hers who was heavily dependent upon both illicit fentanyl and alcohol. A peer worker like Angela Kokinos, and knowledgeable about drug use and treatment options, this woman was, also like Kokinos, alternately abstinent and relapsing. Having tried the addiction medications Suboxone and methadone as well as less well-evidenced treatments, she had found nothing that kept her effectively off the illicit drug market. This left her at extremely high risk of death.

"She was pretty much overdosing every day." In desperation, she told Lauren, "I've done [detox and medication-based treatment] so many times. It doesn't work for me."

And yet, despite the intensity and destructiveness of her dependence upon illicit fentanyl, she knew that opioid dependence could also look very different for her.

"Heroin had been her drug for years and years, with no overdoses then," Lauren explains.

Before fentanyl and other contaminants flooded the Canadian drug supply, she was basically okay; her function, including the ability to work, was good when she had a stable source of uncontaminated heroin. And now she wanted to treat her co-existing dependence on alcohol with detox, a positive personal choice. But as rules for the alcohol treatment program prohibited her from taking other drugs,[8] she would be forced to undergo fentanyl withdrawal at the same time as alcohol detox. And then she'd be sent on her way, with dangerously lowered opioid tolerance at a very vulnerable time.

"It's an ethical dilemma from being restricted from doing what's right because of absolutely nonsensical drug policy that was never put in place to protect our health," Lauren says. Her friend's husband was afraid to leave for work in case his wife were to relapse and overdose alone.

Lauren reached out to the illicit market, which she knew well as a user herself, and acquired uncontaminated heroin for her friend, a week's worth. After that, she was able to connect her with a doctor able — because such programs do exist in Canada, although they have so far been limited and difficult to access — to prescribe an injectable opioid. Lauren could have gone to jail for what she did, lost her job in healthcare, or worse. She also likely saved her friend's life.

After I returned from my short trip to Portugal, I began to look deeper into the variety of models that would be an improvement on the current global war on drugs — in particular, for the ways that people who use drugs are themselves coming up with ideas about what they need and ways of working together to meet those needs. There are many of these, from the woman-led centre for women who use drugs in Barcelona I dreamed of visiting, to an illicit, user-run supervised consumption site in Italy that by 2019 had operated without reported overdose deaths for more than a decade.

Imagine a different sort of recovery for people who have been harmed by drugs (or by the consequences of using drugs in our current society, or who are just drug users who have been harmed by society), a grassroots recovery where users help each other, but not the same as the Narcotics Anonymous twelve-step peer model.

Harm Reduction Works-HRW—a practice founded by veteran harm reduction workers Jess Tilley and Albie Park—is one such model quietly gaining traction in the US. The organization Tilley and Park founded, HRH413, offers free scripts and exercises for meetings that anyone can start to bring people together to learn about harm reduction and apply its principles. The idea is to create an easily accessed, easily replicated model of mutual support for people who use alcohol or other drugs—taking the community-based support of twelve-step programs like NA, but skipping their insistence on abstinence (which becomes just one option on the menu, as it must be under a true harm reduction approach). On their website they write, "Each group is independent. Collectively, all groups are interdependent."[9]

It's a kind of recovery that can go in many directions: moderating use, using safely, and not using at all. Regardless, this sort of "treatment" is non-professional, non-clinical, non-hierarchical. It involves cooperation, equality, knowledge, and support.

Imagine, then, that you make a range of opioids available—ensuring lower-potency opioids like heroin are as affordable and accessible as illicit fentanyl. This would begin to open the possibility for people who are dependent on very high doses of illicit fentanyl to gradually lower their tolerance and move from the dangerous illicit supply on the street to lower-strength, regulated heroin.

"There's groups of us who don't want fentanyl," Lauren tells me. "We've got to stop the bleed [from illicit fentanyl overdose]. We go from fentanyl backwards."

It seems to me that Lauren is an advocate of moderation for a substance about which moderation is popularly believed to be impossible.

To think forward to a world without prohibition, we might imagine, as Lauren does, a future where poppies are grown locally in Canada to produce essential medicines including heroin. She is not the only one: drug legalization activist Dana Larsen has floated the idea of (legally, under current laws) giving away opium poppy seeds and then "crowdsourcing" the sap from poppies grown in gardens across Canada to produce an unadulterated opium supply; Fair Price Pharma, a new company founded by Dr. Perry Kendall, British Columbia's first provincial health officer, and Dr. Martin Schechter, the lead researcher behind NAOMI, Canada's heroin-assisted treatment clinical trial, aims to become the country's first domestic producer of injectable, prescription heroin, with a medicine wonderfully named Opiax.[10]

Or—and this is where I see great potential to redress the twin harms of capitalism and prohibition, systems that have grown up together—a partnership with Mexican farmers would allow for fair trade across borders as an alternative to the war on drugs. Others see that potential too. A series of academic working groups, informal conversations, and networks have sprung up independent of each other, each an attempt to start charting a different future, one of international solidarity in the face of legacies of war on drugs policies: legacies like environmental damage, forced migration, and the insecurity that inspires the cult of Santa Muerte. Through new trilingual networks like PANDA—the Pan-American Network of Drug-user Activists—drug user organizers from Mexico, Canada, and the United States aim to deepen cross-continental work to address the multiple harms of prohibition and eliminate overdose (or "drug poisoning") deaths.[11] I sit in as a guest in some of their virtual meetings and learn that in northern Mexico, drug users are being kidnapped into "treatment" and not always reappearing. People dependent on illicit drugs have also been sacrificed by rival cartels who have carried out massacres in unregistered rehab centres, sometimes shooting every person in the place.[12] Here the violence that people who use drugs may face upon entering conventional rehab is structural and emotional; there, there's all that and sometimes bullets, too (the guns smuggled south just as the drugs are smuggled north).

Then again, forced unpaid labour (that is, slave labour), denial of contact with family, and other bizarre and cruel abuses of human rights are conditions of "treatment" in the unregulated American drug treatment system as well.[13]

Learning from the public health and social justice failures of alcohol and cannabis legalization could help to ensure that any legalization privileges moderate recreational or needed prescribed use, and that they strengthen public health rather than shareholder profits.

People might not stop at moving down from illicit fentanyl to heroin. They might, if it were available to them, choose to smoke heroin rather than injecting it, which would be a less risky choice (and one made by a number of the people who use heroin who I met in Portugal).

Then again, if they could access and afford OxyContin, they might settle into a maintenance dose with that still-lower-potency opioid. And if opium were available, then extremely low-dose opioids such as those you could buy over the counter in the late nineteenth century would become options as well (perhaps regulated with a view to public and individual health, rather than profit).

So long as people who wish to use drugs, whether to treat pain or to experience pleasure, are treated as "drug-seekers," disordered, or criminal, there is no way for a medical relationship to be therapeutic. Questions about safer use are treated as scandalous, impossible, like a lamp that if rubbed will unleash the fumes of dangerous, uncontrollable drug use — a Pandora's box that punishes the curious. As a result, much factual and useful information is kept from people: therapeutic dosing techniques through which people are taught to use the right amount to enhance function with less risk and fewer side effects, for example, or "chipping," the decades-old technique of restrained recreational use that Matt Johnson practises.

For most of my childhood and adolescence, I skipped the annual physicals that were common then. Too healthy to bother. I didn't visit a single doctor for years on end. Now, though, it is impossible for more than a few hours to forget just how much I rely on an array of medical treatments, and appointments with both my vitally important family doctor and a panoply of specialists.

Every week I inject myself with an immune suppressant — no, not the one that made my hair fall out and gave me psoriasis. The one that makes my thigh swell up unless I take an allergy med as well. By cleverly hampering a very specific part of my self-hating immune system, it suppresses just that part, and has given me back some of my range of movement.

We discuss: What do I do when my tramadol dose reaches the point at which seizures become more likely? There are a few different opioids I can rotate to then. Short-term, I can try to bring down my dose using cannabis, which I find unpleasant, but most other painkillers are either not indicated for inflammatory pain or have already savaged my gut and are now off the list of options. After one of the regular periods when pain and stiffness worsen (what's called a "flare"), my doctor and I added a low dose of a different immune suppressant as well. This one is a chemotherapy drug. It gives me heartburn and carries the risk of blood cancer, but it halted the flare without me having to increase the opioid this time. Since taking it, I've found it easier to hold up my own head. I am no longer in quite such a constant fight against gravity. Although my immune system continues to beat me into the shape of a human question mark, I am actually doing really well.

The exceptional access medications program I'm on due to the high cost of my immune suppressants will pay for morphine, but I hate morphine: it gives me nightmares; it makes me feel sick and dull. I tell my doctor I prefer tramadol, for which I pay a significant portion of my monthly income.

All this, the constant decisions and cost-benefit calculations, we can discuss. Anxiety shortens my breath so I have trouble getting the words out. But my doctor takes pains to let me know that he is on my side, that we are working together for my health and well-being, that my reports on my own experience are relevant and my preferences are important rather than suspect. I remember how Frida Kahlo called her long-time doctor, Leo Eloesser (a thoracic and orthopedic surgeon at Stanford who she consulted when she and Diego Rivera visited San Francisco) her "doctorcito querido"—her beloved little doctor. She dedicated a self-portrait to him and painted his portrait as well, and in many years of correspondence expressed an almost embarrassing gratitude for his kindness and care.

(The relationship wasn't one-sided: in 1941 he gave her a fetus in a glass jar, which she kept in her bedroom.[14])

Such gratitude, though, for someone who was, let's face it, unable to make everything better. Neither can my doctor. But like Kahlo—and like Meg, with the physician we're calling Dr. X—I feel a painful gratitude for his willingness to explore options with me, for not being dismissed, belittled, turned away.

I am very aware that my generally positive experience is rare among pain patients, which is why I'm so anxious, especially when we discuss opioids. Things could change on a dime. My experience is uncommon among my fellow women pain patients in particular, practically unheard of among Black women in pain, Indigenous women in pain. It is, also, unimaginable among poor people who use illicit drugs, regardless of how much emotional or even physical pain they are in. Such basic kindness has been unimaginable for Joe, or S., or Lelena, or Michael, for any of the people I write about. Almost universally, chronic pain patients and people who use drugs come to each new appointment bearing a silent history of humiliating, traumatizing interactions with the medical system.

Michael Eschbach, whose inexperienced doctor makes him travel across town on public transit, in pain, during a pandemic, for the sole purpose of testing his urine, describes his latest appointment: "Carlyn, I give up. [...] The doctor poked her head in to see if it was me and wish me a merry fucking Christmas. I told them I just want to die."

The doctor and resident ignored Eschbach's request to stop morphine, which isn't working, and to return to a different painkiller that worked for him in the past, perhaps because he asked for Percocet by name, which can be considered suspicious, "drug seeking." They ignored his requests to resume taking an anti-anxiety medication that also worked. Without it, just leaving his hotel room is a harrowing experience. He tried to explain but his doctor simply talked right over him. "I can't do this anymore, I really can't," he tells me, crying. "I'd rather not have a doctor than this sort of doctoring. That's all I need, a doctor who understands and I can't for the fucking life of me have one." He believes that it's the note in his chart that says he's homeless that has resulted in the lack of trust and dismissal of his experience and concerns.

Lelena, preparing to fly alone to another state to meet a new doctor who she hopes might take her pain seriously, writes me, "If I see a doctor that is dismissive of me AGAIN? It might break me. [...] I'm so afraid all the time. It burns up all my energy."

This is why Meg's experience with Dr. X is so rare. She has found a doctor whose empathy derives from an understanding of trauma, who understands that in her white coat she may represent a lifetime of interactions that were hurtful, frightening, and oppressive. Dr. X doesn't just believe Meg's own account of her pain. She is also willing to believe in Meg's vision for herself. She is doing something more frightening to many doctors than anything else: ceding control to her patient.

After three doses of tramadol and a day's worth of difficult but joint-loosening movement, the Tin Man becomes human. I'm limber and light-hearted and the night expands with possibilities inconceivable by day. I stay up far too late to prolong the good. At night, once the young teen and pre-teen are finally asleep, I stay up later and later to luxuriate in this peaceful dreamy time.

The writer Haruki Murakami once compared the solitary act of writing to eating fried oysters, which his wife can't stand. He has no choice, therefore, but to cook and eat them by himself.

"I am lonely, but they are delicious," he told the audience at a literary event in Fukushima.[15] "Like the relationship between solitude and freedom, it moves in an endless cycle. Picking out single words that are contained within me is also a solitary act so [writing novels] is similar to eating fried oysters by myself."

It is delicious.

But solitude is more enjoyable when you're not condemned to it. With a daily level and frequency of tramadol that leaves me rarely in serious pain, things have become possible that had felt lost forever. This is when we start thinking of getting a cat. My world of online friends—in which, among both pain patients and people who use illicit drugs, there seems to be an above-average number of cat lovers—is delighted. Joe sends me online listings of cats in need of a home. Lelena asks if she might send me a "kitty care package" of toys and treats (sadly, since I'm hoping to write about her, I can't accept gifts, not even tasty salmon crunchies). While I'm still recovering from my second, brutal bout of positional vertigo, I drop the pretense that the kitten is a concession to my children. In reality, it's for me. Despite my new virtual social life, I am so lonely in my spinning world I think I may die of it. My friend Emily drives me, still wobbly, and the boys to the Humane Society in search of a little black or orange kitty.

As it turns out, the cat who presses her nose to the cage, curiosity trumping caution, is a little brown tabby, long and slender, with funny bits of orange and round, surprised eyes. She is a beautiful six-week-old bit of fluff who begins to purr the minute she is in my arms. She is nearly a year old now and has not stopped. She begins to visibly vibrate, to thrum with it, when she sees me and she cries when I leave the house.

My children are just starting to separate from me, developing their own boundaries, as adolescents should do, whereas before they were loving extensions of my own body. Now my little cat is the one who gazes at me with adoration and seems to understand every word I say. And after the first few days with our new companion, I realize I don't know where all my words went over the past many years of days spent alone: Who did I talk to? Because I am talking to Kinu in a continuous stream.

I have been so torn between fruitful solitude and the gaping black hole of loneliness. Kinu fills part of the hole. And my new friends — every one of them an outcast in some way — are gradually taking over the rest. When something happens to me, they are, increasingly, the ones I think to tell. It is as if I have found the missing chair leg that heroin is for some of the people I've met.

Online, the limitations of a life bounded by pain are less important, the strained tone of my voice less of a turnoff. The ways I can seem inflexible or controlling — bitter experience having taught me precisely how best to save myself pain — come off less like a bad or defeatist attitude. Like many others with long-term, life-eroding health conditions, here, in the sparkling reaches of cold cyberspace, I have made real friends.

Julian Buchanan — the young British parole officer we met earlier who realized that heroin was a solution to his client's problems of unemployment, alienation, and ennui — grew older and now lives near his grandchildren in New Zealand, where he advocates against prohibition, and against the attitudes and understanding of substances that prohibition has instilled in all of us. I speak to him from Toronto across a twelve-hour time difference, and he tells me the rest of the story of how a grandfather who has never used an illicit drug came to have such liberal attitudes to substances as feared as heroin, fentanyl, methamphetamines, or cocaine.

Heroin may have been a sort of solution for his clients all those years ago, but it was not a solution that they could be honest about, not to him. And so young people fresh out of jail would assure him they had no intention of using drugs. With their opioid tolerance reduced by forced detoxification in prison, they would easily overdose when they in fact used heroin as soon as they could get hold of it.

"It was really clear that I was screwing people's lives up by abstinence treatment," Buchanan tells me. Instead, he began to ask his clients, over a cup of coffee, what it was that they enjoyed in their lives, and what was getting them down.

"People broke down in tears," he recalls. "They hadn't had the space for so long for someone to sit down [with]." In that space, they would confide in him: "I enjoy heroin...It takes away the pain...it relaxes me."

And, finally, Buchanan began to understand.

He left his position as a parole officer and eventually found his way to the Liverpool area and psychiatrist John Marks. Working for Dr. Marks, Buchanan became part of a controversial experiment in maintenance heroin prescribing that was carried out between 1982 and 1995, and was initially devised to stem the spread of HIV.

Despite the controversy, this was not as radical as it sounds. From as far back as 1926, heroin maintenance prescribing for "addicts" was studied by a government committee chaired by the president of the country's Royal College of Physicians and declared to be a legitimate medical practice in the UK.[16] It was common practice and called the "British System" until 1967, when it was largely phased out and heroin use began, for really the first time, to be associated with crime.[17] In the 1970s injectable heroin was prescribed at University College Hospital in London,[18] and the practice has never died out completely.

"It helped them stop having to run around like a headless chicken" trying to get drugs, Buchanan says.

Instead, the addicts, now redesignated as patients, simply picked up their prescription—a clean[19] supply of opioids—in the form of injectable or smokable diamorphine (the medical name used in the UK for heroin; in Canada it's usually called diacetylmorphine). At last, Buchanan's young clients could start to assess what they needed in their lives and make plans for a future that had seemed impossibly out of reach. And indeed, once they could manage withdrawal with a regular medication, taken in calm conditions (the assumption today that addiction medication must be supervised was not the case then, and users could take their prescription at home just like any other patient), the symptoms of opioid use disorder or addiction simply went away.

Ultimately, Dr. Marks's practice was closed by the Thatcher government after it received media attention in the United States. There were no drug-related deaths during the years he ran his clinic. But in the two years after it was shuttered, 41 of the 450 patients died. Others lost limbs, contracted HIV, and were forced to return to petty theft or sex work to support addictions that had had very little impact on their daily functioning, relationships, or employment during the years they were prescribed their drug of choice.[20] Due to the dramatically positive outcomes of Dr. Marks's project, though, the idea never died. In fact, diamorphine continued to be prescribed under the radar in the UK to small numbers of people up to the present day. In the 1990s, Switzerland began prescribing heroin to a small subset of heroin-addicted patients with longstanding, destructive addictions and two or more unsuccessful attempts at other forms of treatment. Later, looking at the immensely positive results from the Switzerland trial, the Netherlands followed suit, and then Canada, in a very limited way. Now the UK has initiated a new formal program to bring more visibility and more standardization to clinical practice in heroin prescribing in the country that started it. Results so far are the same as everywhere else this has been tried: really astonishing transformations in people's lives, well beyond the sort of results you see with any other treatment for opioid addiction, except for similar programs that provide the range of similar opioids at adequate doses for heroin users.

We already looked at Ottawa Inner City Health's managed opioids program. In London, Ontario, Dr. Andrea Sereda, along with colleagues like Dr. Nanky Rai in Toronto, pioneered publicly what doctors had started doing on the q.t.: prescribing hydromorphone to patients heavily dependent on heroin or fentanyl. It was still a deeply controversial practice in 2019. That's when Dr. Sereda and her colleagues announced the results of three years of this treatment offered to one hundred patients at high risk of overdose death: the same ridiculously positive impact on overall health and quality of life seen with heroin prescribing. Not until the following year, with the COVID-19 pandemic exacerbating the dangers of the illicit drug supply, did the College of Physicians and Surgeons of Ontario (CPSO) finally issue formal guidance to its members, thus endorsing the practice.[21] It's still controversial. After all, many doctors were distressed when cannabis was legalized for medical use with a prescription: the distinction physicians have always drawn between drug dealer and prescriber is one that they do not like to see blurred. The fervour with which some doctors now push for opioid prescribing to be restricted reflects their angst at the knowledge that the medical profession, somehow duped by pharmaceutical marketers, was guilty of "hooking" chronic pain patients on the drugs. But the CPSO's guidance, and the legitimacy it offers, was a long time coming, given the evidence available and the raging overdose crisis.

Some measures of the success of a treatment are more relevant than others. Buprenorphine and methadone, for example, really do shine at preventing overdose (among those who are able to stick with them, a caveat rarely mentioned out loud). Proponents of abstinence-based treatments tend to tout their success at getting patients off drugs, but rarely mention the extremely high relapse rates or deaths among people who do not respond well to detox or abstinence-based counselling. Where heroin is successful as a prescribed treatment is in restoring a patient's quality of life, along with their relationships and communities. The adherence or retention rate — the number of people sticking with treatment for months or years — is also very high (although this is often portrayed as a bad thing, it is actually considered a good thing for most interventions that improve overall health). Overdose deaths in this highly at-risk population decline to zero. Multiple health measures such as treatment for diabetes, viral hepatitis, or HIV improve.

People whose problem was that they were drug seeking do extremely well, it turns out, when they find the drug they are seeking.

And so Meg seeks fentanyl. And Joe seeks OxyContin or morphine. And Jordan seeks injectable fentanyl. And Lauren seeks heroin. And, if I lost access to my pain medication and was desperate not to lose the life it's given back to me, I might possibly become a seeker of tramadol. Other people I speak with have been able to find function and stability with buprenorphine, sometimes despite the immense disapproval that comes with them using this medication that doesn't even achieve the euphoric and calming effects they really want or need. Still others — Garth, for example — find that stability with methadone. Some do all right with no opioids in the long term, while for many others, abstinence proves fatal.

Thanks to the elaborate structures maintaining prohibition of opioids, among other drugs, it is all but impossible to say clearly just how dangerous these drugs really are. What is clear is that the way they are typically classified does not reflect the intrinsic harms of the substances. Opioids like heroin or morphine provide very good examples of the disconnect between the actual risks of the substance and the risks that relate to the "heroin lifestyle" — or, rather, the extra harms created by the various policies and practices and even beliefs that uphold prohibition.

Dr. David Nutt, a British neuropsychopharmacologist, has tried to evaluate the real intrinsic harms of different psychoactive substances. According to his analysis (published in the *Lancet* in 2010, and focusing on the UK), alcohol comes out as most harmful overall, although crack cocaine followed by heroin are considered to be the most harmful drugs to the users themselves. But his analysis still reflects harms resulting from the world we live in now, not the actual qualities of illicit drugs. For example, one measure he uses — relationship of the drug to crime levels — will vary according to the legal status of the drug in some cases (heroin is associated with violent crime networks due to its high desirability and high illegality) and according to more intrinsic factors in others. Heroin's score for mortality is high, but a quick glance at the mortality statistics for supervised consumption sites tells you that its high death rate is also not intrinsic to the drug. There is, in fact, no overdose mortality at these sites — period. Another hint would be the fact that while illicit fentanyl, not measured in Dr. Nutt's 2010 study, would surely be considered more dangerous even than heroin due to recent overdose death statistics, its chemically identical pharmaceutical version has been widely used as a safe and effective analgesic in hospital settings since the 1970s.

Still, studies have shown intrinsic dangers associated with both short- and long-term use of opioids. We know, for example, that long-term use can cause reduced function of testes or ovaries, or low testosterone, which in turn may cause other problems such as low bone density. If considered a harm in itself, dependence is an obvious harm of long-term opioid use, and as we've discussed, there is evidence that heightened sensitivity to pain could result from short- or long-term use, although it's not clear exactly how the typical laboratory tests of pain sensitivity translate to the experience of a person already living with intractable pain.[22]

What else? Injections, if not done under sterile conditions and with knowledge of how best to do it, can be harmful in many ways (but that's not an intrinsic harm). Opioids can cause chronic and terrible constipation — but while intrinsic, it is a modifiable harm: access to a healthy diet with plenty of fibre, to exercise, and to fresh, clean water can reduce its severity. Luckily for me, tramadol is not as often associated with this common woe of illicit and prescribed users alike. Collapsed veins are a common problem among frequent and long-term injectors, but they are also not intrinsic harms as they can be largely avoided through education on proper injection technique; using only substances intended for intravenous use; and using sharp, sterile needles. And infections like viral hepatitis, tuberculosis, HIV, or endocarditis are all associated with injection opioid use — but again, none of these are intrinsic to the drug itself, only to use contexts like homelessness and deep poverty, unsafe injection practices or dirty rigs (syringes).

The fact is that most studies are looking for evidence of harms rather than considering the mechanism of opioids and asking how their use can be made as safe and beneficial as possible. If you scan the literature associated not with substance use but with analgesia relating to surgery though, you find more of the latter.

Before prohibition, as we've seen, opioids were considered a panacea and used in different formulations — like Mrs. Winslow's Soothing Syrup, Ascatco, Stickney and Poor's Paregoric, or Allenbury's throat pastilles — to treat just about anything that couldn't be treated with, say, alcohol, cannabis indica, or cocaine. Some of these indications for use were a little (or more than a little) far-fetched. But others, like depression, cough, or diarrhea, really do respond to opioids. Opioids can protect the heart in the event of a heart attack. They can, when taken long term, mute the adrenergic system, although I don't know of any research that considers whether sluggish cortisol could be a helpful thing for someone with PTSD. They inhibit constriction of the lower airways. They can reduce inflammation in the brain and gut (among many other positive, as well as negative, effects on the body) — but may also increase it, most likely in cases of tolerance and hyperalgesia.

While there's no way to know what has caused what and when, I later see the more long-term evidence of inflammation in a neurology report of white matter scattered through my brain — an accumulation of harm typically resulting from autoimmune diseases like multiple sclerosis, as well as from the aging process. Might opioids in fact protect me from further harm? Without research designed to objectively investigate potential benefits as well as harms, there's no way to really say.

Addiction to opioids, or opioid use disorder, is often described in shorthand as "persistent use despite negative consequences."

But this is a definition that falls apart at the slightest breeze.

What do you call it when the social context changes such that, with the stroke of a lawmaker's pen, a drug that was illegal becomes legal? People who used cannabis persistently and despite the tension this caused in relationships or the legal or employment woes that resulted, while it was illegal, would have been understood to have cannabis use disorder. Now, where it has been legalized, most laypeople have trouble even taking the diagnosis of cannabis use disorder seriously (it is still a clinical diagnosis). Or they have trouble appreciating that not only is cannabis not the cure-all it's marketed as (like opium before it) but that although it's in fact a relatively safe drug, it, too, can be used in harmful ways as well as positive ones.

The opposite process occurred with the prohibition of opium early in the twentieth century, and with prohibition of alcohol in the 1920s. Suddenly, out of nowhere, merely heavy users of a substance became abusers and criminals. A black market materialized, with all the shady trappings of black markets anywhere. Suddenly, recreational, moderate use wasn't possible and "enjoyment" was a deeply suspect rationale for seeking it out. Suddenly the consequences of use weren't a hangover or a heavy sleep, but incarceration, dispossession, or forced treatment — however strange, ill-founded, or barbaric in nature. The end — getting off this vile substance that a few years previously was merely a simple luxury or mild vice — justified the means.

Because it happened, surely we can picture in our minds the way alcohol prohibition, and more recently and incompletely, cannabis prohibition, came and went. And because we know it happened, it must be possible, also, to imagine the way opium prohibition arose, completely transforming the meaning and nature of opioid use. It's a good time — as governments frantically issue new laws and create new policies, trying to catch up to the coronavirus; as different visions of the world compete — to imagine.

Lockdown: the world outside my head and the world inside my head are finally the same. The pressure is equalized.

The virtual world I have been setting up, the world that some of my friends, too busy to stay in touch, nevertheless disparaged, is now the only world there is, for everyone. For nearly the first time in ten years, my social life feels busy and exciting, my contributions meaningful. I start up an emotional support group among neighbours in my area. I take part in an online choir and an online version of the dance class I love but usually come to already exhausted. I reach out to friends, feeling emboldened by the sense that everyone is having drinks over Zoom these days. I join a novel-writing workshop, held in Spanish once a week by a writer in Mexico City; it becomes a bright spot in my week, two hours talking about literature with others, writers from around the world, who care about nothing more (continuing education was physically impossible for me until everything went virtual). I spend a huge amount of time figuring out meals from what we have in the house and in cleaning, cleaning, cleaning. I have gone from being a mostly single parent to being on duty

24/7 as we stay apart from my children's father at first to protect me from his possible exposure to COVID-19 at work.

When he was four, my younger son once stopped suddenly as we were walking to tell me, "Mummy, you are soft. Like feathers and milk." My older son didn't like stuffed animals when he was very young. "You're my stuffed animal," he'd say. But now these kids are ready to be off in the world, heroes of their own stories, not accessories to mine. They are held back only by COVID-19 and these strange circumstances that force them to spend every minute here, inside, with me. For me, it's a bonus, time I didn't expect to have with them, but it's not easy for them, and so it's not easy for any of us.

In the wake of COVID, overdoses have surged across the country. In my province of Ontario, 1,535 people died of opioid-involved overdose in 2019, reflecting a steady increase each year over the past few years (in 2003 there were less than three hundred such deaths).[23] But since the pandemic sent us into lockdown in March of 2020, opioid-involved overdose deaths here have increased by 40 percent.[24] (The same chief medical officer of health who mismanaged the opioid crisis is now mismanaging the COVID-19 response as well. Like his right-wing, populist boss, Dr. Williams seems confused about how public health and epidemiology work, and indifferent to the pain resulting from preventable deaths.) There were twenty-eight opioid-involved overdose deaths in October 2020 in Toronto alone.[25] In Alberta, which shut down harm reduction services just as the pandemic struck, there were nine hundred overdose deaths within ten months.[26]

That sense of vertigo that Garth Mullins, a Vancouver resident, described — it's multiplied since COVID, almost beyond imagining, for everyone on the frontlines of what's being called a syndemic of overdose and SARS-CoV2.

The single tent I saw at Sanctuary right before our version of lockdown has multiplied, spreading to cover the entire area. It's far safer in tent cities or encampments, where you're not crowded on inadequately spaced cots like in the city's overstuffed shelters. The situation in Toronto is being replicated across North America. Overdose crisis, housing affordability crisis, and rental crisis: these things that were tearing at the body of society before COVID-19 are now gaping wounds (there's no longer a causal link with prescription opioids, as prescribing rates have dropped in the US while overdoses surged). Across the United States, tens of thousands, perhaps hundreds of thousands, are in immediate danger of eviction.

The tenants in the third-floor apartment where Joe lives have taken to tossing garbage out the window, as they are quarantined with COVID-19. One day he sees paramedics in intent conversation with the landlord and wonders if it was another overdose death, or one of the tenants with COVID. "This place is an unending tragedy," he says.

What if parents were no longer told that allowing their injection-drug-using adult children to shoot up in their childhood bedroom is the height of enabling, and instead were counselled on how to best support them to inject safely, with family nearby? What once appeared to be the harms associated with the drug—relationships falling apart, children being apprehended, people ending up on the street—now fall away. You are left with a person who is treating physical or emotional pain with opioids, a person for whom the consequences of drug use are now largely limited to the relatively few intrinsic harms of the drug itself, a person who now has support and time to begin figuring out the best way forward.

So, we can get rid of drug-seeking behaviour by providing the drug sought, or a substitute acceptable to the individual. Can we do the reverse, stimulating addictive or drug-seeking behaviour? What if you take a person like me, with a pain condition successfully managed with prescription opioids. Everything is humming along until your state government imposes new rules ordering drastic cutbacks on opioid prescribing and onerous requirements and oversight. As has occurred across the United States since 2016, frightened or exasperated doctors turn their clinics into no-opioid clinics. They send letters to each of their long-time patients, explaining that they are to be given one last dose of their medication and then sent on their way.

When you receive such a letter expelling you from pain relief and, if nothing but opioids works for you, into an exile of pain, what do you do? Suppose you decide to go it alone, looking up the equivalent medication on the Dark Web and hoping it doesn't poison you when it arrives by USPS. Is this evidence of addiction? In this case, we have taken legal prescribed use, which did not come with negative consequences, and suddenly imposed negative consequences on continued use. Were you addicted all along, including before the definition of use-despite-negative-consequences applied? Or did you become addicted the moment you decided you wanted to stick with the medication regimen that was working for you, even if you have to take some greater risks to do so? What if you ask a friend who has access to street opioids for a little to tide you over, to prevent withdrawal symptoms as you begin the long slog of phoning every clinic in the country in search of a new family doctor who will take you on, and possibly maintain your prescription? You could be arrested for doing so, or you might accidentally kill yourself. These harms are not inherent to the drug, but are socially imposed, capricious, changeable consequences, reflective of the priorities of those with the greatest wealth and power but permeating everyone's understanding, even people who use drugs.

Until COVID-19 forced a loosening of some rules, the dispensing regimens for medication-based treatment for addiction, with their surveillance, their urine tests, their daily attendance, were deeply disruptive of a normal life. Perhaps it's that we consider that anyone who has been "abusing" drugs has so little of a real life that there's not much to disrupt. But if addiction is persistent use despite negative consequences for one's social, family, or work life, then what are we to make of the typical methadone regimen, which makes work virtually impossible, for example. Unpleasantness and social control of the former drug user — rather than therapeutic value or healthy bodily autonomy or comfort or well-being — seem to be the standards we use to be sure we're providing treatment, not pleasure. The main thing is to be sure no one feels too free, too confident, or too happy.

By contrast, if you treat dependence only — not by eliminating it but by accepting it and allowing dependence to be part of a full and satisfying life, just as dependence on insulin, on Prozac, or on a wheelchair can be—the question of compulsive use despite negative consequences seems to sort of melt away.

"Raw opium latex smells like crushed up fresh flowers and dirt," says Matthew, my American opium-smoking correspondent. "It's very natural smelling, it's not like floral perfume or something, it's like real flowers, leaves[,] stems and all. Like you just ripped up a patch of a garden."

Opium poppies grow legally in gardens across North America, but it has become illegal to harvest the white sap that oozes out if you nick their seed pods. Magic mushrooms of various types grow across the British Isles. Cannabis was once anathema and now, in places, is a sort of green gold. Online cannabis sales went up by 600 percent during our lockdown, tripled the day the prime minister announced the border with the US would close, and then more than doubled again when cannabis was declared a non-essential business, temporarily shutting storefront pot shops.[27] Once allowed to reopen, they spring up across Toronto like mushrooms after rain, taking over cafés and restaurants and other businesses that didn't make it through the lockdown. Il Gatto Nero, the Little Italy café where I wrote my first book, shuts down, to be replaced by a cannabis shop. Another one opens a few metres away, and yet another one across the street as companies jockey for market position. Since COVID, alcohol use has gone up,[28] with alcohol sales in the US in March 2020, when lockdowns became widespread, 55 percent higher than the same period the previous year. Some 25 percent of Canadian adults over twenty-five and under thirty-four reported drinking more than usual, and among those who drink normally and who have been staying home more, daily drinking has become the norm.[29]

As things derived from nature go, harvesting drugs for pleasure, energy, or relaxation seems far less obscene than continuing to harvest the remains of eons' worth of fossil plant and animal matter, burning it and as a result threatening the continued existence of current life on Earth. If policies were based on evidence about what is good for society, rather than on quick maximization of profits for a very small group of very rich people (as is happening with cannabis in Canada and has happened with prescription opioids), our world would be unrecognizably different.

The drug war has criminalized the plants that grow in nature and the people who have used them, in culturally moderated ways, for centuries. In response to this hypocrisy, we see a backlash of suspicion, where chemicals found in nature are venerated, while those distilled or produced in a lab are thought to be poison. This — a counter-reaction that is also excessive and misinformed — is one among endless examples of prohibition thinking, in which the targets bear little or in fact no relation to what is actually dangerous and every relation to a whole complicated, shifting network of prejudices, historical forces, influences, and financial interests.

When we imagine a post-prohibition world, there's no reason it needs to be a world like this one. In today's world, the exploitation that occurs within the illicit drug system and results in cartels, drug violence, overdose, and misery has a real parallel in the licit world, where pharmaceutical, cannabis, and alcohol giants manipulate users with misleading advertising while huge profits are made by those who least need them. But why couldn't life post-prohibition be constructed differently? A world in which currently illicit substances are legal (in particular the natural products of evolution, plants, and fungi that play their own unique role in ecosystems, which are interdependent by definition) could be an interdependent world.

Although I'm what my son might call a noob when it comes to drugs, among harm reduction practitioners and people who both use drugs and advocate for human rights and a less crap society, it feels like I have found a messy, diverse, caring group of people who share my values, by and large — even though it's only recently that I've begun applying these values to thinking about drug users. Others, like Lelena and other pain patients, are beginning to join the same conversation. After interacting online for a while, you start to develop a sense of care and responsibility for each other.

One day Meg posts something that sounds depressed, and Lelena, who's commented positively on some things she has written, writes to me privately to ask if she's all right. I text Meg and we chat for a little bit, and then I let my new American friend know that she's okay. I give her a little background — Meg has become a friend in real life, we live in the same city . . . but she isn't exactly a pain patient, well, not like Lelena and me. She's actually dependent on heroin — well, actually not heroin but illicit fentanyl, injected. I hold my breath, expecting moral outrage. But Lelena has already decided that Meg seems sweet, and that is enough for her.

More and more often I see Lelena using the small platform that her kindness has earned her on Twitter to talk about the harms of the racialized war on drugs, which damages pain patients and people who use illegal drugs alike. She may never have met a "junkie," or maybe she has. It doesn't matter. We are starting to depend on each other in the best possible way.

At last, methadone patients in many parts of Canada and the United States can get prescriptions that don't require them to come in every day. Not so long ago, this change, which involves trusting people who have used illicit drugs, was thought to be impossible to make. It's the sort of creative and practical thinking that's become far more necessary, and more prevalent, since COVID's come to town, since we've learned, abruptly, that the impossible is in fact not difficult at all; that the most maligned and poorly paid workers are the essential ones; that it's possible for the rich to get vastly richer even as the economy tanks and unemployment soars (it becomes increasingly hard to understand why thousands of condos sit empty, driving up the price of real estate, while people resort to camping en masse in parks across the city).

For people who use drugs and for those in treatment, as for pain patients, time is the great enemy. Anything that makes life easier, that reduces the amount of struggle you need to go through, is going to reduce pain and chaos, improve stability, and contribute to a real recovery. Virtual appointments are a boon to me and to Joe. Rules had to be changed to make this happen, too: the amazing thing is how easy it suddenly is to change all the rules. People with disabilities have been asking for virtual medical appointments and virtual schooling for years, and have always been told it's sadly just not possible. But COVID teaches us that nothing is real: not money, not work, not rules. Everything has been spun to serve the needs of a few, but none of it was necessary. All of it can change.

Joe's methadone seems to be "losing its legs" (waning in effect) ever more quickly, and continues to mess up his sleep. While it feels for him better than buprenorphine, it also creates a sort of fog in his brain, what he calls the "methadone sludge." COVID-19 prompts him to quit the long slog on public transit and seek out a safer methadone clinic. The new doctor he finds seems interested in what's not working for him, wonders aloud if he might be a fast metabolizer of the opioid, if something like hydromorphone or morphine might provide greater stability and well-being with fewer side effects.

Suddenly finding himself with a practitioner who seems to have interests other than milking him for the government-paid fees for testing his urine for drugs, he summons up the courage to ask for the impossible.

I am afraid to hear how the appointment will go. Despite his low expectations of life, Joe's nervousness comes through in his direct messages. What a relief to hear this from him: "Years of struggle, withdrawal, depression, weight loss, insomnia, hypersomnia, constipation and frustration later—I have a fucking morphine script!!!!"

Four exclamation marks from a guy who practices stoicism like nobody's business (actually, he follows Lao-tzu's Daoism, which is similarly stingy with the exclamation marks, as a rule). Joe's idea of a riotous night is cleaning the house or cooking for his beloved, or making sure his darling orange cat is well-brushed every day without fail. I believe he will put his opioids to good use.

In the bathtub, I touch myself everywhere, glorying most in the forbidden act of touching my own face, putting my fingers on my eyes, scratching an itch near my mouth. I stick my finger up one nostril, work out a bit of dried snot that has been tickling my nose for hours. It feels dirty in the most glorious way. In the bath, with the door locked, kids outside, and cat curling up and stretching her paw through the little space under the door, I have the most privacy I have enjoyed in two and a half months. Contained, enclosed, locked in, is the easiest way now for my mind to be free. I retrace little bits of my escape journeys. Venice. Buenos Aires. Amsterdam. Barcelona. Everywhere I walked, delighting in having nowhere to go and no one to please and everything to absorb. Delighting, like Thomas De Quincey, in being separate within a crowd.

I have not walked so little as I do now, ever. Not since I learned to walk. Each morning I pace my apartment, trying in vain to reach ten thousand steps. The almost scalding water blunts the pain in my shoulders and back, and I sink into it up to my sore neck. As I do I become aware that the painkiller I took around fifty minutes ago is beginning to work its magic. I close my eyes and submerge myself further, like a crocodile. Can I write a book about wandering—from inside my bathtub? I have no other choice.

Other than in the bathtub, the only place I wander is in my mind, after midnight. The kids are up increasingly late. I can't settle down in the silence, just me and the cat, until the early hours of the next day. I work from midnight until two or three a.m. and then kitty follows me to bed and lets me sleep for three or four hours, purring at my feet, before waking me with the sun. That is when I pace the apartment, counting stiff-legged steps on my pedometer app, before going back to bed, letting the internet keep my kids occupied in a way I never wanted. The magic, in this way, is contained within those few calm and quiet hours of the night.

What has happened to Meg—what she has made happen—in the single year since she came in from the cold is just astonishing. I've had the immense good fortune, as a journalist, of stumbling on her at this particular time in her life, and watching, and cheerleading, as she works her way out of a truly dire situation.

After so much success, after so much difficult waiting, to find that the prescribed hydromorphone is useless for her is crushing. She was so, so close. It seems that she has reached a dead end, which could become a literal dead end at any moment.

And then, a wonder occurs. Like Joe with his doctor, Meg sees the possibility of real communication for a change. She returns to Dr. X and explains her situation. She wants to leave her dependence on the illicit market; she doesn't want to, and can't imagine, leaving opioids. Together, she and Dr. X come up with a last-ditch attempt that is in fact the most logical possible solution: a prescription of fentanyl, the exact drug she has been injecting from the street. It's not an approved treatment for addiction, but off-label prescribing (prescribing a drug for something other than its official indication) is common for all sorts of conditions. So, it's legal.

It's elegant: Meg is indeed a drug-seeker. And finally, she has found what she's seeking.

Meg knows that despite her really incredible willpower and determination, her relentless and often ruthless focus on self-understanding, much of the progress she has made has to do with privilege that many of her fellow "junkies" simply don't have. It's a source of guilt, and it propels her. The multiple fentanyl patches she sticks on her body for three days at a time — pain patches because, since this isn't an official addiction treatment yet, legal injectable fentanyl is not available outside a hospital setting[30] — are the final thing she needs.

Meg is quick to put herself on the frontlines, applying for a job working in an isolation-and-recovery shelter for homeless people who have tested positive for COVID-19 in city shelters. This is where Michael Eschbach must have spent his quarantine. Meg leaves Twitter as she begins sleeping all day so as to be awake for the night shift. Our long text and direct message exchanges dwindle in frequency. She is most worried, she tells me, about infecting the handsome tuxedo kitten she adopted from the Humane Society against staff advice, because the little creature had not been adequately socialized. When I adopted Kinu, I avoided any possible extra-work cats, but Meg begged them to let her take the responsibility of teaching the maladjusted ball of fluff about safety and about love. Within maybe a week of her studiously ignoring his presence in her studio apartment, the kitten began to emerge from his hiding places and to ask to play. Within weeks he was as loving and cuddly as Kinu.

At the same time, my conversations with Joe return to daily exchanges. Morphine is treating him well for the most part, although—there's always something—it causes terrible nightmares. It's hard to handle that, but worth it for the greater life he has during the day: an energy and a sense of normalcy he didn't have on buprenorphine, or even on methadone. For him, morphine seems to be the answer.

Sometimes he has heard from Meg and I am glad to know things are okay. Occasionally I can report that she is out in the world that we are locked down from, right in the thick of it, and, we think, doing well. From inside our respective apartments we compare notes on the decline and fall of the American empire, as seen from Toronto via TV and the internet. We see the effects of the pandemic on the populations of substance users and homeless people in different ways.

"It looks weirdly normal outside," Joe writes me one day. "People all over the parks, few masks, construction everywhere. We're pretty damn happy, odd as that is in these circumstances. We thrive in chaos. The rest of the world is having our life now. They don't seem to like it."

After a long silence, I hear again from Meg. She is still working nights, now moved from an active COVID isolation shelter, set up in a repurposed hotel, to another hotel for homeless patients recovering from the disease. COVID is tightening the screws on every situation. Overdoses are out of control. Pain and isolation increase.

Lelena finds a new physician, who restores her prescription. But then her new doctor writes a Twitter post defending the use of opioids for chronic pain. The mother of a young man who died of heroin overdose in a different state happens to notice his post. The doctor's licence is suspended while he is investigated — and Lelena, and thirty-three other patients, lose their pain treatment, prescription, and healthcare. So Lele must go back to looking for a physician who will believe in and treat her pain.

All days are difficult. Some are worse, despite the heart emojis. Lelena still privately helps other pain patients, and now people who use illicit drugs or suffer from addiction, to get through their most desperate and despairing moments. She also comments more and more savvily and unambiguously on the war on drugs, which has caught pain patients in its net.

Jordan, who has the misfortune to live in Alberta, where the government is intent on bringing American attitudes to substance use to Canada, has flourished on injectable opioid agonist therapy, which is now cancelled. Although the lawsuit may ultimately result in the treatment being restored, for now he moves onto extended-release morphine, like Joe. He worries that he won't be able to feel a rush when he picks up on the street (takes street drugs), but is managing so far. He hopes one day not to depend on any substance. Joe, by contrast, is happy to depend on something that serves him so well. Repeatedly, he pushes himself into mild withdrawal: "An opioid addict so thoroughly stabilized he's gotten in the habit of forgetting he needs opioids," as he puts it. One day a new pharmacist accidentally gives him twelve extra morphine pills; he returns them so she won't get in trouble.

Someone overdoses upstairs the very first minute of the new year. Joe's partner calls the ambulance. They are constantly afraid someone will break in. If only their apartment were livable or there were prospects to move to somewhere decent that didn't cost the moon, the couple and their cat might be able to save, consider vet technician school, look forward to a brighter future. As it is, Joe's stoicism and constant caring for partner and kitty will have to do.

Michael Eschbach, repeatedly suicidal from under-treated pain and suffering deep anxiety and panic attacks ever since his time in city shelters, is referred to the Centre for Addiction and Mental Health. By phone, he is asked silly questions about his catastrophizing tendencies. The man is living alone, in pain, coughing up green slime, an apparently long-term effect of the COVID infection the city refused to prevent, in a hotel in the middle of nowhere. He feels that his government tried to kill him. His housing worker has no home to offer. He is fifty-nine years old and has decided that he will not return to a shelter. He would rather die. In what world is all this not a catastrophe? Just as it was for me when I sought help for depression arising from under-treated pain, mental health services are useless for him in the absence of reasonable conditions for mental health. "It gets pretty lonely doing isolation by yourself in a hotel in the middle of nowhere," he writes me, shortly before an outbreak of COVID hits the shelter hotel. "I can only imagine what prisoners all over the world must go through when they are beaten and then thrown into isolation for months, even years. What a messed up world."

I write up my article about homeless people being shuffled around during the COVID pandemic, and overdose deaths resulting from the city's lack of interest in finding out what their clients need to stay safe and well. This is the article for which I interviewed S., who describes her time self-isolating in a motel and in a tent, and then her experiences in two shelter hotels, and, finally, a transitional housing apartment for people with mental health or addiction issues. Though officially a step up, the shared unit in the latter lacks hot water in the shower, smoke detectors, or a lock on the door (S. pushes a table against the door for safety).

After my article is published, S. tells me that the manager at her building is hurt and defensive about what S. said in it. Her comments, the woman tells her, have harmed her organization and its mission of recovery; S. can't stay here anymore, she threatens. S. considers going to an outdoor encampment. She volunteers to help set up shelters in a tent city. But then the plumbing is fixed in her unit. And then a lock is put on the back door of the building. I feel pretty good about being a journalist.

Over the next days and weeks, though, S. is repeatedly harassed by her housing manager, who calls her a "liar" and "manipulative," accuses her of letting squatters into the building and putting glue in the lock. The manager removes the string with bells that S. and her roommate hung from the back door as a makeshift alarm, warning her "not to call the papers." She shuts off S.'s internet. S. messages me from outside a nearby subway station, where she can connect to Wi-Fi. Someone dies, most likely of overdose, in one of the apartments.

The day before Christmas, S. is woken by the manager, who gives her five minutes to dress before simply entering. She is told to pack her bags and leave within two hours.

I no longer feel so good about what I have done.

By Christmas Day, S. is back in a shelter hotel. She says it is quieter and safer there. But this isn't permanent housing, and my article caused her weeks of distress. She tells me, "I don't think you can help. Just keep writing and questioning and finding truth." S. is comfortable with me using her full name, telling me she's not afraid. But I am.

S. wants to get off fentanyl completely, but it's not that simple. She has access to hydromorphone safe supply, but its health-stabilizing potential is no more realizable for her than it was for Meg, because it doesn't provide an adequate dosage for someone dependent on illicit fentanyl. So S. moves in and out of withdrawal depending on what she can afford to buy on the illicit market. "I stress about going to look at apartments because I find the process tiresome and a bit like job interviews, and I will need to not be drug sick to get it done," she explains. "But not high as a kite either."

Like Michael Eschbach, S. has a housing worker who seems unwilling or unable to find her a safe and permanent place to live. S. knows what she needs, and she knows her own goals. And yet they are so far out of reach. She writes:

> One nurse practitioner told me there are a quiet careful
> group of street health advocates, nurses and doctors who
> believe decriminalization of all drugs is the goal, then all

these other safe use and harm reduction methods would logically follow. But he lowered his voice telling me this as it isn't a popular idea among the medical community, who likely benefit from keeping things the way they are, [or doctors are] just afraid of change in general. There still seems to be a need to shame and punish the addict in our society.

When I write, I choose what information I share and how. I control the suspense. This is why people in pain, of whatever kind, need to be doing the writing of their own stories.

This isn't writing as private, individual therapy. It's writing as seizing the means of production (or, as I'm not the only one to coin, the memes of production), of wresting control (to wrest: to forcibly pull from someone's grasp; the wrest is also the key used to make a harp or a piano sing, or, one hopes, a piece of writing). As writers we rarely take full advantage of our power, or rather we use it irresponsibly, telling the same old stories in the same old ways.

Jacques Derrida, in his essay "Plato's Pharmacy," notes that the word *pharmakon* (related to the *pharmakos*, or "scapegoat") means both poison and cure. It's a drug, or a spell, or a poison, just like a modern pharmacy's ambiguous wares. Plato, Derrida tells us, uses it as a metaphor for writing, which is both poison and cure, because it seems like truth and yet can be used to mislead or to lie. Each of my correspondents happens to be a strong writer, skilled with language, expressive, honest, and direct. Their stories are the truth about their lives, and they sing.

Julian Buchanan and his colleague, in a beautiful 2015 paper, argue against abstinence (the condition of *not being dependent on drugs*) or removal from state benefits (the condition of *not being dependent on the state*; for example, for unemployment, disability, or other social welfare benefits) being used as metrics to define recovery from opioid or other drug addiction. What they argue for is a very different vision of recovery that involves changing the conditions which may have led to problematic drug use and that in fact has very little to do with the drug but everything to do with full citizenship in the community, accessing human rights, and subjective well-being:

> Whereas, full recovery arguably occurs when a person has properly regained control of his or her life; is no longer subject to stigma and exclusion; is able to access wider opportunities (education, employment and housing); and is able to participate and enjoy the privileges available to others in society. In all the excitement about ambitious policy objectives and debates over the ownership and understanding of recovery, it is important not to lose sight of the vulnerability of long-term dependent drug users, some of whom will need considerable support and care to rebuild lives that were often badly damaged before drugs became an issue.[31]

Not that you need an academic paper to say what we all know instinctively about ourselves. We all need to belong, but we suffocate if controlled. We all need independence, but we flounder if left alone and excluded. These are truths that are demonstrable in every choice and conflict and dream we have, whether within our families or in the larger community. Jess Tilley and Albie Park write, in their description of their mutual support Harm Reduction Works-HRW model:

> It feels wonderful to build power with other people rooted in esteem, kindness and compassion. Love. It's incredible. When harm reduction is done well, REALLY well with others there is a vibration in the air that can often go unnoticed because the work is exhausting, often painful and soul altering.[32]

Pain is a condition of life, but some of us live under far more or worse conditions than others. People who use drugs, who have begun to organize to change the conditions in which they live, talk about liberation politics. Part of that liberation includes having dignified access to the substances they (we) depend upon.

"The line-up was really orderly and it was really nice," says Garth Mullins. In June of 2020, he'd helped organize around a hundred marchers in protest against incredibly high overdose death numbers (there were 170 such deaths in Vancouver in May alone).

The cops who were present paid little or no attention to this line-up that stretched outside a tent after the main event. The protest might have been raucous, but the line was more orderly than at the Apple store when a new iPhone is released, Mullins says. About 150 people were there, young and old. "London Calling," by The Clash, was playing. It rained for a while and nobody cared.

"It was a great feeling. There was camaraderie. One of the organizers said to me afterwards, 'now, this felt like a little moment of liberation. Look how it is when we organize it ourselves.'"

In the tent, organizers handed out free cocaine and opium, tested for purity with a mass spectrometer.

"You could kind of hear the ripple of disbelief going through" as people realized they were giving out free drugs, illegal drugs. Drugs people need, and drugs they enjoy.

This was the first action of the newly formed Drug Users Liberation Front.

"It's [. . .] about liberation on a whole bunch of levels. From drug laws, from over-policing, from incarceration, but also from the over-policing of medical systems. Liberation is especially important to drug users because we've had so much self-determination stolen from ourselves in our lives."

Confronting racism or patriarchy, fighting for disability or queer rights, all of these things have involved breaking laws in order to be recognized as really human. The 1994 Indigenous-led uprising of the Zapatista

National Liberation Army (EZLN) in Chiapas, Mexico, was part of my early political awakening (years before I first went to Mexico to be with my then-boyfriend). That very local uprising combined demands for Indigenous political autonomy within Mexico with an eloquent and media-savvy call for global solidarity. Subcomandante Marcos, its masked spokesperson, articulated a solid grasp of the economic and power bases of oppression, yet still recognized the importance of individual cultures and identities, of self-identification of needs, of people working together to determine their own destinies. The first Zapatista to appear publicly after the uprising was Comandante Ramona, a chronically ill Tzotzil Maya woman who was part of the Zapatistas' governing committee. She did most of her work on the ground, among rebel-protected, self-governing communities, and through her promotion of women's voices in shaping the movement, keeping women's needs and human dignity at its centre.

As it turns out, Garth Mullins was similarly moved by the 1994 uprising and the Zapatistas' analysis. Thinking back to that inspiration, he says that "I think that people want to align themselves with the kind of movements that are liberating themselves from structures. We're learning politically together."

Despite the music festival vibe Mullins describes, it was both a celebratory and a responsible event with a serious purpose.

"People aren't idiots. When you have drug users running things it is careful."

Although I happen to speak with Mullins, his co-organizer, Erica Thomson, is doing most of the media. Most of the leaders in this movement are women, and many are mothers.

For that short time, this tent and its orderly, self-organized distribution system was, Mullins says, "a place where you could not just be Narcanned back to life,³³ but also get the safe supply. This is like a generational demand."

Not just a demand for drugs. A demand for a world where the most disenfranchised enfranchise themselves. From pain, through opioids, to creating little glimpses of a world that offers what they need to get well.

Liberation (pharmacology)

Liberation is the first step in the process by which medication enters the body and liberates the active ingredient that has been administered. The pharmaceutical drug must separate from the vehicle or the excipient that it was mixed with during manufacture. Some authors split the process of liberation into three steps: disintegration, disaggregation and dissolution.[34]

Could it be that we're in the disintegration stage? In one translation of a famous quote from his *Prison Notebooks*, written from a fascist prison, Italian theorist Antonio Gramsci writes of symptoms of illness (presumably of the body politic) that arise in such a time of transition: "The crisis consists precisely in the fact that the old is dying and the new cannot be born; in this interregnum a great variety of morbid symptoms appear."[35]

In another, by Slavoj Žižek, illness or morbidity is instead translated into monstrosity as "Now is the time of monsters."[36]

We certainly seem to be entering a time of authoritarianism, violence, and mass suffering. We must be careful not to confuse cause with effect, though. The victims of oppression are not the monsters here.

Joe and I send each other direct messages nearly every day as Torontonians begin to step out of their apartments and houses, some in masks, with varying levels of concern about the virus that continues to attack the lungs and vessels and hearts of people around the world. We look at this world on fire — literally on fire: there is a heat wave, nearly 38°C, in Siberia, and the streets of cities across the United States and around the world are on fire with uprisings against white supremacy, police brutality, and anti-Black racism. Statues and monuments to the pillaging of the Earth and its peoples, to a not-unrelated, fundamentally racist war on drugs, are being toppled around the world. Corporations are rushing to issue vapid statements of solidarity while undermining their workers. Everything hangs in the balance. We see the threats to world stability, to justice, to the Earth itself and we fear that the wrong bird will rise from the ashes of this breathtaking, tragic world where opioids are a rare balm for some of those who suffer the greatest pain.

But we can't help hoping. We're all — I'm thinking of all the drug users and pain patients I have met — still in physical pain. We're all still haunted emotionally too, each to different degrees, in different ways. But there is this fragile sense of solidarity that glimmers through the distances between us. Dependence keeps us all well; interdependence gives us something to keep well for.

"Tell them I'm alive," writes Meg. "And see if any of them know what that really means for & to me. Tell them I'm not broken anymore."

By "them," of course, she means you.

I have written every word — except the words about withdrawal — of this book under the influence of opioids. Does this mean I am high?

Being intoxicated or high, Joe continues to argue, simply means experiencing the effects of a drug. And indeed, over the time I have known him, he has moved from buprenorphine-naloxone (Suboxone) to methadone, to morphine. He usually takes the morphine orally, as a pill, sometimes crushes and snorts a smaller amount. He often smokes cannabis, and when the bupe was making him sluggish, he'd sometimes get hold of an amphetamine, which he'd use to power some serious house cleaning. We have had conversations during probably all of these states (maybe not the last one). I can't tell the difference, except via slight shifts in mood. Since he takes whichever opioid he's on in an ongoing way, and I take tramadol without fail, in his conception of it, all of our conversations about drugs, addiction, capitalism, video games, and cats take place while both of us are high. Fair enough. Sure.

"I think it's legally mandatory to have a cat in your lap in order to be officially an Author instead of a mere writer," Joe tells me. For me, being a mere writer is living the dream, but I appreciate the sentiment.

I am on my first long walk on my own in three and a half months. It is early evening, getting close to the longest day of the year. I try to time walks and meds so that I'm not still out when it starts to become hard to stand upright. It's good now. The day was hot but the evening is perfect, the light golden and soft. Normally patios would be full on an early summer day like this. I stop at every white peony, inhaling their heavy, delirious scent through the not-so-protective fabric of my facemask.

My phone starts in my hand at an incoming text. It is Meg. I stand outside a school, named after the prime minister father of our current prime minister. The son is the one who legalized cannabis, and also the one who continues to refuse to decriminalize drugs, even as his government acknowledges that substance use is a health issue, not a criminal justice one. Decriminalization is not a silver bullet, he says, evading the issue.

Like other schools, this one has been closed for the past few months due to the pandemic. The message board outside reads, as it always does, *Tout est possible*. Standing still hurts me, but I am eager to hear from my friend and I walk back and forth in this golden-hour light while I scroll through her long text.

She writes,

> suddenly realizing I have two whole hours with nothing
> to do but the laundry. I sit and sweat. It gets in my eyes
> a little. The cat purrs, wanders, sits, purrs more. Blinking
> the sweat out of my eyes I wonder if this is what tranquility
> is. Moments where you're not consciously aware of counting
> minutes, only of the ticking from the clock on the wall.
> I wonder who might care that these thoughts have been
> thought, or even more particularly that I've thought them.

She says more, and I say more. But our conversation isn't for my book anymore.

Acknowledgements

Suitably, since this is a book about what we depend on, I have many people to thank.

Most importantly, the people who let me speak with them, write down their stories, and follow their lives, especially some who have become my friends: Michael Eschbach, Meg, "Joe," Lelena Peacock, "S.," and others not named here. I have tried so hard to do justice to your stories, personalities, and struggles. Any failures there are all mine, but your words speak for themselves. For more solidarity and thoughtful exchanges, thank you to Garth Mullins, Stefan Kertesz, and Julian Buchanan. And thanks to so many others: Mandy and Edik Zwarenstein, who I love more than words can say and who each teach me something about justice. Same hard-to-put-in-words love and gratitude for my sister and fellow plotter, Lianne Zwarenstein, and literate and elegant sister-in-law, Lauren Butler. Saúl Olmos Hernández for giving me a whole world and exploring it with me, still. My beloved Mexican family and sister-friends. My children, Etien and Theo. Thank you for being with me through all of this. I want to give you all the wonder in the world. My constant and loyal friends, especially Emily Gesner, Sonia Singh, Sarah Lea Altose, Melissa Felder, Ann-Elisabeth Samson, Derek Laventure, Frédéric Kodjayan, Sven Heussner. I don't know what I'd do without you. Thank you to Anna Martin and Fred for photos. For weekly joy that got me through some tough months, Martín Solares and his wonderful writing workshop.

I have been incredibly, incredibly lucky in the editors I got to work with at Goose Lane Editions: Linda Pruessen is some kind of magical, subtle, encouraging author-whisperer; Jess Shulman is so careful and on top of things it's scary, and yet also gentle and flexible. Both of you are so much fun to work with. Julie

Scriver, designer of a truly joy-inducing cover; Alan Sheppard, who seems to make everything happen; and Susanne Alexander, who was willing to take a chance on this book. You gave me confidence and latitude to experiment and feel out my way when we weren't sure what it would look like in the end, and I'm so grateful for that. Tyee Bridge, who started all this. And my bold, caring agent, Marilyn Biderman, for believing in my work and in me as well.

Notes

PART I

Opium Eater: The New Confessions

1. David I. Macht, "The History of Opium and Some of Its Preparations and Alkaloids," *Journal of the American Medical Association* 64, no. 6 (1915): 477–481.
2. Rebecca Solnit, *A Field Guide to Getting Lost* (London: Penguin Books, 2005), 109.
3. W.G. Sebald, *Austerlitz* (New York: Random House, 2001), 85.
4. See, for example, Stephen Kishner, "Opioid Equivalents and Conversions," Medscape, accessed March 4, 2016, http://emedicine.medscape.com /article/2138678-overview.
5. Jonathan Duffy, "When Heroin Was Legal," *BBC News Magazine*, January 26, 2006.
6. Arthur Conan Doyle, "The Sign of Four" in *Sherlock Holmes: The Complete Novels and Stories: Volume 1* (Toronto: Bantam Books, 1986), 107.
7. Thomas De Quincey, *Confessions of an English Opium-Eater*, ed. Joel Faflak (Peterborough: Broadview Press, 2009), 88. This edition reproduces the original, tighter 1821 version rather than De Quincey's revised and lengthened later edition.
8. This is a reproduction from the revised edition De Quincey published in later life. Thomas De Quincey, *Confessions of an English Opium-Eater* (1856), in *The Works of Thomas De Quincey, Volume 2*, ed. Grevel Lindop (London: Routledge, 2020), 99, https://doi .org/10.4324/9780429349034.
9. As Joel Faflak discusses, among other historical themes, in his excellent introduction to Thomas De Quincey's *Confessions of an English Opium-Eater* (Broadview Editions, 2009), 36.
10. De Quincey, *Confessions* (2009), 88.
11. De Quincey, *Confessions* (2009), 89.
12. Eli Lilly, for example—known today as the makers of Prozac—once sold tablets of camphorated tincture of opium among the huge range of completely legal, heavily marketed, and widely sold opium medicines used for a variety of common and mild ailments. Barbara Hodgson's *In the Arms of Morpheus* (Vancouver: Greystone Books, 2001) has a fuller and beautifully illustrated account.
13. De Quincey, *Confessions* (2009), 53.
14. Guidelines for one 0–10 Pain Scale, via Lucile Packard Children's Hospital

Heart Center/CVICU, are explained at https://chsg.org/wp-content/uploads/2017/03/0-10_Pain_Scale.pdf (accessed February 20, 2021).

15. De Quincey, *Confessions* (2009), 100. The town in question is Liverpool, oddly enough (see Robert Morrison, *The English Opium-Eater: A Biography of Thomas De Quincey* [London: Weidenfeld & Nicolson, 2009], 109). Working with newly found primary sources as well as with the previously definitive biography of De Quincey by Grevel Lindop, Robert Morrison has written the most thorough account of De Quincey's life to date. My understanding of De Quincey's character and details of his life history are drawn principally from Morrison's work.

16. J.C. (forum user), "An Opioid World: An Experience with Tramadol (Ultram) (exp23886)," Erowid, May 16, 2005, https://erowid.org/exp/23886.

17. De Quincey, *Confessions* (2009), 226.

18. Morrison, *The English Opium-Eater*, 109.

19. Morrison, *The English Opium-Eater*, 108.

20. Hodgson, *In the Arms of Morpheus*, 4.

21. None of which function in substantially different ways, however.

22. Described for example in January 27, 2016, testimony to Congress by Nora D. Volkow, transcribed as "What Science Tells Us About Opioid Abuse and Addiction," National Institute on Drug Abuse, https://www.drugabuse.gov/about-nida/legislative-activities/testimony-to-congress/2016/what-science-tells-us-about-opioid-abuse-and-addiction.

23. Stats based on a 2014 report no longer accessible on the WHO website, accessed March 5, 2016. For updated stats, see World Health Organization, "Opioid Overdose," August 28, 2020, https://www.who.int/news-room/fact-sheets/detail/opioid-overdose.

24. Stats based on a report no longer accessible on the WHO website, accessed March 5, 2016. As you will see later in this book, things have changed in various ways.

25. See Nora D. Volkow, "Testimony to Congress: What Science Tells Us About Opioid Abuse and Addiction," National Institute on Drug Abuse, January 27, 2016, https://www.drugabuse.gov/about-nida/legislative-activities/testimony-to-congress/2016/what-science-tells-us-about-opioid-abuse-and-addiction.

26. Paul C. Webster, "Medically induced opioid addiction reaching alarming levels," *Canadian Medical Association Journal* 184, no. 3 (2012): 285–286.

27. muidumees (forum user), "Turn Around, Blue Eyes: An Experience with Tramadol (exp38660)," Erowid, December 12, 2005, https://erowid.org/exp/38660.

28. Robert Morrison, "Poe's De Quincey, Poe's Dupin," *Essays in Criticism* 51, no. 4 (2001): 428.

29. This quote from Thomas Trotter's *A View of the Nervous Temperament* was cited in Thomas Dormandy, *Opium: Reality's Dark Dream* (New Haven, CT: Yale University Press, 2012), 77.

30. Find the whole 1819 poem here: John Keats, "Ode on Indolence," http://www.poetryfoundation.org/poem/237806.

31. Alcott and Nightingale's laudanum use is discussed in Dormandy, *Opium: Reality's Dark Dream*, 76–84; and Hodgson, *In the Arms of Morpheus*, 68–74. The Florence Nightingale quote appears in Thomas Dormandy, "Seriously Addictive: A History of Opium," YaleBooks blog, Yale University Press, March 15, 2012, http://yalebooksblog.co.uk/2012/03/15/seriously-addictive-a-history-of-opium-author-article-by-thomas-dormandy/.

32. From the mid-second century CE writings of the physician Arataeus the Cappadocian, [Aret.] SD 1.8, translated by F. Adams (London, 1856) and cited in Dormandy 2012, 78.

33. Dormandy, *Opium: Reality's Dark Dream*, 76–84.

34. The disaster of poor Keats's death is discussed in numerous sources,

including Dormandy, who describes it as "a horror story" (Dormandy, *Opium: Reality's Dark Dream*, 78).

35. From Neil Gaiman's 2012 University of the Arts commencement address, which can be found at http://www.uarts.edu/neil-gaiman-keynote-address-2012.

36. De Quincey, *Confessions* (2009), 91.

37. Oliver Sacks, *Hallucinations* (New York: Alfred A. Knopf, 2012), 113–114.

38. Craig Stevens, "The Evolution of Vertebrate Opioid Receptors," *Frontiers in Bioscience* 14 (January 1, 2009), 1247–1269, http://www.ncbi.nlm.nih.gov/pmc/articles/PMC3070387/. Stevens demonstrates the development of opioid receptors early in vertebrate (not just human) evolution, and then goes further to show that as we evolved, selection pressures seem to have favoured differentiation into different types of opioid receptors with particular pressure toward development in mammals of the euphoria-causing *mu*-receptor — suggesting that *mu*-opioid receptors give us a survival advantage. As these receptors and endorphins do very many things in the body, though, this doesn't actually suggest that feeling a high or having addictive tendencies provides a selective advantage. Also interesting is Gavril Pasternak and Ying-Xian Pan's 2013 article, "Mu Opioids and Their Receptors: Evolution of a Concept," *Pharmacological Reviews* 64, no. 3 (2013): 1257–1317, http://www.ncbi.nlm.nih.gov/pmc/articles/PMC3799236/#B588.

39. Krisztina Berczik et al., "Exercise Addiction: Symptoms, Diagnosis, Epidemiology, and Etiology," *Substance Use & Misuse* 47, no. 4 (2012), http://www.ncbi.nlm.nih.gov/pubmed/22216780. There are other terms for and ways of conceptualizing this phenomenon, and some experiments have challenged the idea that the addictive feeling of a "runner's high" is due to endorphins, e.g., Taylor Hinton, "Does Placebo Response Mediate Runner's High?," *Perceptual and Motor Skills* 62, no. 3 (June 1986), http://www.ncbi.nlm.nih.gov/pubmed/3725516, and much later research has added endocannabinoids, which like endorphins are released during exercise, along with other endogenous chemicals. And in fact, more recent research suggests that the runner's high may not require endorphins at all, as you can block opioid receptors with naltrexone and still produce that calm, euphoric feeling following exercise. See Michael Siebers, Sarah V. Biedermann, Laura Bindila, Beat Lutz, Johannes Fuss, "Exercise-induced euphoria and anxiolysis do not depend on endogenous opioids in humans," *Psychoneuroendocrinology* 126 (April 2021):105173, https://doi.org/10.1016/j.psyneuen.2021.105173.

40. Will Self, "Take to the City Streets for a Walking Adventure," *The Guardian*, February 1, 2015, http://www.theguardian.com/travel/2015/feb/01/great-city-walks-will-self-take-to-the-streets. Self has written on the same subject elsewhere and De Quincey often comes up as a key "literary urbanist" and like-minded spirit. He also discusses De Quincey in his 1995 drug-focused collection of essays, *Junk Mail* (London: Bloomsbury, 1995).

41. John McCall, "Malcolm Cowley, The Art of Fiction No. 70," *The Paris Review* 85 (Fall 1982), http://www.theparisreview.org/interviews/3137/the-art-of-fiction-no-70-malcolm-cowley.

42. De Quincey, *Confessions* (2009), 54.

43. De Quincey, *Confessions* (2009), 125.

44. De Quincey, *Confessions* (2009), 125–126.

45. Guidelines for one 0–10 Pain Scale, via Lucile Packard Children's Hospital Heart Center/CVICU, are explained at https://chsg.org/wp-content/uploads/2017/03/0-10_Pain_Scale.pdf (accessed February 20, 2021).

46. Oliver Burkeman, "Rise and Shine: The Daily Routines of History's Most Creative Minds," *The Guardian*, October 5, 2013, http://www.theguardian.com/science/2013/oct/05/daily-rituals-creative

-minds-mason-currey. Mind you, while Proust did indeed treat his asthma with various things at various times (including caffeine, morphine, and opium), the smoking powders inhaled as an asthma treatment were probably cigarettes of stramonium, lobelia, and potash, the smoke of which was inhaled as an anti-spasmodic—at least according to Mark Jackson's exhaustive medical study on inhalation of various substances to treat asthma, "'Divine Stramonium': The Rise and Fall of Smoking for Asthma," *Medical History* 54, no. 2 (April 2010): 171–194, http://www.ncbi.nlm.nih.gov /pmc/articles/PMC2844275. I'm not clear if this study means that the *Guardian* is wrong in its idea that Proust took opium powder to treat his asthma at any point.

47. "Supply of Opiate Raw Materials and Demand for Opiates for Medical and Scientific Purposes," International Narcotics Control Board (INCB), 2014, http://www.incb.org/documents /Narcotic-Drugs/Technical-Publications /2014/ND_TR_2014_3_SD_EN.pdf. The 620-tonnes figure provided includes INCB demand estimates for morphine-rich (480 tonnes) and thebaine-rich (140 tonnes) opiate raw materials. Tramadol and other non-controlled opioids are not included in this statistic. These estimates will rise and fall each year and sometimes numbers of one opiate will increase while the supply or demand of another decreases. Generally, the trend seems to be distinctly upward.

48. Marilyn Herie and Wayne Skinner, *Substance Abuse in Canada* (Toronto: Oxford University Press, 2010), 200.

49. De Quincey, *Confessions* (2009), 55–56.

50. Dormandy, *Opium: Reality's Dark Dream*, 80. In the introduction to this exhaustive account, Dormandy slips in his own little confession. As a child, he endured a series of operations eased by an injection before surgery. He writes (on pages 3–4): "It transported the present writer into a land of indescribable bliss, never experienced before or since, remembered and cherished between operations long after memories of pain and discomfort had faded. Fortunately he did not realize until many years later that the injection contained a hefty dose of a morphine derivative. Had he known, he would today be an addict or, infinitely more likely, the memory of an addict sadly passed away in his prime. Otherwise his experience has been as a doctor; and he is not animated by any reforming zeal."

51. Agata Blaszczak-Boxe, "Woman's Spontaneous Orgasms Triggered by Parkinson's Drug," *LiveScience.com*, August 5, 2014, http://www.livescience .com/47208-spontaneous-orgasms -parkinsons-drug-rasaginine.html.

52. For all opioids, although not everyone needs dose increases, it is likely that the lowest effective dose will rise gradually over time. In the case of my atypical opioid, there is a ceiling due to seizure risk. For other opioids, if they worked well previously but the patient is now developing tolerance, rotating to a different one to lower tolerance may not be necessary: simply gradually raising the dose, being careful to keep it as low as is effective, and no lower, makes perfect sense.

53. See the hydromorphone reports on the online community Erowid (https:// erowid.org/experiences/subs/exp _Hydromorphone.shtml) for many examples, which are often both astonishing and evocative. The more research I do, the more I find various substances that are considered to be "closest to heroin" and extremely diverse opinions on the quality of experience of the same drug, even at comparable dosages and levels of opioid tolerance.

54. See "User Reviews for Hydromorphone," http://www. drugs.com/comments /hydromorphone, for one example of a forum. Largely chronic pain sufferers here. It's unclear in most of these reports whether addiction is an issue, although physical dependence and tolerance

clearly are. Regardless, this forum is a repository of experiences of patients who are taking the drugs essentially as prescribed, rather than decidedly recreational users, who may be snorting or injecting equivalent or higher doses of the same prescription medicines, or taking them as suppositories.

55. This is my loose translation of a quote attributed to Frida Kahlo: "Quise ahogar mis penas en el licor, pero las condenadas aprendieron a nadar." There are various other versions of the phrase, which may be from a 1927 letter. It's unclear if there is a definitive original source, and I have seen various renderings of the phrase in both English and Spanish.

56. This quote is cited in many accounts of Frida's life, such as in this magazine article based on a biography of Kahlo: "Frida Kahlo: The Palette, the Pain, and the Painter," *Art Forum*, March 1983, https://www.artforum.com/print/198303 /frida-kahlo-the-palette-the-pain-and -the-painter-35514.

57. This is a well-documented discrepancy, well described by Judy Foreman in "Why Women Are Living in the Discomfort Zone," *The Wall Street Journal*, January 31, 2014, http:// www.wsj.com/articles/SB100014240 527023046919045793492123I999548 6. I sense that doctors' treatment of my ankylosing spondylitis—a disease far more common in men—is more respectful and attentive than their treatments of other pain-causing diseases that are more common in women, such as fibromyalgia.

58. Fernando Antelo, "Pain and the Paint-brush: The Life and Art of Frida Kahlo," *Virtual Mentor* 15, no. 5 (2013): 460-465.

59. De Quincey, *Historical and Critical Essays*, 1862, 313.

60. Moondust (forum user), commenting on March 29, 2014, on the thread "Keeping Opiate Tolerance to a Minimum," Bluelight, http://www.bluelight.org /xf/threads/keeping-opiate-tolerance -to-a-minimum.508561. There is lots of debate here by recreational prescription drug abusers on whether addiction is inevitable. As "rachamim," another poster on this forum, notes, most participants here will be recreational drug users/addicts: "Taking medicines under medical supervision is an entirely different thing. Very rarely will anyone in this forum be under any kind of supervision." ("Tramadol 50mg," Bluelight, http://www.bluelight.org/vb /threads/345553-tramadol-50mg/page2.)

61. Irvine Welsh, *Trainspotting* (London: Vintage Books, 2004), 8.

62. De Quincey, *Confessions* (2020), 109.

63. Paul C. Webster, "Indigenous Canadians Confront Prescription Opioid Misuse," *The Lancet* 381, April 27, 2013, 1447–1448, http://www.thelancet.com/journals /lancet/article/PIIS0140-6736(13)60913-7 /fulltext.

64. Colleen Anne Dell et al., "Researching Prescription Drug Misuse among First Nations in Canada: Starting from a Health Promotion Framework," *Substance Abuse: Research and Treatment* 6, 2012, 3–31, http://www.ncbi.nlm.nih .gov/pmc/articles/PMC3411531.

65. "A Pill for Work and Play," *The Economist*, April 18, 2015, http:// www.economist.com/news/middle -east-and-africa/21648690-painkiller -becomes-egypts-favourite-recreational -drug-pill-work-and-play; and Erin Cunningham, "Drug Addiction on the Rise in Besieged Gaza," *The Electronic Intifada*, June 30, 2009, https:// electronicintifada.net/content/drug -addiction-rise-besieged-gaza/8323.

66. Michael "Cetewayo" Tabor, "CAPITALISM PLUS DOPE EQUALS GENOCIDE," Black Panther Party, 1970, https://archive.lib.msu.edu/DMC /AmRad/capitalismplusdope.pdf.

67. This was testimony given by Nora D. Volkow, MD, to the House Committee on Energy and Commerce Subcommittee on Oversight and Investigations on April 29, 2014 (https://archives.drugabuse .gov/testimonies/2014/prescription-opioid -heroin-abuse).

68. Some of these have been widely reported. For an example, see Laura Unger, "Scientists Close in on Non-addictive Opioid Painkillers," *USA Today*, November 17, 2014, http://www.usatoday.com/story/news/nation/2014/11/17/non-addictive-opioids-on-horizon/18810059/.

69. nioreh0422 (forum user), commenting on June 18, 2010, on the thread "Keeping Opiate Tolerance to a Minimum," Bluelight, http://www.bluelight.org/vb/archive/index.php/t-508561.html.

70. Sir Arthur Conan Doyle, "The Twisted Lip," in *Sherlock Holmes: The Complete Novels and Stories, Volume 1* (New York: Bantam Books, 1986), 308–309.

71. For example, in the American Academy of Neurology's position paper taking the first major stand against long-term prescription of opioids for non-cancer pain, dependence, addiction, and overdose are all lumped together—although dependence, like tolerance, is an expected outcome of long-term use. The World Health Organization likewise often uses the terms "addiction" and "dependence" interchangeably. Dependence requiring tapering to avoid withdrawal symptoms is common with other medicines, including SSRI and SNRI antidepressants, benzodiazepines and tryptophan (used for migraines). For more information, see "Opioid Overdose," World Health Organization, August 28, 2020, https://www.who.int/news-room/fact-sheets/detail/opioid-overdose; and Gary M. Franklin, "Opioids for Chronic Noncancer Pain," *Neurology* 83, no. 14 (September 30, 2014), http://www.neurology.org/content/83/14/1277.

72. Herie and Skinner, *Substance Abuse in Canada*, 142.

73. Dormandy, *Opium: Reality's Dark Dream*, 199.

74. Thomas De Quincey, as cited in Robert Morrison, "Opium's Invasion," RobertJHMorrison.com (author website),
October 2015, http://robertjhmorrison.com/post/opiums-invasion/.

75. Thomas De Quincey in a letter to Mary Russell Mitford, as cited in Morrison, *The English Opium-Eater*, 366.

76. Morrison, *The English Opium-Eater*, 198, quoting passages from the 1821 text of De Quincey's *Confessions of an English Opium Eater*.

77. Morrison, *The English Opium-Eater*, 359, quoting the recollections of De Quincey's daughters..

78. Dear footnote-reading friends, you are rewarded for your persistence with your very own drugs-and-pain playlist (many, many more are just a Google and some keywords away). Turn down the lights and wallow away.
The Rolling Stones, "Paint it Black"
Terra Naomi, "Vicodin Song"
Neil Young, "The Needle and the Damage Done"
The Dandy Warhols, "Not if You Were the Last Junkie on Earth"
Marcy Playground, "Poppies"
Vendetta Red, "Opiate Summer"
Ramones, "Take the Pain Away"
Counting Crows, "Round Here"
Lil Wyte, "Oxy Cotton"
Porter Wagoner and Dolly Parton, "The Pain of Loving You"
Red Hot Chili Peppers, "Under the Bridge"
Stromae, "Rail de Musique"
The Tragically Hip, "Opiated"
The Velvet Underground & Nico, "I'm Waiting for the Man"
The Verve, "The Drugs Don't Work"
James Brown, "King Heroin"
Nine Inch Nails, "Hurt"
Gym Class Heroes, "Pillmatic"
Sarah McLachlan, "Angel"
Green Day, "Give Me Novocaine"
Jimmy Eat World, "Pain"
Jon Foreman, "The Cure for Pain"
Lily Allen, "Everyone's At It"
The La's, "There She Goes"
Blur, "Beetlebum"
Elliot Smith, "Needle In the Hay"
Hector Berlioz, "Symphonie Fantastique"

79. One small study comparing psychiatric patients with histories of self-harm with others without that history found significant differences in levels of two kinds of endorphins. Cerebrospinal levels of two of these endogenous opioids were *lower* in the self-injuring group. The authors of this study suggest further research into drugs that act on the opioid system (i.e., opioids) as possible pharmacological treatments for self-injury. Barbara Stanley et al., "Nonsuicidal Self-Injurious Behavior, Endogenous Opioids and Monoamine Neurotransmitters," *J Affect Discord* 124, nos. 1–2 (July 2010): 134–140, https://www.ncbi.nlm.nih.gov/pmc/articles/PMC2875354/.

80. Faflak, "Introduction," 42.

81. De Quincey, *Confessions* (2020), 244.

82. Alan Arkin, *An Improvised Life: A Memoir* (Boston: Da Capo Press, 2011), 24–25.

83. Another possibly apocryphal quote from Frida Kahlo. This one is taken from *Frida & Diego: Quotes* by Maria Tsaneva (Lulu Press, 2013).

84. Christine Burrus, *Frida Kahlo: Painting Her Own Reality*, trans. Ruth Wilson (London: Thames & Hudson, 2008), 102.

85. Description according to Raquel Tiból, cited in Gaby Wood, "Anatomy of an Icon," *The Guardian*, May 15, 2005, http://www.theguardian.com/artanddesign/2005/may/15/art2.

86. From Frida Kahlo's illustrated diary, reproduced at http://www.fridakahlofans.com/LastDiaryEntry.html (English translation mine).

87. This was generally considered to have been Frida Kahlo's last painting, produced in 1954 and finished days before her death, but it has been suggested, because the quality is much higher than most other work created during this final, heavily medicated period, that it was actually painted in 1952, and that the inscription "Viva la Vida" was added in 1954, eight days before she died. There is no dispute about *this* date, as she wrote it on the painting herself. See http://www.fridakahlofans.com/co680.html for an image of the painting.

PART II
Saturn Devouring His Children: A Tale of Instability in Seven Parts

DEATH

1. This is my loose translation of an example of such a card in this article about Santa Muerte: Andrew Chesnut, "Life and Death in the Time of Coronavirus: Santa Muerte, the 'Holy Healer,'" *The Global Catholic Review*, March 24, 2020, https://www.patheos.com/blogs/theglobalcatholicreview/2020/03/life-and-death-in-the-time-of-coronavirus-santa-muerte-the-holy-healer/.

2. For example, Kirk Semple and Paulina Villegas, "Arrest of Top Crime Fighter Stuns Mexico, Where Corruption Is All Too Routine," *New York Times*, December 11, 2019, https://www.nytimes.com/2019/12/11/world/americas/mexico-garcia-luna-indictment.html.

3. "Mexico: Events of 2017," Human Rights Watch, https://www.hrw.org/world-report/2018/country-chapters/mexico.

4. Nick Miroff and William Booth, "Mexico's Drug War is Giving Growers a Great," *Washington Post*, October 23, 2011, https://www.washingtonpost.com/world/americas/mexicos-drug

-war-bypassing-growers/2011/10/20/
gIQAPKv93L_story.html.

5. "Drug and Opioid-Involved Overdose
    Deaths—United States, 2013–2017,"
    Centers for Disease Control and
    Prevention, January 4, 2019, https://
    www.cdc.gov/mmwr/volumes/67/wr
    /mm675152e1.htm?s_cid=mm675152e1_w;
    and Holly Hedegaard, Arialdi Miniño,
    and Margaret Warner, "Drug Overdose
    Deaths in the United States, 1999–2017,"
    Centers for Disease Control and
    Prevention, November 2018, https://
    www.cdc.gov/nchs/products/databriefs
    /db329.htm.

6. "Motor Vehicle Deaths Estimated to
    Have Dropped 2% in 2019," National
    Safety Council, https://www.nsc.org
    /road-safety/safety-topics/fatality
    -estimates.

7. "Opioid- and Stimulant-related Harms
    in Canada," Government of Canada,
    December 2020, https://health-infobase
    .canada.ca/substance-related-harms
    /opioids; and Carly Weeks, "One Person
    Died Every Two Hours of Opioid-related
    Overdose in Canada Last Year, Report
    Says," Globe and Mail, June 13, 2019,
    https://www theglobeandmail.com
    /canada/article-one-person-died-every
    -two-hours-of-an-opioid-related-
    overdose-in/.

8. Marianne Rose Spencer et al., "Drug
    Overdose Deaths Involving Fentanyl,
    2011–2016," U.S. Department of Health
    and Human Services, National Vital
    Statistics Reports 68, no. 3, https://
    www.cdc.gov/nchs/data/nvsr/nvsr68
    /nvsr68_03-508.pdf.

9. For example, Jane A. Buxton et al.
    (in "Changing Landscape of Opioid
    Use in British Columbia, Canada:
    A Shift Towards Fentanyl-Seeking
    Behaviour," abstract presented at Harm
    Reduction International Conference,
    Porto, April 2021, https://www.hri.
    global/abstracts/abstracthr19/1311/print)
    chart a move to accepting its probable
    presence in the drug supply. Increasingly
    in illicit drug sales, "down" is sold as

fentanyl rather than masquerading as
heroin.

10. The term was coined in 1986 by cannabis
    activist Richard Cowan. Filter magazine,
    in a 2018 article by Sarah Beller called
    "Infographic: The 'Iron Law of
    Prohibition,'" offers a wonderfully
    clear graphic at https://filtermag.org
    /infographic-the-iron-law-of-prohibition/
    with some explanation of the concept,
    neatly summarized as "the harder the
    enforcement, the harder the drugs."

11. CDC data shows greatest increases in
    fentanyl deaths among fifty-five- to
    sixty-four-year-olds ("Drug and Opioid-
    Involved Overdose Deaths—United
    States, 2013–2017," Centers for Disease
    Control and Prevention, January 4,
    2019, https://www.cdc.gov/mmwr
    /volumes/67/wr/mm675152e1.
    htm?s_cid=mm675152e1_w).

12. Jeff Guo, "'How Dare You Work on
    Whites': Professors Under Fire for
    Research on White Mortality,"
    Washington Post, April 6, 2017, https://
    www.washingtonpost.com/news/wonk
    /wp/2017/04/06/how-dare-you-work
    -on-whites-professors-under-fire-for
    -research-on-white-mortality/.

13. Still, as Deaton points out in that same
    interview, "People were upset at us for
    not putting black mortality on one
    of our charts, but the reason it's not
    there—which we explain—is that black
    mortality is so high it doesn't fit on the
    graph."

14. Zachary Siegel, "Capitalism is Killing
    Us," The Nation, April 23, 2020.
    Siegel—one of the small group of
    journalists I admire for how they
    write about addiction, drawing on
    evidence, personal experience, and
    humanism—clearly outlines the
    strength of the data and the weakness
    of Anne Case and Angus Deaton's
    prescription in Deaths of Despair and
    the Future of Capitalism (Princeton,
    2020).

15. I looked into the fraught question
    of causality between drug use and

homelessness in the first of a three-part article on homelessness and drug use that I wrote for *Filter* magazine in 2020. You can read it on my website at www.carlynzwarenstein.com/journalism.

16. According to Drugabuse.gov, which cites C.M. Jones, "Heroin Use and Heroin Use Risk Behaviors among Non Medical Users of Prescription Opioid Pain Relievers—United States, 2002–2004 and 2008–2010," *Drug Alcohol Depend* 132, nos. 1–2 (2013): 95–100; and K. Muhuri et al., "Associations of Non Medical Pain Reliever Use and Initiation of Heroin Use in the United States," Substance Abuse and Mental Health Services Administration (SAMSH), *CBHSQ Data Review*, August 2013.

17. According to the (American) 2014 National Survey on Drug Use and Health, SAMHSA, https://www.samhsa.gov/data/sites/default/files/NSDUH-DetTabs2014/NSDUH-DetTabs2014.pdf.

18. Iceland's groundbreaking youth alcohol prevention strategy involves an appropriately paternalistic approach, providing healthy social activities, strongly coordinating between parents and schools, and enforcing curfew among young people, and the great success of the model is now leading to versions elsewhere, including Lanark County, in eastern Ontario in Canada (see "Lanark County Turns to Iceland to Curb Teen Substance Abuse," CBC News, November 28, 2018, https://www.cbc.ca/news/canada/ottawa/lanark-county-iceland-substance-abuse-1.4922688). In 2018 I asked our host in a small town in Iceland not far from Reykjavík how people cope with the long, dark winters. "Alcohol," he told me. Perhaps the next generation will have a different response.

19. I interviewed S. for an article about the way homeless people have been shuffled from one temporary residence to the next during the COVID-19 pandemic, and about how shelters established in hotels rented by the City of Toronto,

an excellent measure to enable physical distancing to prevent infection, have been deadly for some people who use drugs due to a lack of attention to their specific needs.

20. Because of the huge diversity in needle and syringe programs — some requiring one-for-one exchange, some simply focusing on getting sterile drug use paraphernalia into the populations likely to use it, and some being accompanied by a slate of other practices that promote safer drug use — it is hard to compare different studies. This review of systematic reviews on the subject goes over some of the different models and their strengths and weaknesses, and discusses the many possible biases or limitations of different studies: Ricardo M. Fernandes et al., "Effectiveness of Needle and Syringe Programmes in People who Inject Drugs – An Overview of Systematic Reviews," *BMC Public Health* 17 (2017): 309, https://www.ncbi.nlm.nih.gov/pmc/articles/PMC5387338/.

21. See for example Julia Rock and Harry August's March 10, 2020, report at The Appeal, "Undercover Providence Police Faked Withdrawal Symptoms and Solicited Suboxone from People with Prescriptions," https://theappeal.org/undercover-providence-police-faked-withdrawal-symptoms-and-solicited-suboxone-from-people-with-prescriptions.

22. See Sarah E. Wakeman et al., "Comparative Effectiveness of Different Treatment Pathways for Opioid Use Disorder," *JAMA Network Open* 3, no. 2 (February 5, 2020): e1920622, https://jamanetwork.com/journals/jamanetworkopen/fullarticle/2760032.

23. Full disclosure: I support this program in a minor way as a small-scale patron (monthly funder) on Patreon, as well as by talking about it enthusiastically every chance I get. I also take probably undeserved pride in having suggested Dr. Stefan Kertesz to the producers when they were working on their stellar episode on chronic pain patients and

prescription opioid crackdowns. You can hear the episode here: https:// crackdownpod.com/podcast/episode -20-cut-off/.

24. US Drug Enforcement Administration, Diversion Control Division, "DEA Trends & Update. San Juan, Puerto Rico Pharmacy Diversion Awareness Conference. March 26–27, 2017 [slideshow]," US Department of Justice Drug Enforcement Agency, 2017, https:// www.deadiversion.usdoj.gov/mtgs/pharm _awareness/conf_2017/march_2017 /carrion.pdf.

25. Not to be confused with naltrexone, the addiction treatment drug marketed as Vivitrol discussed earlier; we'll discuss it again later on.

26. Or "safer," or "supervised" consumption or injection sites (so SCS or SIS), or sometimes overdose prevention sites, although overdoses occur in these sites — but here, unlike on the street or in one's apartment or a restaurant bathroom, are never fatal. Ideally, such a site will support clients in using by the safest method they are open to, which means having ventilation hoods to allow for smoking — smoking heroin, so long as the dose can be calculated, is generally a lower-risk method than injecting it, for example — as well as other forms of ingestion of both opioids and other drugs. The goal is always to respect users' needs and personal autonomy while making it possible to mitigate harms and to learn safer use practices.

27. For more on safety and effectiveness on a range of measures, see Mary Clare Kennedy, Mohammad Karamouzian, and Thomas Kerr, "Public Health and Public Order Outcomes Associated with Supervised Drug Consumption Facilities: a Systematic Review," *Current HIV/ AIDS Reports* 14 (2017): 161–183, https:// pubmed.ncbi.nlm.nih.gov/28875422/ or this fact sheet: "Supervised Consumption Services," Drug Policy Alliance, 2018, https://drugpolicy.org /resource/supervised-consumption -services.

28. In Toronto, for example, there is just one long-term shelter that admits pets (Fred Victor, https://www.fredvictor .org/what-we-do/housing/shelters/), and in New York shelters will accept emotional support or service animals, but not pets.

LIMITS

1. In his wonderful book *Daily Rituals: Women at Work* (New York: Alfred A. Knopf, 2019), on page 6, Mason Currey quotes from a letter Bishop wrote to fellow poet Robert Lowell: "You can sit up typing all night long and feel wonderful the next day. I wrote two stories in a week."

2. Currey, *Daily Rituals*, 24. Oliver Sacks wrote about his amphetamine use and addiction in several of his works.

3. Currey, *Daily Rituals*, 132–133.

4. Described and quoted in Currey, *Daily Rituals*, 163–164.

5. Julian Barnes, *Keeping an Eye Open: Essays on Art* (Toronto: Random House Canada, 2015), 23.

6. "Slum Tourism," Wikipedia, https:// en.wikipedia.org/wiki/Slum_tourism.

7. Joel Wolfram, "Philadelphia police recruits get up-close tour of Kensington neighborhood," WHYY News, February 20, 2019, https://whyy.org/articles /philadelphia-police-recruits-get-up -close-tour-of-kensington-neighborhood/; and "Heroin Hellscape in Kensington, Philadelphia [video report]," *Philadelphia Inquirer*, April 18, 2017, https://www .youtube.com/watch?v=k2PUYVBU7aM.

8. Again, not to be confused with the addiction treatment naltrexone.

9. I'm thinking of Maia Szalawitz in NYC, Christopher Moraff in Philadelphia, and Zachary Siegel in Chicago, as well as Brooke Feldman — also in Philly — and

Elizabeth Brico, currently writing out of Florida.

10. Mike Riggs, "Up Close and Personal with Philadelphia's Heroin Crisis," *Reason*, August/September 2018, https://reason.com/2018/07/31/up-close-and-personal-with-phi/.

11. Lelena is a nickname she's used for twenty years to avoid online harassment; Peacock is her married name.

12. Elizabeth Oliva, et al., "Associations between Stopping Prescriptions for Opioids, Length of Opioid Treatment, and Overdose or Suicide Deaths in US Veterans: Observational Evaluation," *BMJ* (2020): 368, https://www.bmj.com/content/368/bmj.m283.

13. See for example Michele Buonara et al., "Race and Gender Are Associated with Opioid Dose Reduction Among Patients on Chronic Opioid Therapy," *Pain Med* 20, no.8 (August 1, 2019): 1519–1527, https://pubmed.ncbi.nlm.nih.gov/30032197/. There have been many similar studies.

14. Joshua J. Fenton et al., "Trends and Rapidity of Dose Tapering among Patients Prescribed Long-term Opioid Therapy, 2008-2017," *JAMA Network Open* 2, no. 11 (2019), https://www.ncbi.nlm.nih.gov/pmc/articles/PMC6902834/.

15. Alexandra Johnson, *The Hidden Writer: Diaries and the Creative Life* (New York: Doubleday, 1997), 13.

16. "Emails Show Officials Blocked Coronavirus Testing During Outbreak at Mesa Verde ICE Jail," *Democracy Now!*, August 7, 2020, https://www.democracynow.org/2020/8/7/headlines/emails_show_officials_blocked_coronavirus_testing_during_outbreak_at_mesa_verde_ice_jail.

17. Stuart Hughes, "Adam Maier-Clayton's Controversial Right-to-Die Campaign," BBC News, July 18, 2017, https://www.bbc.com/news/world-us-canada-40546632.

18. Mary Oliver, "The Summer Day," available online at https://www.loc.gov/poetry/180/133.html, from *New and Selected Poems* (Boston: Beacon Press, 1992).

VERTIGO

1. Dawn Marie Paley, "Crackdown Podcast: Capitalism, Prohibition and Crisis," *Toward Freedom*, November 2, 2019, https://towardfreedom.org/story/crackdown-podcast-capitalism-prohibition-and-crisis/.

QUAKE

1. Salman Rushdie, *The Ground Beneath Her Feet* (Toronto: Knopf Canada, 1999), 13.

2. Among the first caught in a wave of renovictions and false landlord-own-use evictions that have swept Toronto and fundamentally transformed the composition of the city, in which the high value of real estate, low availability of rental units, and lack of protections for tenants encouraged landlords to evict existing tenants under any pretense in order to raise the rent. Increasingly, precarious and low-wage workers must commute from outside the downtown or even outside the city to provide services to the high earners and those with inherited wealth who can afford to live here. It's a pattern that has occurred in city after city.

3. Maté uses this phrasing in many places in talks and in his writing, but I took this particular quote from an essay on his website, "Beyond Drugs: The Universal Experience of Addiction," April 5, 2017 (posted by Stephanie Lee

but purports to be written by Gabor Maté), https://drgabormate.com /opioids-universal-experience-addiction/.

4. Louise Hay, *Heal Your Body: The Mental Causes for Physical Illness and the Metaphysical Way to Overcome Them* (Hay House, 1984).

5. Addiction psychologist Stanton Peele is worth reading on this. Importantly, he argues that despite its progressive allure and appeal to harm reductionists, Maté's model in fact constitutes a new version of the poorly evidenced, reductive brain disease model of addiction. See, for example, his article "The Seductive, But Dangerous, Allure of Gabor Maté," *Psychology Today*, December 5, 2011, https:// www.psychologytoday.com/ca/blog /addiction-in-society/201112/the -seductive-dangerous-allure-gabor-mat.

6. Such as in the video "Why Capitalism Makes Us Sick" (Kindred Media, October 13, 2017, https://www .kindredmedia.org/2017/10/capitalism -makes-us-sick-video-gabor-mate/) and related interviews, and likely in some form in his book on societal causes of illness (such as materialism and perhaps capitalism), *The Myth of Normal: Illness and Health in an Insane Culture*, not yet published as I write this but due out in 2021.

7. Tweeted on April 8, 2020.

8. I'm not the only one to wonder about this. See Elon Eisenberg, Erica Suzan, and Dorit Pud, "Opioid-Induced Hyperalgesia (OIH): A Real Clinical Problem or Just an Experimental Phenomenon?," *Journal of Pain and Symptom Management* 49, no. 3 (March 2015), https://pubmed.ncbi.nlm.nih .gov/25128284/.

9. Editorial by Jan M. Keppel Hesselink and Michael Shactman, "'But That is Your Opinion': The Dark Side of Postmodern Pain Medicine Creating a Postmodern Patient Autonomy," *Journal of Pain Research*, no. 11 (2018): 2847–2851.

MONSTERS

1. Greg Woodfield, "OPIOID HELL: The Zombies of a USA City with a Hopeless Addiction that's Set to Come to UK," *Daily Express*, March 19, 2018, https:// www.express.co.uk/news/uk/933478 /opioid-addiction-zombies-USA-fentanyl -coming-UK-painkillers.

2. Although Meg's is her real first name, "Joe" is a pseudonym.

3. Elizabeth Brico's entire article is worth a read. Find it at "Witnessed Urine Screens in Drug Treatment: Humiliating and Harmful," *Filter* magazine, October 28, 2019, https://filtermag.org/urine-screen -drug-treatment/.

4. Such as one called Proof+, available on the Google Play store. Its tagline is *Anytime. Anywhere. Anyone,* and as of April 2020 it recorded audio and video evidence of specimen collection of breath samples and saliva, with video-witnessed urine tests coming soon.

5. Bill Kinkle, "Why My Nursing License Hasn't Been Reinstated [blog post]," April 7, 2020, https://billkinkle.weebly .com/bills-blog/why-my-nursing-license -hasnt-been-reinstated.

6. I've elaborated here on less detailed examples Petra Schultz mentioned in our June 2020 interview, so the details come from me, not her, nor are they from Johann Hari, although he does mention most of them in his way in his book.

7. Carolyn C. Shadle and John L. Meyer, "Pets, Vets, and Opioids," *American Veterinarian* 3, no. 3 (April 2018), https://www.americanveterinarian .com/journals/amvet/2018/april2018 /pets-vets-and-opioids.

8. Dan Taekema, "Drugs Make Her a 'Monster': A Hamilton Family's Cry for Help Fighting Addiction," CBC News, July 18, 2019, https://www.cbc.ca/news

/canada/hamilton/addiction-hamilton
-fentanyl-crystal-meth-1.5168438.

9. *Chasing the Dragon: The Life of an Opiate Addict* [transcript]," FBI, n.d., https://www.fbi.gov/video-repository/chasing_dragon_trailer.mp4/view.

10. Simon Shuster, "The World's Deadliest Drug: Inside a Krokodil Cookhouse," *TIME*, December 5, 2013, https://time.com/3398086/the-worlds-deadliest-drug-inside-a-krokodil-cookhouse/.

11. Susan Zielinski, "Drug Use Turns Red Deer Bridge into 'Zombie Apocalypse,'" *Red Deer Advocate*, November 7, 2018, https://www.reddeeradvocate.com/news/drug-use-turns-red-deer-bridge-into-zombie-apocalypse/. This article came to my attention as a link in Allison Barker and Kali Sedgemore's really exceptional article on fear, hatred, and portrayals of stimulant users (the authors both use methamphetamines and work in stimulant harm reduction): "The Monster Smash: Breaking Down the 'Meth Epidemic' and Barriers to Stimulant Safe Supply," The Volcano, October 31, 2019, http://thevolcano.org/2019/10/31/the-monster-smash-breaking-down-the-meth-epidemic-and-barriers-to-stimulant-safe-supply/. Although my focus here is principally opioids, Barker and Sedgemore's very detailed essay is the most outstanding account I have seen of the ways in which monster or zombie characterizations are used to justify oppression of poor and racialized people who use methamphetamines and other stimulants specifically, all of it excellent and much of it relevant to other drugs as well.

12. "Duterte Willing to Unleash a Hitler on PHL Criminals," GMA News Online, September 30, 2016, https://www.gmanetwork.com/news/news/nation/583282/duterte-willing-to-unleash-a-hitler-on-phl-criminals/story/.

13. John Cassidy, "Piketty's Inequality Story in Six Charts," *The New Yorker,* March 26, 2014, https://www.newyorker.com/news/john-cassidy/pikettys-inequality-story-in-six-charts.

14. Thomas Piketty, *Capital in the Twenty-First Century*, trans. Arthur Goldhammer (Cambridge, MA: Harvard University Press, 2017), 265.

DROSS

1. Described in complex but interesting detail in Steffen Rimner's *Opium's Long Shadow: From Asian Revolt to Global Drug Control* (Cambridge, MA: Harvard University Press, 2018).

2. This process of criminalization of poor opioid users, as well as the moderate and widespread use of opioids in China (and elsewhere) before prohibition, is described and supported with extensive documentation in the book *Narcotic Culture: A History of Drugs in China* by Frank Dikötter, Lars Laamann, and Zhou Xun (Hong Kong: Hong Kong University Press, 2004), which relies on mostly Chinese-language primary sources, both published and archival sources such as personal letters, marketing material, or legislation, to describe prevalent use and how it changed as prohibition occurred.

3. "Pharmakos," Wikipedia, https://en.wikipedia.org/wiki/Pharmakos.

4. You can be charged for growing the seeds in the US. But it's a bit of a legal grey area, as writer Stephanie Pappas puts it here: "Massive Poppy Bust: Why Home-Grown Opium Is Rare," LiveScience, June 12, 2017, https://www.livescience.com/59452-why-opium-is-grown-outside-us.html.

5. Turgenev quoted by Alphonse Daudet in an incident described by Julian Barnes in his introduction to Alphonse Daudet, *Into the Land of Pain*, trans. and ed. Julian Barnes (Alfred E. Knopf, New York: 2002).

6. All quotations from Daudet are from Julian Barnes's wonderful translation of *Into the Land of Pain*, 14–15, 30, 67.

7. William Shakespeare, *The Merchant of Venice*, act III, scene I.

8. @Chronic_FLKeys, Twitter, January 8, 2020, https://twitter.com/Chronic_FLKeys/status/1215122414952239104.

9. @OnlyTheSnarky, Twitter, January 27, 2016, https://twitter.com/OnlyTheSnarky/status/692250058364948480.

10. @SASTrendy, Twitter, March 4, 2020, https://twitter.com/SasTrendy/status/1235255284152578048.

11. @MaryEllenGust, Twitter, January 27, 2016, https://twitter.com/MaryEllenGust/status/692546492305948672.

12. Rebecca Ahrnsbrak et al., "Key Substance Use and Mental Health Indicators in the United States: Results from the 2016 National Survey on Drug Use and Health," Center for Behavioral Health Statistics and Quality (SAMHSA), 2017, https://www.samhsa.gov/data/sites/default/files/NSDUH-FFR1-2016/NSDUH-FFR1-2016.htm; and "Module 5: Assessing and Addressing Opioid Use Disorder (OUD)" Centers for Disease Control and Prevention, n.d., https://www.cdc.gov/drugoverdose/training/oud/accessible/index.html.

13. "Results from the 2014 National Survey on Drug Use and Health: Detailed Tables," SAMHSA, 2015, https://www.samhsa.gov/data/report/results-2014-national-survey-drug-use-and-health-detailed-tables.

14. @EschbachMichael, Twitter, June 20, 2020, used with permission.

15. Wikipedia offers a decent summary with links to research and accounts of different usages of the phrase at "Nothing About Us Without Us," https://en.wikipedia.org/wiki/Nothing_About_Us_Without_Us.

SATURNALIA

1. Norman Ohler, *Blitzed*, trans. Shaun Whiteside (Allen Lane UK, 2016).

2. Ohler, *Blitzed*, 16.

3. Ohler, *Blitzed*, 16.

4. Ohler, *Blitzed*, 20, with reference to his footnote 26.

5. Peter Hayes, *Industry and Ideology: IG Farben in the Nazi Era* (Cambridge: Cambridge University Press, 2001).

6. "Bayer," The Holocaust Encyclopedia, United States Holocaust Memorial Museum, June 13, 2019, https://encyclopedia.ushmm.org/content/en/article/bayer.

7. Ohler, *Blitzed*, 21.

8. Nathan Yerby, "The Justice Department Considered Using Fentanyl To Execute Prisoners," Addiction Center, September 19, 2019, https://www.addictioncenter.com/news/2019/09/fentanyl-execute-prisoners/.

9. "Spain's Struggle with Gentrification, Tourism and Globalisation," Madrid No Frills, August 23, 2019, https://madridnofrills.com/gentrification/.

10. Andrew Russel, "B.C. Announces Public Inquiry into Dirty Money—What's the Rest of Canada Doing?," Global News, May 15, 2019, https://globalnews.ca/news/5280174/bc-public-inquiry-money-laundering-rest-of-canada/.

11. "Colau y Buch discrepan sobre cómo combatir los narcopisos de Ciutat Vella," *La Vanguardia*, September 14, 2018, https://www.lavanguardia.com/local/barcelona/20180914/451798456626/colau-buch-discrepan-narcopisos-ciutat-vella.html.

12. Isabelle Aguelovski et al., "Global Cities Like Barcelona and Boston Reveal Health Risks of Gentrification," Barcelona Laboratory for Urban Environmental Justice and Sustainability, November 8, 2018, http://www.bcnuej.org/2018/11/08/global-cities-like

-barcelona-and-boston-reveal-health
-risks-of-gentrification/.

13. Tweet to @fauxillustrado by Teodoro "Teddy Boy" Locsin Jr. (@teddyboylocsin), August 21, 2016, 11.33 p.m., screenshot at https://twitter.com /SanhoTree/status/1306244654443245568 /photo/4.

14. Betsy Pearl, "Ending the War on Drugs: By the Numbers," Center for American Progress, June 27, 2018, https://www .americanprogress.org/issues/criminal -justice/reports/2018/06/27/452819 /ending-war-drugs-numbers/.

15. Rachel Browne, "Black and Indigenous People are Overrepresented in Canada's Weed Arrests," VICE News, April 18, 2018, https://www.vice.com/en_ca /article/d35eyq/black-and-indigenous -people-are-overrepresented-in-canadas -weed-arrests.

16. "Saturnalia," Encyclopedia Britannica, https://www.britannica.com/topic /Saturnalia-Roman-festival.

17. Freud refused opioids even as he died painfully of cancer, in order to stay lucid and aware of the dying process to the last. His death is beautifully described along with other notable writer deaths in Katie Roiphe's unique book, *The Violet Hour: Great Writers at the End* (New York: The Dial Press, 2016).

PART III
The Quarantine of the Opium Eater: Notes on Getting Well

DEPENDENCE

1. Franz Kafka, *The Metamorphosis*, trans. Stanley Corngold (New York: Penguin Random House, 1972).

2. @DawnMGibson, Twitter, December 10, 2019:
   Me: Ouch! Why does my back hurt like that?
   Also me <laughing bitterly>: Silly rabbit. Did you really forget about your #SpondyloArthritis?
   Me: You're the worst! Why are you mocking me?
   Also me: Who forgets the feeling of radioactive badgers and termites chewing on their bones?

3. This is the exact title of several grants awarded by NIDA in collaboration with other granting bodies to one researcher on the topic, Mark E. Vonzastrow, to research opioid receptor interactions with and within the cell to which they bind. So you could say that drug trafficking goes on at the societal and subcellular levels. Drugs (as always) are winning the war on drugs. (See Mark E. Vonzastrow, "Membrane Trafficking of Opioid Receptors," Grantome, http://grantome.com/grant/NIH/R37 -DA010711-15.) See also, just as an example with some description of what membrane trafficking actually means, Bihua Via and Zhizhong Z. Pang, "Trafficking of central opioid receptors and descending pain inhibition," *Molecular Pain* 3 (2007): 37, https:// www.ncbi.nlm.nih.gov/pmc/articles /PMC2219988/.

4. As Richard J. Miller describes in his helpful book *Drugged: The Science and Culture Behind Psychotropic Drugs* (New York: Oxford University Press, 2015), experiments on guinea pig small intestine and on the vas deferens of mice provided the first clear picture of exactly what morphine and other opioids do in the body, not just in the brain.

5. Mike Jay, *This Way Lies Madness: The Asylum and Beyond* (London: Thames & Hudson and the Wellcome Collection, 2016), 193.

6. As, for example, when trying cognitive-behavioral therapy. Those phrases, and

the attitude of insisting the patient is doing it wrong or is too negative if they attempt to express their experience of pain or inadequate response to this treatment, are drawn from a WebMD article about CBT for pain called "Managing Chronic Pain: A Cognitive-Behavioral Therapy Approach" (by Elizabeth Shimer Bowers, June 27, 2011, https://www.webmd.com/pain-management/features/cognitive-behavioral). It reflects many experiences of pain patients with real-life providers of CBT or with doctors who push it for long-term pain based on short-term evidence.

7. "Fix" is an informal term for a dose of a narcotic upon which one is dependent.

8. For more on Miltown, which I learned about through an episode of Geoff Turner's wonderful *On Drugs* podcast on Canada's CBC, see Andrea Tone, *The Age of Anxiety: A History of America's Turbulent Affair with Tranquilizers* (New York: Basic Books, 2008), on which that episode was based.

9. There is a nice overview of hedonics, or the experience of pleasure and displeasure, in Susanne Becker et al., "The Role of Hedonics in the Human Affectome," *Neuroscience and Biobehavoral Reviews* 102 (July 2019): 221–241. For the clearest detailed overview I've found of the various interactions, or signalling events, that occur when opioid receptors are activated, see Tuan Trang et al., "Pain and Poppies: The Good, the Bad, and the Ugly of Opioid Analgesics," *Journal of Neuroscience* 35, no. 41 (October 14, 2015), https://www.ncbi.nlm.nih.gov/pmc/articles/PMC4604226/.

10. Veteran journalist Maia Szalavitz advanced this synthesis of various lines of research on addiction (along with her own experience of addiction to heroin and cocaine) in her book *Unbroken Brain* (New York: St. Martin's Press, 2016). The fact that most addictions start in one's teens or early adulthood and often ease by one's thirties is part of her contention that the habits of addiction are learned responses.

11. John Kersey and Edward Phillips, *The New World of Words: or, Universal English Dictionary* (London: Printed for J. Phillips, 1706).

12. Bronwyn Tarr, et al., "Naltrexone Blocks Endorphins Released When Dancing in Synchrony," *Adaptive Human Behavior and Physiology* 3 (2017): 241–254, https://link.springer.com/article/10.1007/s40750-017-0067-y; Bronwyn Tarr, Jacques Launay, and Robin M. Dunbar, "Silent Disco: Dancing in Synchrony Leads to Elevated Pain Thresholds and Social Closeness," *Evolution and Human Behavior* 37, no. 5 (September 2016): 343–349, https://pubmed.ncbi.nlm.nih.gov/27540276/.

13. See for example A.K. Mangak, G.M. Schmolzer, and W.K. Kraft, "Pharmacological and Non-pharmacological Treatments for the Neonatal Abstinence Syndrome (NAS)," *Seminars in Fetal & Neonatal Medecine* 24, no. 2 (April 2019): 133–141, https://www.ncbi.nlm.nih.gov/pmc/articles/PMC6451887/.

14. Direct message from Joe to me, January 28, 2020, quoted with permission.

15. Direct message from Joe to me, January 29, 2020, quoted with permission.

16. Not actually morphine in my case, at the moment, but the opioid tramadol.

17. William Burroughs, *Junky*, ed, Oliver Harris (New York: Penguin Books, 2003), xxxviii (first published in 1953).

18. This quote comes from an epigraph to Chaim Potok's novel, *The Chosen* (New York: Ballantine Books, 1967).

19. As described here: Ryan Ting-A-Kee and Derek van der Kooy, "The Neurobiology of Opiate Motivation," *Cold Spring Harbor Perspectives in Medicine*, no. 2 (2012), http://perspectivesinmedicine.cshlp.org/content/2/10/a012096.full; and Hector Vargas-Perez et al., "Ventral Tegmental Area BDNF Induces an Opiate-Dependent–Like Reward State in Naïve Rats," *Science* 324, no. 5935 (June 26, 2009), https://science

.sciencemag.org/content/324/5935/1732.full, for example. I've vastly simplified structures and processes here.

20. Direct message from Joe to me, January 29, 2020, quoted with permission.

21. Edward St. Aubyn, *The Complete Patrick Melrose Novels* (Picador: New York, 2015), 169.

22. Tina Rosenberg, "The shelter that gives wine to alcoholics," *The Guardian*, April 26, 2016, https://www.theguardian.com/society/2016/apr/26/homeless-shelter-ottawa-gives-wine-to-alcoholics.

23. Despite a much-cited study showing that users could not distinguish injectable hydromorphone from heroin, it is not actually correct to say that it's the same high. Habitual opioid users know that every opioid has a distinctly different feel, and most people, including the nurse I spoke with at the MOP, see hydromorphone as the next best thing to heroin, which is simply too difficult to acquire legally for their patients. Stephanie Muron told me that many of her patients at the MOP would in fact benefit from heroin, which would make dosing easier and better achieve the feeling they seek in using opioids.

24. I used this quote in the article I wrote for the *Walrus*, a Canadian general interest magazine, called "Saying No to Drugs Isn't an Answer to Addiction," (August 29, 2018).

25. Though that may have changed by the time you read this. See Andrea Woo, "Prof, former public health officer launch company to produce legal heroin for treatment," *Globe and Mail*, July 12, 2020, https://www.theglobeandmail.com/canada/british-columbia/article-prof-former-public-health-officer-launch-company-to-produce-legal/.

26. Brianna Lee, Danielle Renwick, and Rocio Cara, "Mexico's Drug War [backgrounder]," Council on Foreign Relations, 2019, https://www.cfr.org/backgrounder/mexicos-drug-war.

27. I say seemingly because it is difficult to compare. Patients who get access to heroin or hydromorphone are usually those with the most severe opioid use disorder, and they have usually "failed" methadone or buprenorphine or both before trying. The full agonist (heroin or hydromorphone) studies also involve far fewer people. But the results are almost universally dramatically positive on numerous important measures, whereas the main thing we can demonstrate for the less euphoric opioids is that they are extremely effective, compared to other treatments not including heroin or hydromorphone, in preventing overdose death. It seems to me that there is ample evidence to expect that these latter treatments would be more effective for more people across more measures of well-being and recovery, certainly enough to warrant further comparative trials and lower barrier access to them.

INDEPENDENCE

1. Dr. Gabriel E. Sella, in an editorial called "The Practicality of Pain Acceptance" in *Practical Pain Management* 18, no. 4 (August 7, 2018), https://www.practicalpainmanagement.com/resources/clinical-practice-guidelines/editorial-practicality-pain-acceptance.

2. Audre Lorde, "Learning from the 60s," a 1982 address given at Harvard University, transcript at https://www.blackpast.org/african-american-history/1982-audre-lorde-learning-60s/.

3. Amanda Leduc, "Monster or Marvel? A Disabled Life in a Superhero Universe," *Literary Hub*, April 26, 2019, https://lithub.com/monster-or-marvel-a-disabled-life-in-a-superhero-universe/.

4. As a leading anti-prescription-opioid crusader indelicately calls them. It's because this is indeed indelicate that we do not similarly refer to a child's ADHD

medication as "speed pills." It *is* true that they are low doses of a similar substance which does have similar effects, but as Paracelsus said, "the dose makes the poison." In the case of opioids, that should be amended to more accurately say "the dose, relative to the patient's tolerance, makes the poison." It's really all relative.

5. Marcus Aurelius, *The Meditations*, Book VIII (47). Many versions of this float around the internet, all saying roughly the same thing but translated slightly differently from the original. This version is one for which I haven't been able to find a good attribution, but it's probably the most familiar one, copy and pasted by every two-bit pop philosopher with a blog. Here is another version, translated by Arthur Spenser Loat Farquharson and published in 1944 and available at https://sites.google.com /site/thestoiclife/the_teachers/maurcus -aurelius/meditations/08: "When thou art vexed at some external cross, it is not the thing itself that troubles thee, but thy judgment on it. And this thou canst annul in a moment."

6. Demetrios Karaberopoulos, Marianna Karamanou, and George Androutsos, "The Theriac in Antiquity," *The Lancet: Perspectives/The Art of Medicine* 379, no. 9830 (2012): 1942–1943.

7. Daudet, *In the Land of Pain*, 49 and 43.

8. L. Desveaux et al., "Understanding the Behavioural Determinants of Opioid Prescribing among Family Physicians: A Qualitative Study." *BMC Family Practice* 20, article 59 (2019).

9. Desveaux et al., "Understanding the Behavioural Determinants."

10. @RoseCottageCre1, Twitter, June 17, 2017, https://twitter.com/RoseCottage Cre1/status/1273465364005949440.

11. Garth Mullins (@garthmullins), Twitter, May 21, 2020, https://twitter .com/garthmullins/status /1263539490154442752.

12. Although injectable opioids for injection are far safer than oral opioids crushed and injected, which can increase risk of endocarditis.

13. Although most studies of treatments of all kinds, including opioids, for pain are limited in that they tend to be of short duration—often as little as three months and rarely as long as a year, let alone the decades or lifetimes over which chronic pain patients need at least periodic relief—methadone provides good evidence of effectiveness with relatively stable dose over the long term. So does pain relief experienced by opioid use disorder patients receiving long-acting morphine (Kadian) over years, and, where diacetylmorphine (heroin) is prescribed long-term to such patients who often have co-existing pain conditions, we have another potential source of data on the subject.

14. Lee N. Robins, Darlene H. Davis, and David H. Nurco, "How Permanent was Vietnam Drug Addiction?," *American Journal of Public Health* Supplement, vol. 64 (December 1974), https://ajph .aphapublications.org/doi/pdf/10.2105 /AJPH.64.12_Suppl.38.

15. As described in this Cochrane commentary: Cathy Stannard and Andrew Moore, "Traditional Opioids for Chronic Non-Cancer Pain: Untidy, Unsatisfactory, and Probably Unsuitable," Cochrane UK, n.d., https://uk.cochrane. org/news/traditional-opioids-chronic -non-cancer-pain-untidy-unsatisfactory -and-probably-unsuitable.

16. The typically high drop-out rate in these studies, which may be exacerbated by the use of overly high starting doses, provoking avoidable side effects, is one reason why there are so few reliable long-term studies of the use of prescription opioids for pain, leading to suggestions that they don't work, when it's far more likely that they aren't the right treatment for most people, but are an irreplaceable treatment for a minority of pain patients for whom other options are not tolerable or effective.

17. "Mission," National Institute on Drug Abuse, 2018, https://www.nih.gov

/about-nih/what-we-do/nih-almanac
/national-institute-drug-abuse-nida.
18. Ingrid Walker, personal communication,
March 7, 2020. This widely quoted
figure (Dr. Carl Hart uses it, for
example, in his really excellent memoir
High Price [New York: HarperCollins,
2013]) was calculated by Walker, who
went through National Survey on Drug
Use and Health reports dating back to
the 1980s.
19. Priya Shetty, "Nora Volkow—
Challenging the Myths about Drug
Addiction," *The Lancet (Perspectives/*

Profile) 378, no. 9790 (August 6, 2011),
https://www.thelancet.com/journals
/lancet/article/PIIS0140-6736(11)61239-7
/fulltext.
20. Dr. Walker is the author of *High: Drugs,
Desire, and a Nation of Users* (Seattle:
University of Washington Press, 2017),
which looks at the US's dual-pronged
drug policy—on one hand, prohibition
of some substances, and on the other,
an also-problematic medicalization that
has made some substances central to
American life and culture.

INTERDEPENDENCE

1. Antonin Artaud, "Opium Traffic,"
trans. Richard Grossman, *La Révolution
Surréaliste* (1925), reproduced at
Conjunctions, http://www.conjunctions
.com/online/article/antonin-artaud
-01-16-1998.
2. This is the last stanza of Coleridge's
unfinished poem. After "drunk the
milk of Paradise," the poem stops,
due (according to the preface Coleridge
wrote to the poem) to the arrival of an
unnamed "person from Porlock" just as
he was recording the opium-influenced
dream from which he'd awoken. This
inconvenient visitor from Porlock
disturbed his fragile connection with
the reverie and Coleridge forgot the last
lines he'd planned to write. The poem
can be found at Project Gutenberg
(Ernest Hartley Coleridge, ed., *The
Complete Poetical Works of Samuel
Taylor Coleridge, Including Poems Now
Published for the First Time* [in two
volumes; Oxford: Clarendon Press, 1912],
https://onlinebooks.library.upenn.edu
/webbin/gutbook/lookup?num=29090)
or in any collected works of Coleridge.
3. As quoted at length in Horace B. Day's
1868 book, *The Opium Habit*, reproduced
at http://www.dominiopublico.gov.br
/download/texto/guoo7293.pdf.
4. Lena (forum user), "Subsonic
Information: An Experience with

Opium (exp331)," Erowid, September 11,
2000, https://erowid.org/exp/331.
5. Frederick Brown, as described in this
review of Brown's Flaubert biography:
James Wood, "The Man behind Bovary,"
New York Times, April 16, 2006, https://
www.nytimes.com/2006/04/16/books
/review/the-man-behind-bovary.html.
6. De Quincey, *Confessions* (2020), 202.
7. "Portugal Country Drug Report 2019,"
European Monitoring Centre for
Drugs and Drug Addiction, https://
www.emcdda.europa.eu/system/files
/publications/11331/portugal-cdr-2019
_0.pdf; Puja Seth et al., "Quantifying
the Epidemic of Prescription Opioid
Overdose Deaths," *American Journal of
Public Health* 108, no. 4 (2018): 500–502,
https://www.ncbi.nlm.nih.gov/pmc
/articles/PMC5844400/. The United
States' population is 107 times larger
than Portugal's, so roughly three
thousand deaths would have been a
proportional number.
8. Many drug treatment programs and
recovery houses make "recovery"
impossible by making participation
conditional on abstinence from all
substances. In particular, programs
that seek to promote healthy lifestyle
by banning cigarette smoking or forcing
people to withdraw from nicotine and
opioids simultaneously all too often

alienate potential patients or have high dropout rates. It sounds good, to get people off the cancer sticks and the smack at the same time, but people are dying of opioid overdose as a result of unreasonable requirements that force them to quickly and brutally get off everything that gives them a bit of comfort and good feeling.

9. Harm Reduction Works-HRW, https://www.hrh413.org/foundationsstart-here-2.

10. I spoke with Larsen and reported on this briefly in an article, but he explains the idea in more detail in his own words in "Why Opium Poppies?" on his website for Overgrow Canada, http://overgrowcanada.com/poppies/why-opium-poppies/. On Fair Price Pharma, Andrea Woo wrote "Prof, Former Public Health Officer Launch Company to Produce Legal Heroin for Treatment," *Globe and Mail*, July 12, 2020, https://www.theglobeandmail.com/canada/british-columbia/article-prof-former-public-health-officer-launch-company-to-produce-legal/.

11. Natasha Touesnard and Matthew Bonn, "PANDA: The Birth of a Pan-American Drug User Alliance," *Filter* Magazine, July 20, 2020.

12. See also Alicia Yolanda Harvey-Vera et al., "Risk of Violence in Drug Rehabilitation Centers: Perceptions of People who Inject Drugs in Tijuana, Mexico," *Substance Abuse Treatment, Prevention, and Policy* 11, article 5 (2016), https://substanceabusepolicy.biomedcentral.com/articles/10.1186/s13011-015-0044-z.

13. See, for example, Elizabeth Nolan Brown, "The Real Modern Slavery? Inside America's Court-Ordered Corporate Labor Camps," *Reason*, May 10, 2017, https://reason.com/2017/10/05/human-trafficked-by-uncle-sam/.

14. Catherine Reef, "Leo and Frida: The Doctor and the Artist," *Stanford Medicine*, Summer 2013, http://sm.stanford.edu/archive/stanmed/2013summer/article8.html. Eloesser

sounds a bit like a doppelganger of the Canadian thoracic surgeon and communist Norman Bethune, who, like Eloesser, went to Spain to serve as a physician in the fight against the fascists in the Spanish Civil War.

15. The story and quotes are from Justin McCurry, "Librarians in Uproar after Borrowing Record of Haruki Murakami Is Leaked," *The Guardian*, December 2, 2015, https://www.theguardian.com/books/2015/dec/02/librarians-in-uproar-after-borrowing-record-of-haruki-murakami-is-leaked.

16. Tony Sheldon, "More Than a Quick Fix," *BMJ* 336, no. 7365 (2008): 68–69, https://www.ncbi.nlm.nih.gov/pmc/articles/PMC2190259/.

17. Andy Gregory, "'Saved From a Horrible Fate': Legal Heroin Prescribed to Hundreds of UK Drug Users, Figures Reveal," *The Independent*, August 17, 2019, https://www.independent.co.uk/news/uk/home-news/heroin-addiction-diamorphine-treatment-british-system-hat-leap-harm-reduction-a9061556.html.

18. Sheldon, "More Than a Quick Fix."

19. The clean/dirty dichotomy is used often when we talk about substances. But no person is dirty because of what substance they ingest or inject. No person is clean because they are abstinent from a particular molecule. The only time that "clean" makes sense is when we are talking about uncontaminated drugs, and the only time "dirty" makes sense is when we're literally talking about dirt, as in a dirty syringe that must be re-used or shared because of rules limiting availability of syringes, resulting in the spread of infections like HIV or viral hepatitis.

20. Johann Hari describes outcomes of the closure of Dr. Marks's clinic in his book, *Chasing the Scream: The First and Last Days of the War on Drugs* (London and New York: Bloomsbury, 2015).

21. "Advice to the Profession: Prescribing Drugs," College of Physicians and Surgeons of Ontario, n.d., https://www.cpso.on.ca/Physicians/Policies-Guidance

/Policies/Prescribing-Drugs/Advice-to
-the-Profession-Prescribing-Drugs.

22. These typically include very specific
tests such as researchers pinching
subjects' skin, applying cold cylinders
to various body parts, asking subjects
to touch an increasingly hot object until
it becomes intolerable, or asking the
subject to distinguish between pin pricks
and blunt contact—measures which,
taken together, are used to estimate some
general level of sensitivity to pain. As I
have described, I took part in one such
study and have difficulty relating my
experience of pin pricks to my varying
tolerance to unmedicated labour and
childbirth, to chronic pain localized to
my shoulder joints and spine, or to the
flu-like body aches of withdrawal.

23. "Substance Use-Related Harms and Risk
Factors during Periods of Disruption,"
Public Health Ontario, July 28, 2020,
https://www.publichealthontario.ca
/-/media/documents/ncov/main/2020/08
/substance-use-related-harms-disruption.
pdf.

24. "Overdose Deaths in Ontario Climb
by Up to 40% Since Pandemic Started:
Chief Coroner," *Canadian Press*,
September 24, 2020, https://toronto
.citynews.ca/2020/09/24/overdose-deaths
-in-ontario-climb-by-up-to-40-since
-pandemic-started-chief-coroner/.

25. "Preliminary Patterns in Circumstances
Surrounding Opioid-Related Deaths
in Ontario during the COVID-19
Pandemic," Public Health Ontario,
November 2020, https://www
.publichealthontario.ca/-/media
/documents/o/2020/opioid-mortality
-covid-surveillance-report.pdf.

26. Janet French, "More Than 900
Albertans Died from Opioid Poisoning
in First Ten Months of 2020," CBC
News, December 18, 2020, https://
www.cbc.ca/news/canada/edmonton
/900-albertans-opioid-poisoning-1
.5846860. It is no coincidence that
the governments that have ignored
experts in order to carry out a right-
wing ideological program in response
to overdose deaths are the same
governments that have delayed and
obfuscated their COVID-19 response,
ignoring evidence of what works
in favour of wishful thinking and
maximizing private profit for their
friends. The results—around the
world—are measured out in body
bags, refrigerated trucks, and grieving
families.

27. David George-Cosh, "Ontario Online
Pot Purchases Jump 600% amid
COVID-19 Pandemic Data Show,"
BNN Bloomberg, April 16, 2020, https://
www.bnnbloomberg.ca/ontario-online
-pot-purchases-jump-600-amid-covid
-19-pandemic-data-shows-1.1422369.

28. Lindsey M. Rodriguez, Dana M. Litt,
and Sherry H. Stewart, "Drinking to
Cope with the Pandemic," *Addictive
Behaviors* 110 (November 2020), https://
www.sciencedirect.com/science/article
/pii/S0306460320306626?via%3Dihub.

29. "More than 1 in 5 Canadians Who Drink
Alcohol and Have Been Staying at Home
More Have Been Drinking Once a Day
since the Beginning of May," Canadian
Centre on Substance Use and Addiction,
June 9, 2020, https://www.ccsa.ca/more
-1-5-canadians-who-drink-alcohol-and
-have-been-staying-home-more-have
-been-drinking-once-day.

30. It's hard to keep up with the innovations
and bold ideas developed for harm
reduction, which must change to respond
to changing needs and circumstances.
Some months after Meg and her doctor
dream up this solution, the Canadian
Association for Safe Supply (CASS)
released the world's first "support tool"
for prescribers interested in off-label
prescribing of transdermal fentanyl
patches for injection or inhalation as safe
supply for people at risk of illicit fentanyl
overdose ("Ethical Fentanyl Prescribing:
A Supportive Guideline for Ethical
Transdermal Fentanyl Prescribers and
a Harm Reduction Guide for Patients,"
CASS, December 2020, https://
d3n8a8pro7vhmx.cloudfront.net
/unitedforsafesupply/pages/1049

/attachments/original/1608178235
/reportEFP121620.pdf). It explains how
to reduce the substantial risks of trying
to use a pain patch in this way.

31. Julian Buchanan and Alastair Roy,
"The Paradoxes of Recovery Policy:
Exploring the Impact of Austerity and
Responsibilisation for the Citizenship
Claims of People with Drug Problems,"
Social Policy & Administration 50, no. 3
(May 2016): 398–413, https://onlinelibrary
.wiley.com/doi/abs/10.1111/spol.12139.

32. "How to Start a Harm Reduction
Works-HRW Meeting," HRH413.org,
n.d., https://www.hrh413.org
/foundationsstart-here-2.

33. I.e., given naloxone to reverse an overdose.

34. "Liberation (pharmacology)," Wikipedia,
accessed January 5, 2021, https://en
.wikipedia.org/wiki/Liberation
_(pharmacology).

35. Antonio Gramsci, *Prison Notebooks*, 1930,
in Susan Radcliffe, ed., *Oxford Essential
Quotations*, 5th ed. (Oxford University
Press, 2017).

36 Slavoj Žižek, "A Permanent Economic
Emergency," *New Left Review* 64 (July
/August 2010), https://newleftreview
.org/issues/ii64/articles/slavoj-zizek-a
-permanent-economic-emergency.

Bibliography

Antelo, Fernando. "Pain and the Paintbrush: The Life and Art of Frida Kahlo," *Virtual Mentor* 15, no. 5 (2013): 460–465.

Berczik, Krisztina, Attila Szabó, Mark D. Griffiths, Tamás Kurimay, Bernadette Kun, Róbert Urbán, and Zsolt Demetrovics. "Exercise Addiction: Symptoms, Diagnosis, Epidemiology, and Etiology." *Substance Use & Misuse* 47, no. 4 (2012): 403–417.

Blackhurst, Chris. "Self Admits Taking Heroin on PM's Jet." *The Independent*, April 19, 1997.

Blaszczak-Boxe, Agata. "Woman's Spontaneous Orgasms Triggered by Parkinson's Drug." *LiveScience.com*, August 5, 2014.

Burkeman, Oliver. "Rise and Shine: The Daily Routines of History's Most Creative Minds." *The Guardian Online*, October 5, 2013.

Burrus, Christina. *Frida Kahlo: Painting Her Own Reality.* London: Thames & Hudson, 2008.

Cunningham, Erin. "Drug Addiction on the Rise in Besieged Gaza." *The Electronic Intifada*, June 30, 2009.

De Quincey, Thomas. *Confessions of an English Opium-Eater.* Edited by Joel Faflak. Peterborough: Broadview Press, 2009.

———. *Confessions of an English Opium-Eater* (1856). In *The Works of Thomas De Quincey, Volume 2*, ed. Grevel Lindop, 88–278. London: Routledge, 2020. https://doi.org/10.4324/9780429349034.

———. *Historical and Critical Essays Vol. II.* Boston: Ticknor & Fields, 1862.

Dell, Colleen Anne, Gary Roberts, Jennifer Kilty, Kelli Taylor, Mitch Daschuk, Carol Hopkins, and Debra Dell. "Researching Prescription Drug Misuse among First Nations in Canada: Starting from a Health Promotion Framework." *Substance Abuse: Research and Treatment* 6 (2012): 3–31.

Dormandy, Thomas. *Opium: Reality's Dark Dream.* New Haven, CT: Yale University Press, 2012.

Duffy, Jonathan. "When Heroin Was Legal." *BBC News Magazine*, January 26, 2006.

Faflak, Joel. "Introduction." In *Confessions of an English Opium-Eater and Related Writings* by Thomas de Quincey, 9–45. Broadview Editions, 2009.

Hayter, Alethea. *Opium and the Romantic Imagination*. London: Faber and Faber, 1968.

Herie, Marilyn, and Wayne Skinner. *Substance Abuse in Canada*. Toronto: Oxford University Press, 2010.

Hodgson, Barbara. *In the Arms of Morpheus*. Vancouver: Greystone Books, 2001.

Macht, David I. "The History of Opium and Some of Its Preparations and Alkaloids." *Journal of the American Medical Association* 64, no. 6 (1915): 477–481.

McCall, John. "Malcolm Cowley, The Art of Fiction No. 70." *The Paris Review* 85 (Fall 1982).

McCarthy, Rory. "Hamas Burns Tramadol Painkillers Smuggled into Gaza." *The Guardian*, April 20, 2016.

Morrison, Robert. "Poe's De Quincey, Poe's Dupin." *Essays in Criticism* 51, no. 4 (2001): 424–441.

———. *The English Opium-Eater: A Biography of Thomas De Quincey*. London: Weidenfeld & Nicolson, 2009.

Page, H.A. *Thomas De Quincey, His Life and Writings: With Unpublished Correspondence*. London: John Hogg & Co, 1877.

Sacks, Oliver. *Hallucinations*. New York: Alfred A. Knopf, 2012.

Sebald, W.G. *Austerlitz*. New York: Random House, 2001.

Self, Will. "Take to the City Streets for a Walking Adventure." *The Guardian Online*, February 1, 2015.

Solnit, Rebecca. *A Field Guide to Getting Lost*. London: Penguin Books, 2005.

Stevens, Craig W. "The Evolution of Vertebrate Opioid Receptors." *Frontiers in Bioscience* 14, no. 4 (2009): 1247–1269.

Webster, Paul C. "Indigenous Canadians Confront Prescription Opioid Misuse." *The Lancet* 381, no. 9876 (2013): 1447–1448.

———. "Medically Induced Opioid Addiction Reaching Alarming Levels." *Canadian Medical Association Journal* 184, no. 3 (2012): 285–286.

Welsh, Irvine. *Trainspotting*. London: Vintage Books, 2004.

Wood, Gaby. "Anatomy of an Icon." *The Guardian*, May 15, 2005.

CARLYN ZWARENSTEIN is a Toronto-based writer. Her essays, journalism, and fiction cover topics such as pain, drugs, and the nature of dependence. She also writes about literature, travel, and social movements, and the wonder to be found in the natural world, society, and art.

Her first book, *Opium Eater: The New Confessions*, was a finalist for the Science Writers and Communicators of Canada Book Award. It was also a *Globe and Mail* Top 100 Book, where it was described as "that rare thing: a dispassionate account informed by deeply personal experience." *Room* magazine called it "a sensuous and compelling meditation."

Zwarenstein's writing has appeared in the *Washington Post*, the *Walrus*, the *Guardian*, the *Globe and Mail*, in Spanish and English editions of *Vice*, and other magazines and journals. *On Opium* is her second book.